Frommer's®
New Orleans

17th Edition

WILEY

John Wiley & Sons, Inc.

Published by:
John Wiley & Sons, Inc.
111 River St.
Hoboken, NJ 07030-5774

ISBN 978-1-118-07406-0 (paper); ISBN 978-1-118-16151-7 (ebk); ISBN 978-1-118-16152-4 (ebk); ISBN 978-1-118-16154-8(ebk)

Editor: Cate Latting
Production Editor: M. Faunette Johnston
Cartographer: Guy Ruggiero
Photo Editor: Alden Gewirtz
Cover Photo Editor: Richard Fox
Design and Layout by Vertigo Design
Graphics and Prepress by Wiley Indianapolis Composition Services

Front cover photo: French Quarter, stage with drum kit © Cosmo Condina/Alamy Images.

Back cover photo: LEFT: Man performing on trumpet © DreamPictures/Blend Images/Corbis; MIDDLE: French Quarter, detail of green shutters and glass windows © Patrick Filet/hemis.fr/Alamy Images; RIGHT: Crawfish on plate © Simon Reddy/Alamy Images.

For information on our other products and services or to obtain technical support, please contact our Customer Care Department within the U.S. at 877/762-2974, outside the U.S. at 317/572-3993 or fax 317/572-4002.
Wiley also publishes its books in a variety of electronic formats. Some content that appears in print may not be available in electronic formats.
Manufactured in China
5 4 3 2 1

CONTENTS

LIST OF MAPS

HOW TO CONTACT US

In researching this book, we discovered many wonderful places—hotels, restaurants, shops, and more. We're sure you'll find others. Please tell us about them, so we can share the information with your fellow travelers in upcoming editions. If you were disappointed with a recommendation, we'd love to know that, too. Please write to:

Frommer's New Orleans, 17th Edition
John Wiley & Sons, Inc. • 111 River St. • Hoboken, NJ 07030-5774
frommersfeedback@wiley.com

ADVISORY & DISCLAIMER

Travel information can change quickly and unexpectedly, and we strongly advise you to confirm important details locally before traveling, including information on visas, health and safety, traffic and transport, accommodations, shopping, and eating out. We also encourage you to stay alert while traveling and to remain aware of your surroundings. Avoid civil disturbances, and keep a close eye on cameras, purses, wallets, and other valuables.

While we have endeavored to ensure that the information contained within this guide is accurate and up-to-date at the time of publication, we make no representations or warranties with respect to the accuracy or completeness of the contents of this work and specifically disclaim all warranties, including without limitation warranties of fitness for a particular purpose. We accept no responsibility or liability for any inaccuracy or errors or omissions, or for any inconvenience, loss, damage, costs, or expenses of any nature whatsoever incurred or suffered by anyone as a result of any advice or information contained in this guide.

The inclusion of a company, organization, or website in this guide as a service provider and/or potential source of further information does not mean that we endorse them or the information they provide. Be aware that information provided through some websites may be unreliable and can change without notice. Neither the publisher nor author shall be liable for any damages arising herefrom.

ABOUT THE AUTHOR

Diana Schwam fell for New Orleans like a klutz. She traveled the state, scoured the city, and eventually set down roots in Mid-City, convenient to the Jazz Fest Fair Grounds and Angelo Brocato's ice-cream parlor. A strategic marketing consultant and writer, Diana contributes to several trade publications and blogs, splits her time between New Orleans and Southern California, and currently sports a silver Gulf oyster pendant.

ACKNOWLEDGMENTS

For Milan. Let's all go to the Mardi Gras!

Thank you to the city and people of New Orleans for indelibly and continually intoxicating me with your charms (and may we now and forever retire the adjective "resilient"). Thanks to Cate Latting, Andrea Kahn, Alexis Lipsitz, and everyone at Wiley: the red Sharpie is dead, long live the red Sharpie. Thanks and love to the Fat Pack (Chuck, Fiona, John, Nettie, Robin, Steve, and Wesly) and the Plumpettes (Gary, Linda, Mark, and Paula) for frequent dessert bombing and fervent Midnight Disturbing. Thanks always to Harch, LaLisa, and Scot, and love ever to Dave and Mary. Thanks to the Hoseboat Gals (Apple, Chris, JoAnn, Lesley, and Mary)—U (we) did it! I love the North Rendon All Stars, and I love our house, even the garage of the unknown hoarder. With love to the Schwams, Dileos, Beers, Zuckerbergs, and Moonpies.

FROMMER'S STAR RATINGS, ICONS & ABBREVIATIONS

Every hotel, restaurant, and attraction listing in this guide has been ranked for quality, value, service, amenities, and special features using a star-rating system. In country, state, and regional guides, we also rate towns and regions to help you narrow down your choices and budget your time accordingly. Hotels and restaurants are rated on a scale of zero (recommended) to three stars (exceptional). Attractions, shopping, nightlife, towns, and regions are rated according to the following scale: zero stars (recommended), one star (highly recommended), two stars (very highly recommended), and three stars (must-see).

In addition to the star-rating system, we also use seven feature icons that point you to the great deals, in-the-know advice, and unique experiences that separate travelers from tourists. Throughout the book, look for:

Special finds—those places only insiders know about

Fun facts—details that make travelers more informed and their trips more fun

Kids—best bets for kids and advice for the whole family

Special moments—those experiences that memories are made of

Overrated—places or experiences not worth your time or money

insider tips—great ways to save time and money

Great values—where to get the best deals

The following **abbreviations** are used for credit cards:

AE	American Express	**DISC**	Discover	**V**	Visa
DC	Diners Club	**MC**	MasterCard		

TRAVEL RESOURCES AT FROMMERS.COM

Frommer's travel resources don't end with this guide. Frommer's website, www.frommers.com, has travel information on more than 4,000 destinations. We update features regularly, giving you access to the most current trip-planning information and the best airfare, lodging, and car-rental bargains. You can also listen to podcasts, connect with other Frommers.com members through our active-reader forums, share your travel photos, read blogs from guidebook editors and fellow travelers, and much more.

THE BEST OF NEW ORLEANS

New Orleans should come with a warning label. Not about hurricanes, but about the city's seductive powers, and the *never lefts*—the people who came for Mardi Gras, Jazz Fest, or a convention, fell prey to the city's magic—and never left. They danced in Frenchmen Street clubs. They kissed in the French Quarter, ate beignets at Café du Monde. Then they ignored their tickets home. They came for a vacation—and never left. You, too, should go, see, hear, and taste for yourself. Just don't blame us if one day you discover that you, too, never left.

Things to Do Check out the artists, fortune tellers, and street performers in the **French Quarter's Jackson Square.** Spy elegant homes in the **Garden District.** Stroll the tranquil walkway along the **Mississippi River** toward **Audubon Aquarium. City Park,** an oasis of towering mossy Spanish oaks, offers **Storyland Amusement Park** and the **Museum of Art.** Nearby are the picturesque, above-ground **cemeteries.** A short ride from town you can tour stately **plantation homes** or scout for alligators on a **swamp tour.**

Shopping Gift hunt for Mardi Gras trinkets, voodoo dolls, or fleur-de-lis jewelry at the **French Market.** Across town, art fans browse the galleries along **Julia Street** in the **Warehouse District.** The quirky-to-elegant boutiques lining **Magazine Street** will satisfy fashion and home decor fans, while the terrific shops in **Canal Place** and **Riverfront Mall** are blessedly air-conditioned. Hop a streetcar to **Riverbend** and **Oak Street** to browse a variety of quirky shops. Don't leave without stocking up on **pralines** and **Creole spices.**

Nightlife & Entertainment The birthplace of jazz still swings hard. There's old-time tradition at **Preservation Hall,** while Rebirth Brass Band rocks the **Maple Leaf.** Revel on Bourbon Street with a Hurricane at **Pat O'Brien's** and a set at **Irvin Mayfield's** stylish **Jazz Playhouse.** A **Frenchmen Street** club crawl must include **d.b.a.** and the **Spotted Cat,** and it's a quick cab ride to famed **Tipitina's** or the backyard repose of **Bacchanal.** The **New Orleans Opera Association** and the **Louisiana Philharmonic Orchestra** present excellent performances.

Restaurants & Dining The rich, flavorful **Creole fare** is famed for inventions like **Antoine's** baked oysters Rockefeller and **Brennan's** rum-infused bananas Foster. Spicy Cajun is represented by **gumbo,** a muscular stew combining seafood, poultry, or sausage. Freshly shucked Gulf oysters at **Acme Oyster Bar,** po' boy sandwiches from **Parkway Bakery,** or turtle soup at **Commander's Palace** should not be missed, while contemporary cuisine—like that at **Herbsaint, Emeril's, Cochon, Green Goddess,** and **Coquette**—riffs on culinary tradition in delectable new ways.

PREVIOUS PAGE: **The Zulu Queen sits atop a Mardi Gras float.**

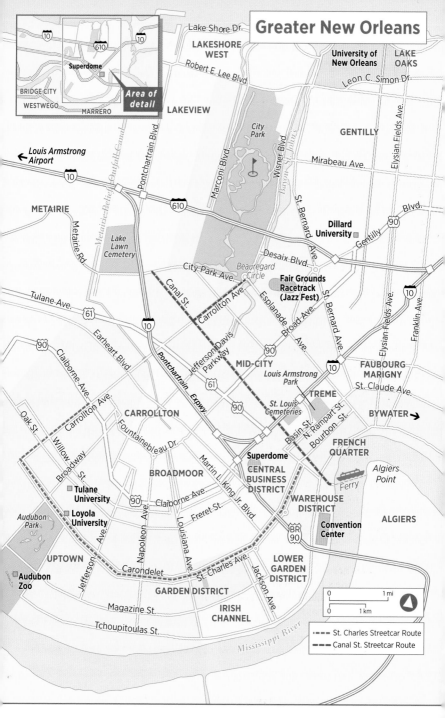

Greater New Orleans

← Louis Armstrong Airport

Lake Shore Dr.

LAKESHORE WEST

Robert E. Lee Blvd.

University of New Orleans

LAKE OAKS

Leon C. Simon Dr.

LAKEVIEW

City Park

GENTILLY

Mirabeau Ave.

Elysian Fields Ave.

Superdome

BRIDGE CITY

WESTWEGO

MARRERO

Area of detail

METAIRIE

Metairie Rd.

Lake Lawn Cemetery

Marconi Blvd.

Wisner Blvd.

Bayou St. John

St. Bernard Ave.

Blvd.

Dillard University

Gentilly

Tulane Ave.

Earheart Blvd.

City Park Ave.

Canal St.

Carrollton Ave.

Desaix Blvd.

Beauregard Circle

Fair Grounds Racetrack (Jazz Fest)

Esplanade Ave.

Broad Ave.

St. Bernard Ave.

Elysian Fields Ave.

Franklin Ave.

Pontchartrain Expwy.

Jefferson Davis Parkway

MID-CITY

Louis Armstrong Park

TREME

FAUBOURG MARIGNY

St. Claude Ave.

BYWATER →

Claiborne Ave.

Carrollton Ave.

CARROLLTON

Fountainebleau Dr.

St. Louis Cemeteries

Basin St.

N. Rampart St.

Bourbon St.

FRENCH QUARTER

Oak St.

Willow St.

Broadway St.

BROADMOOR

Martin Luther King Jr. Blvd.

Claiborne Ave.

Freret St.

Napoleon Ave.

Louisiana Ave.

Superdome

CENTRAL BUSINESS DISTRICT

WAREHOUSE DISTRICT

Ferry

Algiers Point

ALGIERS

Tulane University

Loyola University

Convention Center

Audubon Park

UPTOWN

Jefferson

Carondelet

St. Charles Ave.

Jackson Ave.

LOWER GARDEN DISTRICT

Audubon Zoo

GARDEN DISTRICT

Magazine St.

IRISH CHANNEL

Tchoupitoulas St.

Mississippi River

0   1 mi
0   1 km

····· St. Charles Streetcar Route
----- Canal St. Streetcar Route

3

THE best FIRST-TIME NEW ORLEANS EXPERIENCES

o **Beignets & Café au Lait at Café du Monde:** Sit on the crowded patio gazing at the action on Decatur Street and Jackson Square. Gorge on hot French-style doughnuts liberally coated in powdered sugar (everyone will know what you've been doing from the sprinkles on your shirt) chased by potent chicory coffee. And do it at any hour of the day—3pm or 3am. It's open 24 hours! See p. 154.

o **Jazz at Preservation Hall:** Drop your 12 bucks in the hat and squeeze into one of the country's time-honored jazz institutions. Your feet will be moving and your ears will be happy, even if they never knew they liked jazz before. See p. 280.

o **A Crowded Night at the Maple Leaf:** The epitome of "New Orleans" clubs, it's a terrific place to hang out. On nights when popular bands fill the place to hot, sweaty capacity and the crowd spills over into the street and dances right on the sidewalk, it's sublime. See p. 287.

o **Dinner at Commander's Palace:** For 130 years, this romantic, attentive grande dame has served up the inimitable combination of graciousness, indulgence, and exuberance that defines New Orleans dining. Also, it's delicious. See p. 147.

o **A Cemetery Tour:** New Orleans's odd, beautiful, aboveground tombs are positively memorable, and touring these ghostly cities of the dead brings a unique perspective on the city's history and culture. See p. 209.

o **Street Spontaneity:** If a wailing trumpet catches your ear, follow the sound till you find it. If the swing band playing in the middle of Royal Street inspires you to give your partner a whirl, by all means whirl (and drop a few bucks in their hat). And if you're lucky enough to happen upon a second line parade passing by, don't dare watch from the sidewalk. Jump in and high-step it down the street.

There's nothing like an order of beignets and a chicory coffee at the Café du Monde.

Be sure to take a cemetery tour while visiting New Orleans.

Buying a book from Faulkner House Books lets you take a little New Orleans home with you.

- **A Stroll Through the Garden District:** These elegant old homes, nestled among lush trees, are wonderful to gaze at and covet. At the right time of day, you might have the streets largely to yourself and feel you've slipped back in time—or into a Gothic novel. See p. 232.

- **A Stroll Along St. John's Bayou:** Most tourists don't get much beyond the Quarter or they speed past this low-slung body of water as they head for City Park. Slow down local-style to meander along the bayou and admire the less high-profile but no less romantic neighborhood around it. See p. 178.

- **Bourbon Street After Dark:** Even if you end up hating it, you have to see it at least once. Music spurts out of windows and doors, drinkers reign supreme, and sex is widely available—on paper, on stage, and on video. It's wild, disgusting, and strangely exhilarating. See chapter 10.

- **Club Hopping in the Frenchmen Section:** This portion of the Faubourg Marigny (the neighborhood that borders the French Quarter to the north and east) features nearly a dozen clubs and bars, each with its own personality and charm. Dip in for tastes, or just listen to the music pouring out the doors. See chapter 10.

- **Dancing to Rebirth Brass Band, John Boutté &/or Kermit Ruffins:** Dancing to three of the best musical acts New Orleans has to offer (a brass band, an astonishing soul crooner, and a jazz trumpeter in the tradition of Louis Armstrong, respectively) is the physical manifestation of the word *fun*—and the truest spirit of New Orleans. See chapter 10.

THE best TRIP MEMENTOS

The following are a few New Orleans souvenir ideas beyond T-shirts and snow globes, and are more welcome than a couple of extra pounds around your hips.

- **A Book from Faulkner House,** 624 Pirates Alley (𝄢 **504/524-2940**): Consider picking up a couple of books (see the list on p. 23) from this jewel of that vanishing species, the independent bookstore. Tucked into the bottom floor of the house where William Faulkner lived and wrote *Mosquitoes* and *Soldiers' Pay,* this charming shop is crammed with New Orleans– and Louisiana-related tomes, and the genteel staff will help you find your selection. Many an author has tried, with varying success, to capture New Orleans on the page, and their efforts may help you get a little fix back home when you begin to know what it means to miss New Orleans. Where better to buy it than at a local institution with a literary history? See p. 256.

- **A Photo or Art Book from A Gallery for Fine Photography,** 241 Chartres St. (𝄢 **504/568-1313**): The owner calls his impressive shop "the only museum where you can buy the art." Many famous photographers are represented here, but consider investing in a local artist's work such as E. J. Bellocq's famous Storyville boudoir photos, or possibly more affordably, atmospheric cemetery images from Sandra Russell Clark, or Michael P. Smith's vivid Jazz Fest moments. Consider Herman Leonard's classic takes on Billie Holiday, Ella Fitzgerald, and Dizzy Gillespie, or even the fine works by owner Joshua Mann Pailet. If an original isn't feasible, they also carry a range of photo art books. See p. 253.

o **A Southern Scent from Hove,** 434 Chartres St. (© **504/525-7827**): A perfumery since the 1930s, Hove creates their own unique perfumes and soaps (like Bayou D'Amor and Creole Days) and carries some traditional scents. We got hooked on sachet-favorite vetiver, described as "smelling like the South." Locals also adore the scents made from the indigenous sweet olive. And they have gentlemanly scents, too! See p. 255.

o **A Razor from Aidan Gill:** Manly and mannerly, the selection of hand-sculpted razors will charm even the most diehard disposable dude, and up his style quotient in a single stroke. Shaving cups, neckties, and other gentlemen's accessories fill this classic shop, or you could just take home some smooth cheeks courtesy of an ultraluxe straight-razor shave. See p. 255.

o **A CD from Louisiana Music Factory,** 210 Decatur St. (© **504/586-1094**): A visitor might think of the sights or tastes of New Orleans as the primary sensory experience, but its soundtrack is an essential component. Bring some of it home with you, courtesy of an independent store that houses a funky spirit and the city's best music selection. Check our recommendations in chapter 2, or ask the supremely informed salespeople. See p. 263.

o **Mardi Gras Beads:** It's an interesting phenomenon: You go to New Orleans for Mardi Gras, and are saturated with beads. They are like leaves on the ground—valueless by reason of their ubiquity and seasonality. But hand a friend at home a few cheap strands, and they light up, because outside of the parades they are novel. Buy them in shops around the Quarter, unless you're amassing souvenirs in bulk—then trek to the source, **Accent Annex,** 1009 McDermott Rd., Metairie (© **888/394-5537** or 504/391-3900), for considerable savings. Check the smaller antiques stores on Magazine, and Decatur near Esplanade for a mélange of used beads or pricier antique Czech glass beads.

o **Christmas Tree Ornaments & Other Handicrafts:** The Poor Claire nuns make everything in their little gift shop, from rosaries and ceramic statues to Sister Olivia's amazing Christmas tree ornaments. Iconic New Orleans landmarks (the Cathedral, a Lucky Dog cart, Mardi Gras floats) are meticulously re-created in architecturally accurate, scaled detail, and hand-painted on balsa wood.

Ask a salesperson at Lousiana Music Factory for great local music recommendations.

Prices are so low it feels sinful—buy a lot, to ease your conscience. The **Monastery Gift Shop** is at 720 Henry Clay Ave. (© 504/895-2019); ring the bell at the sliding window inside the building for gift shop access.

○ **Glasswork from Studio Inferno,** 3000 Royal St. (© 504/945-1878): This art gallery/shop features playful New Orleans–inspired pieces—cocktail glasses with a fleur-de-lis in the stem, heart-shaped *milagros* with flames shooting out of them, spicy peppers on cords to wear as a necklace—at prices that will allow you to fill up your gift list. See p. 255.

○ **A Hat from Meyer,** 120 St. Charles Ave. (© 504/525-1045): We're mad about Meyer, for the selection, the service, and the 100-year-plus history. These people are hat whisperers—they know just how to top every head—from a straw boater to a hipster fedora. You're in the South, *chère*; you can rock some class headgear. See p. 262.

○ **A "Be Nice or Leave" Sign:** Dr. Bob's colorful, bottle cap–edged signs may have overtaken Rodrigue's Blue Dog in terms of sheer ubiquity, but they're still true, local works of folk art. Handmade with found materials, they're available in a variety of sizes, materials, and sentiments—including the Saints-loving "Who Dat or Leave." Sold in the French Quarter at Pop City, 940 Decatur St. (© 504/528-8559), and Uptown at Funrock'n, 3109 Magazine St. (© 504/895-4102). Other works are on view at Bob's Bywater studio, 3027 Chartres St. (© 504/945 2225); free tours are offered "by chance or appointment."

THE FIVE best CLASSIC NEW ORLEANS DRINKS

Keep this in mind: Hurricanes are for tourists; Sazeracs are for natives.

This is a town that knows its booze, for sure, and it has contributed a few cocktails to the pantheon. You can drink beer anywhere, so try a few indigenous cocktails. (Thanks to Chuck Taggart and Wesly Moore, who regularly report on cocktails and New Orleans at www.gumbopages.com, for input to this list.)

○ **Sazerac:** This is the quintessential New Orleans cocktail, the Official State Cocktail of Louisiana (yes, really), one of the first, and perhaps the greatest ever. The combination of rye whiskey, Peychaud's Bitters, a touch of sugar, a hint of Herbsaint anise liqueur, and a breath of lemon oil create a symphony of flavor, and it plays new movements as the drink warms up.

○ **Ramos Gin Fizz:** There was a time when there were 35 bar-back boys shaking gin fizzes behind the bar at Henry C. Ramos's Stag Saloon, and Huey P. Long took his favorite bartender to Washington with him so that he would never be deprived of his beloved gin fizz. It's a frothy delight of gin, egg whites, orange flower water, lemon and lime juice, soda water, and cream that not everyone can (or will) prepare. Make it your mission to find those who can (start with the "Best Bars Beyond Bourbon," below).

○ **Vieux Carré Cocktail:** Unjustly forgotten except for a growing number of cocktailians and the bartenders, this wonderful, potent whisky and cognac creation was created by Walter Bergeron of the Hotel Monteleone in the 1930s. And we thank him.

A bust of Napoleon oversees the bar at Napoleon House, where Pimm's Cups are the specialty.

A hurricane on the patio at Pat O'Brien's is a quintessential New Orleans experience.

o **Pimm's Cup:** It's not a New Orleans original, but it's such a refreshing beverage on those languid N'Awlins summer days that we're pretty sure Blanche Dubois would have drunk these in better days. The signature drink of the Napoleon House, one sip will have you calling strangers dahlin'. Cucumber, gin-based Pimm's No. 1, mint, and sweetness brings out the drawl. Do try this at home.

o **Hurricane:** Okay, so we diss the Hurricane sometimes, but when done right, it's a fruity, deviously stealthy drink (as you can't really taste the alcohol). The powdered, premixed stuff is a far cry from what Charlie Cantrell first concocted out of rum and passion fruit back in the 1940s, but a Hurricane on the patio at Pat O'Brien's is such a quintessential New Orleans experience that it merits inclusion . . . and hey, it beats the Hand Grenade.

THE best BARS BEYOND BOURBON

If you're ready to branch out of your drinking environment as well as your choice of drinks, you'll find no lack of options. Given the rise of the craft cocktail movement, the choices are plentiful. We've suffered through the legwork for you to devise this short-list.

o **French 75 Bar at Arnaud's,** 813 Bienville St. (© 504/523-5433): A beautiful, intimate bar space in one of the Quarter's most venerable restaurants, it feels like drinking in New Orleans should: both classic and classy (and cigar-smoky later in the eve). Acclaimed bartender Chris Hannah and others are equally adept at vintage cocktails and original concoctions, including a perfect Ramos Gin Fizz and the namesake French 75 champagne cocktail. *Tip:* Order a side of Arnaud's dreamy soufflé potatoes to munch on. See p. 120.

o **Napoleon House,** 500 Chartres St. (© 504/524-9752): Set in a landmark building, this is a New Orleans must-do. It looks its age (over a century) and seems too perfect to be real—surely it must be constructed just for tourists—but it's not. Even locals like it here. Classical and jazz music play gently in the cave-dark room—making it all the better to sip their house cocktail (the glass of summer known as a Pimm's Cup) and chow on their popular warm muffuletta. See p. 131.

o **Carousel Bar at the Monteleone Hotel,** 214 Royal St. (✆ **504/523-3341**): No, you're not drunk (or maybe you are). The bar is actually spinning; the stools rotate around the central hub of the Carousel Bar (one drink per rotation is the purported ratio—don't worry, it spins slo-o-o-wly). It's a great place for a grown-up cocktail (with prices to match), particularly the Vieux Carré Cocktail, their signature drink for nearly 75 years. See p. 87.

o **Cure,** 4905 Freret St. (✆ **504/302-2357**): This mixologist's mecca helped instigate the resurgence of both craft cocktails in New Orleans and of Freret Street. The anachronistic oasis of sleek boasts great small plates and some of the most knowledgeable bar chefs in town, who blend fine spirits, house-made infusions, and friendly chat—if you can get near them through the thick crowds. Try going early.

o **The Columns,** 3811 St. Charles Ave. (✆ **504/899-9308**): The interior substituted for the brothel in the movie *Pretty Baby,* but there's no substitute for the warm, Southern, summer night, mint julep–sipping fantasies you can satisfy while outside on the wide, oak-shaded veranda. Their ravishing bloody marys will satisfy other needs. See p. 109.

o **Sazerac Bar at the Roosevelt,** 123 Baronne St. (✆ **504/529-4733**): In terms of New Orleans cocktail royalty, the 2009 reopening of the Sazerac Bar was the Mafia equivalent of unearthing Jimmy Hoffa, alive and well, counting wads of cash and sipping Barolo. The sinuous wood walls and Deco-era murals here have surely heard stories, seen stars, and launched scandals too numerous to count (but start with that bullet hole above the back kitchen door—it wasn't touched in the hotel's $170-million renovation). You're here for all that panache as much as the namesake cocktail. See p. 100.

Enjoy a swanky cocktail at the sophisticated and sultry Sazerac Bar at the Roosevelt Hotel.

The centuries-old bar at Tujagues was brought from France to New Orleans.

o **Swizzle Stick Bar at Café Adelaide,** 300 Poydras St., in the Loews Hotel (☎ 504/595-3305): It's classy, art-filled, and a tad sassy, and equally comfortable for solo visitors and those on a date. Revered mixologist Lu Brow blends stellar pre-Prohibition classics: the playful Swizzle Stick cocktail (with a "special ingredient"), and the infamous Corpse Reviver No. 2. Wafflers can order the Trouble Tree, with branches of cocktail shots. Excellent bar food comes from Café Adelaide. See p. 140.

o **Bar Tonique,** 820 N. Rampart St. (☎ 504/324-6045): Please, oh please, move Tonique next door to me, for it is the neighborhood bar of my dreams. Candles bounce off the original brick walls in the small, comfortable room, which is flanked by a smattering of smoochy booths and a swankier offshoot room. The superbly poured cocktails, from well-selected, hand-squeezed, and house-made ingredients, are served with authenticity, not attitude. The classics are in good hands here, particularly the Dark and Stormy made with fresh ginger juice. Their own Tru Kick and the Blanche Dubois rocked our bar stools. There's a short but thoughtful beer and wine list, daily specials, and reasonable prices (but no food). Maybe we'll just move next door to Tonique.

o **Three Muses,** 536 Frenchmen St. (☎ 504/298-8746): Sophisticated modern lounge meets classic 1920s saloon, and we likey. The muses (owners) each contribute an essential expertise: beautifully balanced cocktails, mouthwatering (quite) small plates, and a songstress supreme with loads of talented friends. Serving new-timey cocktails and cuisine to old-timey (and acoustic) tunes, this smallish room is just what the Frenchmen Street scene needed. It's usually packed, and rightly so. See p. 282.

o **Tujagues,** 823 Decatur St. (☎ 504/525-8676): The attraction here is the centuries-old bar with the wall-size mirror, which was essentially hand carried—whole—from France to New Orleans (well, there was some sailing involved). The bartenders will gladly tell the remarkable tale, while pouring some of the better classic cocktails in town. In fact, after extensive personal research, we've ranked their Sazerac in our top five—above some far more hoity locales. There are no seats here but usually some colorful characters worth sidling up to. See p. 126.

1

THE BEST OF NEW ORLEANS | The Best Bars Beyond Bourbon

NEW
ORLEANS
IN DEPTH

Throughout this book, we'll talk about the mystique of New Orleans and its ineffable essence. But first, it's time for some stats. The largest city in Louisiana (even post-Katrina) and one of the chief cities of the South, New Orleans is nearly 100 miles above the mouth of the Mississippi River system and stretches along a strip of land 5 to 8 miles wide between the Mississippi and Lake Pontchartrain. Surrounded by a river and a lake, the city is largely under sea level. The highest natural point is in City Park, a whopping 35 feet above sea level.

Prior to 2005, the city was perhaps best known for its jazz-infused joie de vivre, a place where antebellum-meets-bohemia in a high-stepping dance of life, lived fully and out loud. Post-2005, its recent history is marked by a series of well-known difficulties.

First, the city's federal levee system failed following Hurricane Katrina on August 29, 2005, which resulted in flooding that was responsible for 1,836 recorded deaths and all forms of astounding, horrifying loss. Second, an oil spill occurred at the Deepwater Horizon oil rig in the Gulf of Mexico on April 20, 2010. New Orleans is some 100 miles inland from the Gulf coast, and thus was not directly impacted—but the perception was otherwise. Compound this with the economic downturn, and Louisiana's floods of 2011, and it would seem hard to get past the word "grim."

Remarkably, that is not at all the case. Certainly, all here will be forever designated either B.K. or A.K. (Before Katrina or After Katrina). But the place and its people have seemingly unending reserves of pluck and vivacity, which visitors continue to tap right into. In this chapter, we briefly recount the area's rich history, starting with today and then reaching back to its foundation, to help explain how New Orleanians got their resilient, life-affirming "yatitude" (from "Where y'at?"—the local version of "How ya doin'?").

NEW ORLEANS TODAY

In 2010, the New Orleans Saints football team, at long last, came marching in with their first-ever Super Bowl victory. The long-derided 'Aints restored what billions in rebuilding funds couldn't: civic pride.

The effects of this real and symbolic victory cannot be understated, and the celebration was beyond ecstatic. It was one of many high points in 2010: The *prior* week, Mitch Landrieu won the mayoral race with 66% of the vote, marking the end to the prior administration's fumbling, inertia, and corruption. The week *after* the Saints victory, the largest Mardi Gras crowds in 25 years watched

PREVIOUS PAGE: **Architectural detail in the French Quarter.**

the hyperexultant parades roll. Two months later, a record half-million revelers packed the streets for the French Quarter Fest.

Further, a new entrepreneurial drive was taking hold: in increased residency, tourism, and convention numbers; construction cranes crisscrossing the airspace; and cameras and booms appearing seemingly everywhere as the local film industry, well, boomed. Such rebuilding and start-up projects, in fact, likely served to stymie the worst effects of the economic downturn.

The Frenchmen Street club scene was hopping, new restaurants were opening weekly, and HBO debuted *Treme* to stellar reviews—revealing the best and worst of New Orleans with a spot-on eye and soundtrack.

Along with the long discussed, long delayed, long heralded, erstwhile "new New Orleans," an aura of possibility—of bigger, better things for the city—seemed to have permeated the silken air. The streets are proving it. Visitors to a transformed Oak Street will be amazed at its gussied up shops and restaurants. The once-derelict Freret Street is next: Pioneered by Cure (hipster cocktail central), a half-dozen promising new restaurants are under construction there. And the public schools, rebuilt largely as charters, have the test numbers to confirm that the possible is provable. Time had come to drag out the bootstraps and gumbo metaphors again: The scattered pieces of a healing New Orleans had come together to reform a city that is better than the sum of its parts.

And then, the whammy. Again. (Eye roll, headshake.)

The BP Deepwater Horizon oil spill hit, with potent imagery again painting New Orleans black with a wide, crude brush. In truth, New Orleans is some 150 miles from the spill, and those images of taint were far worse than the reality. Unlike, unfortunately, its state-mates in the severely affected areas, New Orleans remains utterly unsullied, and the sumptuous Gulf seafood—now with added safety testing—remains plentiful. Just ask the 2011 Mardi Gras and French Quarter Festival crowds, which rebroke 2010 records. Oil? Recession? Not here.

Which is not to say that the city has fully recovered. Despite much growth, pristine, rebuilt homes still sit next to abandoned blights, and redevelopment in the Lower 9th Ward is scant. Now a massive tabula rasa cleared of its upended homes, it's populated by a few pioneering resettlers and the architectural anachronisms of Brad Pitt's Make It Right homes. Yet amid their stark backdrop, these homes and their owners embrace their in-your-face presence, as if to proclaim, "Damn right we're here. And we've got *solar panels*." And perhaps the dual disasters will result in some much-needed system-wide improvements.

Meanwhile, across town, rebuilt communities have taken hold as tenants moved into pretty new homes where decayed tenements once sat. Galvanized once again, the citywide mood change is palpable and the progress continues to be tangible, evidenced by groundbreaking on an ambitious biomedical industry corridor. New Orleans is undoubtedly back at last, buoyant, secure, and optimistic.

Because through it all, New Orleanians just do what they do: tidy up, mix a cocktail, and exclaim their undying love for their city. And we're right there with them.

Yes, the indomitable spirit is intact. The oysters are still sweet, the jasmine air still sultry. Kermit Ruffins still plays Vaughan's on Thursdays, and parades seem to erupt at random. New Orleans is still the best city in the United States, and the *bons temps*—like those beloved Saints of field and song—go marching in and on.

As should you. Go, and be in that number.

HISTORY 101
In the Beginning

Two French-Canadian brothers found this spot at the turn of the 18th century. Pierre Le Moyne, Sieur d'Iberville, led an expedition from France to rediscover the mouth of the Mississippi in 1699. René Robert Cavelier, Sieur de la Salle, had claimed the region for France in 1682. (He was murdered in Texas in 1687 by his own party because his lack of navigational and leadership skills risked many of their lives.) Iberville's expedition succeeded, and he planted a cross at a dramatic bend in the river near where La Salle had stopped almost 2 decades before. On his voyage, Iberville also established a fort at Biloxi, naming it the capital of France's new and uncharted territory. His brother, 18-year-old Jean Baptiste Le Moyne, Sieur de Bienville, stayed behind in Biloxi and quickly became commanding officer of the territory. For the next 20 years, he harbored thoughts of returning up the river and establishing a new capital city at the spot where he and his brother had stopped.

A view of 19th–century New Orleans.

In 1718 Bienville got his chance. The previous year, Louisiana had been entrusted to the Company of the West (also known as Company of the Indies or the Mississippi Company) for development as a populated colony. The company was headed by John Law, a Scottish entrepreneur who had convinced the French monarch and many stockholders in his company that fortunes were to be had in the new land. The company authorized Bienville to

DATELINE

1682 Sieur de la Salle stops near the present site while traveling down the Mississippi River from the Great Lakes region and plants a cross claiming the territory for Louis XIV.

1699 Pierre Le Moyne, Sieur d'Iberville, rediscovers and secures the mouth of the Mississippi—on Mardi Gras day, appropriately.

1718 The first governor of Louisiana, Iberville's brother, Jean-Baptiste Le Moyne, Sieur de Bienville, founds New Orleans.

1723 New Orleans replaces Biloxi as the capital of Louisiana.

1726 Capuchin monastery erected.

1752 Ursuline Convent completed.

1762 Louis XV secretly cedes New Orleans and all of Louisiana west of the Mississippi to Spain.

1768 French residents in New Orleans banish Spanish commissioner Don Antonio de Ulloa, proclaiming independence from Spain.

1769 The Spanish return.

1783 Treaty of Paris confirms Spanish possession.

find a suitable location for a settlement on the river at a spot that would also protect France's holdings in the New World from British expansion.

Bienville quickly settled on high ground at the site he had previously seen, and not only because the bend in the river would be relatively easy to defend: Although it was some 100 miles inland along the river from the Gulf of Mexico, the site was near St. John's Bayou, which provided easy water transportation directly into Lake Pontchartrain. It was convenient from a military standpoint—providing a "back door" for defense or escape should the fortunes of war turn against the French—and it gave the site great potential as a trade route because it would allow relatively easy access to the Gulf.

Jean-Baptiste Le Moyne, Sieur de Bienville; founder of New Orleans.

The new town was named New Orleans in honor of the duc d'Orléans, then the regent of France. Following the plan of a late French medieval town, a central square (the Place d'Armes) was laid out with streets forming a grid around it. A church, government office, priest's house, and official residences fronted the square, and earthen ramparts dotted with forts were built around the perimeter. A tiny wooden levee was raised against the river, which still flooded periodically and turned the streets into rivers of mud. Today this area of original settlement is known as the Vieux Carré ("old square") and the Place d'Armes as Jackson Square.

1788–94 Fires destroy much of the city; new brick buildings replace wood.

1794 Planter Etienne de Boré granulates sugar from cane for the first time, spawning a boom in the industry.

1795 Treaty of Madrid opens port to Americans; trade thrives.

1800 Louisiana again becomes a French possession.

1803 France officially takes possession of the territory. United States then purchases it and takes possession.

1805 New Orleans incorporates as a city; first elections are held.

1812 The *New Orleans,* the first steam vessel to travel the Mississippi, arrives from Pittsburgh. Louisiana admitted as a U.S. state.

1815 Battle of New Orleans.

1831 The first (horse-drawn) railway west of the Alleghenies is completed, linking New Orleans and Milneburg.

1832–33 Yellow fever and cholera epidemic kills 10,000 people in 2 years.

continues

A Melting Pot

In its first few years, New Orleans was a community of French officials, adventurers, merchants, slaves, soldiers, and convicts from French prisons, all living in rude huts of cypress, moss, and clay. These were the first ingredients of New Orleans's population gumbo. The city's commerce was mainly limited to trade with native tribes and to beginning agricultural production.

To supply people and capital to the colony, John Law's company began what was essentially the first real estate scam in the New World. The territory and the city were marketed on the Continent as Heaven on Earth, full of immediate and boundless opportunities for wealth and luxury. The value of real estate in the territory rose dramatically with the spreading of these lies as wealthy Europeans, aristocrats, merchants, exiles, soldiers, and a large contingent of German farmers arrived—to find only mosquitoes, a raw frontier existence, and swampy land. Ultimately, the company's scheme nearly bankrupted the French nation. It did succeed, however, in swelling the population of the territory and of New Orleans; in 1723, the city replaced Biloxi as the capital of the Louisiana territory.

In 1724 Bienville approved the Code Noir, which set forth the laws under which African slaves were to be treated and established Catholicism as the territory's official religion. While it codified slavery and banished Jews from Louisiana, the code did provide slaves recognition and a degree of protection under the law.

One significant natural barrier to development of the population and society in Louisiana remained: a lack of potential wives. In 1727, a small contingent of Ursuline nuns arrived in the city and set about establishing a convent. While they weren't exactly eligible, they did provide a temporary home and education to many shiploads of *les filles à la cassette*. The "cassette girls" or "casket girls"—named for the government-issue *cassettes* or casketlike trunks in which they carried their possessions—were young women of appropriate character sent to Louisiana by the French government to be courted and married by the colonists. (If we're to believe the current residents of the city, the plan was remarkably

DATELINE continued

1834 Medical College of Louisiana (forerunner of Tulane University) founded.	**1850** Booming commerce totals $200 million; cotton accounts for 45% of total trade. City becomes largest slave market in the country.
1837 First newspaper coverage of a Mardi Gras parade.	**1852** Consolidation of municipal government; New Orleans annexes city of Lafayette.
1840 Antoine Alciatore, founder of Antoine's restaurant, arrives from Marseille. New Orleans is the fourth-largest city in the United States and is second only to New York as a port.	**1853–55** Yellow fever epidemic during the summer; 12% of the population killed in 1853 in roughly 2 months.
1849 The Place d'Armes renamed Jackson Square.	**1861–62** Louisiana secedes from the Union; city captured by Admiral David Farragut. General Benjamin Butler assumes command of the

successful: Nearly everyone in New Orleans claims descent from the casket girls or from Spanish or French nobility, which makes one wonder at the terrible infertility of the colony's earlier population of convicts and "fallen women.")

John Law's company relinquished its governance of Louisiana in 1731, and the French monarch regained direct control of the territory. In the following decades, a number of planters established estates up and down the river from New Orleans. In the city, wealthier society began to develop a courtly atmosphere on the French model. In the midst of the rough-and-tumble frontier, families competed to see who could throw the most elegant and opulent parties.

Farther afield, westward along the Gulf of Mexico, other French speakers were creating a very different kind of society in a decidedly more rural mode. During the 18th century, many French colonists, displaced by British rule from Acadia, Nova Scotia, formed an outpost in the new French territory along the coastland. Today you'll find the Acadians' descendants living a little to the west of New Orleans, still engaged in farming and trapping, some still speaking their unique brand of French, and proudly calling themselves "Cajuns."

New Orleans experienced only modest commercial development in its first decades, in large part due to trading restrictions imposed by France: The colony could trade only with the mother country. Colonists quickly found ways around the restrictions, however, and smugglers and pirates provided alternative markets and transportation for the region's agricultural products, furs, bricks, and tar.

Despite the awkward relationship with France, New Orleanians were greatly disturbed to learn in 1764 that 2 years earlier (news traveled right slow back then) Louis XV had given their city and all of Louisiana west of the Mississippi to his cousin Charles III of Spain, in the secret Treaty of Fontainebleau. The Spanish, in turn, took 2 more years to send a governor, Don Antonio de Ulloa, who made few friends among local residents. By 1768, a large number of French residents of New Orleans and outlying areas assembled to demand Ulloa's removal. Some proposed the formation of a Louisiana republic. Ulloa was sent packing, and for nearly 2 years, New Orleans and Louisiana were effectively independent of any

	city and earns a reputation for harsh and unfriendly governance.
1865–77	Reconstruction; "carpetbaggers" swarm into the city, and tensions climax in clashes between the Crescent White League and government forces.
1870	Algiers and Jefferson City annexed.
1872	Carrollton annexed.
1884–85	Cotton Centennial Exposition (World's Fair) held at the present site of Audubon Park.
1890	Jelly Roll Morton born.
1890	Creole of color Homer Plessy gets arrested riding a train recently segregated by Jim Crow laws. He sues the state, an effort that culminates in the landmark U.S. Supreme Court decision *Plessy v. Ferguson.*
1892	First electric streetcar operates along St. Charles Avenue.
1897	Sidney Bechet born. Storyville established.
1901	Louis Armstrong born in New Orleans.

continues

Tiled panels at the Spanish Plaza commemorate Spain's shared history with New Orleans.

foreign power. This episode ended in 1769 when Don Alexander O'Reilly (known as "Bloody O'Reilly") and 3,000 soldiers arrived in the city, dispatched by the Spanish Crown. What had been a relatively peaceful rebellion was extinguished, its leaders were executed, and Spanish rule was reimposed. With a Gallic shrug, French aristocracy mingled with Spanish nobility, intermarried, and helped to create a new "Creole" culture.

Devastating fires struck in 1788 (when more than 850 buildings were destroyed) and again in 1794 in the midst of rebuilding. From the ashes emerged a new architecture dominated by the proud Spanish style of brick-and-plaster buildings replete with arches, courtyards, balconies, and, of course, attached slave quarters. Even today you'll see tile markers giving Spanish street names at every corner in the French Quarter.

DATELINE continued

1911 Razzy Dazzy Spasm Band performs in New York, where its name is changed to Razzy Dazzy Jazz Band.

1917 Original Dixieland Jazz Band attains height of popularity.

1921 Inner-Harbor Navigational Canal built, connecting Lake Pontchartrain and the Mississippi.

1928 Colorful Huey P. Long elected governor of Louisiana; 4 years later he is elected to U.S. Senate.

1935 Long is shot dead.

1938 Tennessee Williams arrives in New Orleans. Huey P. Long Bridge built over Mississippi River.

1939 French Quarter Residents Association formed as an agent for preservation.

1956 Lake Pontchartrain Causeway, world's longest bridge, completed.

1960 The city's public schools integrated.

The city of New Orleans was coveted by the English and the Americans—and the French, though the trade to Spain was partly motivated because the unsuccessful colony was costing them money and they could no longer afford it. The Spanish imposed the same kind of trade restrictions on the city that the French had, with even less success (these were boom years for pirates and buccaneers like the infamous Jean Lafitte and his brother Pierre). This being a period of intense imperial conflict and maneuvering, Spain did allow some American revolutionaries to trade through the city in support of the colonists' fight against Britain. France regained possession of the territory in 1800 with a surprisingly quiet transfer of ownership, and held on for 3 years while Napoleon negotiated the Louisiana Purchase with the United States for the paltry (as it turned out) sum of $15 million. For Creole society, the return to French rule was unpleasant enough because France had long been facing serious financial troubles, but a sale to America was anathema. To their minds, it meant the end of a European lifestyle in the Vieux Carré.

Thus, when Americans arrived in the city, the upper classes made it known that they were welcome to settle—but across Canal Street (so named because a drainage canal was once planned along its route, although it was never constructed), away from the old city and Creole society. And so it was that New Orleans came to be two parallel cities. The American section spread outward from Canal Street along St. Charles Avenue; business and cultural institutions centered in the Central Business District, and mansions rose in what is now the Garden District, which was a separate, incorporated city until 1852. French and Creole society dominated the Quarter for the rest of the 19th century, extending toward the lake along Esplanade Avenue. Soon, however, the Americans (crass though they may have seemed) brought commercial success to the city, which quickly warmed relations—the Americans sought the vitality of downtown society, and the Creoles sought the profit of American business. They also had occasion to join forces against hurricanes, yellow-fever epidemics, and floods.

1973 Parades banned in the Vieux Carré, changing the character of the city's observance of Mardi Gras.

1975 Superdome opens.

1977 Ernest N. "Dutch" Morial becomes first African-American mayor.

1984 Louisiana World Expo draws disappointing crowds but spurs redevelopment of the riverside area between Canal and Poydras streets.

1988 Anne Rice moves back to New Orleans, which has enormous impact on the city.

1999 Harrah's opens new casino.

2000 The National World War II Museum opens along with Jazzland, a new theme park just outside the city. Mardi Gras 2000 draws record crowds.

2005 Hurricane Katrina hits August 29.

2010 Underdog Saints win NFL Super Bowl championship for first time in the team's 43-year history; city exults in proud "Who Dat" frenzy. *Treme* TV series debuts, focusing on city's unique culture. BP Deepwater Horizon oil spill despoils Gulf of Mexico—worst offshore spill in U.S. history.

From the Battle of New Orleans to the Civil War

Perhaps nothing helped to cement a sense of community more than the Battle of New Orleans, during the War of 1812. The great turning point in Creole-American relations was the cooperation of Andrew Jackson and Jean Lafitte. To save the city, Jackson set aside his disdain for the pirate, and Lafitte turned down offers to fight for the British, instead supplying the Americans with cannons and ammunition that helped swing the battle in their favor. When Jackson called for volunteers, some 5,000 citizens from both sides of Canal Street responded. Battle was joined on January 8, 1815, in a field a few miles downstream from the city, and approximately 2,000 British troops and 20 Americans were killed or wounded. The dramatic battle made a local and national hero of Jackson. Ironically, though, neither Jackson nor the British had been aware that a treaty concluding the war had been signed a full 2 weeks before, on December 24, 1814.

From then until the Civil War, New Orleans was a boomtown. Colonial trade restrictions had evaporated with the Louisiana Purchase, and more importantly, the era of steam-powered river travel arrived in 1812 with the first riverboat, the aptly named *New Orleans,* delivered from a Pittsburgh shipyard. River commerce exploded, peaking in the 1840s and putting New Orleans's port on par with New York's. Cotton and sugar made many fortunes in New Orleans and its environs; wealthy planters joined the city merchants in building luxurious town houses and attending festivals, opera, theater, banquets, parades, and spectacular balls (including "Quadroon Balls," where beautiful mulatto girls were displayed to the male gentry as possible mistresses). As always, politics and gambling were dominant pastimes of these citizens and visitors.

By the middle of the century, cotton-related business was responsible for nearly half of the total commerce in New Orleans, so it's no surprise that the city housed one of the nation's largest and most ruthless slave markets. Paradoxically, New Orleans also had one of the most extended and established populations of "free men (and women) of color" in the American South. Furthermore, racial distinctions within the city increasingly became difficult to determine; people could often trace their ancestry back to two or even three different continents. Adding to the diversity, waves of Irish and German immigrants arrived in New Orleans during this period, supplying important sources of labor to support the city's growth.

This growth—upriver and downriver from the original center and away from the river toward Lake Pontchartrain—required extensive drainage of swamps and the construction

The Mississippi River plays a central role in New Orleans's history.

of a system of canals and levees. The only major impediments to the development of the city in these decades were occasional yellow-fever epidemics, which killed thousands of residents and visitors. Despite the clearing of swampland, the mosquito-borne disease persisted until the final decades of the 19th century.

Reconstruction & Beyond

The boom era ended rather abruptly with the Civil War and Louisiana's secession from the United States in 1861. Federal troops marched into the city in 1862 and stayed until 1877, through the bitter Reconstruction period. As was the case elsewhere in the South, this period saw violent clashes between armed white groups and the state's Reconstruction forces.

After the war, the city went about the business of rebuilding its economic life—this time without slavery. By 1880, a number of annexations had rounded out the city limits, port activity had begun to pick up, and railroads were establishing their importance to the local and national economies. Also, a new group of immigrants, Italians this time, came to put their unique mark on the city. Through it all, an undiminished enthusiasm for fun survived. Gambling again thrived in more than 80 establishments, there were almost 800 saloons, and scores of "bawdy houses" engaged in prostitution, which was illegal but uncontrolled. New Orleans was earning an international reputation for open vice, much to the chagrin of the city's polite society.

In 1897, Alderman Sidney Story thought he had figured out how to improve the city's tarnishing image. He moved all illegal (but highly profitable) activities into a restricted district along Basin Street, next door to the French Quarter. Quickly nicknamed Storyville, the district boasted fancy "sporting palaces" with elaborate decor, musical entertainment, and a wide variety of ladies of pleasure. Visitors and residents could purchase a directory (the *Blue Book*) that listed alphabetically the names, addresses, and races of more than 700 prostitutes, ranging from those in the "palaces" to the poorer inhabitants of wretched, decaying shacks (called "cribs") on the blocks behind Basin Street. Black musicians such as Jelly Roll Morton played the earliest form of jazz in some of Basin Street's ornate bordellos. Although jazz predates Storyville, here it gained popularity before moving upriver and into record collections everywhere. When the secretary of the Navy decreed in 1917 that armed forces should not be exposed to so much open vice, Storyville closed and disappeared without a trace. None of the fancy sporting houses remains.

The 20th Century

The 20th century found the city's port becoming the largest in the United States and the second-busiest in the world (after Amsterdam), with goods coming in by barge and rail. Drainage problems were conquered by means of high levees, canals, pumping stations, and great spillways, which are opened to direct floodwater away from the city. Bridges were built across the Mississippi River, including the Huey P. Long Bridge, named after Louisiana's famous politician and demagogue. New Orleans's emergence as a regional financial center, with more than 50 commercial banks, led to the construction of soaring office buildings, mostly in the Central Business District.

As in most other American cities, the city's population spread outward through the 20th century, filling suburbs and nearby municipalities. Unlike other cities, however, New Orleans has been able to preserve its original town center and much of its historic architecture.

Hurricane Katrina

This rich, complex, maddening city had 300 years of history before August 29, 2005, and yet New Orleans is now indelibly identified with that one day. The third-strongest hurricane to make landfall in U.S. history, it was "only" a Category 3 when it hit the coast, about 63 miles to the southeast of New Orleans, with winds of 125 mph. However, the time spent out in the Gulf as a Category 5 (175-mph winds) caused the storm surge that inflicted the worst damage. Despite the ferocious wind, New Orleans escaped major problems from the storm itself and initially felt it had "dodged the bullet." But the surge was too much for the poorly constructed levee system (since the disaster, it has been revealed that the Army Corps of Engineers, who constructed the system in the first place, had not done the job properly). Several levees were breached, along with breaks in the Mississippi River Gulf Outlet, a little-used shipping lane. These failures caused flooding in 80% of the city, though the best-known areas, including the French Quarter and the Garden District, did not flood at all. While Mayor Ray Nagin ordered mandatory evacuations on August 28, there were no plans in place to enforce this, nor provisions to enable many of the city's poorest people (as many as 112,000 of whom were without transportation) to do so. The Superdome was designated as a "shelter of last resort," and 28,000 people took refuge there. With inadequate facilities and some roof loss during the storm, plus no additional aid nor rescue for 5 days following the storm, the former grand sports arena became a scene of suffering and misery. Images of residents stranded on rooftops as their houses flooded, or at the Convention Center awaiting rescue, were broadcast around the world. Overnight New Orleans was transformed from a quaint historical relic and/or party destination to a brutal wake-up call about poverty and class limitations in America. It took weeks for the floodwaters to be pumped out—months, in the case of the worst-hit Lower 9th Ward—and the city is still recovering.

A new home, built by the Make it Right program, on a site badly damaged by Hurricane Katrina and its aftermath.

NEW ORLEANS IN POPULAR CULTURE

Books

You can fill many bookcases with New Orleans literature and authors, so the following list is just considered a starter kit. Get more recommendations at the fine shops listed on p. 256.

GENERAL FICTION

There are many examples of early fiction that give a good flavor of old-time New Orleans life. George Washington Cable's stories are revealing and colorful, as in *Old Creole Days* (1879). Grace King answered Cable's not-always-flattering portrait of the Creoles with *The Pleasant Ways of St. Médard* (1916). Perhaps the best writer to touch on the lives of the earliest Creoles is Kate Chopin, whose late-1800s work, including the revered *The Awakening,* are set in Louisiana.

Frances Parkinson Keyes lived on Chartres Street for more than 25 years. Her most famous works are *Dinner at Antoine's* and *Madame Castel's Lodger,* and each has curious descriptions of life in the city at that time, along with excellent descriptions of food.

Ellen Gilchrist's contemporary fiction, including the short story collection *In the Land of Dreamy Dreams,* portrays life in wealthy uptown New Orleans. Sheila Bosworth's wonderful tragicomedies perfectly sum up the city and its collection of characters—check out our all-time favorites *Almost Innocent* and *Slow Poison.* Other possibilities are Nancy Lemann's delightful *Lives of the Saints* and Michael Ondaatje's controversial *Coming Through Slaughter,* a fictionalized account of Buddy Bolden and the early New Orleans jazz era.

New Orleans native Poppy Z. Brite's comic novels set in the New Orleans restaurant world are stuffed full of NOLA (and the chef biz) verisimilitude, starting with *Liquor.*

New Orleans, Mon Amour by poet and essayist Andrei Codrescu captures his adopted city's appeal, while misfit detective Dave Roubicheaux solves crime in a small Cajun town in the popular series by James Lee Burke.

And then, of course, there is the cottage industry known as Anne Rice, who undeniably ignited the current era of pop vampire culture (bow to the master, *True Blood* and *Twilight*). Rice does an arguably underrated job of capturing the city's essence, no doubt driving unknown numbers to fall in love with New Orleans from one of her books. Her *Vampire Chronicles,* set in New Orleans, are her best-known works, but *The Witching Hour* and the well-researched *Feast of All Saints* are also worthy.

HISTORY

Lyle Saxon's *Fabulous New Orleans* is the most charming place to start learning about the city's past. (Saxon was director of the writer's program under the WPA.) From there, move on to his collaboration with Edward Dreyer and Robert Tallant, *Gumbo Ya-Ya.* Roark Bradford's Civil War novel, *Kingdom Coming,* contains a lot of information about voodoo. Mark Twain visited the city often in his riverboat days, and his *Life on the Mississippi* has a good number of tales about New Orleans and its riverfront life. *The WPA Guide to New Orleans* also contains some excellent social and historical background and provides a fascinating picture of the city in 1938. *Beautiful Crescent,* by Joan Garvey and Mary Lou Widmer, is a solid reference book on the history of New Orleans. Those who loved *Gangs of New York* will be pleased to learn Herbert Asbury gave the same highly entertaining, not terribly factual treatment to New Orleans in *The French Quarter: An Informal History of the New Orleans Underworld.* New Orleans's favorite patroness, the Baroness de Pontalba, gets the biography treatment in Christina Vella's *Intimate Enemies.* In *The Last Madam: A Life in the New Orleans Underworld,* Christine Wiltz reveals a bawdy bygone era, much of it conveyed through the unpublished words of Norma Wallace. Wiltz had access to the famed brothel owner's audiotaped memoirs, recorded 2 years before her 1974 suicide.

Ned Sublette's *The World That Made New Orleans* is an eminently readable history, focusing on the cultural influences of European, African, and Caribbean settlers.

There are many guides to Mardi Gras. The definitive account is Henri Schindler's *Mardi Gras New Orleans.* Schindler produced balls and parades for Mardi Gras for 20 years and is considered Carnival's foremost historian. *Mardi Gras in New Orleans: An Illustrated History* is a concise history of the celebration from ancient times to 2001, produced by *Mardi Gras Guide* publisher Arthur Hardy.

Sara Roahen's charming *Gumbo Tales: Finding My Place at the New Orleans Table* left us hungering for more of her uproarious outsider's insights, as the recent transplant to New Orleans discovers the culture through its distinctive food and drink.

LITERATURE

William Faulkner came to New Orleans, lived on Pirates Alley, and penned *Soldiers' Pay.* Several other Faulkner novels and short stories are set in New Orleans. Tennessee Williams became a devoted New Orleans fan, living in the city on and off for many years. It inspired him to write *A Streetcar Named Desire,* one of the best-known New Orleans tales. He also set *The Rose Tattoo* in the city.

Other notable New Orleans writers include Walker Percy and Shirley Ann Grau. Percy's novels, including *The Moviegoer* and *Love in the Ruins,* are classic portrayals of the idiosyncrasies of New Orleans and its residents. Grau's most famous novel, *The Keepers of the House,* won the Pulitzer Prize in 1964. John Kennedy Toole also received a Pulitzer, but he wasn't around to know about it, having committed suicide years before. At the time of his death, none of his works had even been published. Toole's *A Confederacy of Dunces* is a timeless New Orleans tragicomedy that'll have you laughing out loud.

Robert Penn Warren's classic novel *All the King's Men,* an exceedingly loose telling of the story of Huey P. Long, makes the list because it's so good—and because it gives a portrait of the performance art known as Louisiana politics.

A further notable modern writer is Robert Olen Butler, who won the Pulitzer in 1993 for his collection of stories, *A Good Scent from a Strange Mountain,* set primarily in New Orleans's Vietnamese community.

POST-KATRINA LITERATURE

It's true that from great tragedy comes great art, and the following help give a picture of pre- and post-flood New Orleans. Tom Piazza's *Why New Orleans Matters* is a love letter to and about the city, reminding all who love it why they do and encouraging a similar love in novices. Rosemary James, of Faulkner House Books, edited *My New Orleans,* a collection of essays by locals ranging from writers to restaurateurs and raconteurs, attempting to pin down just what it is about

Tennessee Williams.

William Faulkner.

this place that keeps them here, come hell or high water. Local historian Douglas Brinkley's meticulous *The Great Deluge* may not end up the definitive postmortem examination of Katrina, but it will be hard to top. *Times-Picayune* columnist Chris Rose collected his heartbreaking personal essays, written as he and his colleagues covered their flooded city, in *1 Dead in Attic*.

Zeitoun, Dave Eggers's gripping narrative nonfiction, recounts the tale of one man's horror and a nation's injustice, while *New Yorker* columnist Dan Baum weaves together differing perspectives to illustrate how the multihued city unifies nine diverse narratives in *Nine Lives*.

Finally, fans of football and motivational memoirs may enjoy *Home Team* by Saints coach Sean Payton or Drew Brees's *Coming Back Stronger*.

BOOKS ABOUT MUSIC

We highly recommend Ann Allen Savoy's *Cajun Music Vol. 1*, a combination songbook and oral history. It features previously untranscribed Cajun music with lyrics in French (including a pronunciation guide) and English. A labor of many years, it's an invaluable resource.

For a look at specific time periods, people, and places in the history of New Orleans jazz, you have a number of choices. They include William Carter's *Preservation Hall*; John Chilton's *Sidney Bechet: The Wizard of Jazz*; Gunther Schuller's *Early Jazz: Its Roots and Musical Development*; *A Trumpet Around the Corner: The Story of New Orleans Jazz*, by Samuel Charters; *New Orleans Jazz, A Revised History,* by R. Collins; and *New Orleans Style,* by Bill Russell. Al Rose's *Storyville, New Orleans* is an excellent source of information about the very beginnings of jazz; while *Up From the Cradle of Jazz* tells its story post WWII.

If you prefer primary sources, read Louis Armstrong's *Satchmo: My Life in New Orleans,* or *Satchmo: The Wonderful World and Art of Louis Armstrong,* which is a bio by way of his own artworks. Two other suggestions are Sidney Bechet's *Treat It Gentle,* and the story of Mac Rebennack's (aka Dr. John) wild life as reflected in *Under a Hoodoo Moon.*

Film & Television

In a place that oozes character and seems to hide a story behind every iron gate, it's no surprise that film and TV shows about or set in New Orleans are plentiful. Most recently, the HBO series *Treme* has perhaps captured the place most accurately, but if you come across the stellar, little-seen series *Frank's Place* (1987–88), don't miss it. *True Blood* is filmed mostly in Baton Rouge, but that's okay. And with charm and mystery to spare, all forms of water and roadways, new and old architecture, and attractive tax incentives, there's a veritable production boom here. Skip the seriously flawed *The Big Easy*, but consider watching these for some pre- or post-visit flavor:

There are the classics like Brando in *A Streetcar Named Desire* (1951), Betty Davis in *Jezebel* (1938), the kitschy but decent Elvis vehicle *King Creole* (1958), and counterculture Mardi Gras freak-out *Easy Rider*. *Belizaire the Cajun* (1986) tells of the violence between 19th-century Cajuns and English speakers; Tom Waits bums around the city, the countryside, and jail in the indie *Down by Law* (1986); and a young Brooke Shields navigates a Storyville childhood in Louis Malle's *Pretty Baby* (1978). Then there's New Orleans resident Brad Pitt aging backwards in *The Curious Case of Benjamin Button* (2008) or going fang-to-fang with Tom Cruise in *Interview with the Vampire* (1994). Lastly, for kids of any age there's *Abbott & Costello Go to Mars* (1953)—alas, they end up at Mardi Gras. Close, but no cigar.

Documentaries about the Katrina experience cover every angle, notably in Spike Lee's *When the Levees Broke*; the remarkable, Oscar-nominated *Trouble the Water* and superb *Faubourg Treme: The Untold Story of Black New Orleans*; and Harry Shearer's exposé *The Big Uneasy.*

Recordings

The selections listed below should give you a good start, though we could fill pages more (and we're not even touching on the many fine pop, rock, or folk contributions—just to keep the focus on more New Orleans–oriented works). For more advice or recommendations, drop by or call the **Louisiana Music Factory,** 210 Decatur St. (© **504/586-1094**), in New Orleans, or **Floyd's Record Shop,** 434 E. Main St., Ville Platte (© **337/363-2138**). (Floyd's is about 3 hr. from New Orleans—see chapter 11, "Side Trips from New Orleans," for more info.)

ANTHOLOGIES

There are many collections and anthologies of New Orleans and Louisiana music available, including the 1990s Alligator Stomp series by Rhino Records. The most comprehensive, critically acclaimed is *Doctors, Professors, Kings & Queens: The Big Ol' Box of New Orleans,* a four-disc package released in 2004 by Shout! Factory and the one collection that touches all the bases of the diverse musical gumbo that is the Crescent City. For a more modest taste, order up the *Treme, Season 1* soundtrack (Geffen, 2011), which covers a bit of the same fertile, funky ground, albeit just from recent years.

POST-KATRINA RECORDINGS

A, pardon the expression, flood of benefit albums emerged in the wake of the, uh, flood. Notable among them are *Our New Orleans,* with all-new recordings by Allen Toussaint, Dr. John, Randy Newman, and others (Nonesuch Records, 2005), and *Sing Me Back Home,* by the New Orleans Social Club, a "supergroup" of heavy-hitting Crescent City funksters (Burgundy Records/Sony BMG, 2006). Many NOLA stalwarts found inspiration in their experiences. Irma Thomas made one of the strongest albums of her long career with the earthy, Grammy Award–winning *After the Rain* (Rounder Records, 2006). The Dirty Dozen Brass Band reinterpreted Marvin Gaye's ever-more-pertinent 1971 *What's Going On* album (Shout! Factory, 2006). Toussaint and Elvis Costello teamed up for the spectacular *The River in Reverse* (Verve/Forecast, 2006). *A Tale of God's Will (A Requiem for Katrina)* (Blue Note, 2006) is Terence Blanchard's Grammy-winning haunting suite from his score for the documentary *When the Levees Broke.*

One profound post-K music development has been the advent of Threadhead Records, which grew from a bunch of NOLA-lovers helping some locals to fund recording projects to a full-fledged label—with each release financed via fan micro-loans. Of particular note are recordings by Paul Sanchez (formerly of the band Cowboy Mouth), John Boutté (arguably the best jazz-soul singer currently in the city), and Susan Cowsill (yes, of those Cowsills), each of whom truly found his or her artistic voice through their experiences with the trauma and fitful recovery.

JAZZ

Most of Louis Armstrong's recordings are in print and readily available, and there are great sessions from every period of his life, though the early Hot Fives and Hot Sevens recordings are *the* essentials of any collection. For the early jazz sound, the following are recommended: *Streets and Scenes of New Orleans* (Good Time Jazz), by the Silver Leaf Jazz Band; *New Orleans Rhythm Kings* (Milestone); *King Oliver with Louis Armstrong* (Milestone); and the anthologies *New Orleans* (Atlantic Jazz), *Recorded in New Orleans Volumes 1 and 2* (Good Time Jazz), and *New Orleans Jazz* (Arhoolie). A series of CDs being put out by the essential traditional jazz club, Preservation Hall—which of late has moved into a wider repertoire—yields impressively appealing results.

Building on those traditions, Wynton Marsalis and Harry Connick, Jr., have led the way with more recent generations, certainly in terms of international renown. Trumpeter Irvin Mayfield, clarinetist Tim Laughlin, and such old-time revivalists as the New Orleans Jazz Vipers and Loose Marbles are more local phenoms, but well worth checking out. Allen Toussaint doesn't dabble, he delves—as demonstrated by *The Bright Mississippi,* his fine jazz foray. The latest breakout star is Troy "Trombone Shorty" Andrews, though he's reached well beyond jazz into funk and even rock with his monster-hit "Backatown" (Verve, 2009). Finally, though it's not truly a jazz CD, singer-songwriter-multi-instrumentalist Theresa Andersson's *Hummingbird, Go* (Basin Street, 2008), which exposed her to a much broader audience, is certainly innovative enough to fit the category.

BRASS BANDS

The tradition of brass-oriented street bands predates Louis Armstrong but underwent a spectacular revival in the 1980s and 1990s with the revitalization of such long-term presences as the Olympia Brass Band and the arrival of such newcomers as the Dirty Dozen Brass Band, who took the sound global and collaborated with stars ranging from Dizzy Gillespie to Elvis Costello and Norah Jones. The anthology *This Is the Dirty Dozen Brass Band* (Shout! Factory, 2005) spans 25 years of recordings. They inspired a younger and funkier generation, with the Rebirth Brass Band, the New Birth Brass Band, the Hot 8, up-and-comers TCB, and the Soul Rebels, the best of the crowd. It's all better live, so try *The Main Event: Live at the Maple Leaf* (Louisiana Red Hot, 1999). The loose, bumping *Rock with the Hot 8* (2007), New Birth's moving tribute to late co-founder Tuba Fats *New Birth Family* (Fat Back Records, 2004), and Tremé Brass Band's *Gimme My Money Back* (Arhoolie, 1995) are all irresistible.

RHYTHM & BLUES

Don't miss Dr. John's *Gris-Gris* (Atco, 1968), *Gumbo* (Atco, 1972), and *Mos Scocious: The Dr. John Anthology* (Rhino, 1993). Also try the Wild Tchoupitoulas's *The Wild Tchoupitoulas* (Antilles, 1976) for Mardi Gras Indian funk, and the Meters' *Cissy Strut* (Island, 1975) and *Rejuvenation* (Reprise, 1974). You can't go wrong with hometown heroes the Neville Brothers' *Yellow Moon* (A&M, 1989) and *Treacherous: A History of the Neville Brothers, 1955–1985* (Rhino, 1986), or producer/writer Allen Toussaint's *The Complete 'Tousan' Sessions* (Bear Family Records, 1992). He's a legend for a reason. We can't overlook Professor Longhair's *New Orleans Piano* (Atco, 1953) and *'Fess: The Professor Longhair Anthology* (Rhino, 1993), and fellow key wizard James Booker's *Classified* (Rounder, 1982). Worthwhile anthologies include *The Best of New Orleans Rhythm & Blues Volumes 1 and 2* (Rhino, 1988) and *The Mardi Gras Indians Super Sunday Showdown* (Rounder, 1992). Ivan Neville's Dumpstaphunk is keeping the funk alive, while Galactic might be funk, might be jazz, could be rock or jam— but is never uninteresting. Start with *Ruckus* (Sanctuary, 2003).

HIP-HOP & BOUNCE

New Orleans is home to several noted hip-hop and rap artists, and a home-grown subgenre: booty-dropping, second-line-influenced bounce music that only translates in a live setting. Breakout dirty Southerner Juvenile's *400 Degreez* (Uptown, 1998) is a classic, while hip-hop star Lil Wayne came back strong with *I Am Not a Human Being* (Cash Money, 2010). Mystikal's risqué rhymes broke some musical ground before legal troubles sidelined his career; rumor is something new is brewing.

EATING & DRINKING

Where oh where to start? Is there any other American city so revered, so identified with the glory of gluttony and the joy of the juice than New Orleans? Perhaps, but none with a truly indigenous cuisine (or two), none that lay claim (rightly or not) to inventing the cocktail, and surely none that does it with such unbridled gusto. As the oft-repeated homily goes: In most places, people eat to live; in New Orleans, people live to eat. What we say is, you're only visiting, so make the most of it: Convince your tortured psyche that it's okay, you can resume a sensible diet when you get home (and there are plenty of stylish travel garments with elastic waistbands). We've known even the most strident vegan to give it up for a few days while here (yes, really), though most chefs, and certainly those in the better restaurants, are adept at adapting to any specified "isms" or dietary restriction. Of course those who must can seek out the usual, benign ethnic restaurants. The single most important thing to know? *Make reservations.*

Chapter 6 has much more about Cajun and Creole food, including a food glossary. Chapters 1 and 10 are more than half full of cocktailing info.

WHEN TO GO

With the possible exception of July and August (unless you thrive on heat and humidity—and some really exceptional hotel deals!), just about any time is the right time to go to New Orleans. Mardi Gras is, of course, the time of year when it's hardest to get a hotel room, but it can also be difficult during the various music festivals throughout the year, especially the Jazz & Heritage Festival. (See chapter 3.)

Crawfish are a regional specialty in New Orleans.

It's important to know what's going on when; the city's landscape can change dramatically depending on what festival or convention is happening and prices can also reflect that. We love the warm, jasmine-infused nights and warmer days of mid-fall, and even relish the occasional high drama of a good thunderstorm. But the best time of year may just be December. The town is gussied up with decorations, there are all kinds of holiday special events, the weather is nice—but for some reason, tourists become scarce. Hotels, eager to lure any business, lower their rates dramatically, and most restaurants are so empty that you can walk in just about anywhere without a reservation. Take advantage of it.

The Weather

The average mean temperature in New Orleans is an inviting 70°F (21°C), but it can drop or rise considerably in a single day. (We've experienced 40°F/4°C and rain one day, 80°F/27°C and humidity the next.) Conditions depend primarily on whether it rains and whether there is direct sunlight or cloud cover. Rain can provide slight and temporary relief on a hot day; it tends to hit in sudden (and sometimes dramatically heavy) showers, which disappear as quickly as they arrive. In unimpeded sun it gets much warmer. The high humidity can intensify even mild warms and colds. Still, the semitropical climate is part of New Orleans's appeal—the slight moistness makes for lush, sensual air.

New Orleans should be pleasant most of the year except July and August, which can be exceptionally hot and muggy. During those bargain months, follow the natives' example: stay out of the noonday sun and duck from one air-conditioned building to another. June and September can still be humid and warm; early spring and mid-fall are glorious. Winter is mild by American standards but is punctuated by an occasional freeze-level cold snap. But *unpredictable* and flexible are the watchwords. The whims of the weather gods are at play, so be ready to adjust accordingly.

hot time IN THE CITY

If you can stand it, do consider braving the summer; the town is often slow, which produces hotel bargains. On a recent July visit, high-end hotels were offering rooms from $59 to $129 (way, way below their regular rates), sometimes with additional perks thrown in. You can often get upgrades to fancy suites for a song—ask when you check in. The past few years local restaurants have run "COOL-inary" specials during August and September, three-course meals for set fees, under $20 for lunch and under $35 for dinner. Yeah, it's hot and humid, but bearable for all but the most sensitive, and there are plenty of air-conditioned respites to duck into. In fact, the biggest climate problem can sometimes be the air-conditioning overcompensation that chills rooms to near–meat locker temps!

Hurricane season runs June 1 to mid-November. Obviously, there are no guarantees, but despite their unpredictability and the high drama of recent years, hurricanes actually don't happen too terribly often. In the dead of summer, T-shirts and shorts are absolutely acceptable everywhere except the finest restaurants. In the spring and fall, something a little warmer is in order; in the winter, you should plan to carry a lightweight coat or jacket and pack a folding umbrella (though they're available everywhere, as are cheap rain jackets, for those who get caught in an unexpected downpour). Also note that many restaurants are overzealous with air-conditioning, so bring those light wraps along even on warm nights.

New Orleans Average Temperatures & Rainfall

	JAN	FEB	MAR	APR	MAY	JUNE	JULY	AUG	SEPT	OCT	NOV	DEC
HIGH (°F)	62	65	71	78	85	89	91	90	87	80	71	65
HIGH (°C)	17	18	22	26	29	32	33	32	31	27	22	18
LOW (°F)	43	46	52	58	66	71	73	73	70	60	50	45
LOW (°C)	6	8	11	14	19	22	23	23	21	16	10	7
DAYS OF RAINFALL	10	9	9	7	8	11	14	13	10	6	7	10

Calendar of Events

For more information on **Mardi Gras, Jazz Fest, Festivals Acadiens,** and other major area events, see chapter 3, "Mardi Gras, Jazz Fest & Other Festivals." For general information, contact the **New Orleans Metropolitan Convention and Visitors Bureau,** 2020 St. Charles Ave., New Orleans, LA 70130 (✆ **800/672-6124** or 504/566-5011; www.neworleanscvb.com). For a list of other Louisiana festivals, visit www.laffnet.org.

For an exhaustive list of events beyond those listed here, check http://events.frommers.com, where you'll find a searchable, up-to-the-minute roster of what's happening in cities all over the world.

JANUARY

Allstate Sugar Bowl Classic. First held in 1934, this is New Orleans's oldest yearly sporting occasion. The football game in the Superdome is the main event, but there are other activities. ✆ **504/828-2440;** www.allstatesugarbowl.org. January 2, 2012, 2013, and 2014.

BCS Championship. The top two college football teams will meet at the New Orleans Superdome in 2012, where one will become champion. www.ncaa.org. January 9, 2012.

FEBRUARY

Lundi Gras. This recently revived tradition brings a free, outdoors music and food celebration to Spanish Plaza (Poydras St. at the river), including a jazz competition. The big event is at 6pm: the ceremonial, waterfront arrival of the kings of Rex and Zulu, marking the beginning of Mardi Gras. They're welcomed by the mayor and a fireworks display over the river. ✆ **504/522-1555.** See also p. 30. Monday before Mardi Gras. February 20, 2012.

Mardi Gras. The culmination of the 2-month-long carnival season, Mardi Gras is the big annual citywide blowout of a party. Each year the eyes of the world are on New Orleans, as the entire city stops working (sometimes days in advance!) and starts partying, and the streets are taken over by awe-inspiring parades. See chapter 3, "Mardi Gras, Jazz Fest & Other Festivals." Day before Ash Wednesday. February 21, 2012.

St. Patrick's Day Parades. There are several, with dates (like the paraders) usually staggered. Since St. Patty's falls on a Saturday in 2012, two parades are on the big day, March 17, 2012: the biggie, which starts in the Irish Channel neighborhood at 1pm at Jackson Avenue and Magazine Street, goes uptown via St. Charles Avenue, Louisiana Avenue, and back to Jackson Avenue. It has the flavor of Mardi Gras, but instead of beads, watchers are pelted with veggies, including the coveted cabbages (see www.irish channelno.org). The downtown parade begins at 7pm at Burgundy and Piety in the Bywater and stumbles along a route to Bourbon Street (☎ **504/525-5169**). A funky third parade kicks off in the French Quarter at Molly's at the Market (1107 Decatur St.) on Friday at 6:30pm (☎ **504/525-5169;** www.stpatricks dayneworleans.com).

St. Joseph's Day Parade. This is another fascinating, little-known, city-centric festivity. St. Joseph is the patron saint of families and working men. His veneration was brought to New Orleans by Italian and Sicilian immigrants. On his saint's day, in addition to a parade, which takes place the weekend around March 19, altars devoted to St. Joseph are erected. These moving, elaborate works of art featuring food, candles, statues, and such, can be viewed at various churches and private homes around the city (where you might also get fed), and at the American Italian Museum, 537 S. Peters St. Locations are listed in the *Times-Picayune* classified section and on www.nola.com in the days just prior to the event. For more information, call ☎ **504/522-7294.**

Super Sunday. This annual Mardi Gras Indians showdown takes place on the Sunday nearest St. Joseph's Day (Mar 19). The more organized "uptown" event is in A. L. Davis Park, Washington Avenue and LaSalle Street, from about noon till late afternoon. At this incredible event, many Indian tribes are gathered in one place (a rarity), in full, feathered regalia, and the chanting is plentiful. There's a second-line parade, plus food and music of course. The "downtown" Indians have a much looser street meeting, determined by weather or whim (of the Big Chief); the gathering can happen any time from a few weeks to even a few months later, usually on Bayou St. John at Orleans Avenue, but sometimes elsewhere. It is intentionally underannounced and there are no contact numbers, but try checking with the Backstreet Museum (p. 180), www.nola. com, or in the Community Events listings at www.wwoz.org. Mid-March. More on p. 31.

Tennessee Williams New Orleans Literary Festival. This 5-day series celebrates New Orleans's rich literary heritage with theatrical performances, readings, discussion panels, master classes, musical events, and walking tours dedicated to the playwright. The focus is not exclusive to Williams, and the roster of writers and publishers participating is impressive. Events take place at venues throughout the city, culminating with the ever-popular Stella Shouting Contest. For info, call ☎ **504/581-1144** or go to www.tennesseewilliams.net. March 28 to April 1, 2012.

The Stella Shouting Contest takes place during the Tennessee Williams New Orleans Literary Festival.

Spring Fiesta. This cultural heritage celebration, which begins with the presentation of the Spring Fiesta queen, is nearly 75 years old and takes place throughout the city—from the Garden District to the French Quarter to Uptown and beyond. Historical and architectural tours of many of the city's private homes, courtyards, and plantation homes are highlights. For the schedule, contact the Spring Fiesta Association (✆ **504/581-1367;** www.springfiesta. com). March 23 to April 1, 2012.

Final Four. The NCAA men's Division I basketball finals will be held in the New Orleans Superdome in 2012. www.ncaa. org. March 31 to April 2, 2012.

APRIL

French Quarter Festival. For fans of New Orleans music from jazz to funk, this free event has become wildly popular. There's an extended description on p. 55. ✆ **504/522-5730;** www.fqfi.org. April 12 to April 15, 2012.

The Crescent City Classic. This 10k race, from Jackson Square to Audubon Park, brings an international field of top (and lesser) runners to the city. ✆ **504/861-8686;** www.ccc10k.com. Saturday before Easter. April 7, 2012.

New Orleans Jazz & Heritage Festival presented by Shell (Jazz Fest). A 10-day event that draws musicians, cooks, and craftspeople and their fans to celebrate music and life, Jazz Fest rivals Mardi Gras in popularity. Much more information on p. ###. ✆ **504/410-4100;** www. nojazzfest.com. April 27 to May 6, 2012.

Festival International de Louisiane. Some people split their festing between Jazz Fest and Festival International in Lafayette. The free, 5-day street fair overlaps with the first weekend of Jazz Fest, so it dovetails nicely. It's a popular event (2011 attendance: 375,000!), focusing on French music and culture. ✆ **337/232-8086;** www.festival international.com. April 25 to 29, 2012.

MAY

New Orleans Wine & Food Experience. This 5-day gourmandistic pleasure fest has over 150 vintners, 75 restaurants, and myriad chefs featuring their wines and wares via tastings, seminars, and vintner dinners. The culmination is a grand, 2-day tasting held in the Superdome, but the party might really hit its stride with the Royal Street Stroll, where revelers indulge their way from one tasting station to the next along the closed street. Expect some particularly festive additions for 2012; it's their 20th anniversary. ✆ **504/529-9463;** www. nowfe.com. May 22 to 26, 2012.

Mid-City Bayou Boogaloo. Another weekend, another laid-back New Orleans music, art, and food fest. This one's themeless, with the pretty location along Bayou St. John being the draw for the largely local crowd (well, and the rubber ducky derby in said waterway). A blanket, a parasol, some cash for snacks and brews, are all you need. Done. ✆ **504/488-3865;** www.thebayou boogaloo.com. Late May/early June.

JUNE

Vieux-to-Do. Creole Tomato, Seafood Festival. This triple-threat fest combines the Creole Tomato Festival with the WWOZ-sponsored Cajun-Zydeco Festival and the Louisiana Seafood Festival in 2 days of music, food, cooking demos, arts markets, and kids' activities. Music stages and booths stretch from Esplanade through the historic French Market. ✆ **504/522-2621;** www.french market.org and www.wwoz.org. June 8 to June 10, 2012.

JULY

Go Fourth on the River. The annual Fourth of July celebration begins in the morning at the riverfront and continues into the night, culminating in a spectacular fireworks display. For details, go to www.go4thontheriver.com or ✆ **800/672-6124.** July 4th weekend.

Essence Music Festival. This 3-day event, sponsored by *Essence* magazine, features top names in African-American entertainment and empowerment seminars. See p. 55 for extended listing. www.essencemusicfestival.com. July 6 to July 8, 2012.

Tales of the Cocktail. The first mixed drink was invented in New Orleans, and as you may have noticed, they've been perfecting the craft ever since. Perhaps the best-known event for cocktailians from around the world, it's not a drunk fest but a serious gathering of leading experts in the field (well, there's some imbibing, too). There's an extended description on p. 56. See www.talesof thecocktail.com. July 24 to July 29, 2012.

AUGUST

Satchmo Summerfest. Louis Armstrong, hometown boy made very good, is now celebrated with his own festival, held around his real birthday (he claimed to be born on July 4th, but records prove otherwise). It includes the usual local food and music in Satchmo's honor, with the emphasis on jazz entertainment and education, including activities for kids, to ensure Satchmo lives on for generations to come. For location updates and information, go to ☎ **504/522-5730** or www. fqfi.org. August 2 to August 5, 2012.

SEPTEMBER

Southern Decadence. The pinnacle of gay New Orleans, where more than 100,000 gay men (and some women) from around the world come to town to flaunt it, whether they got it or not. The multiday-and-night dance and more party hits its frenzied peak during a bar-studded parade route. In 2010, a long-overdue lesbian event was added on Sunday. Book rooms early, and consider getting a weekend ticket package in advance to save time waiting in line. First-timer hint: Even if *you're* not too hot for leather, September in New Orleans is. www.southern-decadence.net or ***Ambush Magazine*** (☎ **504/522-8047**). Labor Day weekend, August 31 to September 2, 2012.

The Pimm's Cup, an oft-served libation at Napoleon House, is one of New Orleans's signature cocktails.

Ponderosa Stomp. Now in its 10th year, this weekend celebration of early American rock music has become a mecca for fans and students of all things roots—blues, twang, swamp, thrash, or beyond. A scholarly conference anchors the days, and seminal performers you won't likely see on tour pack the Howlin' Wolf at night to give every imaginable subgenre its (long over-) due. The stomp highlights and sometimes revitalizes the careers of many unheralded greats. Past performers range from Bobby Charles to Barbara Lynn, and ? (of the Mysterians) to Link Wray. ☎ **504/810-9116;** www. ponderosastompfoundation.org. September 20 to September 22, 2012 (tentative dates).

OCTOBER

Art for Arts' Sake. The arts season begins on October 1 with gallery openings throughout the city. Julia, Magazine, and Royal streets are where the action is. ☎ **504/523-1216;** www.cacno.org. Throughout the month.

Gumbo Festival. This festival showcases one of the region's signature dishes and celebrates Cajun culture to boot. It's 3 days of gumbo-related events (including the presentation of the royal court of King and Miss Creole Gumbo), plus hours of Cajun music, held in Bridge City about a 20-minute drive from New Orleans. © **504/436-4712;** www.hgaparish.org/gumbofestival.htm. Second weekend in October.

Festivals Acadiens. This weekend series of happenings in Lafayette celebrates Cajun music, food, crafts, and culture. For more information, see p. 55 or contact the **Lafayette Convention and Visitors Commission** (© **800/346-1958** in the U.S., 800/543-5340 in Canada, or 337/232-3737; www.festivalsacadiens.com). October 12 to October 14, 2012.

New Orleans Film Festival. The ultra-plush Canal Place Cinemas and other theaters throughout the city screen award-winning local and international films and host writers, actors, and directors over the course of a week. Admission ranges from $9 per screening to $200 for a full festival pass—with discounts for members. © **504/309-6633;** www.neworleansfilmsociety.org. October 19 to October 25, 2012 (tentative dates).

Halloween. Rivaling Mardi Gras in terms of costumes, Halloween is celebrated especially grandly here (New Orleans does have a way with ghosts). The French Quarter, of course, is the center of the Halloween-night universe, but there is ghoulish action all over the city, including Boo-at-the-Zoo (end of Oct) for children, formal and informal costume extravaganzas (including a Monster Bash at the Ernest N. Morial Convention Center), museum exhibits, and haunted houses (notably the truly terrifying House of Shock [www.houseofshock.com]). Halloween is also a huge magnet for LGBT visitors to New Orleans. October 31.

Voodoo Music Experience. This major 3-day music festival, set in its own area of oak-strewn City Park, is the biggest music festival for a younger demographic, with an eclectic indie, rock, and dance lineup. And you can wear a costume. Extended description on p. 56. www.thevoodooexperience.com. Last weekend in October.

Swamp Festival. Sponsored by the Audubon Institute, there are long days of live swamp music performances, lots of good zydeco, as well as hands-on contact with Louisiana swamp animals. Admission is free with zoo admission. © **504/861-2537;** www.auduboninstitute.org. First weekend in November.

The Rayne Frog Festival. Cajuns can always find an excuse to hold a party, and the lowly frog is the excuse here for a *fais-do-do* (dance), waltz competition, frog races, and frog-jumping and -eating contests. For the amphibian-deprived, there's a Rent-a-Frog service. © **800/346-1958** in the U.S., 800/543-5340 in Canada, or 337/232-3808; www.raynefrogfestival.com. Mid-November.

Words & Music: A Literary Fest in New Orleans. This highly ambitious literary and music conference (originated largely by the folks behind Faulkner House Books) offers 5 days' worth of round-table discussions with eminent authors (with varying connections to the city), original drama, poetry readings, and master classes, plus great music and food. For authors seeking guidance and inspiration and for book lovers in general, call © **504/586-1609** or visit www.wordsandmusic.org. Mid-November.

Christmas New Orleans–Style. It's no surprise that the ever-celebratory New Orleanians do Christmas really well. The town is decorated to a fare-thee-well, there is an evening of candlelit caroling in Jackson Square, bonfires line the levees along the River Road on Christmas Eve (to guide Papa Noël, in his sled drawn by alligators), and house tours offer glimpses of stunningly turned-out residences. Restaurants create special, multicourse Réveillon dinners, which, with "Papa Noël" hotel rates, make it an economically *and* architecturally attractive time to visit. © **504/522-5730;** www.neworleansonline.com/christmas.

Celebration in the Oaks. Lights and lighted figures designed to illustrate holiday themes bedeck sections of City Park, and a walking and miniature train tour lets you take in the charm and grandeur at your leisure. For $7 per person, it's simple, nostalgic winter wonderment for the whole family. Ice-skating and classic carousel and amusement park rides are additional. © **544/482-4888; www.neworleanscitypark.com.** Late November to early January.

New Year's Eve. The countdown takes place in Jackson Square and is a big, reliable street party. In the Southern equivalent of New York's Times Square, revelers watch a lighted ball drop from the top of Jackson Brewery. December 31.

RESPONSIBLE TOURISM

For many visitors, responsible tourism in New Orleans starts the minute they leave the airport: If they take the Airport Shuttle to their hotel, they may be riding in a propane-powered hybrid vehicle. If they're in town for Mardi Gras, chances are good that they'll see biodiesel-powered floats, and if they watch the Rex parade, Mistah might throw them some beads on biodegradable string—to help the strands fall from the tree branches.

While eco-tourism hasn't emerged as a major movement in New Orleans, there are many ways to visit responsibly, some requiring little effort. It's a walking town, the classic streetcars run on key routes, and nearby attractions are easily accessed by tour bus. With little need for a rental car, visitors wishing to reduce their carbon footprint are already a step ahead. Although there are few bike paths, bicycling is becoming more prevalent, and drivers are becoming more cyclist-aware. Several bike rental and tour companies geared to tourists are thriving (p. 347), and it's a good way to see the mostly flat city (if you're comfortable navigating the traffic and potholes).

In terms of caloric intake, a visit to New Orleans is decidedly *ir*responsible. While the tourist areas don't boast many vegetarian or vegan restaurants, the usual Middle Eastern and Asian dining options are readily available. Better yet, any restaurant will accommodate their diners' dietary preferences (though it may pain them to do so). Further, many of the fine dining establishments (and simpler ones as well) have long embraced the farm-to-table movement, sourcing ingredients from local purveyors, supporting farmers' markets, and in some cases even planting their own farms and gardens. Given the bounteous supply of produce and seafood in and around New Orleans, it's no surprise that "buy local" is a longstanding practice. Some "name" chefs who actively promote localism and *terroir*, with menus reflecting their passion for local ingredients, include:

- **John Besh:** Besh Steakhouse, Domenica, Restaurant August
- **Frank Brigtsen:** Brigtsen's, Charlie's Seafood
- **Emeril Lagasse:** Delmonico, Emeril's, NOLA
- **Donald Link:** Butcher, Cochon, Herbsaint
- **Dominique Macquet:** Dominique's on Magazine
- **Tory McPhail:** Commander's Palace
- **Slade Rushing and Allison Vines-Rushing:** MiLa
- **Susan Spicer:** Bayona, Mondo

Many of these restaurants are listed in the "Where to Eat" chapter.

Given the Gulf oil spill, indulging heartily in the local seafood is itself a tasty act of responsible tourism. The seafood supplies may have been diminished, but they were by no means decimated (despite reactionary reports to the contrary). Rigorous testing and source tracing ensures that everything that hits the plate is absolutely safe. So sustaining the seafood industry is a responsible act that any tourist can happily undertake (several times daily, even).

As for responsible lodging, hotels, for the most part, have not been quick to wholly embrace sustainable practices. They may be centuries old or in historically protected buildings or both, such that improvements like solar panels, for example, are prohibited by structural ability or regulation. Unless a property is virtually built or rebuilt from the core (like the recently renovated Roosevelt [p. 100], which incorporated significant smart energy features), major green retrofitting is rare.

Still, many hotels have instituted modest sustainability programs, like replacing light bulbs, recycling, and on-demand linen replacement. Some of the larger hotels and chains, such as the Ritz-Carlton (p. 83) and Harrah's (p. 97), are a bit further along, thanks to corporate-wide programs.

Ironically, Hurricane Katrina and the Deepwater oil spill actually had some environmental upsides: Locals and tourists alike became more aware of the need to support locally owned businesses as a means of rebuilding the local economy and maintaining the unique culture of the city. The Urban Conservancy's **Stay Local** program (www.staylocal.org) has a searchable directory of locally owned businesses to patronize—a superb, still relevant resource.

Second, the voluntourism movement coalesced, and remains active. Before committing to a volunteer program, find out about the type of work you'll be doing to make sure it's a good fit for you, and ascertain that any donations truly go back to the local community. **Volunteer International** (www.volunteerinternational.org) has a helpful list of questions to ask. **Habitat for Humanity** accepts volunteers for a day, a year, or any term. The respected organization is creating the Musicians Village for artists who lost their homes in the flood. Contact them at www.habitat-nola.org, or at 7100 St. Charles Ave., New Orleans, LA 70118 (✆ **504/861-2077**).

Other rebuilding efforts include **Common Ground** (1800 Deslonde St., New Orleans, LA 70117; ✆ **504/218-1729**; www.commongroundrelief.org); the **United Saints Recovery Project** (2309 Dryades St., New Orleans, LA 70113; ✆ **504/895-2922**, ext. 108; www.unitedsaints.org); and **Hands On New Orleans** (1050 S. Jefferson Davis Pkwy., New Orleans, LA 70125; ✆ **504/483-7041**; www.handsonneworleans.org), whose website serves as an opportunity clearinghouse of sorts. All three organizations accept volunteers of any skill level. Larger groups can also work through the **New Orleans Metropolitan Convention and Visitors Bureau** (p. 359). All potential volunteers should plan at least 1 to 2 weeks ahead, to complete applications and paperwork before beginning. In some cases, volunteers may be responsible for certain expenses and accommodations.

Common Ground (see above), in conjunction with **Bayou Rebirth,** also has seasonal opportunities for volunteers to join with **coastal and wetlands restoration projects,** including nursery assistance and seedling plantings.

Given the tribulations that New Orleans and Louisiana have undergone the last few years, the most important act of responsible travel may simply be going, spending, enjoying, and encouraging others to do the same.

3

MARDI GRAS, JAZZ FEST & OTHER FESTIVALS

Everybody knows that New Orleans loves a good party. For many, what they know about the city begins and ends with Mardi Gras—the biggest street party in America (never mind all that stuff about history and culture and architecture and so on). It's understandable, given that New Orleanians know what makes a great party: really good food and music, and lots of it—plus a rollicking, party-ready attitude. That's what you'll find at any festival in Louisiana—regardless of what it is ostensibly celebrating. Anything is an excuse for a party here: Festivals center on swamps, gumbo, crawfish, frogs, tomatoes, architecture, and, oh yeah, jazz and heritage, of course. And believe it or not, they're pretty much all a good time. Just consider the city the hostess with the mostess, and commence to getting on your good foot.

This chapter covers some of the largest festivals in New Orleans and the outlying areas; others are listed in the "Calendar of Events" in chapter 2, "New Orleans in Depth."

You can get information on many of the events in both chapters, and others, by contacting the **New Orleans Metropolitan Convention and Visitors Bureau,** 2020 St. Charles Ave., New Orleans, LA 70130 (© **800/672-6124** or 504/566-5011; www.neworleanscvb.com).

MARDI GRAS

Obviously, the granddaddy of all New Orleans celebrations is Mardi Gras. Thanks to sensational media accounts that zero in on the salacious aspects of this Carnival, its rep as a *Girls Gone Wild*–style spring break persists, and these accounts have attracted masses of *Real World: New Orleans* wannabes looking for decadent X-rated action rather than tradition. If that's your thang, by all means go forth and partay (just remember, Facebook is *forever*). Truth is, Mardi Gras remains one of the most exciting times to visit New Orleans, for people from all walks. You can spend days admiring and reveling in the city's traditions and never even venture into the frat-party atmosphere of Bourbon Street.

In the post-Katrina days, there was some silly talk of cancelling the Mardi Gras 2006 in deference to the somberness of the times. Pshaw, said just about everyone—and 6 months to the virtual day after Katrina, most krewes paraded as usual, albeit along slightly altered routes. But the beads and throws were even more plentiful, as were the crowds. Locals returning from exile and visitors (the gruesomely curious and/or those intent on helping rebuild, via tourism dollars spent) made for record attendance. More to the point, the spirit was immeasurably high,

PREVIOUS PAGE: **Revelers dance in the streets at a Mardi Gras parade.**

A Mardi Gras street scene.

as New Orleanians and lovers of the city alike turned out in their most glittery or satirical costumes, exalted in a moment that some feared would never come again. They had survived, and they were filled with hope that their city would, too.

Characters abound throughout the city on Mardi Gras.

Cut to 2010, when Mardi Gras parades rolled just 9 days after the city's beloved Saints had won the Super Bowl (and 3 days after Mitch Landrieu was elected mayor). Eager to celebrate perhaps the city's most triumphant victory since the Battle of New Orleans, the crowds turned out in record numbers, and many said the enthusiasm exceeded all that had come before. In 2011, a late-season Mardi Gras coincided with spring break, making for yet another monstrous, monstrously fun day.

There is so much more to Carnival than the media-hyped wanton action. Knowledge of some of the long and fascinating history of Mardi Gras may help put matters in perspective. First of all, it's both a day and a time period: French for "Fat Tuesday," it's the day before Ash Wednesday, when Lent begins, and it refers to the 5- to 8-week stretch from Twelfth Night (Jan 6) to Mardi Gras Day (which varies, and falls on Feb 21 in 2012). The idea was that good Christians would eat as much as they could in preparation for their impending denial during Lent.

The party's origins can be traced to the Roman **Lupercalia festival:** 2 days when all sexual and social order disappeared, cross-dressing was mandatory, and the population ran riot (sound familiar?). The early Christian church was naturally appalled by this but was unable to stop it (as someone later said about Storyville and prostitution, you can make it illegal but you can't make it unpopular). Grafting Lupercalia to the beginning of Lent may have been a compromise to bribe everyone into observing Lent, and they may have needed those 40 days to recover!

Carnival (from a Latin word roughly meaning "farewell to flesh") and its lavish masked balls and other revels became popular in Italy and France, and the tradition followed the Creoles to New Orleans. The first Carnival balls occurred in 1743. By the mid-1800s, Mardi Gras mischief had grown so ugly (the habit of tossing flour on revelers gradually turned into throwing bricks at them) that everyone predicted the end of the tradition. (The more things change, the more they stay the same.)

THE BIRTH OF THE KREWES Everything changed in 1856. Tired of being left out of the Creoles' Mardi Gras, a group of Americans who belonged to a secret society called Cowbellians formed the Mystick Krewe of Comus (named after the hero of a John Milton poem). On Mardi Gras evening, they presented a torchlit parade, seemingly out of nowhere, that was breathtaking in its design, effects, and imagination. A new tradition was born. Every Mardi Gras night thereafter (with some exceptions) climaxed with the appearance of Comus, each time grander and more astounding.

And so the new standard was set. It marked the height of the social season for **"krewes,"** made up of prominent society and business types. After Comus emerged Rex, the King of Carnival. Rex paraded in the morning and later paid public homage to Comus. Their meeting became the high point of Mardi Gras, and for many the über-ritualized, televised moment still is.

The **royal colors**—purple for justice, green for faith, and gold for power—were adopted as the festival's official colors, and more krewes arose, each throwing a lavish ball along with its parade and all with exclusive membership.

After the Civil War put a temporary halt to things, two new enduring customs were added. Members threw trinkets to onlookers, and a "queen" reigned over their ball.

As an elite Old South institution, Mardi Gras eschewed racial equality or harmony. African Americans participated in parades only by carrying torches to illuminate the route (the *flambeaux,* as the torches are known, are still around, an atmospheric if still controversial tradition). In 1909, a black man named William Storey mocked the elaborately garbed Rex by prancing after his float wearing a lard can for a crown. Storey was promptly dubbed "King Zulu." Thus begat the Krewe of Zulu (officially the Zulu Social Aid and Pleasure Club), which parodied Rex and mocked racial stereotypes. The Zulu parade quickly became one of the most popular aspects of Mardi Gras, famously crowning Louis Armstrong as King Zulu in 1949.

Unfortunately, most krewes still excluded blacks, Jews, and women. Eventually the public, which could not join the krewes but paid taxes for post-parade cleanup, demanded equality. A 1992 ordinance denies a parade permit to any group that discriminates on the basis of race or religion. (Krewes are still not required to integrate along gender lines, a choice of the all-female krewes as much as the male, though men in drag are common.)

Paradegoers vie for throws as a krewe float passes by.

Rex acceded to the new regulations, but mighty Comus, in a move that many still feel marked the beginning of the end of classic Mardi Gras, canceled its parade. Proteus and Momus followed.

Then as now, the krewes and traditions of Mardi Gras change. Today there are dozens of unofficial krewes and "sub-krewe" spinoffs, and more crop up with some regularity.

SPECTACLE & BEAUTY Parades were always things of spectacle and beauty with wooden-wheeled, 19th-century caissons for floats. But the processions outgrew the narrow Quarter streets—and now some have become things of outrageousness, too. New "superkrewes" emerged, like Orpheus (founded by musician and lifelong Mardi Gras enthusiast Harry Connick, Jr.), Bacchus, and Endymion, with nonexclusive memberships and block-long floats. The largest parades can have more than 20 floats, celebrity guests, marching bands, dancing groups, motorcycle squads, celebrity kings, and thousands of participants.

The trinkets known as **throws** fly thick and fast from the floats. The ubiquitous plastic beads were originally glass, often from Czechoslovakia. **Doubloons,** the oversize aluminum coins stamped with the year and the krewe's coat of arms, are collector's items for natives. Other throws include **stuffed animals, plastic krewe cups,** and especially the cherished **Zulu coconuts.**

Alas, the traditional cry of "Throw me something, Mister!" to obtain a trinket is occasionally reduced to the request/demand, "Show me your tits!" But truth is, a cute kid, an eager grandma, and a genuinely friendly face are equally likely to score copious throws.

Kickin' Up Your Heels: Mardi Gras Activities

Mardi Gras can be whatever you want. The exhibitionism and drunken orgies are largely confined to Bourbon Street. If that's what you want, go there. But if you avoid Bourbon Street (or visit a few weeks before Fat Tuesday), you can have an entirely different experience.

THE SEASON The date of Fat Tuesday is different each year, but Carnival season always starts on **Twelfth Night,** January 6, when the Phunny Phorty Phellows kick off the season with a streetcar party cruise.

Over the following weeks, the city celebrates, often with **King Cakes.** This round, coffeecake-like confection, dusted with Mardi Gras purple-, green-, and gold-colored sugar, contains a plastic baby baked right in. Getting the piece with the baby can be a good omen or can mean you have to throw the next King Cake party. For the high-society crowd, the season brings dozens of invitation-only parties, some harking back to the traditional, 19th-century masked balls. Each krewe throws a ball, ostensibly to introduce its royalty for the year.

Two or three weeks before Mardi Gras itself, the parading (and parodying) begins. Adorable canines parade in the **Mystick Krewe of Barkus,** often with their humans in matching costumes, and the hilarious **Krewe du Vieux** outrages with un-family-friendly decadence. If you want to experience Mardi Gras but don't want to face the full force of craziness, consider coming for the weekend 10 days before Fat Tuesday (the season officially begins the Fri of this weekend). You can count on 10 to 15 small to midsize parades, and easily manageable crowds.

The following weekend there are another 15 parades. The parades are bigger, the crowds are bigger—everything's bigger. By this point, the city has succumbed to Carnival fever. After a day of screaming for beads, you'll probably find yourself heading somewhere to get a drink or three. The French Quarter, the center of late-night revelry, will be packed. If you've traveled uptown or to Mid-City for a parade, consider staying put at a nearby joint. If you opt for more reserved revelry and a nice evening out, book well in advance, and make sure your route to the restaurant won't be impeded by the parades. The last parade each day (on both weekends) is usually scheduled to end around 9:30pm but can run way later; you might be exhausted by the time you get back to the hotel.

LUNDI GRAS From 1874 to 1917, Rex's **King of Carnival** arrived downtown from the Mississippi River on Lundi Gras, the Monday before Fat Tuesday. After years of neglect, the event is a big deal once again. Festivities begin at the riverfront in the afternoon with lots of drink and live music. King Zulu arrives around 5pm, followed by the masked King of Rex. The two meet and are greeted by the mayor, and the ceremony is followed by a huge fireworks display over the river. That night **Proteus** and the **Krewe of Orpheus** (known for their generous throws) hold their parades. Because Lent begins the following night (Tues) at midnight, a good portion of the city pulls an all-nighter on Monday.

MARDI GRAS DAY The two biggest parades, **Zulu** and **Rex,** run back to back to kick things off. Zulu starts near the Central Business District at 8:30am; Rex starts uptown at 10am. Across town, the Bohemian Societé of St. Anne starts mustering around 9am near Burgundy and Peity Streets in the Bywater area. The walking club (no floats) is known for its madcap, au courant, and sometimes risqué costumes.

Throughout the early morning, in between the parades, you can see other elaborately costumed Mardi Gras **walking or marching clubs,** such as the Jefferson City Buzzards, the Pete Fountain Half Fast, and Mondo Kayo (identifiable by their tropical/banana theme). They walk (or stroll, or stumble), accompanied by marching. Catch the "marchers" anywhere along St. Charles Avenue between Poydras Street and Washington Avenue.

Mardi Gras Indians wear elaborate handmade suits made from beads, feathers, and other colorful adornments.

Also keep a watch out for unofficial and rogue krewes and marching clubs like the Julus, which includes members of the New Orleans Klezmer All-Stars and throws painted bagels, the sci-fi Krewe of Chewbacchus, or the legume-adorned Krewe of Red Beans. They're sometimes announced on WWOZ.org or in Gambit (www.bestofneworleans.com). These can be groups formed among friends, within a neighborhood, or around any random theme.

By early afternoon, Rex spills into the Central Business District. Nearby at about this time, you may be able to find some of the most elusive New Orleans figures, the **Mardi Gras Indians.** The "tribes" of New Orleans are small communities of African Americans and black Creoles (some of whom have Native American ancestors), mostly from the inner city. The tribes have an established hierarchy and deep-seated traditions, including enormous, elaborate beaded and feathered costumes. They're entirely made by hand, and a great source of pride, each attempting to out-outlandish the next. The men work on them all year in preparation for Mardi Gras and St. Joseph's Day (p. 31), and then turn around and start working on next year's suit.

The timing is loose, but traditionally, tribes converge throughout the day, in their neighborhoods, at main intersections along the Claiborne Avenue median (underneath the interstate), and at St. Augustine's church in the Treme. Crowds of locals mill around to see the spectacle: When two tribes meet, they'll stage a mock confrontation, resettling their territory and common borders. After marching in various parades, they reconvene around midafternoon on Claiborne, where a party gets going. Play it cool, however—this is not your neighborhood, nor a sideshow act put on for your benefit. It is a ritual deserving of respect. Also, Indian suits are copyrighted works of art; photos of them can't be sold without permission. Ask locals for rumors about times and intersections, and then bike, walk, or drive around (it's probably the only time a car is useful on Mardi Gras), keeping eyes and ears open for feathers and drums. You can also try to catch these confrontations during St. Joseph's Day (p. 31), at parties and at Jazz Fest.

After the parades, the action picks up in the Quarter. En route, you'll see that Mardi Gras is still very much a family tradition, with whole families dressing up in similar costumes. Marvel at how an entire city has shut down so that every citizen can join in the celebrations—on the streets, on their balconies watching the action below, or barbecuing in their courtyards. If you are lucky and seem like the right sort, you might well get invited in.

In the Quarter, the frat-party action is largely confined to Bourbon Street. The more interesting activity is in the lower Quarter and the Frenchmen section of the Faubourg Marigny (just east of the Quarter), where the artists and the gay community celebrate in their elaborate, work-of-art costumes. It's boisterous and enthusiastic, but not (for the most part) obnoxious.

As you make your way through the streets, keep your eyes peeled for members of the legendary **Krewe of Comus.** They will be men dressed in tuxes with brooms over their shoulders, holding cowbells. Ask them if they are Comus, and they will deny it, insisting they are Cowbellians. But if they hand you a vintage Comus doubloon, the truth will be out.

If you can, try to stay until midnight when the police come through the Quarter, efficiently, officially shutting down Mardi Gras. If you can't, tune in to WYES (Channel 12) for live coverage of the Rex Ball—it's serious pomp.

Doing Mardi Gras

LODGING During Mardi Gras, accommodations in the city and the nearby suburbs are booked solid, *so make your plans well ahead and book a room as early as possible*—a year or more in advance is quite common. Prices are usually much higher during Mardi Gras, and most hotels and guesthouses impose minimum-stay requirements. Some hotels along the parade routes offer packages including bleacher or balcony seats where you can view the action almost hassle-free. They're popular but pricey.

CLOTHING For the parades before Mardi Gras day, dress comfortably and prepare for whatever weather is forecast (which can vary widely). A wig or mask makes it fun, but most don't dress up. Fat Tuesday is a different story. As with anything in New Orleans, you must join in if you want to have the best time. That means a **costume** and **mask,** which automatically makes you a participant (and it's more fun). (Tellingly, the Bourbon Street participants usually do not wear costumes. Just skin.) You needn't do anything fancy; scan the thrift stores for something loud and you're good to go. But anything goes, so fly your freak flag if you're so inclined.

If you've come unprepared, see p. 258 for shops that specialize in Mardi Gras costumes and masks, or try the secondhand stores along Magazine Street and in the Bywater that stock inexpensive costumes from previous years.

DINING If you want to eat at a restaurant during Mardi Gras, make reservations as early as possible. And pay attention to **parade routes** (map on p. 47), because if there is one between you and your restaurant, you may not be able to drive or park nearby, or even cross the street, and you can kiss your dinner goodbye. Thus, restaurants often have a high no-show rate during Mardi Gras, so a well-timed drop-in may work to the nonplanner's advantage.

DRIVING & PARKING Traffic and navigating during Mardi Gras is horrendous. So our admonition against ever renting a car is even stronger during Mardi Gras. **Don't drive.** Instead, relax, take a cab, walk, or pedal (see p. 347, and call well in advance for a bike reservation). Parking along parade routes is not allowed 2 hours before and 2 hours after the parade. Parking on the neutral ground (median strip) is illegal (despite what you may see), and chances are good that you'll be towed. ***Note:*** Taxis are very busy, and while some streetcars and buses do run during Mardi Gras, they may have radically altered schedules and routes during that time (none run on St. Charles Ave.). Contact the Regional Transit Authority (RTA; ☎ **504/248-3900;** www. norta.com) for more information.

FACILITIES Restrooms are notoriously scant along the parade routes. Take advantage of the facilities when you come across them, such as at a lunch or bar break. Otherwise it's the ever-popular porta-potty, so bring tissues.

THE DAY PLAN It's not necessary to make a plan for the big day, but it might help. It also helps to know that you'll probably adjust the plan, or throw it out altogether, as the day goes on. Go with the flow. Don't get irritated. The fun is everywhere—but with limited transportation and facilities available (and until you've done it enough to determine a satisfying routine), you'll have to make some choices about what you intend to do. Read the rest of this section, and check the route maps. Then decide if you want to head uptown, downtown, to the Quarter, the Bywater, Claiborne Avenue, or some combination of the above, as your stamina dictates.

SAFETY Many, many cops are out, making the walk from uptown to downtown safer than at other times of year, but not surprisingly, the streets of New Orleans are a haven for pickpockets during Mardi Gras. Take precautions.

SEATING A limited number of bleachers are erected along the downtown parade route. Most are reserved for private use, but some are sold to the public—you'll pay dearly for the convenience. Start checking Ticketmaster and www.neworleansparadetickets.com in December. Some enterprising folks buy cheap folding chairs at local drug stores, which typically don't make it home. Many just bring a blanket or tarp (we find that lightweight sarongs fold down well and serve multiple purposes). You might find a spot to use them on the Uptown routes; downtown, you'll probably be standing. The longest parades can last 3-plus hours, so plan in accordance with your staying power.

KIDS Though it may seem contrarian, you can bring the kids to Mardi Gras if you stick to the Uptown locales (you'll see hundreds of local kids seated atop custom-rigged ladders, the better to catch throws). It's a long day so make sure to bring supplies and diversions for between parades. While there may be some schlepping involved, their delight increases everyone's enjoyment considerably.

WHAT ELSE TO BRING The usual dilemma applies: You'll want to stay unencumbered, but well-supplied. Much depends on whether you plan to stay in one place or make tracks. A starter set of beverages and snacks is called for, or a full picnic if you desire (food carts and trucks, and enterprising homeowners-turned-delis are usually available along the routes; many locals set up elaborate barbecue rigs). Toilet tissue and hand sanitizer are good ideas, and don't forget a bag for those beads.

 Save the Date

Mardi Gras falls exactly 47 days before Easter: that's February 21, 2012; February 12, 2013; March 4, 2014; February 17, 2015; and February 9, 2016.

How to Spend the Big Day

Despite the popular impression of Mardi Gras, the parades don't even go down Bourbon Street. Your Carnival experience will depend on where you go and whom you hang out with. Here are three ways of doing it: nice, naughty, and nasty. Us? We prefer a mix of the first two.

NICE Hang out exclusively Uptown with the families. Find a spot on St. Charles Avenue (which is entirely closed that day) between Napoleon Avenue and Lee Circle, and set up camp with a blanket and a picnic lunch for **Rex,** the truck parades, and walking clubs. Dressed-up families are all around. One side of St. Charles is for the parades and the other is open only to foot traffic, so you can wander about, admire the scene, and angle for an invitation to a barbecue or balcony party. New Orleans kids assure us that Mardi Gras is more fun than Halloween, and we can see why.

    Zulu's route starts at Jackson and goes downriver, so those further uptown will miss out. Staking out a spot downtown is another option; the crowds are a bit thicker and rowdier.

    For an utterly different experience, head out around 9am-ish and look for the **Mardi Gras Indian** tribes meeting. It's a hit-or-miss proposition; the Indians themselves never know in advance when or where the gatherings occur. But running across them on their own turf is one of the great sights and experiences of Mardi Gras. See p. 43.

NAUGHTY Try to be near the corner of Burgundy and St. Ann streets at noon for the **Bourbon Street** awards. You may not get close enough to actually see the judging, but the participants are all around you so that you can gawk up at their sometimes R- and X-rated costumes. As you wander the Quarter, keep an eye out (or ask around) for the **Krewe of Kosmic Debris** and the **Society of St. Anne,** no floats, just marvelously costumed revelers. After the awards (about midafternoon), head over to the Frenchmen section, where street dancing to tribal drums celebrates Carnival well into the night.

NASTY Stay strictly on **Bourbon Street.** Yep, it's every bit as crowded, vulgar, and obscene as you've heard (and the floats are nowhere nearby). The street is full of drunks (and the occasional bewildered soul), few in costume, with

DO YOUR homework

You'll enjoy Mardi Gras more if you've done a little homework before your trip. Contact the **New Orleans Metropolitan Convention and Visitors Bureau,** 2020 St. Charles Ave., New Orleans, LA 70130 (☏ **800/672-6124** or 504/566-5011; www.neworleanscvb.com), and ask for current Mardi Gras info.

    You'll also want to get your hands on the latest edition of *Arthur Hardy's Mardi Gras Guide.* Order through www.mardigrasguide.com, or pick it up nearly anywhere around town. Schedules and routes occasionally change, and this will have updated information, among much other useful information. Also get their helpful free app, and the real-time parade tracker app from wwl.tv.

Major Mardi Gras Parade Routes

CITY PARK

Endymion starts here

City Park Avenue

Canal St.

N. Alexander St.

N. Solomon St.

MID-CITY

Esplanade Ave.

Fair Grounds Racetrack (Jazz Fest)

Gentilly Blvd.

N. Broad St.

Law St.
N. Dorgenois St.
N. Rocheblave St.

St. Bernard Ave.

S. Carrollton Ave.

S. Pierce St.

Orleans Ave.

Hagan St.

Ursulines Ave.

90

N. Tonti St.

N. Miro St.

N. Galvez St.

10

Bienville

Iberville Parkway

N. Lopez St.

N. Gayoso St.

N. White St.

Orleans St.

N. Broad Ave.

N. Dorgenois St.

N. Rocheblave St.

Esplanade Ave.

Ursulines Ave.

N. Derbigny St.

St. Bernard Ave.

Kerlerec St.

Urquhart St.

St. Claude Ave.

Area of detail

Lake Pontchartrain

CITY PARK

10

610

Fair Grounds Racetrack

Superdome

Mississippi

S. Clark St.

Jefferson

Tulane Ave.

Banks St.

Cleveland Ave.

Canal Ave.

S. Iberville St.

Bienville

Bienville St.

N. Galvez

Conti St.

Durhaine Ave.

St. Ann Ave.

N. Robertson St.

LOUIS ARMSTRONG PARK

N. Rampart St.

Bourbon St.

Esplanade Ave.

Gravier St.

Perdido St.

90

Galvez St.

S. Poydras

10

Zulu ends here

Basin St.

FRENCH QUARTER

Pontchartrain Expressway

Earhart Blvd.

S. Rendon Ave.

S. Broad Ave.

Erato St.

M.L. King Blvd.

Endymion starts here

Superdome

Duncan Plaza Civic Center

Girod

Rex ends here

Krewe d'Etat ends here

Magazine St.

Poydras

BROADMOOR

S. Galvez St.

Toledano Ave.

3rd St.

S. Claiborne Ave.

Zulu starts here

Julia

Union Passenger Terminal

Loyola Ave.

Girod

Julia

Howard

Iris ends here

Iris starts here

Rex starts here

Clara St.

Jackson Ave.

4th St.

2nd St.

1st St.

Melpomene Ave.

Lee Circle

Muses ends here

Orpheus & Bacchus end here

Magnolia St.

Freret St.

S. Washington

LaSalle St.

Loyola Ave.

St. Charles

10

CENTRAL BUSINESS DISTRICT

Jena St.

Cadiz St.

Napoleon Ave.

Loyola Ave.

Danneel St.

Baronne St.

Jackson Ave.

Camp St.

Magazine St.

Constance St.

Annunciation St.

Religious

Danneel St.

Dryades St.

St. Charles

Felicity

Muses & Krewe d'Etat start here

Perrier St.

GARDEN DISTRICT

Magazine St.

Louisiana Ave.

LOWER GARDEN DISTRICT

Tchoupitoulas

Mississippi River

Orpheus & Bacchus start here

Jena St.

0   1/4 mi

0   0.25 km

BR 90

Prime Bead Catching Area

Endymion Parade Route

Zulu Route

Other Routes

mardi gras memories: **RIDING A FLOAT**

Sure, it's fun to watch a Mardi Gras parade, but we all yearn to actually be in one, to ride one of those glorious floats in a fabulous, shiny costume, wearing a mask, tossing beads to an adoring public. Even lifelong New Orleanians almost never get to have that experience, as only a few krewes invite outsiders to ride. So when the krewe of Orpheus generously offered to let this former *Frommer's New Orleans* author join their 1999 Mardi Gras parade, she didn't hesitate. She recounts it here:

The theme was "Premieres of the French Opera," an homage to the beloved building that burned down in the 1920s. The floats were conceived by master float designer Henri Schindler. I would be riding on *Le Cid* (an opera by Jules Massenet). I had to send in measurements for my costume (float riders must be masked and costumed throughout the parade) and purchase beads to throw. Many, many beads. How many? "Oh, about 50 or 60 gross."

"That's more than 7,000 strands!" I said, calculating that this was going to set me back several hundred bucks.

"Yeah, you're right—you might want to get a few more."

Orpheus parades on Lundi Gras night, starting at 6pm. I show up at 10am at the convention center to load my beads on the float. Several other float riders do the same, and before long, we are surrounded by little fortresses of beads and other throws. My neighbors, noticing my thrifty (read: cheap) beads (the better-quality beads cost a lot more, especially for 7,000 of them), graciously share a few good strands with me so I may bestow them on especially worthy people. I resolve to throw only to people who don't have many beads, who've been overlooked by other float riders, who aren't cute college girls—in short, people like me. (I'd been frustrated all week by float riders who seemed to find me invisible.)

I try on my costume, which is vaguely knightlike (that is, if knights wore shiny metallic fabric and orange polyester). We finally get on the floats at 3:30pm, ready to head to the parade route. My husband, in mandatory tux, will meet me at the finish line near the convention center, home of the Orpheus Ball.

4pm: The floats start to move toward the starting point on Tchoupitoulas.

4:30pm: Our float stops. The float in front of us has a flat tire.

4:31pm: Everyone around me starts drinking.

5pm: Float starts to move again.

5:20pm: Float stops moving.

5:45pm: Pizzas (dinner) are delivered to the float. Only in New Orleans.

6pm: Parade starts. It doesn't really affect us. We are float 24, and it's a long, long time until we hit the starting line.

6:05 to 7:35pm: People still drinking.

7:35pm: Float starts to move again.

7:37pm: Float stops.

8pm: Float starts again. We can see the starting point.

8:05pm: So much for moving.

8:30pm: Everyone is deeply, crushingly bored.

9pm: Even the drinkers have stopped drinking.

9:17pm: I think of my husband at the ball and wonder if I will ever see him again.

9:30pm: Here we go! And it's mayhem. Thousands of people, waving hands, screaming, shrieking, pleading, crying,

"Please, Mister, throw me something; throw me something, Mister!" I start to grin and don't stop for hours. I throw beads, feeling, at last, like a queen tossing largesse to the populace. I am sparing in my generosity, however, minding advice not to go overboard too early, lest I run out of beads. I discover my aim isn't bad, and from my upper-level vantage point, I can throw quite far out, to specific people in the back. I also learn that from atop the float, you can see everybody, no matter how small, so if it seems like float riders are ignoring you, it's because they are.

9:35pm: One heavily endowed young woman flashes me and looks expectant, but I say, "Put those away!"

10pm: As we turn onto St. Charles, I hear someone shout my name. It's my cousin's son, a Tulane med student whom I've never actually met before. Of course, since I'm masked and costumed, he still doesn't know what I look like.

10:15pm: Orpheus is known for its generosity, so by now every paradegoer's neck is already thickly covered in beads. There is no bead-challenged person to throw to. Worse, because so many floats have already gone by, everyone only wants the really good beads, not the utilitarian stuff I'm throwing. Oh, dear.

10:45pm: I notice how my friend Ann is really good at taunting the crowd with the good beads. She holds out long, thick strands, shows them off, whips the crowd into a frenzy, then shakes her head sadly and puts them away to await more worthy types.

11pm: The crowd's impatience is high whenever the float comes to a halt—that's when riders supposedly throw the really good stuff. The crowd threatens to turn ugly when I don't. The occasional

good strand given by a sympathetic co-rider means I can then appease the angry mob. Lacking a worthy target, I choose to turn my back and throw blindly. Meanwhile, my neat fortress of beads is now in shambles, and I slip and slide on loose strands, frantically trying to get some to throw before revelers scale the float to rip them from me.

11:04pm: I never want to see another bead as long as I live.

11:05pm: Oh, goody, only about halfway there!

11:06pm to 12:35am: Pleasemisterthrow mesomethingpleasemisterpleasemister c'monmisterheymisterpleasemisterpleas emisterpleasepleaseplease*mistaaaahhh!*

12:40am: I make a horrifying discovery. With less than one-third of the parade to go, I still have several thousand beads left. These are worthless once the parade is over (particularly my crappy cheap beads), so as we hit Canal Street, I start to heave them at a great rate, by the dozen, and sometimes entire packages of several dozen. Suddenly, I am *very* popular.

1:30am: We arrive at the convention center. Although these people have been watching floats arrive for at least 3 hours, they are still surprisingly fresh and enthusiastic. This howling mob of gowned women and tuxedoed men stands on chairs and tables and shrieks for beads. Among them is my husband, who catches the camera I toss him, so he can take a picture of my dirty, bedraggled self.

1:35am: I descend from the float and proceed to the party. "How was it?" my husband's new friends (he's been sitting there a long time) inquire. "Ask me tomorrow," I say.

by Mary Herczog

balconies full of the same, dangling beads (some with X-rated anatomical features), which they will hand over in exchange for a glimpse of flesh (by the way, flashing the usual parts is technically illegal). It's the "anything goes" attitude of Carnival, and while it's worth getting a quick peep at, it grows boring more quickly than you might think.

Parade Watch

A Mardi Gras parade works a spell on people. There's no other way to explain why thousands of otherwise rational men and women scream, plead, and sometimes expose themselves for no more reward than a plastic trinket. Don't worry—nobody goes home empty-handed (even the trees end up laden with glittery goods). In your zeal to catch beads, don't forget to actually look at the amazing floats. When the nighttime floats are lit by flambeaux torch bearers, it is easy to envision a time when Mardi Gras meant mystery and magic.

These are just a few of the major parades of the last days of Carnival. Also see the route map on p. 47, and the guide advice on p. 46.

- **Muses** (founded 2000): This popular all-gals krewe honors New Orleans's artistic community—and shoes. Their glittery, decorated shoes are highly sought throws. Muses parades on the Thursday evening before Mardi Gras.

- **Krewe d'Etat** (founded 1996): Social satire is the Krewe specialty, with no current event left unscathed. It parades on the Friday evening before Mardi Gras, and their hilarious float designs are often talked about all week.

- **Iris** (founded 1917): This women's krewe follows traditional Carnival rules of costume and behavior. It parades on the Saturday afternoon before Mardi Gras.

- **Endymion** (founded 1967): This became one of the early "superkrewes" in the 1970s by featuring a glut of floats and celebrity guests such as Alice Cooper, Tom Jones, Dolly Parton, John Goodman, and Kevin Costner. It runs in Mid-City Saturday evening, concluding with a big party in the Superdome.

- **Bacchus** (founded 1968): The original "superkrewe," Bacchus was the first to host international celebrities, especially as grand marshals. It traditionally runs the Sunday before Mardi Gras, from Uptown to the convention center.

- **Orpheus** (founded 1994): Another youngish krewe, it was founded by a group that includes Harry Connick, Jr., and tries to adhere to classic krewe traditions, and is popular for its many stunning floats and generous throws. They parade on Lundi Gras evening and follow the Bacchus route.

- **Zulu** (founded 1916): Lively Zulu has float riders decked out in woolly wigs and blackface. They carry the most prized of Mardi Gras souvenirs: glittery gold-and-black hand-painted coconuts. These status symbols must be placed in your hands, not tossed, so go right up to the float and do your best begging. The parade runs on Mardi Gras morning.

- **Rex** (founded 1872): Rex, the original Mardi Gras daytime parade, follows Zulu down St. Charles. It features the King of Carnival and some of the classic floats of Carnival. Various independent walking clubs often precede Rex.

CAJUN MARDI GRAS

If Mardi Gras in New Orleans sounds like too much for you no matter how low-key you keep it, consider driving out to Cajun Country, where Mardi Gras traditions are just as strong but considerably more, er, wholesome. **Lafayette,** the capital of French Acadiana, celebrates Carnival in a manner that reflects the Cajun heritage and spirit. The 3-day event is second in size only to New Orleans's celebration. There's one *big* difference, though: Their final pageant and ball are open to the general public. Don your formal wear and join right in!

The Lafayette festivities are ruled by King Gabriel and Queen Evangeline, the fictional hero and heroine of Henry Wadsworth Longfellow's epic poem *Evangeline,* set in these locales (p. 319).

Things get off to a joyous start with a Friday night parade and then kick into high gear with the **Children's Krewe** and **Krewe of Bonaparte** parades and ball, held on the Saturday before Mardi Gras, following a full day of celebration at Cajun Field. On Monday night Queen Evangeline is honored at the **Queen's Parade.** The **King's Parade,** held the following morning, honors King Gabriel and opens a full day of merriment. Lafayette's African-American community stages the **Lafayette Mardi Gras Festival Parade,** honoring King Toussaint L'Ouverture and Queen Suzanne Simonne at about 1pm, just after the King's Parade. Then the **Krewe of Lafayette** invites everyone to get into the act as its **Independent Parade** winds through the streets. Krewe participants trot along on foot or ride in the vehicle of their choice—some very imaginative modes of transportation turn up every year. The Mardi Gras climax, a formal ball presided over by the king and queen and their royal court, takes place that night. Everything stops promptly at midnight, as Cajuns and visitors alike depart to begin their observance of Lent.

MASKED MEN & A BIG GUMBO In the Cajun countryside outside Lafayette, there's yet another celebration, the Courir de Mardi Gras, tied to the traditional rural lifestyle. Bands of masked men dressed in raggedy patchwork costumes and peaked *capichon* hats set off on Mardi Gras morning on horseback, led by their *capitaine.* They ride from farm to farm, asking at each, *"Voulez-vous recevoir le Mardi Gras?"* ("Will you receive the Mardi Gras?"). *"Oui,"* comes the invariable reply. Each farmyard then becomes a miniature festival as the revelers *faire le macaque* ("make monkeyshines") with song, dance, much drinking of beer, and other antics. As payment for their pageantry, they get "a fat little chicken to make a big gumbo" (or sometimes a bag of rice or other ingredients).

When each band has visited its allotted farmyards, all head back to town where everyone else has already begun cooking, dancing, game-playing, storytelling, and the like. This lasts into the wee hours, and yes, all those fat little chickens do indeed go into a *gumbo gros* pot to make a very big gumbo.

Get particulars on both the urban (Lafayette) and rural celebrations (**Eunice** and **Mamou** stage some of the most enjoyable ones) from the **Lafayette Parish Convention and Visitors Commission** (© **800/346-1958** in the U.S., 800/543-5340 in Canada, or 337/232-3737; www.lafayettetravel.com).

NEW ORLEANS JAZZ & HERITAGE FESTIVAL

What began in 1969 as a small gathering in Congo Square to celebrate the music of New Orleans now ranks as one of the best attended, most respected, and most musically comprehensive festivals in the world. Although people call it Jazz Fest, the full name is **New Orleans Jazz & Heritage Festival presented by Shell,** and the "heritage" part is broadly interpreted. Each of the 12 stages showcases a musical genre or three—at times likening a walk through Fest to a miniature world tour. A walk will also mean catching the tantalizing aromas of a dozen or so different food offerings, and meeting a United Nations–like spectrum of fellow festgoers all at once.

Jazz Fest has come to encompass everything the city has to offer, in terms of music, food, and culture. That, and it's a hell of a party. Shell Oil stepped in to sponsor Jazz Fest in 2006, securing its return after Katrina and instigating a moment of resurrection for the city, highlighted by an emotional, resonant set by Bruce Springsteen and his Seeger Sessions band. Such musical and emotional epiphanies abound at Fest. While such headliners as Arcade Fire, Pearl Jam, Stevie Wonder, Van Morrison, Dave Matthews, My Morning Jacket, Bob Dylan, and the Roots have drawn record-setting crowds in recent years, serious Festers savor the lesser-known acts. They range from the avant-garde to old-time Delta bluesmen, from African artists making rare U.S. appearances to Bohemian street folkies, and from the top zydeco players to gospel mass choirs. And, of course, jazz.

Filling the infield of the Fair Grounds horse-racing track up near City Park, the festival covers 2 long weekends, the last in April and the first in May (for 2012, that's Apr 27–29 and May 3–6). It's set up about as well as such an event can be. When the crowds get thick, though—especially the popular second Saturday—it can be tough to move around, more so if the grounds are muddy from rain. Lines at the most popular of the several dozen food booths can be frustratingly long, but they're worth the wait. Although the crowds can diminish the fun some, they are generally remarkably well behaved.

Attending Jazz Fest means making a few decisions. Hotels, restaurants, and flights fill up months (if not a year) in advance, but the schedule is not announced until a couple of months before the event. Just about every day at Jazz Fest is a good day regardless of who is playing, however, and you can always go for both weekends. The Thursday before the second weekend traditionally has more locals, on stage and in the audience, and smaller crowds. It's a great time to hit the best food booths and to check out the crafts areas.

Dr. John is a fan favorite at Jazz Fest.

Jazz Fest draws huge crowds.

Jazz Fest Pointers

"It's a marathon, not a sprint" as the saying goes. With music in every direction, you can plot out your day or just wander from stage to stage, catching a few songs by just about everyone—some of the best Jazz Fest experiences come from discovering a hitherto unknown (at least to you) band or otherwise stumbling across a gem of a musical moment. Or you can jettison the jetting about and instead set up camp at just one stage—from the big ones, which feature famous headliners, to the gospel tent, where musical miracles are pretty much a given. We liken the choice to sit-down dining versus a buffet: Both have their advantages.

On a typical Jazz Fest day, you'll arrive sometime after the gates open at 11am and stay until you are pooped or they close at 7pm. Incredibly, the whole thing usually runs as efficiently as a Swiss train. After you leave, get some dinner, and hit the clubs. Every club in the city has Jazz Fest–related bookings (of special note are Piano Night at the House of Blues, Tipitina's Instruments a Comin' benefit, and the jam-heavy shows produced by Superfly [www.superflypresents. com]). Alternatively, sleep.

The excellent nonmusical aspects of Jazz Fest are plentiful. Local craftspeople and juried artisans fill a sizable area with products and demonstrations. You might see Louisiana Native American basket making; Cajun accordion, fiddle, and triangle making; and/or Mardi Gras Indian beading. Contemporary arts and crafts—such as jewelry, hand-blown glass, and painting—are also abundant, and an open marketplace at Congo Square is filled with African (and African-influenced) crafts. Most vendors will pack and ship goods to your home (and there's a U.S. Post Office on site, too).

And then, as always in New Orleans, there's the food. There are local standbys, and we don't mean burgers and dogs; you'll find none of that here. We *do* mean red beans and rice, jambalaya, étouffée, gumbo, and more interesting choices such as oyster sacks, the hugely popular sausage bread, *cochon de lait* (a mouthwatering roast-pig sandwich), a fried soft-shell crab po' boy, and quail and pheasant gumbo. There's crawfish every way, in sushi, enchiladas, and the divine crawfish Monica (a white-cream sauce over pasta). And that's not even discussing the various Caribbean, African, Spanish, and vegetarian dishes available. The kids' area has PB&J, mac and cheese, and other easy-pleasing faves. Dessert?

Mai oui: fresh strawberry shortcake, white chocolate bread pudding, Key lime tarts, fruity snoballs with condensed milk—oh, my! We highly recommend trying at least one new thing daily, and also sharing, so you can sample more variety and decide which booths to revisit. ***Tip:*** There's copious cold beer, but the lines can get long. Smaller stages = shorter lines, and it's often worth it to trek there.

But wait, there's more! Cultural presentations on topics like folklore, traditions, and local food (complete with tastes!) are held daily. These little jewels are easily overlooked. We encourage you to either buy a program (which lists everything being offered and has food coupons, too) or drop by one of the information booths to look over the listings. And yes, there's an app for that, with schedules and descriptions. Link to it from the Fest website, **www.nojazzfest.com**.

Experienced Fest-goers also know that the Grandstand is the best-kept secret; it's air-conditioned, full of art and photography exhibits, and has cooking demonstrations by the city's best chefs. The upstairs Heritage Stage features interviews and short performances by some of the acts in a more intimate setting. We once saw Elvis Costello and Allen Toussaint with only a handful of people, compared with the thousands who struggled to see their full set later in the day.

Wear and bring as little as possible, you'll want to be comfy and unencumbered. But do bring sun protection, something that tells time, a poncho if rain is forecast (they sell them there, but for double what you'll pay at a souvenir store), moola (cash only for food; credit okay for crafts), and a camera if that's your thing (no video- or audio-taping allowed, though). Wear comfy, supportive, well broken-in shoes, whether (for you) that means sandals or hiking boots. You know your feet, and plan accordingly.

Note: No outside beverages (apart from 1 liter of water) are allowed at Jazz Fest. Though there are seats in the two jazz tents and the gospel tent, and some bleachers at *fais-do-do,* people either sit on the ground, stand, or bring blankets or folding chairs. When left vacant, these become annoying space hogs. Kind Fest-goers invite others to use their space when they leave temporarily, but don't be shy about asking.

Purchase tickets when they go on sale in late fall or early winter, when they are the cheapest. They're available through **Ticketmaster** (✆ **800/745-3000;** www.ticketmaster.com), online or at any Ticketmaster outlet. Admission for adults in 2011 was $40 in advance (when purchasing a full weekend's worth), $60 at the gate, $5 for children (plus Ticketmaster's ample handling fees). There are also various VIP packages available, with a range of swanky seating, access, and amenities including the elevated "Big Chief" VIP seating area (nearly $1,000 per weekend). The good news is that general admission Fest tickets are always available at the gate (there is no sellout, except for the VIP packages). The bad news is that tickets are always available at the gate, which can lead to major crowds. For more information, contact **New Orleans Jazz & Heritage Festival** (✆ **504/410-4100;** www.nojazzfest.com).

JAZZ FEST PARKING & TRANSPORTATION The only parking at the Fair Grounds is for people with disabilities at $50 a day, first-come, first-served. We strongly recommend that you take public transportation or one of the available shuttles. The **Regional Transit Authority** operates bus routes from various pickup points to the Fair Grounds. For schedules, contact ✆ **504/248-3900** (www.norta.com). Taxis, though busy, charge a special-event rate of $5 per person (or the meter reading if it's higher); try **United Cabs** (✆ **504/524-9606**). Gray Line's **Jazz Fest Express** (✆ **800/535-**

7786 or 504/569-1401; www.graylineneworleans.com) operates shuttles from the steamboat *Natchez* dock in the French Quarter, the Sheraton at 500 Canal St., and City Park. It's $17 round-trip and you must have your Jazz Fest ticket already in hand to ride (you can add them to your Ticketmaster ticket order, see above).

Note: The **Canal Street streetcar line** will be packed, but it's another option from the Quarter. Take it to the Carrollton line, which then gets you close to the Fair Grounds' City Park entrance.

PACKAGE DEALS **Festival Tours International,** 15237 Sunset Blvd., Ste. 17, Pacific Palisades, CA 90272 (ⓒ **310/454-4080;** www.gumbopages.com/festivaltours), designs tour packages that include accommodations and tickets for Jazz Fest, plus a midweek visit to Cajun Country for unique personal encounters with local musicians.

If you're flying to New Orleans specifically for the Jazz & Heritage Festival, visit **www.nojazzfest.com** to get a Jazz Fest promotional code from a list of airlines that offer special fares during the event.

OTHER TOP FESTIVALS
The French Quarter Festival

The 3½-day French Quarter Festival in April celebrates local music of the traditional jazz, brass band, Cajun/zydeco, or funk variety. The diversity of music isn't anything like Jazz Fest's but it's become wildly popular, largely because it's free: In 2011, over 533,000 took in the scores of outdoor concerts, art shows, children's activities, tours, and seminars. Stages are set throughout the Quarter (making it easy to return to your hotel room for a rest, though some stages are at far-flung ends of the Quarter). Breeze-blown stages along the river help keep the crowds cool, and food booths everywhere represent about 60 local restaurants. Book travel early, this one's becoming a victim of its own success.

For details, see **French Quarter Festivals** (ⓒ **800/673-5725** or 504/522-5730; www.fqfi.org).

Festivals Acadiens et Creoles

While much smaller than the nearby, Francophone-focused **Festival International** (p. 32), this one doesn't conflict with Jazz Fest. It's several Cajun Country celebrations combined: the **Bayou Food Festival, Festival de Musique Acadienne,** and **Louisiana Native Crafts Festival,** held during the second weekend of October in Girard Park in downtown Lafayette. Players, bring your instruments—there's a jam tent. We also like the cooking demo stage. It's fun, easygoing, tasty, and free, so spend freely to help keep it going. Details via the **Lafayette Conventions and Visitors Center** (ⓒ **800/346-1958** in the U.S., 800/543-5340 in Canada, or 337/232-3737; www.festivalsacadiens.com).

Essence Music Festival

This massive, 3-day July event, sponsored by the venerable *Essence* magazine, consistently presents a stellar lineup of R&B, soul, and hip-hop musicians in evening concerts. The 2011 lineup featured Mary J. Blige, Kanye West, Boys 2 Men, Fantasia, and Jill Scott, plus classic artists like Chaka Khan and George Clinton for cross-generation appeal. During the day, this "party with a purpose" offers

Earth, Wind & Fire playing at the *Essence* Music Festival.

educational and empowerment seminars featuring A-list (Cosby! Oprah!) speakers and celebs, crafts and trade fairs, and other activities, not to mention huge crowds. Evening tickets get you a reserved seat for the main stage, admission to the smaller, clublike "Super Lounges," and access to the daytime seminars. Daytime food is just your average concession-stand fare, but local caterers and restaurants dish it up at night. Ticket prices vary widely from $58 for a single-day ticket to $3,000 for V.I.P. weekend packages. For more information, go to www. essencemusicfestival.com.

Tales of the Cocktail

The cocktail revolution has come full circle—from the invention of the cocktail in New Orleans to this 5-day, mid-July mixtravaganza celebrating all things liquor-based. Based at the Monteleone Hotel but pouring over into other venues, it's no booze fest, but a scholarly gathering of serious mixologists and admirers of the cocktail culture who, well, drink a lot, too. Its popularity has exploded, what with clever classes; quirky competitions; bar tours; tastings; "Spirited Dinners" (when many of the finest restaurants in town create special menus pairing cocktails and cuisine); and panels featuring restaurateurs, chefs, mixologists, and authors. It's a big deal and getting bigger—the popular events fill up well in advance. Individual seminars cost around $40 each; Spirited Dinners run $70 to $100. Contact ☏ **504/948-0511** or go to www.talesofthecocktail.com.

Voodoo Experience

Halloween is huge in New Orleans, and nowhere more than in City Park, where about 60,000 youngish people daily attend this monstrous 3-day festival, filling six stages and a huge dance space. Its diverse line-up features major stars and up-and-comers spanning hip-hop, hard rock, and electronic music, plus a solid line-up of local sounds. Past headliners have included everyone from Ozzy to Eminem to deadmau5 and the Chili Peppers among the 100-plus acts. Having grown exponentially, it's crowded (expect long food lines) but still doable. Cool art installations, crafty stuff, an eclectic circus tent with trapeze artists, burlesque, and other exotica, plus costumed people-watching and food provide diversions (skip the burgers and pizza, head for the Creole stuff). The gorgeous, moss-dripping oak trees and nearby bayou lend just the right eeriness to the occasion. Early-bird tickets in 2011 started at $175 for the weekend. More info at www.thevoodoo experience.com.

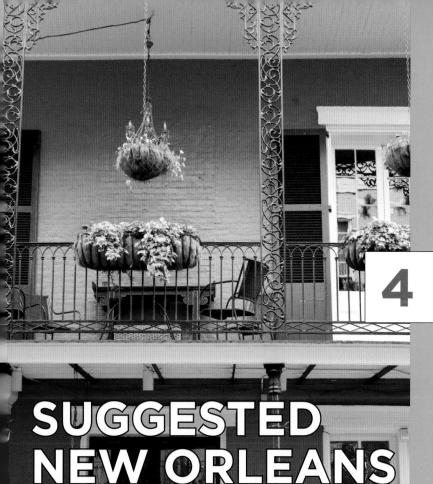

4

SUGGESTED NEW ORLEANS ITINERARIES

N ew Orleans has plenty of landmarks and sights to see—but truly, the whole city is also like one big sight. You could spend your time wandering aimlessly, and that would be just fine (we encourage it, in fact). But there are some quirky spots of interest, curious little nooks you probably shouldn't miss, plus there is the risk that without direction, you might duck into a club and not be heard from again until your flight home. Nothing wrong with that. All the same, the following may help you to navigate the city and make the most of your time in it.

THE NEIGHBORHOODS IN BRIEF

"Where y'at?" goes the traditional local greeting. "Where" is easy enough when you are in the French Quarter, the site of the original settlement. A 13-block-long grid between Canal Street and Esplanade Avenue, running from the Mississippi River to North Rampart Street, it's the closest the city comes to a geographic center.

After that, all bets are off. Because of the bend in the river, the streets are laid out at angles and curves that render north, south, east, and west useless. Readjust your thinking to New Orleans's compass points: *lakeside, riverside, uptown,* and *downtown.* You'll catch on quickly if you keep in mind that North Rampart Street is the *lakeside* boundary of the Quarter and that St. Charles Avenue extends from the French Quarter, *downtown,* to Tulane University, *uptown.*

Canal Street forms the boundary between new and old New Orleans. Street names change when they cross Canal (Bourbon St., for example, becomes Carondelet St.), and addresses begin at 100 on either side of Canal. In the Quarter, street numbers begin at 400 at the river because 4 blocks of numbered buildings were lost to the river before the levee was built.

MAPS You can't get along without one, so we've equipped you with a good one in this book. If you need more, get them free from the Convention and Visitors Bureau, 2020 St. Charles Ave., New Orleans, LA 70130 (©**800/672-6124** or 504/566-5011; www.neworleanscvb.com), the Visitor Information Center, 529 St. Ann St. (©**504/568-5661**), or at most hotel desks and rental car agencies.

STREET NAMES The streets themselves are colorful enough, as are the street names, from Felicity to the jawbreaker Tchoupitoulas (Chop-i-*too*-las). Some of the fanciful monikers came from overeducated city fathers who named streets after Greek muses (Calliope and Terpsichore). Some immortalize long-dead women (Julia was a free woman of color, but who was Felicity?). Many streets in the French Quarter—Burgundy, Dauphine, Toulouse, and Dumaine—honor French royalty or nobility, while St. Peter and St.

PREVIOUS PAGE: Tennessee Williams wrote *A Streetcar Named Desire* at 632 Peter St.

Ann were favorite baptismal names of the Orleans family. The Faubourg (or "suburb") Marigny neighborhood was once part of the Marigny (say *Mare-i-nee*) family plantation. After scion Bernard gambled away his family's fortune, he sold off parcels to the city, naming the streets after his favorite things: Desire, Piety, Poets, Duels, Craps, and so forth.

Even with a French accent, you may not nail the pronunciation: Chartres is *Chart*-ers, Burgundy is Bur-*gun*-dee, Gallier is *Gaul*-ee-er, and of course Calliope is Cal-lee-*ope*. Oh, never mind, just ask a local. They're used to it. For more fun with street names, pick up the book *Frenchmen, Desire, Good Children* by John Churchill Chase.

City Layout

THE FRENCH QUARTER Made up of about 90 square blocks, this section is also known as the Vieux Carré (Old Square) and is bordered by Canal Street, North Rampart Street, the Mississippi River, and Esplanade Avenue. The Quarter is full of clubs, bars, stores, residences, and museums; its major public area is Jackson Square, bounded by Chartres, Decatur, St. Peter, and St. Ann streets. The most historic and best-preserved area in the city, a survivor of two major fires in the 1700s in addition to Katrina, it's the focal point of most first-time visitors.

STORYVILLE North of the Quarter (just above Rampart St.) is Basin Street, the birthplace of jazz—or, at least, that's the legend. In fact, jazz probably predates the rise of Storyville (the old red-light district along Basin St.) by some years. To give credit where credit is due, however, Storyville's "sporting houses" did expose the music to a wide segment of the public who went there to enjoy the houses', uh, services. Jazz greats King Oliver, Jelly Roll Morton, and Louis Armstrong got their starts in the Basin Street brothels.

St. Louis Cathedral faces Jackson Square.

The City at a Glance

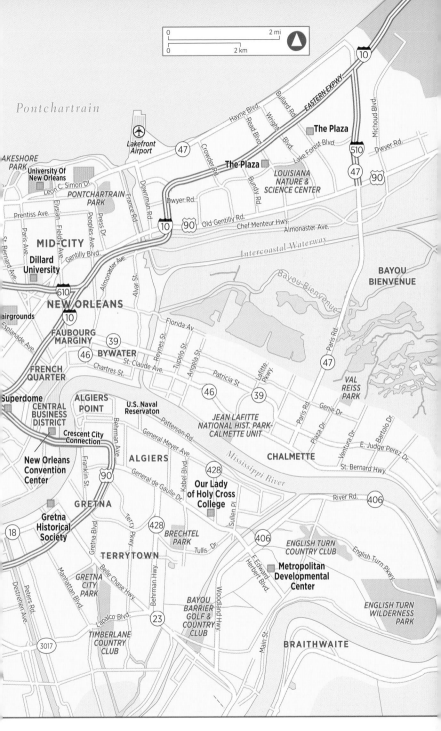

Pontchartrain

AKESHORE
PARK

University Of
New Orleans

Lakefront
Airport

47

PONTCHARTRAIN
PARK

The Plaza

The Plaza

LOUISIANA
NATURE &
SCIENCE CENTER

Michoud Blvd.

EASTERN EXPWY.

10

510

47

90

Dwyer Rd.

Hayne Blvd.
Read Blvd.
Bullard Rd.
Wright Blvd.
Lake Forest Blvd.
Crowder Rd.
Bundy Rd.

Leon C. Simon Dr.

France Rd.

Downman Rd.

Dwyer Rd.

Prentiss Ave.

Elysian Fields Ave.

Peoples Ave.

Press Dr.

10

90

Old Gentilly Rd.

Chef Menteur Hwy.

Almonaster Ave.

Gentilly Blvd.

MID-CITY

Dillard
University

Paris Ave.

St. Bernard Ave.

Almonaster Ave.

Aver St.

610

NEW ORLEANS

10

Intercoastal Waterway

Bayou Bienvenue

BAYOU
BIENVENUE

Paris Rd.

VAL
REISS
PARK

fairgrounds

E. Esplanade Ave.

FAUBOURG
MARGINY

39

46

BYWATER

FRENCH
QUARTER

Florida Av.

Reynes St.

Tupelo St.

Angela St.

Patricia St

Lafitte Pkwy.

46

39

47

Chartres St.

St. Claude Ave.

Superdome

CENTRAL
BUSINESS
DISTRICT

ALGIERS
POINT

U.S. Naval
Reservaton

Patterson Rd.

JEAN LAFITTE
NATIONAL HIST. PARK-
CALMETTE UNIT

CHALMETTE

Paris Rd.

Genie Dr.

Plaza Dr.

Ventura Dr.

Bartolo Dr.

E. Judge Perez Dr.

Behrman Ave.

Crescent City
Connection

General Meyer Ave.

Mississippi River

St. Bernard Hwy.

New Orleans
Convention
Center

Franklin St.

90

ALGIERS

General de Gaulle Dr.

428

Our Lady
of Holy Cross
College

Kabel Blvd.

Sullen Pl.

River Rd.

406

GRETNA

18

Gretna
Historical
Society

Terry Pkwy.

Gretna Blvd.

428

BRECHTEL
PARK

Tullis Dr.

406

ENGLISH TURN
COUNTRY CLUB

English Turn Pkwy.

TERRYTOWN

Belle Chase Hwy.

GRETNA
CITY
PARK

Manhattan Blvd.

Behrman Hwy.

BAYOU
BARRIER
GOLF &
COUNTRY
CLUB

Woodland Hwy.

E. Edward
Herbert Blvd.

Metropolitan
Developmental
Center

ENGLISH TURN
WILDERNESS
PARK

Destrehan Rd.

Peters Rd.

Lapalco Blvd.

23

TIMBERLANE
COUNTRY
CLUB

Main St.

BRAITHWAITE

3017

0   2 mi
0   2 km

Apart from a couple of non-descript buildings, no trace of the old Storyville survives. A low-income public housing project now sprawls over much of the site (and unfortunately it is not a safe neighborhood), where statues depicting Latin American heroes like Simón Bolívar dot the landscape.

FAUBOURG MARIGNY This area is east of the French Quarter, across Esplanade Avenue. Over the past decade, the Marigny has emerged as one of the city's vital centers of activity, with Frenchmen Street, the main drag, becoming a must-visit nighttime haunt for music lovers and anyone seeking a scene. A small Creole suburb, many old-time residents remain here, with younger urban dwellers who have moved in recently.

The Miltenberger House in the French Quarter exudes quintessential French Quarter charm.

Little gem bars, restaurants, and coffeehouses are tucked into its haphazard folds. Along with the adjacent sections of the French Quarter, the Marigny is also a social center for the city's gay and lesbian communities.

BYWATER This riverside neighborhood is past the Faubourg Marigny and is bounded on the east by an industrial canal. The Bywater has its share of rundown homes—as well as plenty of nice, modest residential sections (it's actually something of a hotbed of renovation). Historically, the area was also home to artisans, immigrants, and free people of color, and today many artists' studios are splashed amid the urban decay. Worthy bars and cafes dot the neighborhood, including **Elizabeth's** (p. 134), **Satsuma Café** (3218 Dauphine St.; C **504/304-5962**), the **Joint BBQ** restaurant (p. 153), and **Bacchanal** wine bar, with its funky garden and killer sandwiches (600 Poland Ave.; C **504/948-9111**).

MID-CITY/ESPLANADE RIDGE Stretching north from the French Quarter to City Park, Esplanade Ridge hugs either side of Esplanade Avenue, once the grande avenue of New Orleans's Creole society—the St. Charles Avenue of downriver. Many of the lavish 19th-century houses along it have seen better days, though plenty are still showy, and the ancient oak trees form a leafy canopy over the road. If you head toward City Park along Esplanade (see Walking Tour 3, "Esplanade Ridge," p. 240), you can measure the progress of the avenue's development in the styles of its houses. Eventually you'll cross **Bayou St. John**—the lovely **Faubourg St. John** neighborhood adjacent to the historic waterway—and more Mid-City neighborhoods stretching outward toward the lake.

The oldest section of Esplanade Ridge, **Faubourg Treme,** is directly across Rampart Street from the French Quarter. It was and remains one of the most vibrant African-American neighborhoods in New Orleans, home to many of the city's best brass bands and other musicians. Like the Quarter, it was a dense 19th-century Creole community. Unlike the Quarter, Treme (pronounced Treh-*may*) has remained almost untouched by preservationists, apart from some plucky folks who have beautifully restored their turn-of-the-20th-century and older houses. This trend has raised some fear of post-Katrina gentrification. For now, fortunately, it continues to be a dynamic, organic residential community, as highlighted in the HBO series named for the area. Although it's no longer a scary dangerous neighborhood, it has its share of crime, and it is not advisable to walk through at night or solo.

CENTRAL BUSINESS DISTRICT Historically, **Canal Street** has been New Orleans's main street. In the 19th century it divided the French and American sections of the city. (By the way, there's no canal—the one that was planned for the spot never came to be.) It's a far cry from the days of yore when white-gloved ladies and seersuckered men shopped this grand avenue, but street improvements have helped to lure some better businesses and sidewalk cafes, in addition to several fine hotels and restaurants already in place. Even the classic Saenger Theatre has a comeback in the works. Admire the streetlights on the neutral ground (you might know it as the meridian); they were a gift from France. When they were first lit, none other than Thomas Edison himself threw the switch, making Canal Street the most illuminated street in the world.

The **CBD** is roughly bounded by Canal Street and the elevated Pontchartrain Expressway (Business Rte. U.S. 90) between Loyola Avenue and the Mississippi River. Some of the most elegant luxury hotels and best restaurants are in this area.

Within the CBD is the **Warehouse District.** More than 20 years ago, this area was nothing more than abandoned warehouses. With the efforts of some dedicated individuals and institutions, it's evolved into a thriving residential neighborhood, dotted with cool loft conversions, a plethora of terrific restaurants, and hot music clubs. The area also houses the city's thriving arts district, with myriad galleries along **Julia Street** (see chapter 9, "Shopping"); the Ogden Museum, Contemporary Arts Center, and Louisiana Children's Museum (p. 184, 301, and 214); and the terrific World War II Museum (p. 182).

UPTOWN/THE GARDEN DISTRICT Bounded by St. Charles Avenue (lakeside) and Magazine Street (riverside) between Jackson and Louisiana avenues, the Garden District remains one of the most picturesque areas in the city. Originally the site of a plantation, it was subdivided and developed as a residential neighborhood for wealthy Americans. Throughout the middle of the 19th century, developers built the Victorian, Italianate, and Greek Revival homes that still line the streets. A few of the once elaborate lawns and gardens still exist. The Garden District is located uptown (as opposed to the CBD, which is downtown); the neighborhood west of the Garden District is often called Uptown (not to be confused with the directions people often use here: The Garden District is located uptown from both the Quarter and CBD and is *in* what is collectively referred to as Uptown). (See chapter 8, "City Strolls," for a suggested walking tour of this area.)

THE IRISH CHANNEL The area bounded by Magazine Street and the Mississippi River, Louisiana Avenue, and the Central Business District got its name during the 1800s when more than 100,000 Irish immigrated to New Orleans and found (mostly blue-collar) work.

HOW TO MAKE LIKE THE locals DO

Sure, we recommend many popular yet deserving spots, but by and large this book avoids cheesy tourist traps. In fact, it features many a spot that has prompted a local to say, "You've got that place in there?! No one knows about that!" Here are a few more residents-only suggestions that have their own traditional following. Be aware that making like a local sometimes means heading into areas that will prompt your cabdriver (yes, take a cab if you don't have your own car) to shake his or her head about your foolhardy behavior. Ignore them, though do please be cautious.

ARGUE ABOUT THE BEST PO' BOY

Some of these are off the beaten paths, but you can't go wrong with any of them.

Crabby Jack's Best known for the roast duck po' boy, but we go for the panéed rabbit. Monster fried shrimp and oyster sammies, too. 428 Jefferson Hwy. (☏ **504/833-2722**).

Domilise Wait in line at this old-school institution; take a number; order your fried catfish, shrimp, or oyster po' boy. Wait some more while they fry to order. Worth it. 5240 Annunciation St. (☏ **504/899-9126**).

Gene's A serious dive with one serious po' boy—the classic, house-made Creole hot sausage patty with American cheese. No chips, no dessert. Comes with a soda. That's all you need to know. Trust us. 1040 Elysian Fields (☏ **504/943-3861**).

Liuzza's by the Track The BBQ shrimp po' boy is their specialty and others swear by their roast beef, but our choice is the garlic oyster. Superb gumbo, too. 1518 N. Lopez St. (☏ **504/218-7888**).

Mahony's The peacemaker, or pacemaker as it might be better known (fried oysters, cheddar, and bacon), is our 'boy of choice here, followed by the fried chicken liver with stellar slaw (yeah, really), plus onion rings, followed by the gym. 3454 Magazine St. (☏ **504/899-3374**).

Parkway Bakery Our choice for a dripping-with-juice roast beef po' boy.

There, we've said it. Let the fighting begin. Another good option for fried oyster or shrimp, too. 538 Hagan Ave. (☏ **504/482-3047**).

Sammy's So good it's worth renting a car for (it's a good ways from the tourist zones). The Ray-Ray (fried chicken, grilled ham, Swiss cheese) is so much better than it sounds that one health-conscious skeptic just laughed out loud upon first bite. 3000 Elysian Fields Ave. (☏ **504/947-0675**).

Tracey's vs. Parasol's Go into either rival po' boy shop (both have their advocates). Order a roast beef, dressed. Ask the server (or anyone), "So what's the deal between Parasol's and Tracey's?" and let the fireworks begin. Tracey's, 2604 Magazine St. (☏ **504/897-5413**); Parasol's, 533 Constance St., (☏ **504/899-2054**).

A REAL GOSPEL BRUNCH

Why see the slick, so-called "Gospel Brunch" at the House of Blues? Go see the real thing in a real place of worship. Don't expect fancy robes or masses of choir members, just rooms and rooms full of spirit. Try **Zion Hill Missionary Baptist Church,** 1126 N. Robertson St. (☏ **504/525-0507**). It's humble, right, and true (and Pastor Joshua's preaching can get pretty fiery). You may well be the only nonparishioner there, but the modest congregation is welcoming; show some mutual respect when the collection plate comes 'round. Sunday services are at 10:30am to noonish; communion service on the first Sunday of the month runs longer. You'll find a similar experience closer to the Garden District (but not in a great area) at **Guiding Light Missionary Baptist Church,** 2012 Washington Ave. (✆ **504/891-7654**). Worship is Sunday at 7:30am and 9am (smaller choir).

For a different musical religious experience, take in the Sunday 10am jazz Mass at historic **St. Augustine's,** 1210 Governor Nicholls St. (✆ **504/525-5934;** www.staugustinecatholicchurch neworleans.org; p. 186). Home church for many a famous local musician, like Sidney Bechet, masses now incorporate New Orleans–tinged music and cultural color. *Tip:* Right afterward (at noon), the talented **Holy Faith Baptist Temple** band seriously rocks the house of worship just up the street at 1225 Governor Nicholls St. (✆ **504/525-0856**).

FRIED CHICKEN FROM MCHARDY'S

Friends of ours served fried chicken from **McHardy's,** 1458 N. Broad St. (✆ **504/949-0000**), at their wedding reception. And no fancy-pants expensive, catered extravaganza had better food. This family-owned establishment serves stellar bird—moist, tender, slightly crispy skin, perfectly seasoned. Sold in increments of five, an order works out to about 96¢ a piece.

"THURSDAYS AT TWILIGHT" CONCERTS IN CITY PARK

If you're in town between March and October, you couldn't ask for a nicer way to spend an evening (a bold statement, considering all the options) than sipping a cool mint julep among the green lawns or windowed Pavilion of City Park's Botanical Gardens, while chilling out to some of the city's best local artists. Tasty vittles are available (no outside picnics allowed, though). Concerts are on Thursdays from 5 to 8pm; admission is $8 for adults, $4 for kids 5 to 12. In City Park, Esplanade and North Carrollton avenues (✆ **504/483-9386;** www.neworleanscitypark.com).

BANH MI ME

Sandwich fiends may come here for po' boys, but New Orleans's large Vietnamese community knows a good sandwich, too—and local foodies look eastward for them at **Dong Phuong,** 14207 Chef Menteur Hwy. (✆ **504/254-0296;** www.dpbanhmi.com). There are many versions of *banh mi*, but the classic ham, pâté, aioli, pickled daikon, and jalapeño on crusty bread does it for us.

SNAKE & JAKE'S CHRISTMAS CLUB LOUNGE

Tiny. Cramped. Full of Christmas twinkle lights and locals drinking and some out-of-towners, also drinking, because they consider it their own local lounge when they come to town. See p. 297.

SUPER SUNDAY

All year long, the Mardi Gras Indians work on their elaborate suits of hand-sewn beaded mosaics and feathers, creating concoctions that even Cher would envy. They parade on Mardi Gras and once a year (in Mar, see p. 31) they meet on their home turfs to prove, via chants, drums, and costumes, which tribe is the most glorious and who is the prettiest. All that work for nothing but honor, pride, and beauty. Watching them square off is one of the great sights of New Orleans. More about the Indians on p. 43.

A look back at New Orleans from aboard the ferry to Algiers.

The area's quiet residential neighborhoods mix the run-down with the fixed-up.

ALGIERS POINT Directly across the Mississippi River and connected by the Canal Street Ferry, Algiers Point is another largely unchanged, original Creole suburb. Today you can't see many signs of the area's once-booming railroad and dry-docking industries, but you can see some of the best-preserved small gingerbread and Creole cottages in New Orleans. (See chapter 7, "Sights to See & Places to Be," for tips on how to get here.)

THE BEST OF NEW ORLEANS IN 1 DAY

If you have only a day in New Orleans, you might as well spend it largely in the **French Quarter**—after all, you could easily spend a much longer trip entirely within its confines. (But we won't let you do so if you have the additional time.) This day will include all the important factors of a New Orleans visit: eating, walking, drinking, soaking in the history, eating some more, listening to music, and dancing. ***Start:*** *River side of Jackson Square.*

1 Café du Monde ★★★

Downing a cup of chicory coffee and some powdered sugar–covered beignets is the ideal way to start a New Orleans day. You can watch this city come to lazy life and the carriage drivers line up across the street. But wear white, the better to camouflage any stray powdered sugar. See p. 154.

2 Take a Walking Tour of the Quarter ★★★

Get the overall lay of the land with the map and walking tour in chapter 8, or take an official one from Historic New Orleans Tours (p. 204). Our tour gives you a bit of history in addition to pointing out individual buildings,

The Best of New Orleans in 1 Day

1 Café du Monde ☕
2 Take a Walking Tour of the Quarter
3 St. Louis Cathedral
4 Central Grocery ☕
5 Stroll the Moonwalk
6 The Cabildo
7 The Presbytère
8 Shop the Quarter 🎁
9 Take a Walk on Bourbon Street
10 Commander's Palace ☕
11 While Away an Evening in
   New Orleans 🎵🌟

and it also helps you slow down and admire the architecture of this unique neighborhood. As you wander, take notice of how the building exteriors, apart from the ironwork (mostly slave-made, originally), are rather plain. The Creoles saved the embellishments for their indoor living quarters.

3 St. Louis Cathedral ★

It's a humdrum ecclesiastical building, but it is the center of spiritual life for a town that is surprisingly devoutly Catholic (it's always a shock to note how many foreheads soberly bear ashes the day after the frantic party antics of Mardi Gras). Go around the back to the garden, a serene oasis (though usually locked) that legend has it was a favorite haunt of good Catholic Marie Laveau (the infamous Pere Antoine, sent to New Orleans by none other

St. Louis Cathedral.

Central Grocery is famous for its muffuletta sandwiches.

than the office of the Inquisition, urged her to forsake voodoo—to no avail). The imposing statue of Jesus lost a thumb and the garden lost its sweeping oaks to Katrina. There are plans to redesign the landscape to reflect the original early-1800s design. See p. 168.

4 Central Grocery ★★★

Get a muffuletta for lunch at Central Grocery (split it with somebody; they're gigantic) and thread your way through the buildings across the street to eat it by the banks of the Mississippi River. 923 Decatur St. ℂ **504/523-1620.** See p. 132.

5 Stroll the Moonwalk ★★★

Walk off your lunch on a stroll down the Moonwalk, the park and pedestrian walkway that runs along the river, stopping to notice some of the curious public art installations and local cultural monuments along the way. Ol' Man River will keep rolling along, and you can watch riverboats, cruise ships, and cargo vessels sail by, much like they have for centuries. See p. 177.

6 The Cabildo ★★★

The site of the signing of the Louisiana Purchase, this is one of two buildings erected by the Baroness Pontalba's father, who thus set the tone for the Place D'Armes—as Jackson Square was originally known. It has fine exhibits illustrating New Orleans and Louisiana history and culture. But we love the Napoleon death mask here the best. See p. 172.

7 The Presbytère ★★★

The former home of the priests who worked at St. Louis Cathedral has been turned into a museum housing the terrific *Living with Hurricanes* exhibit (details on p. 176), which is well worth an hour of anyone's time.

8 Shop the Quarter

You are released from sightseeing and freed up for browsing through some of the curious shops in the Quarter. We suggest starting in nearby Pirate's Alley, at **Faulkner House Books** (p. 256), to choose a literary souvenir. Then walk down Royal Street and admire the antiques. Head around the corner to Chartres and Bienville

A night out on Bourbon Street is a must for a first-time visitor to New Orleans.

streets and drop in at **A Gallery for Fine Photography** (p. 253); with its stunning pictorial representations of local culture and history. Swing by the shops toward the Esplanade Avenue end of Decatur Street, with its mélange of edgy, antiquey, and artsy goods (all considerably less posh than those on Royal St.).

9 Take a Walk on Bourbon Street

Dusk is the best time to do this, between the too tame and the too rowdy hours. Sure, it's gaudy, loud, and kind of disgusting and comes off as a combination giant T-shirt shop and bar. At the right time, when things are heating up but the obnoxious drunks aren't too plentiful, when different kinds of music pour from every door, it's also seductive and exhilarating. Everyone has to do it once, and some people need to do it often. Have a predinner drink at the darkly mysterious **Lafitte's Blacksmith Shop** (the oldest building in town, at the end of the business part of the street; p. 292) or sample a Hurricane at the not-so-dark-but-always-lively **Pat O'Brien's** (p. 290), or get off Bourbon and go to the crumbly romantic **Napoleon House** bar and cafe (p. 131).

10 Commander's Palace 🍴 ★★

Food is a very, very important part of your time in New Orleans. Tonight we are forcing you out of the Quarter, just for variety's sake. Try the deservedly famous and long-lived Commander's Palace, which serves excellent examples of nouveau Orleans cuisine that have influenced the cooking of many a local chef. 1403 Washington Ave. ℂ **504/899-8221.** See p. 147.

11 While Away an Evening in New Orleans ★★★

Nightlife is too important a part of this city to leave it off your list. Do not miss hearing some jazz at **Preservation Hall** (p. 280)—it's cheap, and it's the real McCoy. You may also want to navigate Bourbon Street; now that night has fallen, the scene will have truly kicked in. For fun without the frat party, head to the **Frenchmen** section of the Faubourg Marigny, where at least a dozen clubs and bars are within a few blocks (p. 266). Wander from one to another, mingle with the crowds, people-watch, and maybe even go inside. Hungry again? Head back to **Acme Oyster House** (p. 129) or **Felix's Restaurant & Oyster Bar** (p. 131) for a couple dozen raw. Have you exercised restraint and missed a bar or two? Go now. If you don't collapse exhausted—and full—in your bed, you haven't done your day properly.

THE BEST OF NEW ORLEANS IN 2 DAYS

Get out of the Quarter, *get out of the Quarter*, **get out of the Quarter.** Are we getting through to you? You can come back; you probably still have serious shopping (or eating, or drinking) to do. On Day 1 you stayed close to the French Quarter, but today you must begin to see what else New Orleans has to offer. We've constructed this tour so that the sights mentioned follow a logical geographic order, but if you have limited time, just take the streetcar/bus ride/tour, a short stroll through the Garden District, and visit the **National World War II Museum** (p. 182). ***Start:*** *St. Charles Streetcar line, Canal Street stop.*

1 St. Charles Avenue Streetcar ★★★

Hop on the oldest continuously operating wooden streetcar in the country—and that means no air-conditioning (or wheelchairs), so doing this in the cool of the morning is a good idea. Don't forget to have exact change ($1.25). Admire the gorgeous homes along the way and remember which side of the car you rode on so that you can get on the other side for the ride back. See p. 348.

2 Take a Walking Tour of the Garden District ★★★

Aside from its historical significance and interest, this neighborhood, full of fabulous houses and lush greenery, is just plain beautiful. Contrast the plain exteriors of the "French" Quarter with these grand, ornamented "American district" spectacles. Use our walking tour in chapter 8 or take a guided tour from Historic New Orleans Tours. See p. 204.

Taking a ride on the St. Charles streetcar is a great way to get around town while doing some sightseeing along the way.

4

SUGGESTED ITINERARIES · The Best of New Orleans in 2 Days

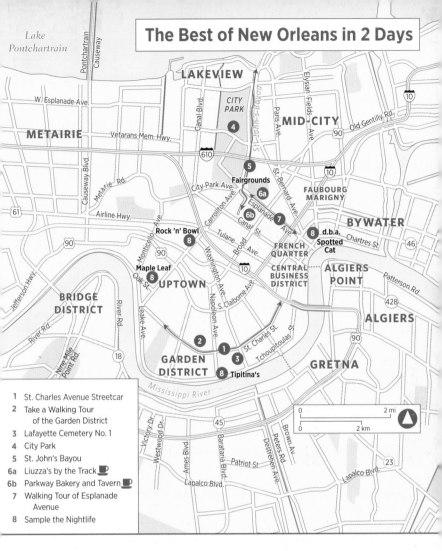

The Best of New Orleans in 2 Days

Lake Pontchartrain

LAKEVIEW

CITY PARK

❹

MID-CITY

METAIRIE

Vetarans Mem. Hwy.

W. Esplanade Ave.

Pontchartrain Causeway

Canal Blvd.

Paris Ave.

Elysian Fields Ave.

Old Gentilly Rd.

610

❺

Fairgrounds

FAUBOURG MARIGNY

Metairie Rd.

Airline Hwy.

City Park Ave.

❻a

St. Bernard Ave.

BYWATER

Causeway Blvd.

Carrollton Ave.

Esplanade Ave.

❻b

❼

❽ d.b.a.
Spotted Cat

Chartres St.

Rock 'n' Bowl ❽

Tulane Ave.

Canal St.

FRENCH QUARTER

Monticello Ave.

Broad Ave.

Washington Ave.

CENTRAL BUSINESS DISTRICT

ALGIERS POINT

Patterson Rd.

Maple Leaf ❽

Oak St.

UPTOWN

Napoleon Ave.

S. Claiborne Ave.

ALGIERS

BRIDGE DISTRICT

River Rd.

Leake Ave.

St. Charles St.

Tchoupitoulas Ave.

GRETNA

Jefferson Hwy.

Nine Mile Point Rd.

❷

❶

❸

GARDEN DISTRICT

St. Charles St.

❽ Tipitina's

Mississippi River

Victory Dr.

Westwood Dr.

Ames Blvd.

Barataria Blvd.

Patriot St.

Lapalco Blvd.

Peters Rd.

Destrehan Ave.

Brown Ave.

Lapalco Blvd.

0   2 mi
0   2 km

1 St. Charles Avenue Streetcar
2 Take a Walking Tour
   of the Garden District
3 Lafayette Cemetery No. 1
4 City Park
5 St. John's Bayou
6a Liuzza's by the Track
6b Parkway Bakery and Tavern
7 Walking Tour of Esplanade
   Avenue
8 Sample the Nightlife

3   Lafayette Cemetery No. 1

The "little cities of the dead" are part of the iconic landscape of New Orleans. (St. Louis No. 1 is older and has more historic graves, and you may consider going there instead, particularly with a guided tour so you won't miss some of the more significant tombs.) But this cemetery, which catered to the Uptown folks, is perhaps prettier, thanks to the foliage and the larger square footage. (Like many of the cemeteries, it is in great need of maintenance, and there are scant funds to do so.) Notice the tombs with French or German writing, and the four matching mausoleums in the far left corner, which belong to four boyhood friends (one a Civil War vet) who used to play together in that corner of the graveyard. See p. 197.

Take the St. Charles streetcar line to the end and transfer to the City Park streetcar line, which ends at the entrance to:

4 City Park ★★★

City Park is full of all sorts of sights, from the Spanish moss–draped giant live oaks to the **New Orleans Museum of Art,** to the **Sculpture Garden,** to pedal boats in the lake, to the kids' amusement park and **Storybook Land.** The lush **Botanical Gardens** include the **Train Gardens,** a sort of melted Dr. Seuss

Head to City Park to take a break from city sightseeing.

replica of the city in miniature, complete with model trains (not to mention enormous lily pads). See p. 192.

5 St. John's Bayou ★★★

Just outside the gates of City Park lies this former bustling canal turned scenic body of water. A stroll here is one of the lesser-known delights of the city. Stand outside the Pitot House (p. 189) and imagine owning one of the former plantation homes around here. Keep your eyes peeled for local wildlife, like herons, pelicans, nutria—and kayakers. See p. 178.

6 Liuzza's by the Track or Parkway Bakery and Tavern 🍴 ★★

Head down Esplanade Avenue and turn left on Lopez to get some lunch at the popular Liuzza's by the Track. You'll find authentic local food—excellent gumbo, wonderful po' boys, and large, well-constructed salads—but it can get crowded at lunch. 1518 N. Lopez St. ✆ **504/218-7888.** See p. 137. Or stay put. Right off the Bayou, Parkway Bakery and Tavern has some of the best po' boys (and atmosphere) in town. 538 Hagan St. ✆ **504/482-3047.** See p. 138.

7 Walking Tour of Esplanade Avenue

Follow our nice walking tour in chapter 8 (if you do this itinerary in chronological order, follow our walking tour in reverse order). Architecturally similar to the Garden District, the area includes at least one home with a French connection—the birthplace of Impressionist Edgar Degas's mother and grandmother, and the only studio belonging to the former artist that is open to the public. See p. 242.

At the end of the tour, you can take any bus marked RAMPART back to the Quarter.

8 Sample the Nightlife

Once you've eaten, if you go to **Mid City Lanes**—otherwise known as **Rock 'n' Bowl** (p. 284)—you can bowl as well as listen to some zydeco and other local music. Or head to **Tipitina's** (p. 288), or the **Maple Leaf Bar** (p. 287), or to Frenchmen Street, paying special attention to the **Spotted Cat** (p. 281) and **d.b.a.** (p. 285) for more local music.

THE BEST OF NEW ORLEANS IN 3 DAYS

Yes, we are dragging you out of the Quarter again, but we will let you come back later. We're also recommending quite a few museums, which can be time-consuming if you enjoy more than a browse. Pick and choose based on your interests. **Start:** *Taxi to Algiers Point Ferry Terminal or Canal Streetcar line to Convention Center Boulevard.*

1 A Ferry Ride to Algiers

Not so much because Algiers is so great, but because it's a free ride across the Mississippi. Wind in your face, visions of Tom and Huck, all that. The neighborhood itself is worth strolling, as it's a more or less undisturbed turn-of-the-20th-century suburb. And the ride back across on the ferry will give you a wonderful view of the New Orleans skyline. See p. 190.

2 Audubon Aquarium of the Americas ★★★

Here's a fine refuge for a rainy (or for that matter, overly warm) day, and a perfect outing for kids, who will want to see the jellyfish, giggle at the sea otters, touch the manta rays, and marvel at the enormous river fish. Get here early to avoid the busloads of schoolchildren. Consider taking in the excellent **Audubon Insectarium ★★★**, the largest free-standing museum in the world devoted to creepies, crawlies, and flutterers. See p. 163.

Take the riverboat to Audubon Park.

3 Audubon Park ★★ & Audubon Zoo ★★★

You may or may not want to visit the zoo, which is small but sweetly developed, but if you do and it's a hot day, plan on coming here before any other activity if you want to see anything other than a pile of snoozing fur in the shade. Even if you don't visit the zoo, do stroll through Audubon Park. See p. 191 and p. 194 respectively.

The Audubon Aquarium of the Americas is an ideal destination for families.

4   Lilette or Creole Creamery 🍵 ★★

Owned by one of the most interesting and creative chefs in town, Lilette is a charming—and popular—spot for lunch. 3637 Magazine St. ℂ **504/895-1636.** See p. 151. If you just want a sweet, sample some of the myriad flavors concocted at Creole Creamery, including lavender honey, red velvet, and pepper. 4924 Prytania St. ℂ **504/894-8680.**

5   Shop Magazine Street

The sometimes swanky, sometimes quirky shops along Magazine are a mix of antiques stores (affordable and not), home decor tchotchke shops, shops of no particular theme, and good clothing stores. A good stretch runs from roughly the 3500 to 4200 blocks, through the very hip Lower Garden District. The no. 11 Magazine Street bus line begins at Audubon Park. See p. 248.

6   National World War II Museum ★★★

Begun with an emphasis on D-day, but gradually turning its focus to all of World War II, this was the inspiration of historian (and *Saving Private Ryan* consultant) Stephen Ambrose. D-day vets often volunteer, taking tickets and doing other jobs—say thank you for us, please. By afternoon the crowds get thinner, but if you have a special interest in the subject, allow a good 3 hours. You can take the no. 11 Magazine Street bus and exit as close to Calliope as you can get. See p. 182.

7   The Ogden Museum of Southern Art ★★★ & the Galleries on Julia Street

The premier collection of Southern art in the country is at the Ogden Museum. After viewing the art in the museum, walk around the corner to the galleries on Julia Street to see works (mostly contemporary, Southern art) by artists who may someday grace the Ogden's walls, and some that already do. Take the no. 11 Magazine Street bus from the Lower Garden District (exit as close to St. Joseph as you can), or walk from the National World War II Museum or in from the Quarter. See p. 184 for the Ogden and p. 251 for the Julia Street galleries.

Explore the fascinating memorabilia on exhibit at the National World War II Museum.

The Best of New Orleans in 3 Days

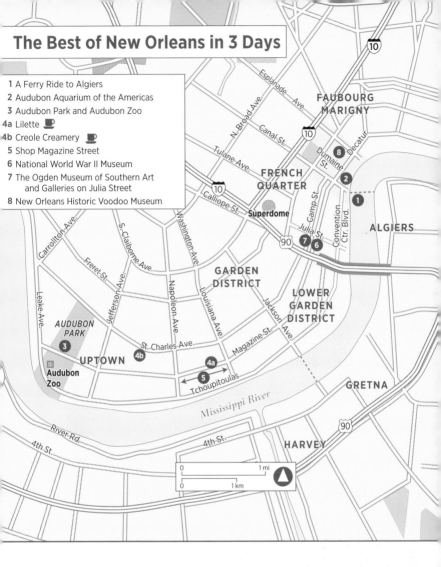

1 A Ferry Ride to Algiers
2 Audubon Aquarium of the Americas
3 Audubon Park and Audubon Zoo
4a Lilette
4b Creole Creamery
5 Shop Magazine Street
6 National World War II Museum
7 The Ogden Museum of Southern Art
   and Galleries on Julia Street
8 New Orleans Historic Voodoo Museum

8 New Orleans Historic Voodoo Museum

It's not like you can visit voodoo—it's a religion, not a place—but you can tour the musty and a bit touristy **New Orleans Historic Voodoo Museum** (p. 175), which has some informative exhibits and a staff that should be able to give you a tour if you ask nicely. Combine a visit here with one to the **Voodoo Spiritual Temple** (p. 200).

9 Eat. Yes, Again.

It's what you do in New Orleans. Skipping a meal is tantamount to sacrilege, no matter how tired you are after a day packed with sightseeing. You need sustenance, so take your pick from the recommendations in chapter 6.

5

WHERE TO STAY

f you're doing your New Orleans trip right, you shouldn't be doing much sleeping. But you do have to put your change of clothes somewhere. Fortunately, New Orleans is bursting with hotels of every variety (though increasingly of the brand-name chain sort), so you should be able to find something that fits your preferences.

Given a choice, we tend to favor slightly faded, ever-so-faintly decayed, just-this-side-of-elegant locales. A new, sterile chain or even a luxury hotel doesn't seem right for New Orleans, where atmosphere is everything. Slightly tattered lace curtains; faded antiques; mossy courtyards with banana trees and fountains; a musty, Miss Havisham air—to us, it's all part of the fun. We prefer to stay in a Tennessee Williams play, if not an Anne Rice novel (though in summertime, we'll take air-conditioning, thank you very much).

Understandably, this may not appeal to you. It may, in fact, describe your own home, and who wants to stay in one's home on vacation? Meanwhile, here are a few tips. Don't stay on Bourbon Street unless you absolutely have to or don't mind sleepless nights. The open-air frat party that is this thoroughfare does mean a free show below your window, but it is hardly conducive to . . . well, just about anything other than participation in the same. On the other hand, making a night of it on your balcony, people-watching—and people-egging-on—is an activity with its own merits, one enjoyed by a number of happy tourists. If you must stay on Bourbon Street, try to get a room away from the street.

We think accommodations in the French Quarter make the most sense for first-time visitors. We adore the feeling of being ensconced in the essence of the city every time we step out of the hotel—besides, you'll probably spend the bulk of your time there. That said, if you'd prefer to get away from it all or simply see a neighborhood whose raison d'être isn't to entertain first-time visitors, try the beautiful Garden District instead. It's an easy streetcar ride away from the Quarter and close to a number of wonderful clubs and restaurants. Finally, staying in the increasingly interesting Mid-City, Marigny, or Bywater neighborhoods will give you more of a local's perspective.

All the guesthouses in this chapter have their merits. If you want more information, we recommend **PIANO,** the Professional Innkeepers Association of New Orleans. Its website (**www.bbnola.com**) will provide you with brief descriptions and photos of a variety of B&Bs, inns, and more, with quick links. All members must be licensed by the city and inspected by a state official.

Tourism is the city's largest industry, so to be on the safe side, always book ahead in spring and fall. And if your trip coincides with a major event, book *way* ahead, up to a year in advance if you want to ensure a room. We can't stress this enough, especially for the biggies: Mardi Gras, Jazz Fest, Essence Fest, French Quarter Fest, Southern Decadence, Halloween, and Sugar Bowl. *Please* look at "Calendar of Events," in chapter 2, to make sure. Also, there's always the chance that a big convention or sports event will be in town, making it difficult to find

FACING PAGE: **The Bienville House.**

New Orleans Hotels

Southern Baptist Hospital

BROADMOOR

New Orleans Arena

Union Passenger Terminal (Amtrak)

UPTOWN

GARDEN DISTRICT

Lee Circle

Ferry Service to Algiers Point

Riverfront streetcar route/stops

St. Charles streetcar route/stops

Vieux Carre loop route/stops

Canal St. streetcar route/stops

See also "Uptown Hotels & Restaurants" map.

Ashtons Bed & Breakfast **42**
B&W Courtyards Bed & Breakfast **47**
Best Western St. Christopher **25**
The Chimes B & B **4**
Comfort Suites **38**
Country Inn and Suites by Carlson **27**
Courtyard by Marriott **18**
Degas House Bed & Breakfast **41**
Drury Inn & Suites **37**

Embassy Suites **17**
The Frenchmen Hotel **45**
The Grand Victorian Bed & Breakfast **6**
Hampton Inn and Suites **13**
Hampton Inn Garden District **5**
Harrah's **20**
Hilton New Orleans Riverside Hotel **20**

Hilton St. Charles **34**
Holiday Inn Express **35**
Homewood Suites **36**
Hyatt Regency **14**
InterContinental New Orleans
International House **31**
JW Marriott Hotel New Orleans **30**
Lafayette Hotel **33**

La Quinta Inn and Suites **32**	Park View Guest House **2**	SpringHill Suites by Marriott **16**
Le Pavillion Hotel **37**	Prytania Park Hotel **12**	St. Charles Guest House **9**
Loews New Orleans Hotel **22**	Quality Inn **39**	St. James Hotel **24**
Loft 523 **28**	Queen Anne **10**	Sully Mansion **7**
Magnolia Mansion **8**	Renaissance Arts Hotel **19**	The Whitney – A Wyndham
Maison de Macarty **46**	Residence Inn by Marriott **15**	Historic Hotel **26**
Maison Dubois **43**	The Roosevelt **40**	Windsor Court **23**
Maison Perrier Bed & Breakfast **1**	Royal Street Inn & R Bar **44**	W New Orleans **21**
The McKendrick-Breaux House **10**	Sheraton **29**	

a room. (Though we have to admit that's often when the maligned anonymous chain hotels do come in handy. If a convention hasn't taken one over with block booking, there is often an extra room for a decent rate floating around. See the box "Spending the Night in Chains," later in this chapter.) You should also be aware that rates frequently jump more than a notch or two for Mardi Gras and other festival times (sometimes even doubling), and in most cases hotels require a minimum 4- or 5-night stay during those periods.

If you want to miss the crowds and the lodgings squeeze that mark the big festivals, consider coming in the month immediately following Mardi Gras or, if you can stand the heat and humidity, in the summer, when the streets are not nearly as thronged. December, before the Sugar Bowl and New Year's activities, is a good time, too, but it can get a bit chilly and rainy. In both cases, hotel prices fall dramatically and great deals can be had just about everywhere.

There are no recommendable inexpensive *hotels* in the French Quarter. If you're on a budget and must stay there, consider a guesthouse. On the whole, however, you'll have a better selection of inexpensive lodgings outside the Quarter. New Orleans also has a couple of hostels; check the website **www.hostels.com** for more information.

You'll find a list of our favorite accommodations in a variety of eclectic categories in the first section of this chapter.

The rack rates we've given in this chapter are for double rooms and do not include the city's 13% hotel tax. You may see a wide range of room rates below, which hotels were not eager to break down more specifically for us. Realize that rates often shift according to demand. Unless it includes the caveat "higher rates for special events" (implying higher prices at those times) or "seasonal rates apply" (implying either higher or lower prices during same), the high end of the range is for popular times such as Mardi Gras and Jazz Fest, and the low end is for quieter periods such as the month of December. **Note:** Some of the hotels listed under "Expensive" have some surprisingly low rates at said low end of their range. These could indicate certain times of year—like the height of the hot summer—or even just whim. Therefore, it's worth searching those out and making a call; you might get very lucky!

BEST HOTEL BETS

Selecting just one hotel in New Orleans is a little like picking your favorite flavor of ice cream—there are just so many great options to choose from.

- **Best for a Romantic Getaway:** Take an old indigo plantation some blocks away from the Quarter, outfit it with some of the nicest furnishings in town, add in a full lavish breakfast, and you've got the **House on Bayou Road,** 2275 Bayou Rd. (© **800/882-2968** or 504/945-0992). See p. 94.

- **Best Basic Hotel:** You know, just a hotel, albeit a hotel that looks sufficiently NOLA-like. It's friendly, it's sweet, and it's better than *basic* allows it to sound—it's the **Maison Dupuy,** 1001 Toulouse St. (© **800/535-9177** or 504/586-8000). See p. 88.

- **Best Fabulous B&B:** You need to see the **Magnolia Mansion,** 2127 Prytania St. (© **504/412-9500**), to believe it, from the blood-red entrance hall to the antiques-crammed public rooms to the wonderfully over-the-top accommodations. See p. 106.

- **Best More Modest B&B: Chimes B&B,** 1146 Constantinople St. (© **504/ 899-2621**), is a delightful family-owned guesthouse in the Garden District.

The charming owners have been operating the B&B for over 20 years, generating loyal return guests. See p. 108.

o **Best Moderately Priced Hotel:** The **Bienville House,** 320 Decatur St. (℃ **800/535-7836** or 504/529-2345), features amenities befitting somewhat swankier digs. Though not centrally located, it's within easy walking distance of everything in the Quarter. See p. 89.

o **Best for Families:** The **Richelieu,** 1234 Chartres St. (℃ **800/535-9653** or 504/529-2492), and **Dauphine Orleans,** 415 Dauphine St. (℃ **800/521-7111** or 504/586-1800), are easy, comfortable, midrange French Quarter hotels with pools for the minnows. A suite at the **Sheraton,** 500 Canal St., (℃ **504/525-2500**) adds space and proximity to several family attractions. If more space and a kitchen are must-haves, the **Homewood Suites,** 901 Poydras (℃ **800/225-5466** or 504/581-5599), is the way to go. It's walking distance to the Quarter and Aquarium (for those of post-toddler age) and rates include a hot breakfast buffet.

o **Best for Travelers with Disabilities:** Two of the most accessible and accommodating choices are the **Hotel Monteleone,** 214 Royal St. (℃ **800/535-9595** or 504/523-3341), and the **Windsor Court,** 300 Gravier St. (℃ **800/262-2662** or 504/523-6000). See p. 87 and p. 100.

o **Best Hotel for Hip Executives:** The innovative minimalist style and myriad comforts at the **International House,** 221 Camp St. (℃ **800/633-5770** or 504/553-9550), have justly made this every film- and record-company dude's (and dudette's) favorite hotel. It's the perfect palate cleanser if you can't stand Victorian frills. See p. 102.

o **Best Health Club:** The hands-down winner is the **Hilton New Orleans Riverside Hotel,** 2 Poydras St. (℃ **800/445-8667** or 504/561-0500). Its Rivercenter Racquet and Health Club features outdoor and indoor tennis courts, squash and racquetball courts, a rooftop jogging track, tanning beds, massage, a hair salon, and a golf studio. See p. 98.

o **Best Hotel in the Quarter:** The **Ritz-Carlton,** 921 Canal St. (℃ **800/241-3333** or 504/524-1331)—they know how to do hotels. A top-to-bottom post-K fix-up has only enhanced this already splendid property. And if you want to go even more decadent, stay in the smaller but elegant club-level rooms in their **Maison Orleans** annex. Just say the words "24-hour butler service." You know you want it. See p. 83.

o **Best Funky Little Hotel:** The **Frenchmen Hotel,** 417 Frenchmen St. (℃ **504/948-2166**), is small but full of pure New Orleans charm. Bear in mind, however, that one person's "funky" may be another person's "dingy," though an excellent post-Katrina makeover has addressed some of those concerns. See p. 93.

o **Best Brand-Name Hotel Addition:** A few years ago, we would have said the Loews New Orleans Hotel, still a swell and stylish place to stay. But in late 2009 the venerable **Roosevelt,** 123 Baronne St. (℃ **800/WALDORF** [925-3673] or 504/648-1200), shuttered since 2005, reopened as a Waldorf Astoria property following a basement-to-attic redo. It's stunningly outfitted and comes with a serious pedigree, and even if it's still working out some kinks, it's a luscious stay. See p. 100.

- **Best Hidden Gem:** Back behind a fence at the start of a so-so neighborhood above the Quarter is an enchanting set of renovated old buildings, a series of suites and rooms full of the sort of impossible romantic details that exist only on the pages of novels about New Orleans. And, of course, here at the **Garlands Historic Creole Cottages,** 1129 St. Philip St. (✆ **800/523-1060** or 504/523-1372). See p. 86.

- **In a Class by Itself:** Of all the hotels in New Orleans, the **Windsor Court,** 300 Gravier St. (✆ **800/262-2662** or 504/523-6000), stands head and shoulders above the rest. Most guest rooms are suites with Italian marble bathrooms, balconies or bay windows, living rooms, kitchenettes, and dressing rooms. If you choose one of the two-bedroom penthouse suites, you'll have the added luxury of a private library and a terrace that overlooks the mighty Mississippi from your Central Business District locale. See p. 100.

THE FRENCH QUARTER

For hotels in this section, see the "French Quarter Hotels" map on p. 83.

Very Expensive

The Inn On Bourbon The justification for staying in this too-pricey chain hotel is not the rooms—though they're fine, thanks to a much-needed, eco-friendly refurbishing in 2010—but the location: the former site of the 1859 French Opera House, the first opera house built in the United States (it burned down in 1919). Party animals should note that this means the hotel is right in the middle of the liveliest action on Bourbon, and many rooms (not standards, though) have balconies overlooking the mayhem. If you plan to sleep, choose another place to stay or request an interior room. On the other hand, there are worse ways to spend a N'Awlins evening than having a pizza on your balcony while enjoying the free Bourbon Street show below. Plus, the **Puccini Bar** occasionally features actual opera and beer tastings by the **NOLA Brewing Co.** Bathroom upgrades include granite counters and new tub/shower combos. The **Café de l'Opera** serves Southern-style breakfast and lunch buffets.

541 Bourbon St., New Orleans, LA 70130. www.innonbourbon.com. ✆ **800/272-6232** or 504/524-7611. Fax 504/568-9427. 186 units. $219–$299 double. AE, DC, DISC, MC, V. Valet parking $25. **Amenities:** Restaurant; bar; concierge; fitness room; outdoor pool (unheated). *In room:* A/C, flatscreen TV, hair dryer, minibar, Wi-Fi (free).

Maison Orleans ★★★ This is for those who say, "I'd stay at the Ritz-Carlton if only it were even nicer and had even better service." *Voilà!* This operates at the Ritz's Club Level, but with, get this, 24-hour butler service. Yes, ring a special button, "ask for the sun" (they say themselves), and your own personal Jeeves will fetch it for you.

The rooms here are gorgeous little classics of NOLA style: wood floors, paneling, and furniture; superb moldings; fireplace facades; and bathrooms containing deep hotel tubs and separate showers (rooms whose numbers end with 05s have smaller bathrooms, with tub/shower combinations), quality amenities, and thick bath sheets. You get both local aesthetics *and* modern comforts, though window size can vary. Beds are ultralush, with feather beds, down comforters with soft covers, and a half canopy. All of this doesn't come cheap, to say the least. However, it includes five food servings a day (enough so that you need not

French Quarter Hotels

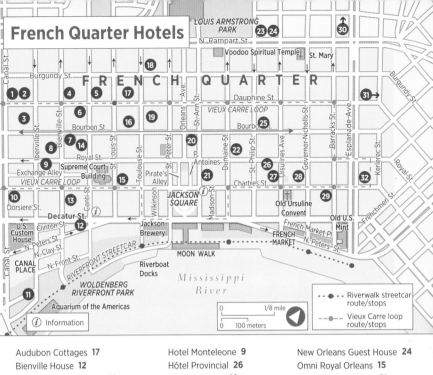

eat anywhere else, though that would be a mistake in New Orleans!), and drinks are free. Summertime can bring incredible specials as well.

904 Iberville St., New Orleans, LA 70112. www.ritzcarlton.com. © **504/670-2900.** Fax 504/670-2910. 75 units. $229–$469 double; call for suite rates. Rates include continental breakfast plus daily snacks/meal presentations. AE, DC, DISC, MC, V. Valet parking $36. **Amenities:** Restaurant; babysitting; health club (complimentary access); Internet (free); room service; spa; Wi-Fi (free). *In room:* A/C, TV/DVD and movie library, CD player and CD library, hair dryer, Internet ($13 per day), minibar (stocked according to personal preference), MP3 docking station.

Ritz-Carlton, New Orleans ★★★ Sentimentalists that we are, we were deeply sad to see the venerable Maison Blanche department store go the way of Woolworth's, D.H. Holmes, and other Canal Street shopping landmarks. But for the city's sake, we are pleased to have the Ritz-Carlton take its place, preserving the classic, glazed terra-cotta building and bringing high-end luxury to the Quarter. Service is sterling. Rooms are light green, purple, and gold in tribute to New Orleans and have lovely beds. King rooms are nicer than doubles, while rooms on the 12th, 14th, and 15th floors are the largest (some ridiculously large), with chaise longues and fancy coffee and tea service in a cleverly designed wooden box. The whole effect is most gracious (even more so at the hotel's Club Level, which includes five food presentations a day plus complimentary drinks). There are a great many elevators and different levels, so getting around does require some zigzagging to and fro. The spa (p. 256) is one of the two best in town (along with the Guerlain, p. 255), and though undeniably expensive, it's gorgeous and the treatments are utter perfection; the fitness center is open 24 hours. Look for fun site-specific events in the courtyard, like crawfish boils and voodoo ceremonies. The entire hotel is nonsmoking.

Staying Safe

There is, of course, considerable concern about personal safety in New Orleans. Your hotel choice, for the most part, need not be influenced by that. Daytime is mostly safe, and at night you will probably be traveling in cabs or, if you're in the French Quarter, in well-populated areas. If you stay above Bourbon Street, closer to Rampart, don't walk back to your hotel alone at night; take a cab or travel in a group.

921 Canal St., New Orleans, LA 70112. www.ritzcarlton.com. © **800/241-3333** or 504/524-1331. Fax 504/524-7675. 452 units. $199–$349 double; $259–$509 executive suite; call for rates on other suites. AE, DC, DISC, MC, V. Valet parking $36. Pets welcome. **Amenities:** Restaurant; 2 bars; concierge; complimentary access to health club (w/resistance pool, Jacuzzi, and personal trainers); room service; top-of-the-line spa; Wi-Fi (free). *In room:* A/C, TV, hair dryer, Internet ($13 per day), minibar.

Royal Sonesta ★★ The contrast between the hurly-burly of Bourbon Street and the Sonesta's elegant lobby couldn't be greater—this is one of the classiest hotels in the Quarter. Inside, all is gracious, and if your room faces the courtyard (complete with a large pool), you are in another world altogether. Big and bustling (a favorite of business travelers, so it always seems busy), this is considered the only acceptable, top-flight Bourbon Street hotel, though noise is still a problem in rooms that face Bourbon (or even the side streets). Rooms are good if not memorable, except for that enormous combo armoire/TV cabinet—it leaves scant few inches between it and the end of the king-size beds. The bathrooms gleam, but don't try to swing a cat inside one (though it's actually a pet-friendly hotel). **Irvin Mayfield's Jazz Playhouse** (p. 278), based in the hotel, is a stellar addition, as is the inexpensive new **P.J.'s Coffee Café. Note:** This is the best place in the Quarter to catch a cab; they line up at the corner.

300 Bourbon St., New Orleans, LA 70130. www.sonesta.com. © **800/766-3782** or 504/586-0300. Fax 504/586-0335. 483 units. $109–$329 double; $400–$2,500 suite. Rates higher during special events. AE, DC, DISC, MC, V. Parking $32 car, $37 oversize. **Amenities:** 2 restaurants; coffee shop; bar; concierge; exercise room; pool; room service. *In room:* A/C, TV, hair dryer, minibar, Wi-Fi ($10).

Soniat House ★★ The recipient of endless tributes from various prestigious travel journals, the wonderful and romantic Soniat House lives up to the hype, though prices can be daunting. Inside the plain, unassuming Creole exterior is a perfect little hideaway, an oasis of calm that seems impossible in the boisterous Quarter. The beyond-efficient staff spoils guests, and the sweet courtyards, candlelit at night, soothe them. The experience here is gracious and adult.

Rooms do vary, if not in quality then at least in distinction. (Be aware that designations such as "junior suite" just mean a room with a sitting area.) All have antiques, but if you want, say, high ceilings and really grand furniture (room no. 23 has a 17th-c. bed), you are better off in the main house or the suite-filled annex across the street (many of the smaller antiques in the rooms are even for sale). The rooms in the old kitchen and other buildings are not quite as smashing by comparison. On the main property, bathrooms are small, though some rooms have their own private balconies. Our only real complaint is the extra charge ($13) for the admittedly delicious, but small, breakfast (fresh-squeezed orange juice and fluffy biscuits made to order)—it seems petty given the already high prices and lack of room service.

1133 Chartres St., New Orleans, LA 70116. www.soniathouse.com. ✆ **800/544-8808** or 504/522-0570. Fax 504/522-7208. 31 unitws. $195–$325 double; $350–$750 suite. Rates higher for special events, lower in summer. AE, MC, V. Valet parking $25. No children 11 or under. **Amenities:** Concierge; access to nearby health club (for additional charge). *In room:* A/C, TV, hair dryer, Wi-Fi (free).

W French Quarter ★★ The groovy, hip vibe of the W never seemed to fit New Orleans all that well—it's a New York thing, isn't it?—but it was okay so long as it was safely tucked away in the CBD with the rest of the businesspeople hotels. But the W folks have neatly melded a more subdued version of the brand into a very New Orleans space, and it doesn't feel jarring at all. It's got the luxury one would want from a more modern hotel, plus a certain sultry, decadent languor that comes from hanging out in a courtyard by a (small) pool or lounging, inside or out, on the W's custom bedding and plush furniture. Rooms (which are grouped around said courtyard and seem to be larger upstairs than down) are done in a more New Orleans–appropriate series of neutrals, with fancy amenities like Bliss Sinkside Six toiletry sets. Bacco is the fine on-site restaurant. If you can snag a room at the lower end of the price range, hop on it.

316 Chartres St., New Orleans, LA 70130. www.whotels.com/wfrenchquarter. ✆ **888/627-8260** or 504/581-1200. Fax 504/523-2910. 98 units. $209–$509 double; suites up to $750. AE, DC, DISC, MC, V. Valet parking $30 and up. **Amenities:** Restaurant; bar; concierge; access to Sheraton health club (2 blocks west at 500 Canal St.); pool; room service. *In room:* A/C, TV/DVD, CD player/MP3 docking station, hair dryer, minibar, Wi-Fi ($15 per day).

Expensive

Chateau Bourbon—A Wyndham Historic Hotel ★★ On the site of the former D.H. Holmes Canal Street department store (1849), the Chateau Bourbon (formerly the Chateau Sonesta) maintains the structure's 1913 facade. Many rooms feature balconies overlooking Bourbon or Dauphine street, which you might want to avoid if you're a light sleeper—or request if you hanker after the party action. High ceilings and a fairly spacious layout, not to mention that proximity to Bourbon, make this a potentially well-priced (if slightly generic) choice, already popular among business groups for its meeting rooms and location. At the Canal Street entrance is a statue of Ignatius Reilly, hero of *A Confederacy of Dunces,* whom we first met when he was waiting, as all of New Orleans once did, "under the clock." The old Holmes clock, now located in the hotel's **Clock Bar,** was for decades the favored rendezvous point for *tout* New Orleanians.

800 Iberville St., New Orleans, LA 70112. www.chateaubourbonneworleans.com. ✆ **877/999-3223** or 504/586-0800. Fax 504/586-1987. 251 units. $99–$350 double; $285–$798 suite. Extra person $20. Children 16 and under stay free in parent's room. AE, DC, DISC, MC, V. Valet parking $28. **Amenities:** Restaurant; bar; babysitting; concierge; exercise room; heated outdoor pool; room service. *In room:* A/C, flatscreen TV w/pay movies, hair dryer, minibar, Wi-Fi ($10 per day).

Chateau LeMoyne—Holiday Inn French Quarter ★ The Chateau LeMoyne has a good location, just around the corner from Bourbon Street but away from the noise and not far from Canal. It's actually a Holiday Inn, and it's a nice surprise to find one housed in century-plus-old buildings. The ambience stops at your room's threshold, however. Once inside, matters look pretty much like they do in every Holiday Inn—too bad. Famed architect James Gallier designed one of these 19th-century buildings, and you can still see bits of old brick, old ovens, and exposed cypress beams here and there, along with a graceful curving outdoor staircase. You wish they'd made more of the space, but even the spacious courtyard feels oddly sterile. Maybe it's the new brick, which seems sandblasted free of pesky (but atmospheric) moss. That said, new paint, bedding, and furnishings in 2010 were more than welcome. Suites aren't much different from standard rooms, just with frillier furniture, though the enormous Executive Suite is probably worth budget busting for its four large (if dark) rooms that include a Jacuzzi and sauna.

301 Dauphine St., New Orleans, LA 70112. www.chateaulemoynefrenchquarter.com. ✆ **800/HOLIDAY** (465-4329) or 504/581-1303. Fax 504/523-5709. 171 units. $89–$339 double; $299–$499 suite, depending on season. AE, DC, DISC, MC, V. Valet parking $30; trucks, vans, oversize $35. **Amenities:** Restaurant (breakfast only); bar; heated saltwater outdoor pool. *In room:* A/C, flatscreen TV, hair dryer, Wi-Fi (free).

Dauphine Orleans Hotel ★ On a relatively quiet and peaceful block of the Quarter, the Dauphine Orleans Hotel is relaxed but not unkempt. It's just a block from the action on Bourbon Street, but you wouldn't know it if you were sitting in any of its three secluded courtyards. Guests tend to like the atmosphere a lot. The hotel's buildings have a colorful history: The license a former owner took out to make the place a bordello is proudly displayed in the bar, and its proprietors are happy to admit that ghosts have been sighted on the premises (nonsmoking ghosts presumably—it's not allowed on property). The hotel's back buildings were once the studio of John James Audubon, and the "patio rooms" across the street from the main building were originally built in 1834 as the home of New Orleans merchant Samuel Hermann. Rooms are fresh, clean, and somewhat modern, with white duvets, plasma TVs, and sleek tubs. The saltwater pool is adequately sized.

415 Dauphine St., New Orleans, LA 70112. www.dauphineorleans.com. ✆ **800/521-7111** or 504/586-1800. Fax 504/586-9630. 111 units. $99–$299 double; $179–$399 suite. Rates include continental breakfast and welcome wine or beer coupon. Extra person $20. Children 17 and under stay free in parent's room. AE, DC, DISC, MC, V. Valet parking $28, oversize vehicle $32. **Amenities:** Bar; coffee lounge; small fitness room; Jacuzzi; outdoor pool. *In room:* A/C, TV, minibar, Wi-Fi (free).

The Garlands Historic Creole Cottages ★★ Here's a hidden gem across a side street from Armstrong Park, which makes it not the best location in town, though the inn itself is completely safe thanks to a good security fence. Please don't let our warning discourage you; this B&B is utterly charming, with some of the nicest accommodations in the city, set on the grounds of the former Claude Treme plantation—plus they've recently given things a fresh coat of paint and updated the bedding. Creole cottages (one with four bedrooms) feature big, sexy canopy beds, wide pine-board floors, exposed brick walls, a fireplace, a big oval soaking tub, and good-taste furniture. Some come with kitchens and small living rooms, while other rooms are smaller (since units vary in size, ask when booking), but all are impeccably maintained, and the whole place is set in small, delightful Southern gardens. The breakfast includes dishes such as curried eggs with crab-meat on puff pastry, and there are often homemade snacks and farmers' market fruit around. Still, you should exercise caution coming home at night, and don't plan on venturing deeper into the Treme neighborhood.

1129 St. Philip St., New Orleans, LA 70116. www.garlandsguesthouse.com. ℂ **800/523-1060** or 504/523-1372. Fax 504/523-1951. 15 units. $135–$500 cottage. Rates include breakfast. AE, DC, DISC, MC, V. Free parking. **Amenities:** Wi-Fi (free). *In room:* A/C, flatscreen TV.

Hotel Monteleone ★★ Opened in 1886, the Monteleone is the largest hotel in the French Quarter (and was home to Truman Capote's parents when he was born!). Because of its size, rooms are often available here when other places are booked. Everyone who stays here loves it, probably because it's a family hotel whose approach to business is reflected by the staff, among the most helpful in town. One guest who stayed here with a child with disabilities raved about the facilities. There are still variations in terms of room size and style: Rooms with numbers from 56 to 59 are slightly bigger, with old high ceilings; rooms with numbers in the 27s have no windows; rooms with numbers in the 60s are near the ice machine. Executive suites are just big rooms that have the nicest new furniture, including four-poster beds and Jacuzzis. The glass fitness room overlooking the city is well stocked with ellipticals and other machines.

One of the city's best-kept secrets is the renovated rooftop pool; on a recent visit, we were among a handful of folks lounging on the deck high above the street noise, with unencumbered views of the city and beyond. It's quite a scene, with snacks served there in the evening.

214 Royal St., New Orleans, LA 70130. www.hotelmonteleone.com. ℂ **800/535-9595** or 504/523-3341. Fax 504/561-5803. 570 units, including 55 suites. $169–$399 double; $339–$3,500 suite. Extra person $25. Children 17 and under stay free in parent's room. Package rates available. AE, DC, DISC, MC, V. Valet parking $30 car, $32 oversize. Pets allowed on the 3rd floor only, for a fee and deposit. **Amenities:** 2 restaurants; bar; concierge; fitness center; heated rooftop pool (year-round); room service. *In room:* A/C, TV, hair dryer, minibar, Wi-Fi ($13 per day).

Lafitte Guest House ★ Here you'll find the best of both worlds: antique living just blocks from Bourbon Street mayhem (though the Lafitte's cute little parlor seems almost antithetical to rowdy merriment). The three-story brick building, with wrought-iron balconies on the second and third floors, was constructed in 1849. Each room has its own mostly Victorian flair, with thoughtful touches such as pralines on the pillow and even white-noise machines to handle the Bourbon Street ruckus, which is an excellent idea. Some rooms have balconies overlooking Bourbon. Room no. 21 has its own sitting room, while *garçonnière* rooms are smaller and probably best for singles. Room no. 5 in the old stables in back has a tiny loft (the ceiling may be a little low for a tall person). It has a wonderful quality, good for couples wanting a little extra privacy. The owners are committed to supporting their city and use many products from local vendors. Altogether, this is a delightful little place, but the prices are a bit steep, considering.

1003 Bourbon St., New Orleans, LA 70116. www.lafitteguesthouse.com. © **800/331-7971** or 504/581-2678. Fax 504/581-2677. 14 units. $179–$269 double. Rates higher for special events, lower in summer. Extra person $25. Rates include morning coffee and biscuits. AE, DISC, MC, V. Parking $15. **Amenities:** 24-hr. concierge. *In room:* A/C, TV, fridge (in some rooms), hair dryer available, Wi-Fi (free).

Maison Dupuy ★ We often forget to recommend this place, but that's a mistake. The Maison Dupuy is a little out of the main French Quarter action and a tad closer than some might like to somewhat dicey Rampart, but that makes for a quiet locale (and the hotel is entirely safe). Comprised of seven town houses surrounding a perfectly pleasant, good-size courtyard and heated pool, it is warm and inviting. Rooms are comfortable if unremarkable, and though floor space and balconies (with either courtyard or street views—the former is quieter) vary, the staff is most friendly and helpful. Proximity to a bar with pool tables (a rarity in town) and a quite good restaurant on-site (**Le Meritage,** p. 124) puts it right in the middle of the "Oh, they've got rooms available? Why not?" category.

1001 Toulouse St., New Orleans, LA 70112. www.maisondupuy.com. © **800/535-9177** or 504/586-8000. Fax 504/525-5334. 200 units. $99–$269 superior double; $149–$299 deluxe double with balcony; $329–$838 suite. AE, DC, DISC, MC, V. Valet parking $28 for cars, $32 for SUVs and trucks when available. **Amenities:** 2 restaurants, including Le Meritage (see review, p. 124); bar; babysitting; exercise room; heated outdoor saltwater pool; room service. *In room:* A/C, TV, hair dryer, Wi-Fi (free).

Omni Royal Orleans ★★ ☺ Despite being part of a chain, this is an elegant hotel that doesn't feel sterile and generic. This is only proper given that it is on the former site of the venerable 1836 St. Louis Exchange Hotel, one of the country's premier hostelries and a center of New Orleans social life until the final years of the Civil War. The original building was finally destroyed by a 1915 hurricane, but the Omni, built in 1960, is a worthy successor, enjoying a prime location smack in the center of the Quarter. Truman Capote and William Styron have stayed here, and there's even a Tennessee Williams suite. Guest rooms are done in grave good taste, full of muted tones and plush furniture, with windows that let you look dreamily out over the Quarter. Room sizes vary, though the smaller rooms were recently expanded, with furnishings that aim for "European traditional opulence." Vast suites make this a good choice for families despite the fancy appearance. Service is swift and conscientious, amenities are ample, and you can often enjoy live piano jazz in the lobby next to the posh **Rib Room** restaurant (p. 126). If you don't stay here yourself, try to cozy up to someone who does—at least long enough to access the rooftop pool and **Observation Bar,** with its stunning 360-degree views. Altogether, an especially worthwhile choice.

> ## Impressions
>
> *There is something left in this people here that makes them like one another, that leads to constant outbursts of the spirit of play, that keeps them from being too confoundedly serious about death and the ballot and reform and other less important things in life.*
>
> —Sherwood Anderson, *New Orleans, the Double Dealer, and the Modern Movement in America.*

621 St. Louis St., New Orleans, LA 70140. www.omniroyalorleans.com. © **800/THE-OMNI** (843-6664) in the U.S. and Canada, or 504/529-5333. Fax 504/529-7089. 346 units. $189–$339 double; $339–$850 suite; $1,200–$1,600 penthouse. Children 17 and under stay free in parent's room. AE, DC, DISC, MC, V. Valet parking $32. **Amenities:** Restaurant, Rib Room (see review, p. 126); 2 bars; babysitting; concierge; health club; heated outdoor pool; room service. *In room:* A/C, TV, hair dryer, minibar, Wi-Fi ($9.95 per day).

St. Louis ★ Right in the heart of the Quarter, the St. Louis is a small hotel that surrounds a lush courtyard with a fountain (wedding crashers note: many are held here). But it's somewhat disappointingly dull for what ought to be a charming boutique hotel. A few third-floor rooms have private balconies overlooking Bienville Street, and all open onto the central courtyard. The exterior is looking a little battered, but the standard quality of the rooms is justifiable if you get in at the low end of its rate card—and we're told room renovations were on tap for 2011. King rooms are smaller than doubles, and there are far more of the latter (leaving queen-sizes for the single rooms). An additional wing with pricey units featuring parlors and kitchenettes has been added. The otherwise uninteresting bathrooms do have bidets. If the price holds, it's a great deal, especially considering the location.

730 Bienville St., New Orleans, LA 70130. www.stlouishotel.com. © **800/535-9111** or 504/581-7300. Fax 504/679-5013. 97 units. $79–$189 double. Rates higher for special events. AE, DISC, MC, V. Valet parking $34. **Amenities:** Restaurant; concierge; pool use at nearby sister hotel. *In room:* A/C, TV, hair dryer, Wi-Fi (free).

Westin New Orleans at Canal Place ★★ At the foot of Canal Street, the Westin is technically *in* the French Quarter—but not quite *of* it. It is literally *above* the Quarter: The grand-scale lobby is on the 11th floor of the **Canal Place** tower. The views of the Mississippi and French Quarter are unparalleled in the city (and will cost you about $25 more per night—it's worth it!). Rooms are equipped with the marshmallow delight that is the Westin Heavenly bed, and have a boring but clean and fresh contemporary look in neutral colors. Bathrooms are adequately sized, but the tub/shower combo is nothing special, despite the double shower head. The restaurant and pool also have those views, while the well-equipped gym has up-to-date equipment. It's an easy walk from here to the Convention Center, for humans and dogs (who are welcome here).

100 Iberville St., New Orleans, LA 70130. www.westinneworleanscanalplace.com. © **504/566-7006.** Fax 504/553-5120. 438 units. $159–$309 double. Ask about specials. AE, DISC, MC, V. Self-parking $18; valet $36. **Amenities:** Restaurant; bar; concierge; fitness center; heated pool; room service. *In room:* A/C, TV, hair dryer, minibar, Wi-Fi ($13 per day).

Moderate

Bienville House ★★ A nice little Quarter hotel, better than most (thanks to a combo of location, price, and room quality), though not as good as some (owing to a lack of specific personality and the odd bit of shabbiness). It's generally sedate, except perhaps during Mardi Gras, when the mad gay revelers take over—as they do everywhere, truth be told. The truly friendly and helpful staff adds a welcoming spirit, for pooches, too. If you can score some of the lower-end rates, nab a spot here. Most rooms have high ceilings, though some don't have windows, and all have comfortable four-poster beds and fresh linens. Some rooms have balconies overlooking the small courtyard with its pretty saltwater pool (open 24 hr. if guests aren't too rowdy!), and all have the standard amenities of a fine hotel. The Iberville Suite is so large it actually made us laugh out loud—in a good way. Also, take note of the excellent restaurant, **Iris** (p. 128).

320 Decatur St., New Orleans, LA 70130. www.bienvillehouse.com. © **800/535-7836** or 504/529-2345. Fax 504/525-6079. 83 units. $99–$189 double; $650 penthouse. Rates higher for special events; call for summer specials. Rates include continental breakfast and afternoon reception with cookies and punch. AE, DC, DISC, MC, V. Parking $20 and up for larger vehicles. **Amenities:** Restaurant, Iris (see review, p. 128); Wi-Fi (free) in lobby; outdoor saltwater pool; room service. *In room:* A/C, TV, hair dryer, Wi-Fi ($9.95 per day).

Bourbon Orleans Hotel ★ This hotel occupies three historic buildings. Ceilings in the rooms feel lower than the frequent high variety found around town, which may be an optical illusion. Beds are too firm while bathrooms are long and narrow with a natty use of stripes and brocades. Small rooms are cozy but not unbearable, though if occupied by two people, they had better like each other. The rooms for the mobility-impaired are well designed. Some rooms have only armoires, no closets, and some have balconies. Rooms with numbers in the 170s have views up Bourbon Street, but if you want to escape the noisy street excitement, ask for an interior room. All rooms are nonsmoking. We are fond of the two-story town-house rooms, with exposed brickwork on the walls, and the beds upstairs in a romantic loft. It's classy sexy, good for a multiple-day stay.

717 Orleans St., New Orleans, LA 70116. www.bourbonorleans.com. © **866/513-9744** or 504/523-2222. Fax 504/525-8166. 218 units. $139–$199 petite queen or twin; $189–$329 deluxe king or double; $239–$599 suite. Rates higher for special events; check for specials. Extra person $30. AE, DC, DISC, MC, V. Valet parking $28, oversize $32. **Amenities:** Restaurant (breakfast only); bar; concierge; outdoor pool; room service (breakfast only). *In room:* A/C, TV, hair dryer, Wi-Fi (free).

Bourgoyne Guest House 🍴 This is an eccentric place with an owner to match. If you dislike stuffy hotels and will happily take things a little worn at the edges (and can live without Wi-Fi) in exchange for a relaxed, hangout atmosphere, come here. Accommodations are arranged around a nicely cluttered courtyard, the right spot to visit and regroup before diving back out onto Bourbon Street (whose main action begins just a few feet away). Studios are adequate little rooms with kitchens and bathrooms that appear grimy but are not (we saw the strong potions housekeeping uses; it's just age). The Green Suite is big and grand, with huge, tall rooms, a second smaller bedroom, a bigger bathroom, a kitchen, and a balcony overlooking Bourbon Street. For price and location, it's a heck of a deal, maybe the best in the Quarter. The first floor can suffer from street noise, depending on the time of year and how far up Bourbon the party travels.

839 Bourbon St., New Orleans, LA 70116. www.bourgoynehouse.com. © **504/525-3983** or 504/524-3621. 5 units. $95 studio; $125 La Petite Suite; $140–$200 Green Suite. AE, MC, V. *In room:* A/C, TV (in suites only), fridge.

Hôtel Provincial ★ Don't mention this to the owners, who are sensitive about it, but word from the ghost tours is that the Provincial is haunted, mostly by soldiers treated here when it was a Civil War hospital. It must not be too much of a problem, though, because guests rave about the place and never mention ghostly visitors. With flickering gas lamps, no elevators, at least five patios, and a tranquil setting, this feels less like a hotel than a guesthouse. Both the quiet and the terrific service belie its size, so it seems smaller and more intimate than it is. It's also in a good part of the Quarter on a quiet street off the beaten path. For views of

WHERE TO STAY | The French Quarter

the river (plus higher ceilings), get a room on the third or fourth floor of the back building. Some rooms have half-tester beds (the furniture is a mix of antiques and reproductions). Regular rooms are dark but roomy. Finally, with such a pretty pool area, it's a shame there isn't much in the way of a lounging area or shade.

1024 Chartres St., New Orleans, LA 70116. www.hotelprovincial.com. ☏ **800/535-7922** or 504/581-4995. Fax 504/581-1018. 92 units. $79–$289 double. Rates higher for special events. Rates include continental breakfast. AE, DC, DISC, MC, V. Valet parking $22. **Amenities:** Restaurant, Stella! (see review, p. 126); bar; pool. In room: A/C, flatscreen TV, hair dryer, Wi-Fi (free).

Hotel St. Marie Location, location, location. Just a little above Bourbon Street on an otherwise quiet street, this hotel could be on your list of "clean and safe backup places to stay if my top choices are full." Surrounding a pretty, foliage-and-light-bedecked courtyard with a small pool (which you will bless the heavens for in summer), rooms are generic New Orleans, with dark colors and standard-issue and mock European hotel furniture. Note that king rooms are more pleasant than doubles, and corner rooms are more spacious, which includes the otherwise dinky bathrooms. Some rooms from the original town house have balconies overlooking the street and courtyard. Hallways are not numbered and can be dim, which could make a tipsy late-night return a challenge.

827 Toulouse St., New Orleans, LA 70112. www.hotelstmarie.com. ☏ **800/366-2743** or 504/561-8951. Fax 504/571-2802. 100 units. $49–$199 double. Rates higher during special events. Rates include continental breakfast. Children 11 and under stay free in parent's room. AE, DC, DISC, MC, V. Valet parking $25. In room: A/C, TV, hair dryer, Wi-Fi (free).

Hotel Villa Convento ★ Local tour guides say this was the original House of the Rising Sun bordello, so if you have a sense of humor (or a theatrical bent), be sure to pose in your bathrobe on your balcony so that you can be pointed out to passing tour groups. With its rather small public spaces and the personal attention that its owners and operators, the Campo family, give to their guests, the Villa Convento has the feel of a small European inn or guesthouse and does a lot of repeat business. The building is a Creole town house; some rooms open onto the tropical patio, others to the street, and many have balconies. There is much to be fond of in this place—though parts can be shabbier than one would like, and truth be told, it can smell like mold. Free garage parking is about 5 blocks away.

616 Ursulines St., New Orleans, LA 70116. www.villaconvento.com. ☏ **504/522-1793.** Fax 504/524-1902. 25 units. $89–$125 double; $125–$155 suite. Rates higher during special events. AE, DC, DISC, MC, V. No children 9 or under allowed. **Amenities:** Wi-Fi (free). In room: A/C, TV, hair dryer, Wi-Fi (free, in some rooms only).

Lamothe House ★ Somehow, a shiny new hotel doesn't seem quite right for New Orleans. More appropriate is slightly faded, somewhat threadbare elegance, and the Lamothe House neatly fits that bill. The plain Creole-style facade of this 1840s town house hides the atmosphere you are looking for—a mossy, brick-lined courtyard with a goldfish fountain and banana trees and rooms filled with antiques that are worn in the right places but not shabby. Despite interior upgrades, rooms can be dark and small, with clashing decor. Room no. 101 is a grand affair with lots of original plaster frills, though we wish there were good wood floors instead of that carpet. Room no. 117 nearly gets it right in terms of size and style. A continental breakfast is served in a second-floor dining room that just screams faded gentility. It's a short walk to the action in the Quarter and just a couple of blocks to the bustling Frenchmen scene in the Faubourg Marigny.

621 Esplanade Ave., New Orleans, LA 70116. www.lamothehouse.com. ☎ **800/367-5858** or 504/947-1161. Fax 504/218-4297. 35 units. $69–$199 double; $79–$299 suite. Rates include continental breakfast. AE, DISC, MC, V. Self-parking $15. **Amenities:** Jacuzzi; pool. *In room:* A/C, TV, hair dryer, Wi-Fi (free).

Le Richelieu Hotel ★ ☺ First a row mansion, then a macaroni factory, then a hotel, and finally a Katrina victim—this building has seen it all, including part of its roof collapsing. But the latter mess allowed for some new paint (or textured wallpaper), carpet, drapes, and beds, and consequently Le Richelieu looks as good as it ever has (though some rooms still look rather motel-like, thanks to dated mirrored walls). Bathrooms are only fair, just like any old hotel. Other rooms are standard high-end motel rooms. Many have balconies, and all overlook either the French Quarter or the courtyard. Le Richelieu is good for families (despite the surcharge for children), being away from the adult action, with a nice pool and multiroom suites. Paul McCartney thought so; he and his family stayed here for some months long ago while Wings was recording an album. Le Richelieu is the only hotel in the French Quarter with free on-premise self-parking. All rooms are nonsmoking.

1234 Chartres St., New Orleans, LA 70116. www.lerichelieuhotel.com. ☎ **800/535-9653** or 504/529-2492. Fax 504/524-8179. 86 units. $95–$180 double; $200–$550 suite. Extra person, including children, $15. Honeymoon and seasonal packages available. AE, DC, DISC, MC, V. Free parking. **Amenities:** Restaurant (breakfast and lunch only); bar; concierge; pool; room service. *In room:* A/C, TV, fridge, hair dryer, Wi-Fi (free).

Place d'Armes Hotel ★ ☺ Parts of this hotel seem a bit grim and old, though a quite large courtyard and an amoeba-shaped pool are ideal for hanging out and may make up for its shortcomings. Plus, it's only half a block from the Café du Monde (p. 154)—very convenient when you need a beignet at 3am. This also makes it a favorite for families with kids. Rooms (all nonsmoking) are homey and furnished in traditional style; however, 32 of them do not have windows and can be cell-like—be sure to ask for a room with a window when you reserve. Breakfast is served in a breakfast room, and the location, just off Jackson Square, makes sightseeing a breeze.

625 St. Ann St., New Orleans, LA 70116. www.placedarmes.com. ☎ **800/366-2743** or 504/524-4531. Fax 504/571-2803. 84 units. $59–$219 double. Rates higher for special events. Rates include continental breakfast. Children 11 and under stay free in parent's room. AE, DC, DISC, MC, V. Valet parking $25. **Amenities:** Concierge; pool. *In room:* A/C, TV, hair dryer, Wi-Fi (free).

Prince Conti Hotel ★ This tiny but friendly hotel is in a great location right off Bourbon and not generally noisy (though thin walls can mean otherwise if you're stuck with an unruly neighbor). Rooms are decorated with attractive reproduction antiques. All have high ceilings, some with ceiling fans and exposed brick walls, and are bright and pretty. Bathrooms can be ultratiny, with the toilet virtually on top of the sink. The continental breakfast is meaningless (the Déjà Vu restaurant across the street is reliable), but the hotel's **Bombay Club** restaurant and bar are well known for their umpteen martini variations and swell piano entertainment.

830 Conti St., New Orleans, LA 70112. www.princecontihotel.com. ☎ **800/366-2743** or 504/529-4172. Fax 504/636-1046. 76 units. $49–$199 double; $119–$299 suite, depending on season. Rates include continental breakfast. Children 11 and under stay free in parent's room. AE, DISC, MC, V. Valet parking $25. **Amenities:** Restaurant; piano bar. *In room:* A/C, flatscreen TV, Wi-Fi (free).

5

The French Quarter

WHERE TO STAY

Inexpensive

New Orleans Guest House ★ Run for many years by Ray Cronk and Alvin Payne, this guesthouse is a little off the beaten path (just outside the French Quarter across N. Rampart St.), but it's painted a startling hot, Pepto-Bismol pink, so it's hard to miss. Top-floor and back rooms have been redone, mostly to fine, funky, and fun effect, all in a way that is classic NOLA guesthouse, in a manner that is being lost to generic good taste. Main-house rooms are dark-colored, sometimes with gaudy new bathrooms, but sweet, and room no. 8 has an outrageous Art Nouveau bedroom suite. The slave quarters are simpler but with interesting antiques and light colors. Some rooms have exposed brick walls, while others open directly on to the green plant-stuffed courtyard, a veritable tropical garden, with some intricately carved old fountains. All rooms are nonsmoking. There is a 24-hour desk clerk and two gray kitties!

1118 Ursulines St., New Orleans, LA 70116. ⓒ **800/562-1177** or 504/566-1177. Fax 504/566-1179. 14 units. $59–$79 double; $69–$99 queen or twin; $89–$109 king or 2 full beds. Rates higher during special events. Rates include continental breakfast. Extra person $15. AE, MC, V. Free off-street parking. *In room:* A/C, TV, hair dryer available, Wi-Fi (free).

THE FAUBOURG MARIGNY

The Faubourg Marigny is very distinct from the French Quarter, though the neighborhoods border each other and are an easy walk apart. This arty and bohemian neighborhood may be better for a younger crowd who wants to be near the French Quarter without actually being in it. If you stay in the farther reaches of the Faubourg, however, please either take a cab or be very cautious returning at night; the neighborhood has suffered from crime problems lately.

For hotels in this section, see the "New Orleans Hotels" map on p. 78.

Moderate

B&W Courtyards Bed & Breakfast ★★ The deceptively simple facade hides a sweet and very hospitable little B&B, complete with two small courtyards and a fountain. It's located in the Faubourg Marigny next to the bustling nighttime Frenchmen scene, a 10-minute walk or short cab ride to the Quarter. Owners Rob Boyd and Kevin Wu went to ingenious lengths to turn six oddly shaped spaces into comfortable rooms. No two rooms are alike—you enter one through its bathroom. Another room is more like a small, two-story apartment with the bedroom upstairs and a virtually full kitchen downstairs. All are carefully and thoughtfully decorated. Rob (who designs jewelry, some of which has been worn by Mary J. Blige, Kanye West, and Oprah) and Kevin (a trained masseuse who can treat you in your room) are adept at giving advice—and strong opinions—about the city and their own local favorites. Breakfast is light (fruit, homemade granola) but beautifully presented. Special rates are given to visiting Habitat for Humanity or St. Bernard Project volunteers.

2425 Chartres St., New Orleans, LA 70117. www.bandwcourtyards.com. ⓒ **800/585-5731** or 504/945-9418. 6 units. $99–$250 double. Rates include continental breakfast. MC, V. Free on-street parking. **Amenities:** Jacuzzi. *In room:* A/C, flatscreen TV, hair dryer, MP3 docking station, Wi-Fi (free).

The Frenchmen Hotel ★ Some see this as a small, sweet, slightly funky inn, very popular with in-the-know regular visitors who think of it as quintessential

New Orleans. Others think it's a total dump. Recent room overhauls please us greatly, in either case. It's just across from the Quarter and a block away from the main drag of the Frenchmen section of the Faubourg Marigny, where all sorts of clubs and happenings make for a lively night scene (and noisy, if your room overlooks the street). Housed in two 19th-century buildings, the rooms vary in size considerably (rooms with two beds are quite large), and some are very small indeed. Each has its own bright and rather eccentric paint color, plus old-timey prints or paintings, and much improved mattresses. First-floor rooms have tile floors, and some rooms have large TVs. It still smells a bit musty, though, like old Quarter hotels. A tropical courtyard has a small pool and Jacuzzi, and the continental breakfast is carb-heavy (muffins, pastries, bagels, cereals).

417 Frenchmen St. (at Esplanade Ave.), New Orleans, LA 70116. www.frenchmenhotel.com. € **504/948-2166.** Fax 504/948-2258. 27 units. $59–$250 double; $89–$299 suite. Rates include continental breakfast. AE, DISC, MC, V. Parking $15. **Amenities:** Jacuzzi; pool. *In room:* A/C, TV, Wi-Fi (free).

Inexpensive

Royal Street Inn & R Bar ★★ This little offbeat establishment lies on the edge of the so-happening Frenchmen Street scene. It's loose but not disorganized (though you can only book rooms online), and there couldn't be a better choice for laid-back travelers. B&B stands for bed-and-*beverage*—the lobby is the highly enjoyable **R Bar** (p. 294), and as a guest, you are entitled to two complimentary cocktails.

A long-overdue stripped-to-the-walls redo of the rooms (converting them all into sometimes rather wee "suites" with separate sitting areas) gave this place the hip, clever, fresh look it totally deserves coupled with a great New Orleans vibe. Leather couches, exposed brickwork, gorgeous gleaming wood floors, geometric colors—sure, most of the rooms are small, and two open onto the street, but if you are looking for something special in New Orleans, this is hard to beat. The attic is a big room with sloping ceilings, pleasing for those with starving-artist garret fantasies. Couples traveling together may love the smashing suite, with two large bedrooms and its own balcony; it's perfect for those wanting a party with its own accessible bar.

1431 Royal St., New Orleans, LA 70116. www.royalstreetinn.com. € **504/948-7499.** 5 units. $75–$250 double. Rates include bar beverages. AE, DISC, MC, V. Street parking available—purchase special permit from management. **Amenities:** Bar. *In room:* A/C, TV/DVD, hair dryer, MP3 docking station, Wi-Fi (free).

MID-CITY/ESPLANADE

For hotels in this section, see the "Mid-City Hotels & Restaurants" map on p. 95.

Expensive

The House on Bayou Road ★★ If you want to stay in a rural and romantic plantation setting but not be far from the action, try what is quite possibly the most smashing guesthouse in town. Tucked away off Esplanade Avenue, this intimate 1700s Creole plantation home, one of the most distinctive accommodations in a city full of curious places to stay, is romantic and peaceful, yet only a

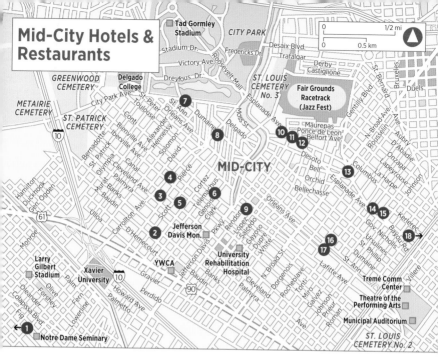

Mid-City Hotels & Restaurants

HOTELS

Ashtons Bed & Breakfast **16**
Degas House Bed and Breakfast **14**
1896 O'Malley House **3**

RESTAURANTS

Angelo Brocato's Ice Cream
& Confectionery **4**
Café Degas **11**
Dooky Chase **17**
Lil' Dizzy's **18**

Liuzza's **6**
Liuzza's by the Track **12**
Lola's **10**
Mandina's **5**
McHardy's Fried Chicken **13**
Mona's Café & Deli **2**
Pandora's **8**
Parkway Bakery and Tavern **9**
Ralph's on the Park **7**
Willie Mae's Scotch House **16**
Ye Olde College Inn **1**

few minutes away by car from the Quarter (and a few minutes in another direction from a not-so-stellar section of town).

Each room has its own charm and is individually decorated to a fare-thee-well—a slightly cluttered, not quite fussy but still lovingly done aesthetic. The Bayou St. John Room (the old library) holds a queen-size four-poster bed and a working fireplace; the Bayou Delacroix has the same kind of bed and a wonderfully large bathtub. The large cottage has four rooms that can be rented separately or together (perfect for a large family). The private cottage was rebuilt post-Katrina, even larger and better than before. The unusually extensive grounds are beautifully manicured, with an outdoor pool, patio, and screened-in porch. Expect a hearty plantation-style breakfast (the New Orleans Cooking Experience classes are held on-site, see p. 210). *Note:* At press time, the property was for sale—though there's hope that a new owner would keep the B&B going. Things could change by the time you read this.

2275 Bayou Rd., New Orleans, LA 70119. www.houseonbayouroad.com. ✆ **504/945-0992.** Fax 504/945-0993. 8 units, 2 cottages. $155–$250 double. Call for summer specials; rates higher during special events. Rates include full breakfast. AE, MC, V. Free off-street parking. Children 13 and older welcome. **Amenities:** Outdoor pool. *In room:* A/C, TV, hair dryer, minibar, Wi-Fi (free).

Moderate

Ashtons Bed & Breakfast ★★ This charming guesthouse represents one of the gutsiest ventures in the city. After devastating Katrina-induced mayhem, it's been fully restored to great beauty and effect, and is a fine and worthy alternative to some of its more costly compatriots. There are pretty custom-paint treatments like shadow striping on top of new molding and chandeliers, and the whole effect is bright, cheerful, and handsome. All the rooms have wide wooden floorboards, inviting beds, and excellent robes, and some have whirlpool tubs. Room no. 4's bed has a half canopy, while room no. 1's bathroom is contained in a curtained-off corner. They put that second *B* in B&B to good use, with such fun as bananas Foster waffles and sweet-potato-stuffed French toast. The so-so stretch of grand Esplanade Avenue is between the French Quarter and City Park (and the Jazz Fest Fair Grounds), and right on the bus line.

2023 Esplanade Ave., New Orleans, LA 70116. www.ashtonsbb.com. ✆ **800/725-4131** or 504/942-7048. 8 units. $159–$189 double; $189–$219 for Mardi Gras and special events; $269–$289 during Jazz Fest. Call for off-season specials. Rates include full breakfast and complimentary soft drinks. AE, DISC, MC, V. Free secure parking. *In room:* A/C, TV, hair dryer, Wi-Fi (free).

Block-Keller House ★★ This inn was extensively restored with an eye toward both guest comfort and preservation of the full Victorian aesthetic. It's a splendid choice for someone who wants both the classic Victorian B&B experience (look for period excess in the front rooms' gorgeous details) and a room with modern amenities (Berber carpet, Jacuzzi tubs, and the like). If that's you, stay upstairs in the absurdly large top-floor rooms. However, if you prefer traditional surroundings, the ground-floor rooms, with fireplaces and grand old beds, should do just fine. You'll find comfy communal sitting areas upstairs and in the bottom level. Room nos. 3 and 5 are large, while room no. 4 has a window seat. The gardens are stunning. Upkeep may have slipped a little of late, and it's a bit out of the thick of it on a rough stretch of Canal Street, but it's close to Mandina's restaurant (p. 137) and right on the Canal streetcar line, making it an easy hop to the Quarter, City Park, and Jazz Fest Fair Grounds. All in all a fine choice for style and service, plus it comes with two sweet dogs.

3620 Canal St., New Orleans, LA 70119. www.blockkellerhouse.com. ✆ **877/588-3033** or 504/483-3033. 5 units. $125–$165 double. Rates for special events higher; seasonal rates lower. Rates include breakfast and coffee and tea service. Special packages on website. AE, MC, V. Free off-street parking. *In room:* A/C, TV, hair dryer, Wi-Fi (free).

1896 O'Malley House ★★ One of the most smashing B&Bs in the city, this place is just a treasure inside, full of gorgeous antiques and repro furniture. Although it's located on a dull stretch of street, this Mid-City neighborhood came back strong from the flood and many restaurants and shops are nearby. The B&B is also mere minutes from the Canal Street streetcar, which goes to the Quarter. Many of the original details, including marvelous tile on the various fireplaces in several of the rooms, are still intact—yet they've paid close attention to green touches, down to the eco-friendly toiletries. The handsome, somewhat masculine (as opposed to frilly) rooms are each meticulously decorated, using clever touches such as vintage (at least appearing) oil paintings, Bali puppets, and European art. Second-floor rooms are larger, and most have Jacuzzi tubs. The third floor is a clever use of design and space, where formerly dull cypress walls have been pickled lighter to striking effect (ask to see the photos of the mysterious science equations found scrawled on one wall). These rooms are smaller and more garretlike, though they pale in desirability only if you really, *really* want that classic high-ceilinged look.

120 S. Pierce St., New Orleans, LA 70119. www.1896omalleyhouse.com. © **866/226-1896** or 504/488-5896. 9 units. $135–$155 double; $200 special events such as Mardi Gras and Jazz Fest. Call for special summer rates. Rates include breakfast, beer, wine, and soft drinks. AE, DISC, MC, V. Free off-street parking. *In room:* A/C, flatscreen TV w/built-in DVD player, hair dryer, Wi-Fi (free).

CENTRAL BUSINESS DISTRICT

At first glance, the CBD seems too generic big city for a proper New Orleans stay. And while it is true that many of its hotels blur together in terms of style, quality is consistent, and you can get very good rates here compared to prices just across Canal. It's an easy walk to the Quarter, but given the increasing number of more moderately priced, and excellent, restaurants in the area, you may not care. For hotels in this section, please see the "New Orleans Hotels" map on p. 78.

Very Expensive

Harrah's ★ If you've had any experience with Vegas hotels, you would know this post-Katrina property was casino-owned. New Orleans doesn't lack for impressive, grand hotels, but there is something so . . . *big* . . . about the Harrah's lobby that it passes right through grand and into something almost too immense to be truly elegant. Which isn't to knock the place; everyone did a good job (and it helps to know that Harrah's has extensive energy efficiency and recycling programs). The rooms are sharp, if a touch generic, though photos by local artist Richard Sexton and splashes of Mardi Gras purple and gold help. Rooms are all pretty much the same size, except for the larger corner suites, which don't offer enough extra to justify the price. Rooms ending in nos. 1 to 10 have romantic river views, while city views aren't anything special. An airy gym with a tall ceiling and windows is well stocked with a good mix of aerobic and weight machines. Naturally, it's right across from the casino. Carnivores have their choice of two good on-site steak options, **Ruth's Chris** and **Besh Steak.** *Tip:* Since this is a casino property, special deals are offered to Harrah's Total Rewards members.

228 Poydras St., New Orleans, LA 70130. www.harrahs.com. © **800/VIP-JAZZ** (847-5299) or 504/533-6000. www.harrahs.com. 450 units. $149–$449 double. Rates can vary depending on events. $30 additional person. AE, DC, DISC, MC, V. Valet and self-parking $34. **Amenities:** Restaurant; 2 bars; babysitting; concierge; gym; room service. *In room:* A/C, TV and Web TV, CD player, fridge, hair dryer, Wi-Fi ($12 per day).

Hilton New Orleans Riverside Hotel ★ ☺ The Hilton is in the neighborhood of the Windsor Court (see below) but in a more central location—right at the riverfront near the New Orleans Convention Center, Aquarium, and Insectarium. It's a self-contained complex of restaurants, bistros, and bars; two gift shops; two pools; a full and exceptional racquet-and-health club; a huge exhibition and conference space; and a sprawling outpost of the legendary **Drago's** restaurant, rightly renowned for its addictive charbroiled oysters. In addition, Harrah's Casino (see above) and the **Riverwalk Marketplace** (p. 249) are accessible from the hotel's lobby, which contains a nine-story atrium. Rooms are spacious (double-bedded rooms are smaller), but a tiny bit dull. Parlor rooms have rather awesome versions of Murphy beds with hydraulic lifts! River views (usually with even-numbered rooms) are astonishing, though higher is better. Given all that, this is a good choice for conventioneers and families—there is much in the way of child-friendly entertainment right in the hotel or nearby—but not terrific for those with mobility issues, given the sheer size of the place.

2 Poydras St., New Orleans, LA 70140. www.neworleans.hilton.com. ℰ **800/445-8667** or 504/561-0500. Fax 504/568-1721. 1,622 units. $109–$409 double; $750–$2,500 suite. Special packages and lower seasonal rates available. AE, DC, DISC, MC, V. Valet parking $38; self-parking $32. **Amenities:** 2 restaurants, including Drago's (p. 144); 2 bars; concierge-level rooms; health club ($12 per day, comped for Hilton Honors Silver, Gold, Diamond members); room service. *In room:* A/C, flatscreen TV, hair dryer, minibar, Wi-Fi ($17 per day).

InterContinental New Orleans ★ The red-granite InterContinental rises from the heart of the Central Business District within walking distance of the French Quarter and the Mississippi River attractions. It's a favorite of groups (including rock groups; the Rolling Stones have stayed here) and conventions. It's an old-fashioned—or what passes for that in this brave new Ian Schrager–ized world—business hotel, clearly targeting a certain kind of traveler who isn't impressed by the hip minimalists springing up everywhere. It's a superb place to camp out for Mardi Gras, since the Rex parade stops right in front. Rooms are done in dark-wood furniture (mattresses are nothing special); bathrooms can be small but dignified. Call it masculine in a slightly frilly way. All the rooms are decently sized, but the doubles (especially corner doubles) are somewhat larger, and "deluxe kings" are larger still, with patio balconies (overlooking office buildings, alas). Some rooms have balconies that overlook the modern and industrial courtyard.

444 St. Charles Ave., New Orleans, LA 70130. www.new-orleans.intercontinental.com. ℰ **800/327-0200** or 504/525-5566. Fax 504/585-4350. 479 units. $200–$429 double; $500–$2,500 suite. AE, DC, DISC, MC, V. Valet parking $29. **Amenities:** Restaurant (dinner only); coffee, sweets, and sandwich bar; bar; concierge; health club; outdoor rooftop pool; room service. *In room:* A/C, flatscreen TV, hair dryer, Internet ($11 per day), minibar.

JW Marriott Hotel New Orleans ★ You can't fault the location on Canal right across from the Quarter (excellent for viewing Mardi Gras parades). Ultimately, though, it's classy but boring—yes, we're spoiled—more for business travelers who don't plan on spending much time in their rooms, though some 2010 upgrades did help hippify the decor. New NOLA-specific touches such as local photos and drawings are appreciated, as are the thickly made beds. The public areas are far grander than the actual rooms. Bathrooms are dinky, though amenities are good. Corner "deluxe" king rooms (usually numbered 04 and 09) have extra windows for an additional view, though higher up is best. The fitness center is decent sized, and the property has a **Don Shula Steakhouse,** as well as a new spa.

614 Canal St., New Orleans, LA 70130. www.jwmarriottneworleans.com. ©**504/525-6500.** Fax 504/586-1543. 494 units. $169–$355 double; $750–$1,500 suite. AE, DC, DISC, MC, V. Valet parking $32. **Amenities:** Restaurant; 2 bars; concierge; health club; heated outdoor pool; room service; spa; Wi-Fi (free). *In room:* A/C, TV, hair dryer, Internet ($15 per day), minibar.

Loft 523 ★ Located in an old carriage and dry-goods warehouse, each of the 18 lofts is a marvel of modern design, sort of a *Jetsons*-futuristic-meets-NYC-minimalist fantasy. They are sleek and handsome, but those wanting plushy and overstuffed will be miserable as soon as they see the concrete floors. Beds are platforms, surprisingly comfortable with Frette linens (but just a chenille throw blanket over that; ask for the down comforters if the night brings a chill). The bathrooms are so big you could fit the entire Rebirth Brass Band inside. Check out that Agape "spoon" tub in the Loft Superior rooms—which are somewhat larger than the Loft Deluxe Rooms. Both have dual showers. Yet throughout are reminders of the building's provenance—old wood planks form the floor downstairs, turn-of-the-20th-century tin ceiling tiles outfit the elevators, and columns from the old warehouse decorate the lounge. Note that there may be some room service, but it's spotty—the food comes from Rambla in the International House

SPENDING THE NIGHT IN chains

For those of you who prefer the predictability of a chain hotel or are gambling that generic lodgings get overlooked during popular events, there's a perfectly okay **Marriott ★** at 555 Canal St., at the edge of the Quarter (©800/654-3990 or 504/581-1000). A **Sheraton** at 500 Canal St. (©504/525-2500) is also a good bet.

In the Central Business District (CBD), check out the smoke-free **Holiday Inn Express** in the historic Cotton Exchange building, 221 Carondelet St. (©504/962-0800). **Residence Inn by Marriott ★**, 345 St. Joseph St. (©800/331-3131 or 504/522-1300), and **Courtyard by Marriott ★**, 300 Julia St. (©888/703-0390 or 504/598-9898), are both a couple of blocks from the convention center (a second Courtyard by Marriott is set to open in the French Quarter in 2012). The **Homewood Suites,** at 901 Poydras St., is pretty dazzling, in a cookie-cutter way (©800/225-5466 or 504/581-5599), while the **Quality Inn,** at 210 O'Keefe Ave., seems clean and fine (©877/525-6900 or 504/525-6800).

Still need a last-minute emergency reservation? Here's a bunch more, all more or less CBD or adjacent: **Comfort Suites** (346 Baronne St.; ©800/524-1140 or 504/524-1140), **Country Inn and Suites by Carlson** (315 Magazine St.; ©800/456-4000 or 504/324-5400), **Embassy Suites** (315 Julia St.; ©504/525-1993), **Hampton Inn and Suites** (1201 Convention Center Blvd.; ©866/311-1200 or 504/566-9990), **La Quinta Inn and Suites** (301 Camp St.; ©800/531-5900 or 504/598-9977), and **SpringHill Suites by Marriott** (301 St. Joseph St.; ©800/287-9400 or 504/522-3100).

And if all the rooms in town are booked, you might try to see if one of the chains down by the airport has something for you.

(its sister property) down the street. Both hotels donate unused bath amenities to Clean the World, which distributes them to impoverished countries and homeless shelters.

523 Gravier St., New Orleans, LA 70130. www.loft523.com. ✆ **800/633-5770** or 504/200-6523. Fax 504/200-6522. 18 units, 3 of them penthouses. $139–$699 double; suites can run into 4 figures, call for rates. Look for deeply discounted online seasonal specials. AE, DC, DISC, MC, V. Valet parking $32, SUVs $38. **Amenities:** Lounge; health club; Internet (free) in lobby. *In room:* A/C, TV/DVD, hair dryer, MP3 docking station, Wi-Fi (free).

The Roosevelt ★★★ There are celebrities, and then there are movie stars. The Roosevelt is a movie star of a hotel: grand, glam, confident, memorable. You don't just enter the gilded, block-long lobby—you *arrive*. The former Fairmont reopened under the Waldorf Astoria banner in 2009, following a $170-million renovation that updated everything down to the legacy. The Roosevelt, after all, has hosted presidents, Elvis, and the illustrious governor Huey P. Long (who had built a highway to the hotel—the better to reach its **Sazerac Bar**. Icons like Louis Armstrong and Sinatra headlined the renowned Blue Room (now, jazz brunches and monthly dinner shows recall the era). Today, all that and all 8,000 strands of chandelier crystal (count 'em) gleam again, as do the luxurious **Guerlain Spa** (p. 255), the Precor-stocked fitness center, and chef John Besh's **Domenica** restaurant (p. 143). Though the updating paid close attention to energy-saving features, it's possible that more attention was paid to facilities than service, as there were some staff infractions early on. More recently that seems to be rectified, though the room service menu and cuisine can still stand some improvement.

Oh, and then there are the guest rooms. They're fittingly formal if somewhat staid, in dark woods and charcoal and gold tones, with pretty mosaic bathroom floors that echo the lobby tile. Room size varies widely, from generous to downright small, though corner Luxury Suites are plenty spacious. Some have clawfoot or standard bathtubs but no showers; some on the upper floors overlook the city or fourth-floor pool—so make your preferences known. Aside from the requisite amenities, the rooms aren't particularly distinctive, save for the beds—oh, those Waldorf beds. You'll want to ship the whole shebang home—mattress, pillows, sheets, and all. After a hard day of touristing, a stroll through that grandiose lobby into the comforting arms of that bed might just justify the rates.

123 Baronne St., New Orleans, LA 70112. www.therooseveltneworleans.com. ✆ **504/648-1200.** Fax 504/585-1295. 504 units, including 132 suites. $159–$499 double; $199–$509 suite. Packages may be available. AE, DC, DISC, MC, V. Valet parking $38. Pets under 20 lb. allowed ($175 fee). **Amenities:** 2 restaurants, including Domenica (see review, p. 143); coffee shop; bar; Blue Room club; concierge; fitness room; Jacuzzi; pool; room service; top-of-the-line spa. *In room:* A/C, flatscreen TV/DVD, small TV in vanity area, hair dryer, minibar, MP3 docking station, Wi-Fi ($13 per day).

Windsor Court ★★ Pre-Katrina, *Condé Nast Traveler* voted the Windsor Court the Best Hotel in North America (and probably did it a disservice—who, after all, could ever live up to such hype?). And post-? It's still mighty fine. There's a reason this remains the center of high New Orleans society, from traditional afternoon tea to fancy dinners before or after some significant society function. It's that kind of place. Two corridors downstairs are minigalleries that display original 17th-, 18th-, and 19th-century art. Everything here is very, very traditional and serene (including the Grill Room, the hotel's fine-dining restaurant), though not unwarm. It's not too stiff for restless children, though it still feels more like a grown-up hotel. The accommodations, admittedly showing a touch of wear, are exceptionally spacious, with classy, not flashy, decor. Almost all are suites (either really big or downright huge) featuring large bay windows or a private balcony overlooking the river (get a river view if at all possible) or the city, a private foyer, a large living room, a bedroom with French doors, a large marble bathroom with particularly luxe amenities, two dressing rooms, and a "petite" kitchen. A club level adds 24/7 concierge service. Some rooms have flatscreen TVs.

300 Gravier St., New Orleans, LA 70130. www.windsorcourthotel.com. ℂ **888/596-0955** or 504/523-6000. Fax 504/596-4749. 322 units. $160–$390 standard double; $195–$440 junior suite; $225–$490 full suite; $290–$645 club-level room. Children 16 and under stay free in parent's room. Packages available. AE, DC, DISC, MC, V. Valet parking $32. **Amenities:** Restaurant; lounge; concierge; health club w/resort-size pool; Jacuzzi; room service. *In room:* A/C, TV, hair dryer, minibar, Wi-Fi (free).

W New Orleans ★★ While we have strong feelings indeed about staying in more New Orleans–appropriate, site-specific accommodations, we cheerfully admit that this is one fun hotel, and what is New Orleans about if not fun? There are certainly no more-playful rooms in town, done up as they are in black, plum, and white—frosty chic, to be sure, but oh, so comfortable, thanks to feather everything (pillows, comforters, beds—and yes, allergy sufferers, they have foam alternatives). There are nifty amenities and gewgaws galore; suites offer little difference from the rooms except more space and, indeed, more of everything (two bigger TVs, two DVD players). Not all rooms have views (and not all suites have Jacuzzis), but the ones that do, especially with views of the river, are outstanding. The ultrachic bar was designed by hip bar/club owner Rande Gerber. We do wish this whole experience wasn't so, well, New York, but then again, we find ourselves having so much fun, it's kinda hard to get all that worked up about it.

333 Poydras St., New Orleans, LA 70130. www.whotels.com/wneworleans. ℂ **800/522-6963** or 504/525-9444. Fax 504/581-7179. 423 units. $179–$469 double; $329–$619 suite. Rates lower in summer. AE, DC, DISC, MC, V. Valet parking $32–$40. **Amenities:** Restaurant; bar; concierge; fitness center; pool; room service. *In room:* A/C, flatscreen TV/DVD, CD player, hair dryer, minibar, MP3 docking station, Wi-Fi ($15 per day).

Expensive

Hilton St. Charles ★ The site of the old Masonic Temple, and the second skyscraper in the city (after the Hypernia building), this establishment is a lot more memorable than the other Hilton in town. Rooms have some pizazz in the form of wild prints and designs, plus black marble vanities in the spacious bathrooms (tubs are small, though), newish bedding, and Lavazza coffee. Corner-room doubles have extra space perfect for noncouple traveling partners. Upgrades to suites start at $60—if that rate's available, go for it. The smashing wood deck that overlooks the city is sure to become a nighttime hot spot, and the wedding chapel (the only hotel-based one in town) still carries its Masonic roots. The John Besh restaurant **Lüke** is reviewed on p. 144.

333 St. Charles Ave., New Orleans, LA 70130. www.hhneworleansstcharles.com. ℂ **800/445-8667** or 504/524-8890. 250 units. $109–$389 double; $169–$450 suite. AE, DC, DISC, MC, V. Valet parking $32. **Amenities:** Restaurant; Lüke (see review, p. 144); bar; concierge; health club; indoor pool; room service. *In room:* A/C, flatscreen TV, hair dryer, MP3 docking station, Wi-Fi ($13 per day).

International House ★★★ The International House sets the local standard for modern hotels with its creative design and meticulous attention to detail, down to the smashing staff uniforms. Record-company and film execs love it, but so should anyone who needs a palate cleanser from all that Victorian sweetness. Here, a wonderful old Beaux Arts bank building has been transformed into a modern space that still pays tribute to its locale. Consequently, in the graceful lobby, classical pilasters stand next to modern wrought-iron chandeliers. Interiors are the embodiment of minimalist chic. Rooms are simple with muted, mono-chromatic (okay, beige) tones, tall ceilings and ceiling fans, up-to-the-minute bathroom fixtures, but also black-and-white photos of local musicians and characters, and other clever decorating touches that anchor the room in its New Orleans setting. The commitment to hip, neat, cool, and groovy means dark corridors and hard-to-read room numbers, and although the big bathrooms boast large tubs or space-age glassed-in showers, they do come off as a bit industrial. The entire hotel is nonsmoking. **Loa,** the lobby bar (p. 294), is one of the best in town for fans of fine mixology, and the restaurant **Rambla** serves excellent small plates.

221 Camp St., New Orleans, LA 70130. www.ihhotel.com. *©* **800/633-5770** or 504/553-9550. Fax 504/553-9560. 117 units. $119–$379 double; $369–$1,799 suite. Look for special deals online. AE, DC, DISC, MC, V. Valet parking $32 cars, $38 SUVs. **Amenities:** Restaurant; bar; concierge; health club; room service. *In room:* A/C, flatscreen TV, fridge, hair dryer, Wi-Fi (free).

Loews New Orleans Hotel ★★ Swanky. Ooh-la-la. These are the words that spring to mind as you enter the stylish Loews hotel. It's a sharp-dressed combo of modern and *moderne,* with judiciously applied sprinkles of New Orleans flavor. Whatever it is, we are quite smitten. The rooms are all spacious, starting with the Deluxe rooms, at 346 square feet—bright and decorated with art by a local photographer, with goose-down comforters and pillows. Bathrooms are small, but granite and wood vanities make up for the lack of space. Luxury rooms step up to 442 square feet; Grand rooms include a seating area and weigh in at 532 square feet; suites add yet more. Views vary from river to partial river plus piazza to New Orleans city skyline, which get better the higher up you go. Note that the hotel's lowest floor is the 11th, so this is not the choice for those with vertigo or other high-floor issues. There is also a steamy indoor pool and a good-size workout room that could use more machines, plus the excellent restaurant **Café Adelaide** (p. 140) and the **Swizzle Stick** bar, with live music on weekend eves. Possibly best of all: Loews has a company-wide "Loews Loves Pets" policy, which practically encourages Fido to come join in the fun.

300 Poydras St., New Orleans, LA 70130. www.loewshotels.com. *©* **800/23-LOEWS** (235-6397) or 504/595-3300. 285 units. $149–$289 double; suites start at $400. AE, DC, DISC, MC, V. Valet parking $29. Pets allowed ($25 pet cleaning fee). **Amenities:** Restaurant, Café Adelaide (see review, p. 140); bar; babysitting; concierge; exercise room; pool; room service; spa. *In room:* A/C, TV, CD player, hair dryer, minibar, Wi-Fi ($13 per day).

Renaissance Arts Hotel ★ The Arts Hotel is so named because it's at the border of the Arts District and attached to a branch of Arthur Rogers, a well-respected local gallery. Don't expect painters in smocks in the lobby, splattering like Pollock or staging suspicious performance-art gags. What "arts" means here is that the designers have made a concerted effort to incorporate art, specifically local art, into the decor. On first glance, it just seems like a throwback to 1970s business hotels (thanks to an atrium) with the simple addition of some brightly colored modern art. But the theme gets stronger once you enter the hallways, and comes into stronger focus in the rooms, which are hung with the works of several Louisiana artists (from Lafayette-based Francis Pavy to New Orleans's highly recommended Studio Inferno glassworks). The rooms are well sized (look for a connecting room to get extra square footage) and include down pillows and covers (foam on request). The hotel has a dull rooftop pool with a view of industrial New Orleans, and a health club with adequate elbow room.

700 Tchoupitoulas St., New Orleans, LA 70130. www.marriott.com/msydt. ✆ **504/613-2330.** Fax 504/613-2331. 217 units. $229–$299 double. Rates higher during special events, lower in summer. AE, DC, DISC, MC, V. Valet parking $28. **Amenities:** Restaurant, LaCôte Brasserie (see review, p. 141); bar; babysitting; concierge; health club; pool; room service. *In room:* A/C, TV, fridge (on 3rd and 4th floors), hair dryer, Wi-Fi ($13 per day covers access to in-room and lobby Wi-Fi).

St. James Hotel ★ The hotel is actually two different buildings. The one in front used to be—get this!—the St. James Infirmary, sung about so memorably by many a mournful jazz musician (well, the New Orleans S.J.I. at least; the original was in London). Before that, it was an old coffee and sugar company. A semi-Caribbean redo gave the place a touch more style than the fresh white-bed generic look around town. Look for parrots, palm trees, and even monkey-shaped pull chains on the lamps. Rooms vary in size and style, and a few lack windows. Rooms in the back building have high ceilings. Rooms have either painted texture or, on the top floor, exposed brick and wood. All have feather beds, soft towels, and marble bathrooms. Two suites and a room share a small, private brick courtyard with a fountain—a nice setup for a small group. There is a teeny-weeny pool—you might be forgiven for considering it really just a large puddle with nice tile. The hotel's restaurant is Cuvée.

330 Magazine St., New Orleans, LA 70130. www.saintjameshotel.com. ✆ **888/211-3447** or 504/304-4000. 86 units. $109–$299 double plus mandatory $3 charge for safe. AE, DC, DISC, MC, V. Valet parking $25. **Amenities:** Restaurant; concierge; pool. *In room:* A/C, TV, CD player, hair dryer, Wi-Fi ($4.95 per day mandatory charge, includes local and domestic long-distance calls).

The Whitney—A Wyndham Historic Hotel ★ A clever and welcome use of space as a grand old bank building has been converted into a fine modern hotel. The unique results include gawk-worthy public spaces; be sure to look up at all the fanciful, wedding-cake-style old plasterwork (they don't make 'em like that anymore—pity) and help us wonder how the heck safecrackers got past those thick slabs of doors. Best of all is the imposing lobby, full of stately pillars (doubtless the grandeur intimidated many a loan applicant of yesteryear), now part restaurant but also still part working bank—it puts other swellegant establishments in town to shame.

Rooms are a little too stately to classify as true business efficient, but also a little too generic to make this a proper romantic getaway. The restaurant is a branch of local Creole/soul favorite **Lil' Dizzy's.** Overall, the Whitney has more character than your average upscale chain, so it ultimately gets a positive vote. And if you are a preservationist, you will probably like it a lot.

610 Poydras St., New Orleans, LA 70130. www.wyndham.com/hotels/MSYWW/main.wnt. ✆ **877/999-3223** or 504/581-4222. 93 units. $79–$399 double. AE, DC, DISC, MC, V. Valet parking $28. **Amenities:** Private dining room; lobby bar; fitness center. *In room:* A/C, TV, CD player, hair dryer, Internet ($9.95 per day).

5

WHERE TO STAY

Central Business District

Moderate

Best Western St. Christopher This place is New Orleans by way of a chain hotel—but a good design, still. Exposed brick walls in rooms slightly relieve the generic quality. Bathrooms feel new if still cramped. Check out the pun-filled painting in the lobby (there's a visual joke; see if you get it), which is attached to a courtyard-inspired (if indoors) bar that works better than you might think. This location is great for Mardi Gras celebrations, with easy access to the Quarter, CBD, and Uptown.

114 Magazine St., New Orleans, LA 70130-2421. www.stchristopherhotel.com. ℰ **504/648-0444.** Fax 504/648-0445. 108 units. $89–$299 double, seasonally. Rates include continental breakfast. AE, DC, DISC, MC, V. Valet parking $28. Pet friendly. **Amenities:** Off-site fitness center. *In room:* A/C, TV, hair dryer, Wi-Fi (free).

Drury Inn & Suites ★ 🦮 This family-owned chain looks all too generic outside, but inside is a pleasant surprise, with grander-than-expected public spaces and rooms that are fancier than those in the average chain. All have high ceilings (except for those on the fifth floor), newish bedding, and a decent amount of square footage, though rooms on the first floor can be dark with zero views. Bathrooms are small (with sinks in the dressing area). The inn has a nice little heated rooftop pool plus a small exercise room. Free popcorn and sodas are offered from 3 to 10pm, and the wine and appetizer service from 5:30 to 7pm is a nice touch that encourages guest socializing. Look for more specials, like 1 hour of free long-distance calling per night. All that plus a friendly staff and a generous comp breakfast make this not a bad little bargain for the area.

820 Poydras St., New Orleans, LA 70112-1016. www.druryhotels.com/properties/neworleans.cfm. ℰ **800/DRURY-INN** (378-7946) or 504/529-7800. Fax 504/581-3328. 156 units. $119 regular room; $139 suite. Rates are higher during special events, lower during summer. Rates include full breakfast and weekday evening beverages. AE, DC, DISC, MC, V. Parking $17 (higher during special events). **Amenities:** Exercise room; heated pool. *In room:* A/C, flatscreen TV, fridge, hair dryer, Wi-Fi (free).

Lafayette Hotel ★ Built as a hotel in 1915, with some of the earliest indoor plumbing and telephones for such an establishment, this is a relatively cute place. The French Regency decor—think pale blues and greens, reproduction photos and paintings, and other simple but thoughtful touches—lends some charm to the most recently redecorated rooms. Some second-floor rooms and suites have balconies, just right for watching Mardi Gras parades. This is the place for those who want something more than a B&B but dislike the generic quality that comes with a chain or business-oriented hotel. Suites offer a living room with foldout couches and have minibars/fridges. The hotel charges a mandatory communications fee of $4.95 per day for phone and Wi-Fi access.

600 St. Charles Ave., New Orleans, LA 70130. www.thelafayettehotel.com. ℰ **800/366-2743** or 504/524-4441. 44 units. $69–$459 double; $110–$499 suite. AE, DISC, MC, V. Valet parking $19. **Amenities:** Concierge. *In room:* A/C, TV, CD player, hair dryer, Wi-Fi ($4.95 per day).

Le Pavillon Hotel ★★ Established in 1907 in a prime CBD location, Le Pavillon was the first hotel in New Orleans to have elevators. It's now a member of Historic Hotels of America, and it feels like elegant old New Orleans in a way that, sadly, so few places do. The lobby is stunning, just what you want in a big, grand hotel, with giant columns and chandeliers. The standard guest rooms are all rather pretty and have similar furnishings, but they differ in size. Deluxe rooms have ceiling fans, detailed ceiling paintings, and black granite bathrooms. Bay Rooms are standard with two double beds and bay windows. Suites are actually hit-or-miss in terms of decor, with the nadir being the mind-bogglingly ugly Art Deco Suite. Much better is the Plantation Suite, decorated in—you guessed it—antiques. The Honeymoon Suite has "Napoleon's" marble bathtub and is a riot of fantasy hilarity. Note the statues by the pool. Late-night peanut-butter-and-jelly sandwiches, one of New Orleans's sweetest traditions, are offered in the lobby, and newer recycling and energy-saving traditions score points. (It's also a nonsmoking building.) *Tip:* Covet those suites? If you are staying during a slow period, ask at check-in about upgrades—they may offer you some incredible deals.

833 Poydras St., New Orleans, LA 70112. www.lepavillon.com. © **800/535-9095** or 504/581-3111. Fax 504/529-4415. 226 units. $149–$319 double; $199–$1,695 suite. AE, DC, DISC, MC, V. Valet parking $28. **Amenities:** Restaurant; bar; babysitting; concierge; fitness center and whirlpool spa; heated outdoor pool; room service; spa service. *In room:* A/C, TV, hair dryer, minibar, Wi-Fi (free).

Inexpensive

The Depot at Madame Julia's ★ 🎁 This is a low-budget alternative to more commercial hotels in the Central Business District. Low prices and a guesthouse environment mean a number of good things—including rooms with character and a proprietor who loves to help guests with all the details of their stay (owned by the same folks who own the St. Charles Guesthouse)—but it also means shared bathrooms, rooms on the small and cozy side, virtually no amenities, and a location that, although quiet on the weekends, can get noisy in the mornings as the working neighborhood gets going. The neighborhood is hit-or-miss, but more of the former thanks to nearby artsy Julia Street. A mere 7 blocks (safe in the daytime) from the Quarter, it's a quick walk or a short streetcar/bus ride, which makes it an affordable alternative to the Quarter's much more expensive accommodations. The budget-conscious and those who prefer their hotels with personality (and can live without Internet service for a few days) will consider this a find.

748 O'Keefe St., New Orleans, LA 70113. www.stcharlesguesthouse.com. © **504/523-6556.** 15 units, all with shared bathrooms. $65–$85 double, much lower for groups. No credit cards. Off-street parking available. *In room:* A/C.

UPTOWN/THE GARDEN DISTRICT

For hotels in this section, see the "Uptown Hotels & Restaurants" map on p. 107 or the "New Orleans Hotels" map on p. 78.

Expensive

The Grand Victorian Bed & Breakfast ★★ A former crumbling Queen Anne–style Victorian mansion on the corner of Washington (2 blocks from Lafayette cemetery and Commander's Palace with a streetcar stop right in front) is now a fine B&B. The location makes its porches and balconies a perfect place to spend Mardi Gras; parade viewing doesn't come any more comfortable or convenient. The stunning rooms are full of antiques (each has an impressive four-poster or wood canopy bed—though a couple are small thanks to their vintage), with the slightly fussy details demanded by big Victorian rooms. Linens, pillows, and towels are ultraplush, and some bathrooms have big Jacuzzi tubs. The largest room—our favorite—overlooks the street corner (and has its own St. Charles–view balcony) and so is potentially noisy—consider requesting one toward the back. A generous continental breakfast is served, and coffee, fruit, and such are always available. Friendly owner Bonnie is ready with suggestions on how to spend your time, though as in any B&B, do not expect 24-hour service.

2727 St. Charles Ave., New Orleans, LA 70130. www.gvbb.com. © **800/977-0008** or 504/895-1104. Fax 504/896-8688. 8 units. $150–$300 double. Rates include continental breakfast. AE, DISC, MC, V. *In room:* A/C, TV, hair dryer, Wi-Fi (free).

Magnolia Mansion ★★ Itching to stay in an archetypal big, white Southern mansion? With a large veranda, perfect for sittin' a spell? Sure you are! This hilarious and alluring B&B features huge public rooms splashed with plaster curlicues and Victorian furniture, while the theatrical guest rooms are the owner's imagination run amok. With the exception of the appropriately named Napoleon's Retreat, downstairs rooms are bigger, with 15-foot ceilings and elaborately explored decor. The black, blood red, and green Vampire's Lair is your Gothic fantasy, while the front bridal room is the largest. Upstairs rooms are smaller and not quite as over-the-top, but are similar bonbons of delight. Some, such as the Bordello Storyville Jazz room, have murals, and a few have extra twin beds. *Note:* No children allowed, and you must be 21 and older to stay here.

2127 Prytania St. (at Jackson), New Orleans, LA 70130. www.magnoliamansion.com. © **504/412-9500.** Fax 504/412-9502. 9 units. $125 and up double, depending on time of year. Rates include continental breakfast. MC, V. Street parking. Guests must be 21 or older; no children. *In room:* A/C, TV w/VCR or DVD, hair dryer, Wi-Fi (free).

Maison Perrier Bed & Breakfast ★★ Decorated with art by local artists and run by the genuinely friendly Tom and Patricia Schoenbrum, the splashy, good-looking rooms feature antique elements (and the breakfast room features Abita Amber on tap). It all adds up to very likable accommodations. The rooms have good beds with high-quality linens and well-appointed bathrooms, and nearly all have whirlpool tubs. The Lillian suite is quite spacious and includes a double Jacuzzi tub, and there are multibed, family-ready rooms as well as one that's pet-friendly. The least impressive room is also the cheapest, a modest space just off the kitchen. A hearty cooked breakfast—with delicacies like praline French toast and puff pancakes—is offered by the resident chef, and the inn has a fully stocked honor bar. Other perks include a weekend wine-and-cheese party and daily snacks like fresh-baked brownies.

4117 Perrier St. (2 blocks riverside from St. Charles Ave., 3 blocks downtown from Napoleon Ave.), New Orleans, LA 70115. www.maisonperrier.com. © **888/610-1807** or 504/897-1807. Fax 504/897-1399. 14 units. $130–$260 double. Rates higher during special events, lower in summer. Rates include tax and breakfast. AE, DISC, MC, V. Parking available on street; free limited on-site parking as well. **Amenities:** Complimentary concierge. *In room:* A/C, TV/DVD, CD player, hair dryer, Wi-Fi (free).

The McKendrick-Breaux House ★★ Each room in this likable B&B is done in impeccable good taste, with high-quality mattresses and pillows, and each has its own style; the ones in the main house have claw-foot tubs and (sadly nonworking) fireplaces. Room no. 36 is the largest but also has the most traffic

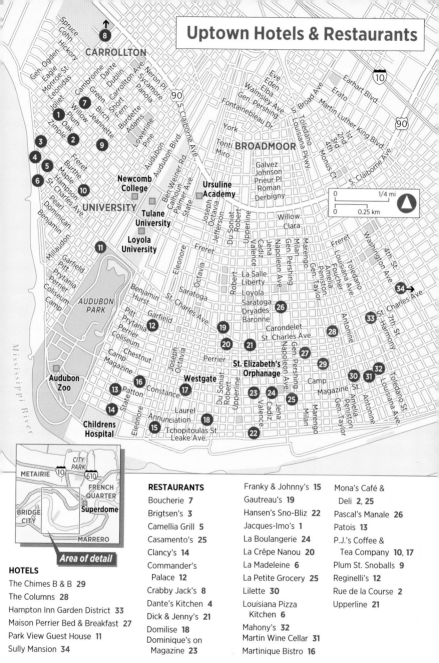

Uptown Hotels & Restaurants

noise. Third-floor rooms (reached by a steep, narrow staircase) evoke classic garret quarters, with exposed brick walls and less of that traffic noise, thanks perhaps to lower ceilings and fewer windows (we swoon over room no. 38). Rooms in the second building are somewhat larger; the first-floor units are slightly more modern in appearance (but have large bathrooms), which is probably why we like the ones on the second floor (especially the front room, and the deep-purple walls and bright-green bathroom wainscoting of the Clio room). A full breakfast featuring local and farmers' market ingredients has been added, and the staff doesn't skimp on suggestions for how to spend your time in the city they love. Smoking is not allowed in the house, but guests may do so on the porch.

1474 Magazine St., New Orleans, LA 70130. www.mckendrick-breaux.com. *(f)* **888/570-1700** or 504/586-1700. 9 units. $145–$245 double. Rates higher for special events. Rates include tax and breakfast. AE, DC, DISC, MC, V; cash or check preferred. Limited free off-street parking. **Amenities:** Jacuzzi in courtyard. *In room:* A/C, TV, hair dryer, Wi-Fi (free).

Queen Anne ★ A somewhat different take on lodging from the same folks who bring you the Prytania Park (see below) and Prytania Oaks Hotels, this was a one-family home for 130 years. The owners had to pass muster with the mayor, the governor, and the park service when they renovated it, and the result is one of the grandest buildings for a B&B in town. Furnishings are a bit sterile, however—hotel-room furniture masquerading as antique (though mattresses are top-of-the-line). The Queen Anne is not our first choice for decor, but the stately rooms (each of which has some exquisite detail like beautifully tiled nonworking fireplaces or 10- to 14-foot ceilings) pull it off. The tiniest room has quite a large bathroom, while the three attic rooms are too conventional to be worth your while. The inn is nicely located near the Mardi Gras parade route. The phones are answered "Prytania Park." **Note:** No children allowed, and you must be over 25 to rent a room here.

1625 Prytania St., New Orleans, LA 70130. Registration is at the Prytania Park Hotel on Terpsichore St. btw. Prytania St. and St. Charles Ave. www.thequeenanne.com. *(f)* **800/862-1984** or 504/524-0427. Fax 504/522-2977. 12 units. $99–$129 double; $159–$179 during special events. Rates include continental breakfast. AE, DC, DISC, MC, V. Free self-parking. **Amenities:** Wi-Fi (free). *In room:* A/C, TV, fridge, hair dryer.

Moderate

Chimes B&B ★★★ 🏨 This is a real hidden gem, one that truly allows you to experience the city away from the typical tourist experience. The Chimes is in a less-fashionable but more neighborhood-like portion of the Garden District, just 2 blocks off St. Charles Avenue. Jill and Charles Abbyad have run this B&B for more than 20 years, and their experience shows. Rooms vary in size from a generous L-shape to a two-story loft type (with a very small bathroom) to some that are downright cozy. All have antiques but are so tastefully underdecorated, particularly in contrast to other B&Bs, that they are positively Zen—as is the relaxing courtyard. An ambitious continental breakfast is served in the hosts' house. The Chimes has made improvements designed for the business traveler, and all we need to say is laptop + courtyard = working bliss. One recent guest, a veteran of many New Orleans hotels, spent 1 night and proclaimed that on subsequent trips she would stay nowhere else but here.

1146 Constantinople St., New Orleans, LA 70115. www.chimesneworleans.com. *(f)* **504/899-2621** or 504/453-2183 (owner's cell). Fax 504/899-9858. 5 units. $130–$160 double in season;

$99–$140 double off season. Rates higher during special events. Rates include breakfast, tax, parking. Look for rates, availability, and featured specials online. AE, MC, V. Limited free off-street parking. Well-behaved pets accepted with prior approval; call to discuss. *In room:* A/C, TV, hair dryer, Wi-Fi (free).

The Columns ★ The Columns interior was used by Louis Malle for his film about Storyville, *Pretty Baby.* Built in 1883, the building is one of the city's greatest examples of a late-19th-century Louisiana residence. The grand, columned porch is a highly popular evening scene thanks to the bar, the **Victorian Lounge.** The immediate interior is utterly smashing; we challenge any other hotel to match the grand staircase and stained-glass-window combination. We wish still more had been done to make the upstairs match that smashing downstairs; it's still a bit too dark and the color schemes are not that great. The totally renovated third floor looks more modern, mostly to good and comfortable effect. The Pretty Baby room has no discernable nods to its ostensible theme (nor does the Bellocq), but it does have a nice garret sitting area. We particularly like room no. 16, with its grand furniture and floor-to-ceiling shutters that lead out to a private, second-story porch. The Columns is worth a stay if you can get a low rate; otherwise, come by for a drink. Smoking is not permitted in the rooms.

3811 St. Charles Ave., New Orleans, LA 70115. www.thecolumns.com. ℂ **800/445-9308** or 504/899-9308. Fax 504/899-8170. 19 units. Aug 16–June 14 $120–$173 double Mon–Thurs, $160–$230 double Fri–Sun; summer rates June 15–Aug 15 $99–$155 double Mon–Thurs, $120–$173 double Fri–Sun. Rates include full breakfast in Albertine's Tea Room. AE, MC, V. Parking available on street. Pet friendly (call to make arrangements). **Amenities:** Bar; Internet (free) in lobby. *In room:* A/C, TV, hair dryer, Wi-Fi (free).

Hampton Inn Garden District This is a top choice for a chain hotel, if you don't mind being a bit out-of-the-way (though it is right on the St. Charles streetcar line). The public areas are slightly more stylish than those found in other chains, and there are welcome touches like free coffee in the lobby and complimentary cheese and tea served daily from 5 to 7pm. The style does not extend to the rooms, however, which are pretty mundane. But they're not *that* bad (mustard-colored walls excepted), with all kinds of personality-enhancing details (decent photos for artwork, ever-so-slight arts-and-crafts detailing on furniture, and big TVs) hidden in that bland color scheme.

3626 St. Charles Ave., New Orleans, LA 70115. www.neworleanshamptoninns.com. ℂ **800/426-7866** or 504/899-9990. Fax 504/899-9908. 100 units. $129–$159 double. Rates higher during special events, lower in summer. Rates include continental breakfast with hot items, free local calls, and free incoming faxes. AE, DC, DISC, MC, V. Free parking. **Amenities:** Small outdoor lap pool. *In room:* A/C, flatscreen TV, fridge, hair dryer, Wi-Fi (free).

Inexpensive

Park View Guest House ★ Built in the late 1800s as a boardinghouse for the World Cotton Exchange, this is an inn crossed with a B&B, which means a front desk staffed 24/7 and proper public areas. But it's way uptown, so if you can't live without Bourbon Street and bars mere steps from your hotel entrance, then this is not the place for you. Otherwise, the stunning location on St. Charles (with a streetcar stop just opposite, so it's easy to get to and from the Quarter), with views right across to Audubon Park and waffles for breakfast, makes it well worth considering. New owners plan room renovations, which should take care of some egregious aesthetic errors, like no. 19, a spacious room with a balcony, claw-foot tub, fireplace with glazed tiles—and some god-awful 1980s motel-room furniture. On the other hand, no. 9 is just fine (with two antique wood beds, a nice old fireplace, a large balcony, and newish bathroom), as is no. 17 (bigger bathroom, better furniture). Most of the rooms are spacious, and those downstairs, while just off the public areas, are grander still. Smoking is allowed outdoors only.

7004 St. Charles Ave., New Orleans, LA 70118. www.parkviewguesthouse.com. © **888/533-0746** or 504/861-7564. Fax 504/861-1225. 21 units, including 2 suites. $119–$169 double. Special-event rates higher. Rates include generous continental breakfast, coffee throughout the day, and complimentary wine and snacks each afternoon. Extra person $10. AE, DISC, MC, V. Parking available. *In room:* A/C, TV, hair dryer available, Wi-Fi (free).

Prytania Park Hotel This 1840s building (which once housed Huey Long's girlfriend) is now equal parts motel and funky simulated Quarter digs. Rooms vary: Some have been redone to the owner's pride (adding darker wood tones and four-poster beds plus bathrooms that still have a Holiday Inn feel), but we kind of prefer the older section with its pine furniture, tall ceilings, and nonworking fireplaces. All rooms have lots of good reading lights. Some units have balconies or loft bedrooms (accessible by spiral staircases). Those without the loft can be small, and the dark-wood furniture makes it a bit ponderous. All rooms were remodeled about a year ago, freshened up with new paint, curtains, furnishings, and mattresses. Rooms closer to the lobby have better Wi-Fi reception.

1525 Prytania St. (enter off Terpsichore St.), New Orleans, LA 70130. www.prytaniaparkhotel.com. © **800/862-1984** or 504/524-0427. Fax 504/522-2977. 62 units. $79–$99 double. Rates higher during special events, lower in summer. Extra person $10. Rates include continental breakfast. Children 17 and under stay free in parent's room. Seasonal rates and special packages available. AE, DC, DISC, MC, V. Free off-street parking available. Must be 21 to check in. *In room:* A/C, TV, fridge, Wi-Fi (free).

St. Charles Guest House ★ This is our first choice for budget travelers or less-than-picky folks, or those comfortable with European pensions who aren't looking for the spick-and-span hotel experience. You can't beat the quiet, pretty location, if only because it gets you out of the engulfing Quarter and into a different part of town. Rooms are plain and vary wildly in size—from reasonably spacious to "small and spartan" (the management's words)—and also range from low-end backpacker with no air-conditioning to larger chambers with air-conditioning and private bathrooms. Room no. A-5, with twin beds in a separate room, is perfect for a family. A bonus is the banana-tree-lined courtyard with a pool. While it's still a little musty smelling, here you can pay very little for a good-size room with a mix of antiques and new furnishings and humble bathrooms with bright green or yellow tile. It's a little crumbly in places, but it's still one of the best values in town. All rooms are nonsmoking.

1748 Prytania St., New Orleans, LA 70130. www.stcharlesguesthouse.com. © **504/523-6556.** 26 units, 22 with private bathroom. $45–$95 double, up to $125 during special events. Rates include continental breakfast. No credit cards. Parking available on street. **Amenities:** Outdoor pool. *In room:* No phone, Wi-Fi (free).

COMMANDER'S
PALACE
RESTAURANT

WE KNOW WHAT IT MEANS...

Lally, Ti, Ella, Dottie
&
The Commander's Palace Gang

WHERE
TO EAT

New Orleans restaurant matriarch Miss Ella Brennan says that whereas in other places, one eats to live, "In New Orleans, we live to eat." It's hard to spoil such a big appetite.

Here, we don't call a friend and ask, "How are you?" Instead, it's the colloquial "Where y'at?" or, more likely, "What're you eatin'?" With the focus so intently on feasting, it's no surprise that there are some 300 more restaurants now than before Katrina. Nor is it unusual that, following a brief absence in some places (during which safety was verified), the gloriously plump, sensuously sweet Gulf oysters have returned to menus all over town, in old and new preparations, and perhaps a bit pricier. In their absence, we saw a distinct uptick in pork belly dishes on menus around town. Now *that's* making some tasty lemonade.

New Orleans is a town dedicated to food, glorious food, with goodness to be found in every direction and on every level—in the centuries-old, grande dame restaurants and the corner po' boy shops; in a gas station with shockingly good steam-table food; and the sleek bistro of a brash upstart chef, a Culinary Institute of America grad fusing grandma's recipes with unpronounceable techniques and ingredients.

There are culinary training grounds like **Café Reconcile** and **Liberty's Kitchen,** serving sturdy meals while training young men and women for careers in food service. And there are fourth-generation chefs working backstreet dives whose menus and ingredients haven't varied in, well, ever.

The city has an amazingly cohesive, supportive food community, dedicated to the culture of New Orleans because here, cuisine *is* culture, as everyone inherently understands.

You are going to want to eat a lot here. And you are going to want to eat here, a lot. And then you are going to want to talk about it. After being in New Orleans for just a short amount of time, you will find yourself talking less about the sights and more about the food—if not *constantly* about the food: what you ate already, what you are going to be eating later, what you wish you had time to eat. We are going to take a stand and say to heck with New York, Chicago, and San Francisco: New Orleans has the best food in the United States. (Some natives will gladly fight you if you say otherwise.)

We have to admit that, historically, neither the cuisine nor the cooking of New Orleans is all that innovative, with some exceptions. Many places are variations on either Creole or Italian (or both), and a certain sameness, if you are paying attention, can creep onto menus. This may sound like we are denigrating the food of New Orleans. Believe us. We don't do that. It will take you a while to notice any menu repetition, about the same amount of time it will take you to emerge from a coma that is brought on by equal parts butter sauce and pleasure.

This is the city where the great chefs of the world come to eat—if they don't work here already. Many people love to do nothing more than wax nostalgic about great meals they have had here, describing entrees in practically pornographic

PREVIOUS PAGE: **Commander's Palace is an iconic New Orleans restaurant.**

detail. It is nearly impossible to have a bad meal; at worst, it will be mediocre, and with proper guidance, you should even be able to avoid that.

Please keep in mind that all prices, hours, and menu items in the following listings are subject to change according to season, availability, or whim. You should call in advance to ensure the accuracy of anything significant to you. Where to eat? You should try everything, then savor a few more, and then plan your return visit so you can sample yet a few others. Some of the restaurateurs have soldiered on for generations, through absurd adversity. Tell them you are glad they are here. And ask 'em where you ought to eat next.

BEST DINING BETS

It's always hard to quantify such things as restaurant comparisons, particularly in a town that has so many wonderful choices. Below is a list to guide you.

○ **Best Innovative Restaurant:** In a town full of shrimp rémoulade atop fried green tomatoes, and crawfish atop Gulf fish (not that there's anything wrong with that!), **Stella!** (p. 126) and **Green Goddess** (p. 127) consistently break the mold, **Le Foret** (p. 141) is blazing its own path, and newcomer **Dominique's on Magazine** (p. 150) is melding new and traditional flavor profiles.

○ **Best Neighborhood Restaurant:** **Elizabeth's** (p. 134) serves monster portions of delicious and curious food (praline bacon!) and is just flat-out wonderful. A little farther to the north is **Liuzza's by the Track** (p. 137), contender for "City's Best Gumbo" and home to gorgeous salads and fat, perfect po' boys. Everything one could want in a neighborhood joint. Uptown, the honor goes to **Joey K's** (p. 152).

○ **Best Neighbahood Restaurant:** You know, the old *neighbahood* where the locals still ask, "Hey, dahwlin', wheah y'at?" This category is a tossup between the Italian and Creole dishes at **Mandina's** (p. 137) and those found at **Liuzza's** (p. 136) though the deep-fried dill pickle slices at the latter may tip the scales.

○ **Best Late-Night Choice:** We go for the burgers and omelets at stalwart **Camellia Grill** (p. 130) and the oysters at **Felix's** (p. 131); both are open till 1am or 2am on weekends. In a pinch, **La Peniche** (p. 134) is open 24 hours (except on Tues) with something to satisfy everyone. For hearty appetites, the insanely good steaks at **La Boca** are available till midnight (p. 140).

○ **Best Wine List:** **Brennan's** (p.122), **Emeril's** (p. 139), and **Commander's Palace** (p. 147) all cellar extensive collections, while the lists at **Bayona** (p. 120) and **Meson 923** (p. 141) are smaller yet well-selected.

○ **Best for Kids:** Take them to **Café du Monde** (p. 154), where getting powdered sugar all over yourself is half the fun, or the counter at **Camellia Grill** (p. 130). For something fancy, **Antoine's** (p. 120) makes a good introduction.

○ **Best Gumbo:** More fighting words, but you can't go wrong at **Liuzza's by the Track** (p. 137), **Galatoire's** (p. 123), or **Herbsaint** (p. 140).

○ **Best Oysters:** Or "ersters," as the locals would say, and then they would insist that **Acme Oyster House** (p. 129) or **Casamento's** (p. 152) is the place. Unless you want charbroiled ersters, in which case head to **Drago's** (p. 144).

○ **Best Contemporary Creole:** We remain fond of **Café Adelaide** (p. 140), as well as lovely **Iris** (p. 128) and long-termer **Brigtsen's,** still doing it so well (p. 146).

○ **Best Contemporary Cajun:** It can only be **Cochon** (p. 143) and its casual offshoot **Cochon Butcher** (p. 145), where you won't find yo mama's Cajun; although many believe **K-Paul's** (p. 124), the originator, still does an excellent job.

○ **Best Italian:** We almost hate to tell you, because it's already too crowded, but New Orleans's traditional Italian presence is best represented at **Irene's Cuisine** (p. 127), with **A Mano** (p. 142) carrying the banner for contemporary Italian.

○ **Best Classic New Orleans Restaurant:** Of the three mainstays of New Orleans dining (the others being Galatoire's and Antoine's; p. 123 and 120), **Arnaud's** (p. 120) is the one where you can count on getting a consistently good (and maybe even great) meal in the same way, and in the exact same surroundings, that generations of New Orleanians have done before you.

○ **Best Desserts:** Desserts in New Orleans tend to run to the familiar, but some places (often run by people named Brennan) stray into more interesting territory, including the white chocolate bread pudding at the **Palace Café** (p. 142), the banana cream pie at **Emeril's** (p. 139), and the rounds of goat-cheese crème fraîche with poached pears at **Lilette** (p. 151).

○ **Best Classic Creole Soul Food:** This traditional local cuisine is well represented at **Lil' Dizzy's** (p. 137) where the lunch specials draw waiting crowds, and legendary **Dooky Chase** (p. 136).

○ **Best Bistro:** Tough choice, given the richness of this category, but **Coquette** (p. 147), **La Petite Grocery** (p. 151), and newcomer **Sylvain** (p. 129), among others, certainly rate a mention.

○ **Best Outdoor Dining:** **Bayona** (p. 120), **Martinique** (p. 148), and **Café Amelie** (p. 126) all have quiet, fairly secluded courtyards, delightful on starry nights or balmy spring afternoons.

○ **Best Po' Boys:** This might start an argument, but we're all about the roast beef po' boy at the **Parkway Bakery and Tavern** (p. 138). Also, see "Argue About The Best Po' Boy" on p. 64 in "Suggested New Orleans Itineraries."

○ **Best Muffulettas:** The originator of this olive-drenched sandwich, and still reigning king, is **Central Grocery** (p. 132). It may be heresy, but the house-made ingredients at **Cochon Butcher** (p. 145) may have tipped our scale in its upstart favor.

○ **Best Sazerac:** This famous locally invented cocktail can be found all over the city, including the namesake **Sazerac Bar** (p. 100) in the Roosevelt Hotel. But we still think that **French 75 in Arnaud's** (p. 120) tops the pack—though the underrated **Tujague's** (p. 126) is right up there.

A TASTE OF NEW ORLEANS

Boy, does this city love to eat. And boy, does it offer visitors a range of choices. Thanks to influences from French, Spanish, Italian, West Indian, African, and Native American cuisines, it covers the whole span from down-home Southern cooking to the most artistic gourmet dishes. New Orleans is one of the few cities in America that can justify a visit solely for cuisine.

Many of the famous dishes here started out as provincial French settlers' recipes. Native Americans introduced the settlers to native herbs and filé (ground sassafras leaves); the Spanish added saffron and peppers to the mix somewhat later. From the West Indies came new vegetables, spices, and sugar cane, and when slave boats arrived, an African influence was added. Out of all this came the distinctive Creole culinary style unique to New Orleans. Later, Italian immigrants added yet another dimension, while many traditional Old South dishes remain on menus. This international mélange has borne a love of exciting culinary combinations, and the city's old-world traditions have instilled an appreciation for fine service in elegant surroundings. Yet ironies abound here; you can get gourmet dishes served in the plainest of settings and simple dishes (such as boiled crawfish or red beans and rice) in the fanciest of eateries. New Orleanians are voracious restaurantgoers and are notoriously strict about quality. If a place is below par, it probably won't last very long. And woe to any classic restaurant that dares to remove a beloved dish!

Impressions

Living in New Orleans is like drinking blubber through a straw. Even the air is caloric.
　　—Andrei Codrescu, *Fantastic Fast*

You Got Your Cajun in My Creole!

Cajun and Creole are the two classic New Orleans cuisines. The difference lies chiefly in distance between city and countryside.

Cajun cooking came from country folk—the Acadians who left France for Nova Scotia in the 1600s and, after being expelled from Canada by the British in the 1700s, made their way to the swamps and bayous of rural Louisiana. French dishes traveled with them, but along the way recipes were adapted to locally available ingredients. Their cuisine tends to be a lot like their music: spicy and robust. Étouffée, a classic dish, features sausage, duck, poultry, pork, or seafood prepared in a rich roux and served over rice, while jambalaya is rice with many of those same ingredients cooked in it. Both demonstrate how to turn a little into a lot, a necessity for an often-poor people. Creole dishes, on the other hand, were developed by French and Spanish city dwellers and feature fancier sauces and ingredients.

In practice, however, the two cuisines have discovered such a happy marriage in New Orleans that it's often difficult to distinguish between them. Two entirely different restaurants might correctly call themselves Creole. Paul Prudhomme of K-Paul's Louisiana

Red beans and rice.

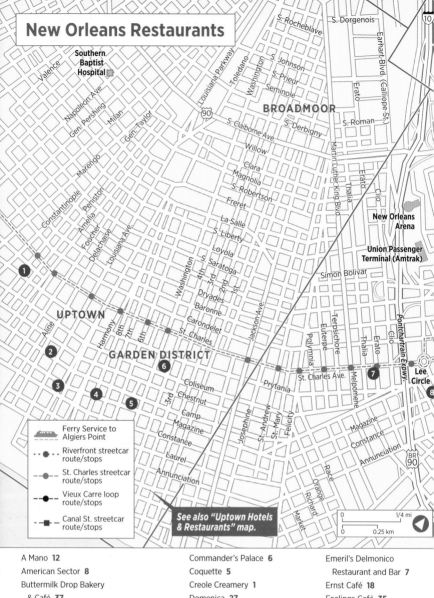

New Orleans Restaurants

Southern Baptist Hospital

BROADMOOR

S. Rocheblave
S. Dorgenois
S. Johnson
S. Prieur
Seminole
Washington
Toledano
Louisiana Parkway
Valence
Napoleon Ave.
Gen. Pershing
Milan
Gen. Taylor
Earhart Blvd. (Calliope St.)
Erato
S. Claiborne Ave.
S. Derbigny
S. Roman
Willow
Clara
Magnolia
S. Robertson
Freret
La Salle
S. Liberty
Loyola
S. Saratoga
Martin Luther King Blvd.
Thalia
Clio
Erato
New Orleans Arena
Union Passenger Terminal (Amtrak)
Marengo
Constantinople
Peniston
Amelia
Foucher
Delachaise
Louisiana Ave.
Washington
4th
3rd
2nd
1st
Dryades
Baronne
Carondelet
St. Charles
Simon Bolivar
Jackson Ave.
UPTOWN
Aline
8th
7th
6th
Harmony
GARDEN DISTRICT
Coliseum
Chestnut
3rd
Camp
Magazine
Constance
Laurel
Annunciation
Josephine
St. Andrew
St. Mary
Felicity
Prytania
St. Charles Ave.
Euterpe
Terpsichore
Polymnia
Melpomene
Thalia
Erato
Clio
Pontchartrain Expwy.
Lee Circle
Magazine
Constance
Annunciation
Orange
Richard
Race
Market
BR 90

See also "Uptown Hotels & Restaurants" map.

Ferry Service to Algiers Point

Riverfront streetcar route/stops

St. Charles streetcar route/stops

Vieux Carre loop route/stops

Canal St. streetcar route/stops

0   1/4 mi
0   0.25 km

Kitchen calls the result of Cajun and Creole cross-fertilization "Louisiana food." He goes on to say, "Nowhere else have all the ethnic groups merged to combine all these different tastes, and the only way you'll know the difference, honey, is to live 'em!" Our advice? Disregard the classifications, try it all, and decide what *you* prefer.

Of Beignets, *Boudin* & Dirty Rice

Many of the foods in New Orleans are unique to the region and consequently may be unfamiliar to first-time visitors. Here's a list that will help you navigate any New Orleans menu:

andouille (ahn-doo-*we*) A spicy Cajun sausage made with pork.

bananas Foster Bananas sautéed in liqueur, brown sugar, cinnamon, and butter, then drenched in rum, set ablaze, and served over vanilla ice cream.

beignet (bin-*yay*) A big, puffy, deep-fried, hole-free doughnut, liberally sprinkled with powdered sugar—the more sugar, the better.

boudin (boo-*dan*) Cajun pork and rice sausage of varying spice levels.

café brûlot (cah-*fay* brew-*low*) Coffee, spices, and liqueurs, served flaming.

crawfish A tiny, lobsterlike creature plentiful in the waters around New Orleans and eaten in every conceivable way. To eat whole and boiled, twist the head apart from the tail; remove the first two sections of the tail shell. Squeeze the tail at its base, and tug the meat out—you'll get the hang of it.

daube Beef or sometimes veal.

debris Rich, juicy bits of roast beef or pork meat, particularly those shreds that fall off when roasted meat is carved. Whole sandwiches can be made of debris, or it can top other dishes.

dirty rice It looks dirty because of the spices and other ingredients in which it's cooked: usually chicken livers and gizzards, onions, chopped celery, green bell pepper, cayenne, black and white peppers, and chicken stock.

dressed "The works": a "dressed" po' boy comes with lettuce, tomato, mayonnaise, and sometimes pickles.

eggs Sardou Legend has it that Antoine Alciatore created this dish of poached eggs, artichoke bottoms, anchovy filets, hollandaise, and truffles or ham especially for French playwright Victorien Sardou (author of *La Tosca*).

étouffée (ay-too-*fay*) A Cajun stew (usually containing crawfish) served with rice.

filé (*fee*-lay) A thickener made of ground sassafras leaves. Filé is frequently used to thicken gumbo.

grillades (gree-*yads*) Thin slices of beef or veal smothered in a tomato-and-beef-flavored gravy, often served with grits.

grits Grains of dried corn that have been ground and hulled (aka polenta). A staple of the Southern breakfast table, grits are most frequently served with butter and salt (not maple syrup or brown sugar), cheese, or red-eye gravy.

gumbo A thick, spicy soup of poultry, seafood, and/or sausage, with okra in a roux base, served with rice.

holy trinity Onions, bell peppers, and celery: the base of much Creole and Cajun cooking.

Hurricane A local drink of rum and passion-fruit punch.

jambalaya (jum-ba-*lie*-ya) A jumble of yellow rice, sausage, seafood, vegetables, and spices.

lagniappe (lan-*yap*) A little something extra: a bonus freebie like the 13th doughnut when you order a dozen.

muffuletta A mountainous sandwich made with Italian deli meats, cheese, and olive salad (pickled olives, celery, carrots, cauliflower, and capers), piled onto a round Italian bread made specially for these incredible sandwiches.

oysters Rockefeller Oysters on the half shell in a creamy spinach sauce, so called because Rockefeller was the only name rich enough to match the taste.

A po'boy is a classic New Orleans sandwich.

pain perdu (pan *pair*-du) Literally "lost bread," this is New Orleans's version of French toast, made with French bread and serviced with a variety of toppings.

po' boy A sandwich on French bread, similar to submarine sandwiches and grinders. Most often filled with fried seafood or roast beef, they can include most anything, from simple ham or turkey to fried eggs or french fries. Yes, french fries.

pralines (*praw*-leens) A sweet confection of brown sugar and pecans.

rémoulade A spicy sauce, usually over shrimp, concocted of mayonnaise, boiled egg yolks, horseradish, Creole mustard, and lemon juice.

roux A mixture of flour and fat that's slowly cooked over low heat, used to thicken stews, soups, and sauces.

Sazerac The official state cocktail of Louisiana, consisting of rye whiskey with sugar and bitters.

shrimp Creole Shrimp in a tomato sauce seasoned with what's known around town as the "holy trinity": onions, bell peppers, and celery.

tasso A local variety of ham. No weak little honey-baked version, this one's smoked and seasoned with red pepper.

THE FRENCH QUARTER

Expensive

Antoine's CREOLE We have a sentimental soft spot for Antoine's. Perhaps that's because it has been owned and operated by the same family for an astonishing 160 years, and is considered one of the first fine dining restaurants in the New World. We love that Thomas Wolfe said he ate the best meal of his life here, and that author Frances Parkinson Keyes immortalized it in her mystery *Dinner at Antoine's*. We love how a New Orleanian friend reminisced about her grandfather's regular visits.

But we also like fabulous food. Which actually isn't what you get here. It's as classic as New Orleans dining gets, and well executed. But to be sure, there's better food (and presentation) to be had elsewhere in the city. Still, if you end up with the right waiter (hi, Johnny!), tour some of the 15 (!) memorabilia-stuffed rooms, and share tales with convivial neighboring guests, it can absolutely be a standout experience. The best strategy is to max out on classics and high drama. Start with the creamy, spinach-soaked baked oysters Rockefeller (invented here), and then order the buttery, crab-topped trout Pontchartrain or rich crawfish étouffée, and a side or two of the hollowed soufflé potato puffs. Finish in dramatic fashion with a *café brûlot* (see "Anythin' Flamin'," p. 146) and the frivolous, football-size (and -shaped) baked Alaska. The three-course, prix-fixe Friday lunch at $20.12 is worth every penny.

713 St. Louis St. ℭ **504/581-4422.** www.antoines.com. Reservations preferred. No shorts, sandals, or T-shirts; collared shirts for gentlemen (jackets no longer required). Main courses $24–$40. AE, DC, MC, V. Mon–Sat 5:30–9:30pm; Mon–Sat 11:30am–2pm; Sun 11am–2:30pm.

Arnaud's ★★ CREOLE ☺ Arnaud's has the lowest profile of all the classic old New Orleans restaurants, undeservedly so, since it tops them in quality. You need to try at least one venerable, properly New Orleans atmospheric establishment, and that one should be Arnaud's, which, while not wildly creative, is doing some of its best culinary work in years. Apart from the signature appetizer, shrimp Arnaud (boiled shrimp topped with a spicy rémoulade sauce) and full-bodied turtle, we love the spicy pompano Duarte, and any filet mignon entree here is often better than what's served in most local steakhouses, in particular the *filet au poivre*. The Quail Elzey is a rich gift of flavors and textures, the petite birds stuffed with foie gras mousse, tied with bacon, and topped with a truffle-inflected wine sauce. It's illegal (or should be) to leave without ordering the delightful soufflé potatoes. For desserts, the bananas Foster, prepared tableside, fills the Anythin' Flamin' (p. 146) counsel, and one crème brûlée fan said Arnaud's was the best she ever had. Allow time to visit the impressive Mardi Gras museum upstairs. A more casual jazz bistro room features nighttime entertainment (and a cover charge added to the check)—all of which makes Arnaud's a good fine dining introduction for well-behaved children.

813 Bienville St. ℭ **866/230-8892** or 504/523-5433. www.arnauds.com. Reservations requested. Business casual. Main courses $23–$40. AE, DC, DISC, MC, V. Sun–Thurs 6–10pm; Fri–Sat 6–10:30pm; Sun brunch 10am–2:30pm.

Bayona ★★ INTERNATIONAL A chef-owner who is a local treasure (and the model for Chef Desautel on HBO's *Treme* series), perennially imaginative, superior food (after 20-plus years), and one of the finest wine lists and loveliest courtyards in the French Quarter are some of the reasons why Bayona hangs

French Quarter Restaurants

FRENCH QUARTER

Area of detail

atop many "Best of" lists. When they're not at their best, service can be the sore point. Begin with the outstanding cream-of-garlic soup, a signature dish. Appetizers include grilled shrimp with corian-

Impressions

The Louisiana diet will kill a man as surely as the sword. —*King of the Hill*

der sauce and black-bean cakes, and delicate, flavorful veal sweetbreads sautéed with scallions and diced potatoes in sherry mustard. Knockout entrees have included medallions of lamb loin with a goat cheese and zinfandel demi-glace; and a faultless grilled pork chop with polenta and roast tomatoes. Lunch brings Bayona's famed smoked-duck with cashew butter and pepper jelly. Superb desserts are fruit-forward: The rich mocha banana torte with caramelized pecans melts us. Saturday's $25 light lunch features a choice of three tapaslike plates.

430 Dauphine St. © **504/525-4455.** www.bayona.com. Reservations required at dinner, recommended at lunch. Main courses $12–$16 lunch, $28–$38 dinner. AE, DC, DISC, MC, V. Wed–Sat 11:30am–2:30pm; Mon–Sat 6–10pm. 3 hr. free parking at Chateau LeMoyne, 301 Dauphine St.

Brennan's ★ FRENCH/CREOLE For more than 40 years, breakfast at Brennan's has been a New Orleans tradition, a feast that has kept many a heart surgeon busy: This multicourse extravaganza is unabashedly sauce- and egg-intensive. It's a special event, dress-up dining, and it's also costly—it's not hard to drop $50 on breakfast—so dine late and make it your main meal of the day. Or limit your choices and outlay by sticking with the fixed-price meal. Think classically prepared eggs Benedict, eggs Portuguese (poached on top of a tomato concoction, served in a puff pastry with hollandaise ladled over the whole), and very fine turtle soup. Though known for breakfasts, it does serve dinner (opt to have it on the gas-lamp-lined balcony) and a good-value weekday lunch special for under $25.

417 Royal St. © **504/525-9711.** www.brennansneworleans.com. Reservations recommended. Main courses $18–$43; fixed-price lunch $36; fixed-price 4-course dinner $48. AE, DC, DISC, MC, V. Mon–Fri 9am–1pm and 6–10pm; Sat–Sun 8am–2:30pm and 6–10pm. Closed for dinner on Christmas Eve and all day Christmas Day.

Broussard's ★ CREOLE It fell pretty deeply into tourist-trap territory for a while, but it's come roaring back, and now makes a very good alternative to some of its similarly well-established peers—and adds more of a nod to contemporary cuisine than a number of them. A very fine meal can be had here, especially in the lovely brick-walled courtyard. We suggest the appetizer of crabmeat Broussard, covered in an artichoke brie sauce and served with Herbsaint-flavored spinach, and for an entree the salmon Jean Lafitte, with a seafood shrimp, crab, and spinach stuffing over wild rice risotto. The desserts are happily heavy and creamy. The bar menu is a nice option for solo diners, and the three-course table d'hôte is a good deal at $33.

819 Conti St. © **504/581-3866.** www.broussards.com. Reservations recommended. No jeans, shorts, sneakers, or T-shirts. Main courses $26–$34. AE, MC, V. Daily 5:30–10pm.

Court of Two Sisters ♨ CREOLE This is probably the prettiest restaurant in town (thanks to a huge, foliage-filled courtyard located in a 2-centuries-old building—both spared any storm-related issues), but even major ambience can't obscure the problems with the mediocre food. You'll find the only daily jazz brunch in town here, but it suffers from the typical buffet problem—too many dishes, of which only the made-to-order items succeed (stick with simple eggs Benedict).

We also give the seafood slaw a thumbs up. Dinner may be even worse; apart from a Caesar salad (made in the traditional style, at tableside), there is little, if anything, to recommend. It's a pity, because you can't ask for a better setting.

613 Royal St. ℂ 504/522-7261. www.courtoftwosisters.com. Reservations highly recommended for dinner and brunch. Main courses $25–$35; brunch $29. AE, DC, DISC, MC, V. Daily 9am–3pm jazz brunch buffet and 5:30–10pm.

Dickie Brennan's Bourbon House Seafood ★★ SEAFOOD Sadly, it's easy to overlook this commendable restaurant, with its sprawling dining room and Bourbon Street location, but don't. It's a modern take on the classic New Orleans fish house, both aesthetically and gastronomically. The *fruits du mer* platter by itself makes a great meal, but the fresh seafood—including a perfect simple grilled redfish—shows their stuff (you can get any fish topped with fresh lump crabmeat for an additional charge, and you should). It serves one of our favorite BBQ shrimp preparations—which, in this city, means shrimp sautéed in a buttery, garlicky spicy sauce (heaven to sop up with bread); theirs is finished in sweet bourbon. Leave room for the frozen bourbon milk punch, the restaurant's swoon-worthy, booze-shake dessert. Naturally they're committed to, and knowledgeable about, all things bourbon, and happy hour features $5 small plates and $1 oysters (and a good shucker show).

144 Bourbon St. ℂ **504/522-0111.** www.bourbonhouse.com. Reservations suggested. Main courses $10–$16 breakfast, $11–$34 lunch, $19–$34 dinner. AE, DISC, MC, V. Daily 6:30–10:30am; Sun–Thurs 11am–10pm; Fri–Sat 11am–11pm.

Dickie Brennan's Steakhouse ★★ STEAK It looks gorgeous, but not as much so as its prime steaks. We are hard-pressed to choose our favorite steak here: the 14-ounce rib-eye, the 16-ounce cast-iron-seared prime strip, or the house filet topped with béarnaise sauce, flash-fried oysters, creamed spinach, and Pontalba potatoes. Each is tender and juicy and seasoned to give it an enhancing kerwallop but not enough to overpower the flavorful meat. Prime rib is less impressive—it's a bit pallid compared with a hearty aged steak. Finding the steaks a bit costly? Split one (they aren't small), and then you can order plenty of sides and appetizers, all of which are sterling as well. And even fish entrees are entirely successful, particularly the grilled redfish, which could be topped with lemon or lobster beurre blanc sauce, and the terrific crab cake appetizer, with nearly no filling. Save room for desserts. ***Note:*** You can also come from 5 to 7pm for the $5 Louisiana-inspired small plates in the bar.

716 Iberville St. ℂ **504/522-2467.** www.dickiebrennanssteakhouse.com. Reservations recommended. Main courses $24–$44 dinner. AE, DISC, MC, V. Daily 5:30–10pm; Fri 11:30am–2:30pm. Bar daily 5–10pm.

Galatoire's ★ FRENCH Hmm, where to start? Galatoire's, you're a time-honored classic and we'll always love you. But Gramps, it may be time to take away the proverbial keys. We're afraid you're becoming a danger. To us, specifically, because you and your clubby cronies will no doubt continue to have a grand old time. Sure, you ooze character; Tennessee Williams supped here (right behind the word RESTAURANT on the window), as did his characters Stella and Blanche in *A Streetcar Named Desire,* and so have generations of old-line families. They still do, getting lavished by waiter John's attention and in-jokes. Meanwhile, if we're lucky enough to be seated in the venerable, no-reservations downstairs dining room, we may get to wait while sipping flavorless mint juleps, eager to experience the ultimate New Orleans tradition—which it surely remains. Start with the fried eggplant fingers with Tabasco and powdered sugar, great gumbo, or the lump crab appetizer. Follow with grilled or meunière-style redfish with crabmeat, terrific creamed spinach, and glorious, puffy soufflé potatoes. Avoid the gloppily sauced dishes. No one comes here for gastronomic greatness. If only one could taste reverence.

209 Bourbon St. ✆ **504/525-2021.** www.galatoires.com. Reservations accepted for upstairs. Jackets required after 5pm and all day Sun. Main courses $19–$34. AE, DC, DISC, MC, V. Tues–Sat 11:30am–10pm; Sun noon–10pm. Closed July 4th, Thanksgiving, and Christmas. Fri lunch: recommend lining up 45-60 min. before opening.

K-Paul's Louisiana Kitchen ★ CAJUN/CREOLE Paul Prudhomme was at the center of the Cajun revolution of the early 1980s, helping to popularize Cajun food throughout the world. His reputation and his retail spice line continue today, but unfortunately, the restaurant's American regional food today is good (quite good, in fact), but not spectacular enough to justify the high cost. Different menu items are offered daily, the best of which may be blackened beef tenders with debris, or classic blackened drum. If you're set on trying something affordable from the Cajun cuisine pioneer, K-Paul's now offers perfectly decent "deli" lunches Thursday through Saturday, ordered at a counter and served on paper.

416 Chartres St. ✆ **504/524-7394.** www.kpauls.com. Reservations recommended for dinner. Business casual. Gentlemen asked to remove hats and caps inside. Main courses $27–$36 dinner, $10–$12 lunch. AE, DC, DISC, MC, V. Thurs–Sat 11am–2pm; Mon–Sat 5:30–10pm.

Le Meritage ★★ CONTEMPORARY SOUTHERN A laudable addition to this end of the Quarter, Le Meritage categorizes its new Southern menu items as though it were a wine list ("spicy reds," "full-bodied whites," and so on). Wise, globe-spanning wine pairings in small and large pours are also proposed for each dish. The approach is decidedly "fine," and—if you and your companions are game—fun, in spite of the slightly bland service and decor. The delicate, beautifully plated cooking is anything but flavorless, however. The divine lump crab and crawfish cakes were nearly solid; the beef carpaccio with horseradish cream was a tender delight. The promising duck two ways was a bit overseasoned. Skip the bland shrimp and grits in favor of sumptuous short ribs with parsnip purée. Leave space for the luxurious coffee crème brûlée. *Note:* Next door, the same kitchen serves up more casual, locally influenced fare in the newer **Bistreaux.**

1001 Toulouse St. (in the Maison Dupuy hotel). ✆ **504/522-8800.** www.lemeritagerestaurant. com. Reservations recommended. Soups, salads, starter small plates $8–$19; main courses $9–$35. AE, DISC, MC, V. Tues–Sat 6–10pm.

Mr. B's Bistro ★ CONTEMPORARY CREOLE A favorite among business-people for lunch, Mr. B's other claim to fame is its BBQ shrimp, with many a joke being made that the "B" stands for butter. The menu these days is fairly standard, so much so that nothing else really stands out—either on it or on the plate. If it's your first introduction to New Orleans restaurants, it's not a bad choice by any means, but if you've been eating pretty well up to this point, it's probably going to be a bit pedestrian. Having said that, those BBQ shrimp *are* plump, though the (yes, buttery) sauce is rather peppery—you might want to drop by just to split a portion.

201 Royal St. ℂ **504/523-2078.** www.mrbsbistro.com. Reservations recommended. No shorts or tank tops; business casual. Main courses $14–$23 lunch, $26–$38 dinner; jazz brunch entrees $30–$35. AE, DC, DISC, MC, V. Mon–Sat 11:30am–2pm; Mon–Thurs 5:30–9pm; Fri–Sat 5:30–9:30pm; Sun jazz brunch 10:30am–2pm.

Muriel's ★ CREOLE According to conventional wisdom, any restaurant this close to tourist-hub Jackson Square is bound to have overpriced, mediocre food. A few years ago, Muriel's not only defied that prognosis but impressed us mightily. Sadly, it has now succumbed to expectations; our last meal was closer to cafeteria Creole (perhaps explained by its booming banquet business), with clunky service to boot. It wasn't bad, per se; it just lacked real finesse and care. Stick with the simple and you'll be fine, like the pecan-crusted puppy drum, double-cut pork chop, or grilled chicken breast. The popular crawfish and goat cheese crepes appear on the three-course table d'hôte menu ($32), but the overly sweet desserts are negligible so it may not be worth it. The Goth-parlor decor and amusing wink to the in-house ghost (a table is set for him) help compensate for the blasé fare. A gluten-free menu is available.

801 Chartres St. (at St. Ann). ℂ **504/568-1885.** Reservations suggested. Main courses $12–$18 lunch, $16–$21 brunch, $17–$35 dinner. AE, DISC, MC, V. Mon–Sat 11:30am–2:30pm; Sun jazz brunch 11am–2pm; Mon–Fri 5:30–10pm; Sat–Sun 5–10pm.

Nola ★ CREOLE/NEW AMERICAN This modern two-story building with a glass-enclosed elevator is the most casual of chef Emeril Lagasse's three restaurants, and the most conveniently located for the average tourist. Unlike Lagasse's other restaurants, the dining experience here can be a bit hit-or-miss. It's never less than good quality (if not excellent, with farm-to-fork ingredients a focus), but it can be unmemorable. Whatever variation on duck pizza (with confit and fried egg with truffle oil, and hickory-roasted with cornbread pudding on a recent visit) is always a sure thing, as are daily soups, such as a nearly fork-able thick roasted garlic–Reggiano Parmesan with basil pesto. But while a recent wood-roasted, garlic drum was sumptuously moist, a glazed pork chop was overly sweet, and the shrimp with grits was rather dull compared with other versions around town. It's also a particularly noisy space in a town not known for hushed dining. The dine-on bar, though, is a convivial choice for single diners.

534 St. Louis St. ℂ **504/522-6652.** www.emerils.com. Reservations recommended. Main courses $11–$25 lunch, $25–$38 dinner. AE, DC, DISC, MC, V. Daily 6–10pm; Thurs–Sun 11:30am–2pm.

The Pelican Club ★ ☺ NEW AMERICAN We're particularly fond of the appetizers here (you could easily make a meal of them), but everything is quite tasty and nicely inventive, and the three rooms are as smartly tailored as the service. Escargots in a mushroom garlic-butter sauce (which will undoubtedly be sopped up with bread) are topped with tiny puff pastries. Oysters garnished with apple-smoked bacon tempt even oysterphobes. Tender lamb comes encrusted in rosemary-flavored bread crumbs with a spicy pepper jelly, and a whole flounder is cooked to perfection. Sides are simple but well-matched, and desserts are certainly standouts. Try the flat (rather than puffy) white-chocolate bread pudding or the creamy chocolate pecan pie. Of note, the children's menu gives kids a chance to try fancy but approachable grown-up food (fried shrimp with pasta in creamy sauce, panéed Gulf fish with lump crabmeat, chicken breast, or filet with truffle mashed potatoes).

615 Bienville St., entrance on Exchange Alley. ☎ **504/523-1504.** www.pelicanclub.com. Reservations recommended. Main courses $23–$34; 3-course prix-fixe menu $48–$55; children's menu $14. AE, DC, DISC, MC, V. Sun–Thurs 5:30–9:30pm; Fri–Sat 5:30–10pm. Closed Easter and July 4th.

Rib Room ★ SEAFOOD/STEAK Historically, this solid, cozy Old English-y room, with the natural brick and open ovens, is where New Orleanians go to eat beef. In truth, the meat is good but not outstanding, and the acclaimed prime rib is a bit tough and lacking in flavor. The menu has the usual other cuts and sauces, plus some seafood dishes. Carnivores and ichthyophobes will be happier here than at one of the city's Creole restaurants, and the old-line servers are charismatic, but it is not the must-do that its reputation would have you believe.

In the Omni Royal Orleans hotel, 621 St. Louis St. ☎ **504/529-7045.** www.omnihotels.com. Reservations recommended. Main courses $24–$38. AE, DC, DISC, MC, V. Daily 6:30–10:30am, 11:30am–2pm, and 6–9pm.

Stella! ★★ INTERNATIONAL We are very fond of this charming Quarter restaurant. The room glows with real and faux candlelight, making it instantly warm; equally appealing is the dedication to locally sourced food. Chef Scott Boswell (2010 James Beard–award finalist) consistently creates clever, arty food of stunning design and construction. Still, some combinations are more successful than others; the less-is-more theory might apply here. On a recent foray we thrilled to an appetizer of foie-gras-and-duck-pâté BLT, a decadently stacked combo. The veal rib-eye with lump crabmeat in a heady caper butter reduction is positively sublime, but the popular duck five ways has some elements that work superbly (the foie-gras wontons) and others that don't quite get there (the lacquered thigh can be dry). A caviar menu and excellent wine list greet splurgers, and desserts and ice creams are laudable.

1032 Chartres St. (in the Hôtel Provincial). ☎ **504/587-0091.** www.restaurantstella.com. Reservations recommended. No shorts or tank tops; business casual. Main courses $33–$46; 7-course tasting menu $125. AE, DC, DISC, MC, V. Daily 5:30–10:30pm.

Tujague's ★ CREOLE Dating back to 1856, Tujague's (pronounced *Two-jacks*) is every bit as venerable and aged as the big-name New Orleans restaurants. It may not be a knockout, but it's authentic and solid, and they mix a perfect Sazerac. Tujague's does not have a menu; instead, it offers a set six-course meal—local food, nothing fancy or nouvelle—and that's what you get. Meals start with a sinus-clearing shrimp rémoulade (with red or white sauce, or both if you can't make up your mind), followed by soup du jour, which may be a fine gumbo (not as thick as some, but that's not a liability), then on to Tujague's famed so-tender-you-cut-it-with-a-fork brisket "appetizer," and then the entree. You have your choice of four daily entrees: an ordinary filet mignon and items such as stuffed shrimp, fine fettuccine, or Bonne Femme chicken, a baked garlic number from the original owner's recipe (you have to ask for it). Finish with the right-on-the-money bread pudding or whatever is on the day's menu.

823 Decatur St. ☎ **504/525-8676.** www.tujagues.com. Reservations recommended. 6-course dinner $36–$45. AE, DC, DISC, MC, V. Daily 5pm–closing.

Moderate

Café Amelie ★ CONTEMPORARY SOUTHERN The picturesque courtyard (a favorite of brides) is the big draw here, along with straightforward, updated

Louisiana cuisine and farmers'-market freshness. Nothing is particularly revelatory (the Key lime pie with a cumulous cloud of fresh whipped cream comes close), but everyone can find something to enjoy, and the relaxing environs fairly scream languor and mint juleps (or fresh lemonade). There's a nice array of salads (senselessly tough to find in the French Quarter), and stellar local bakery La Boulangerie supplies the ciabatta for the chicken-salad BLT sandwich (liberal with the B, thanks). The *cochon* with ultracreamy stone-ground grits works on all cylinders, while catfish (sourced direct from fishermen) comes unfried and not overly blackened.

912 Royal St. ✆ **504/412-8965.** www.cafeamelie.com. Reservations suggested, especially for Sun brunch (not accepted for Sun dinner). Main courses lunch $7–$19, dinner $12–$29, brunch $8–$15. AE, DISC, MC, V. Wed–Sat 11am–4pm; Wed–Sat 5–10pm; Sun 5–9pm; Sun brunch 11am–3pm. Closed occasionally for special events; call ahead to check.

Green Goddess ★★ CONTEMPORARY CREOLE Chef Chris DeBarr's "globetrotting cuisine"—inspired by flavors from Spain to India but featuring local seafood, sausage, and organic produce—makes for some of the most creative and exciting dinners in town (lunch and brunch are handled by the talented chef Paul Artigues). The menu changes constantly, but you might get a wonderfully refreshing chilled melon soup or a terrine of three blue cheeses that had us squealing with delight. For your entree, try a Creole-Hawaiian dish made with smoked pulled pork seasoned with Hawaiian black lava salt; their version of bangers and mash, with local duck sausage and orangey mashed yams; or the blue corn crepes with mushrooms and *huitlacoche* (a wonderful Aztec "truffle" that grows on corn cobs). The beverage and cocktail menus are astonishing (Brazilian cashew fruit juice, anyone?—it's wonderful), the wine list is positively adventurous. The place is tiny, though the alleyway and "wine dungeon" seatings have their charms. What's not to love? Well, we fear Chef DeBarr's cooking may be too good for his own good, as a busy night can result in nothing less than a service meltdown. If your patience is as broad as your palate, perhaps you won't mind. An expansion is in the offing; we just hope the *front* of the house gets the attention paid to the *size* of the house.

307 Exchange Place. ✆ **504/301-3347.** www.greengoddessnola.com. No reservations (prepare to wait). Main courses $7–$16. AE, DISC, MC, V. Wed–Sun 11am–3:30pm; Thurs–Sun 6–11pm.

Irene's Cuisine ★★ FRENCH/ITALIAN Irene's is somewhat off the regular tourist dining path, but just follow the garlic scent until you see a long line. In a constantly changing world, waiting for a table at Irene's is something you can count on, even with reservations. But the French Provincial and Creole-Italian food in this dark, cluttered warren of small, somewhat romantic if tight-packed rooms is worth it. Ultrafriendly waiters and Irene herself provide prompt service.

The menu is heavier on meats and fish than the house-made pasta; locals know that Thursday is *osso buco* day, and we've known duck aficionados to pledge undying allegiance to the Duck St. Phillip (in a raspberry-pancetta demi-glace). We were thrilled by the whole fried soft-shell crab atop pasta with a cream sauce of garlic, crawfish, tomatoes, and wads of whole basil leaves. The panned oysters and grilled shrimp appetizer can be magnificent, and don't forget the *pollo rosemarino*—five pieces of chicken marinated, partly cooked, marinated again, and then cooked a final time. Desserts, alas, are the usual suspects (repeat after me: crème brûlée, bread pudding, chocolate torte . . .).

539 St. Philip St. ℰ **504/529-8811.** Limited reservations accepted if space is available. Main courses $18–$38. AE, MC, V. Mon–Sat 5:30–10pm. Closed New Year's Day, July 4th, Labor Day and the week before to honor the Katrina losses, Thanksgiving and Christmas.

Iris ★ CONTEMPORARY CREOLE This small, pretty little place is helmed by a talented chef-owner whose delicate cooking walks a satisfying line between French, Mediterranean, and local influences. The menu changes daily, but possibilities include a supple ricotta gnudi starter with sweet local peas, red beans, and Creole tomatoes, or a graceful snapper with baby root vegetables in an olive vinaigrette. It's all very pretty, fresh food, meticulously prepared, and while portions are on the modest side, the quality is high and the contrast to heavier Creole fare is welcome.

321 N. Peters St. (in the Bienville House Hotel). ℰ **504/862-5848.** www.irisneworleans.com. Reservations recommended. Main courses $18–$34. AE, DISC, MC, V. Mon and Wed–Sat 6pm–closing; Thurs–Fri 11:30am–2pm.

Louisiana Bistro ★★ CONTEMPORARY CREOLE The vibe here is a bit *arrondissement*: intimate (11 tables), low-ceilinged, and tucked away on an unassuming street. The six entrees on the regular menu are concessions to convention; the real choice is among the three-, four-, and five-course "Feed Me" tasting menus (more on request). This Creole *omakase* is where Bourdain-esque Chef Mars (of Emeril's and the CIA) excels, and the day's ingredients shine. Consider dreamy crawfish beignets in brown beurre, the BP-inspired "pork barrel," braised grillades in a potato cylinder with crisped leeks, or cast-iron-bronzed Louisiana swordfish shocked with a drizzle of jalapeño hollandaise (all subject to change). The wine list is ample, and the service is sassy in a good way—the old-school waiters know when to chat and when to split, but can be a bit slow when busy. Skip dessert; it's not their forte.

337 Rue Dauphine. ℰ **504/525-3335.** www.louisianabistro.net. Reservations recommended. Entrees $22–$34; "Feed Me" tasting menu, 3 courses $39, 5 courses $59. AE, DISC, MC, V. Wed–Sun 6–10pm.

Meauxbar Bistro ★★ BISTRO Rampart Street, nay, *any* street, needs more places like this: a sweet, sophisticated neighborhood cafe that aspires to serve more than just the usual fare. Large and small plates tend toward traditional French bistro, some with Asian accents, like the signature starter of ginger crawfish dumplings in a sesame dipping sauce. The salad Lyonnaise with poached egg alone is worth coming back for. Steak frites are done to a T, and the robust, double-cut pork chop is perfectly grilled. The apple tartin, served in the fall, is like no other apple dish in New Orleans (in spring, go for the pineapple upside-down cake).

942 N. Rampart St. ℰ **504/569-9979.** www.meauxbar.com. Reservations suggested. Main courses $19–$32. AE, DISC, MC, V. Tues–Sat 5:30–10:30pm.

Port of Call ★★ HAMBURGERS When you're sauced and seafooded out, sometimes you just need a burger. There are many theories of what makes an ideal burger. Those who lean toward huge and juicy feel strongly that the half-pound monsters served at this cozy (and we mean it) spot are the best in town. The Port of Call is just a half-step above a dive, but it's a convivial place with a nice staff that can get justly somewhat harried during busy hours (that is, whenever they're open). The steaks are also quite good, but instead of an accompaniment of fries here you get a brawny, loaded baked potato. Expect a wait, and sip on the signature Monsoon, a refreshing but potent citrus-laden rum combo.

838 Esplanade Ave. ℂ **504/523-0120.** http://portofcallnola.com. No reservations. Main courses $10–$26. AE, MC, V. Sun–Thurs 11am–midnight; Fri–Sat 11am–1am.

Red Fish Grill ★ SEAFOOD Red Fish is far better than anything else in its price range on Bourbon Street, and—surprise!—it's another Brennan restaurant. Seafood and local veggies, delivered daily, are spiked with some surprising flavors and accompaniments, like catfish with tasso (ham) flamed in anise-scented Herbsaint liqueur, or a refreshing lump crab starter with rosemary ice on a bed of horseradish slaw. The signature BBQ oysters are quick fried in a spicy sauce and served, winglike, with blue cheese dressing. For lunch, the shrimp and blackened avocado po' boy is so good we don't know why it isn't replicated everywhere; avocado appears again at dinner with tomato pesto and crisped parsnips. The casual, playful atmosphere makes this an easy choice. And yes, the menu has meat and poultry dishes, to which we pay no attention.

115 Bourbon St. ℂ **504/598-1200.** www.redfishgrill.com. Reservations limited. Main courses $12–$27 lunch, $17–$34 dinner. AE, DC, DISC, MC, V. Daily 11am–3pm; Mon–Thurs and Sun 5–10pm; Fri–Sat 5–11pm.

Sylvain ★★ BISTRO Truth be told, there's not a lot of coolness in the French Quarter, restaurant-wise. Sylvain fills the gap, hip without being off-putting. (Well, to start, there's that "where's the entrance?" matter: down the alley on the right.) The Civil War–meets-Soho vibe, friendly servers, and the small bar shoulder-to-shoulder with locals make it welcoming, but the good to very good cooking and reasonable prices make it work. The speckled wood floors were repurposed from an old church roof; the bar manager doubles as a WWOZ DJ (and does very well at both—note the pitch-perfect Americana soundtrack); the chef's grandmother was the Pickle Queen of Alabama (order whatever's pickled!); the absurdly tender beef cheeks are packed with flavor; the chicken liver crostini is lush and generous; the handmade pappardelle Bolognese is a fine preparation of the classic; the wine list is thoughtful. Oh, and it has a ghost with a literary lineage. The menu leans slightly toward the carnivorous—not heavy-handed, but impeding room for dessert, perhaps. Share the chocolate *pot du crème*, then.

625 Chartres St. ℂ **504/265-8123.** www.sylvainnola.com. Reservations recommended. Main courses $16–$24. AE, DC, DISC, MC, V. Fri–Sat 11:30am–2:30pm and 5:30pm–midnight; Mon–Thurs 5:30–11pm; Sun 10:30am–2:30pm and 5:30–10pm.

Inexpensive

Acme Oyster House ★★ SEAFOOD/LIGHT FARE The Quarter's oldest oyster bar needed a $2-million renovation to recover from Katrina, but it looks pretty much as it always did, just spiffier, and they got themselves (and us) an expanded kitchen in the process. There's almost always a line to get into this boisterous, crowded joint, but if you need an oyster fix or you've never tried oyster shooting (taking a raw oyster, possibly doused in sauce, and letting it slide right down your throat), come here. There's nothing quite like standing at the oyster bar and eating a dozen freshly shucked oysters on the half-shell (you can have them at a table, but somehow they taste better at the bar). The garlicky broiled ones are good anywhere. If you can't quite stomach them raw, try the oyster po' boy, with beer, of course.

24 Iberville St. ✆ **504/522-5973.** www.acmeoyster.com. Oysters $19 per dozen raw or char-broiled; po' boys $8–$17; entrees $9–$22. AE, DC, DISC, MC, V. Sun–Thurs 11am–10pm; Fri–Sat 11am–11pm.

Angeli on Decatur ★ ITALIAN/INTERNATIONAL/LIGHT FARE This place serves satisfying, if not particularly New Orleanian, food till 2am, and they deliver: crucial words for hungry locals and tourists—making it convenient and suitable for a light, actually rather healthy meal (!!). Portions are substantial; splitting a Greek salad produced two full plates of fresh, lovely veggies and a couple of pieces of garlic bread. Add to that a small but gooey Mystical pizza—roasted garlic, goat cheese, onions, sun-dried tomatoes—and you've got a tasty, affordable meal, almost anytime or anywhere, for two normal-appetite adults (including Brad and Angie, who order from here occasionally).

1141 Decatur St. (at Governor Nicholls St.). ✆ **504/566-0077.** Main courses $7–$21. AE, MC, V. Sun–Thurs 11am–2am; Fri–Sat 11am–4am. Delivery till 2am.

Antoine's Annex ★ LIGHT FARE/DESSERT This clean, white space with just a few tables (and a few more in the adjacent alleyway) is an easy option for coffee, pastries, and a small selection of perfectly okay sandwiches and salads. Beyond that, it has two important things going for it: 1) you can say you've eaten at Antoine's, kinda (p. 120); and 2) you can get a scoop of Angelo Brocato's superb ice cream (p. 154) in the Quarter. Grownups can even order a booze-infused gelato shake.

513 Royal St. ✆ **504/581-4422.** www.antoines.com/antoines-annex.pdf. Pastries $2.75–$3.50; sandwiches $7.50–$9. AE, DC, DISC, MC, V. Daily 8am–9pm.

Café Beignet ★ CAFE At breakfast, this counter-service bistro-style cafe serves Belgian waffles, an omelet soufflé, bagels and lox, or brioche French toast. Items on the lunch menu include gumbo, vegetable sandwiches, and salads. And, of course, beignets. The latter won't make us forget Café du Monde—nothing will, of course—but if you are here, make the most of it. The Bourbon Street location has a nice patio and live jazz Thursday through Sunday from 1pm until closing.

334B Royal St. ✆ **504/524-5530.** www.cafebeignet.com. Most items under $10. MC, V. Daily 7am–5pm. Also at 311 Bourbon St. ✆ **504/525-2611.** Mon–Wed 8am–3pm; Thurs and Sun 8am–10pm; Fri–Sat 8am–midnight.

Café Maspero ★ CAFE/SEAFOOD/LIGHT FARE Upon hearing complaints about the increasing presence in the Quarter of "foreign" restaurants, such as Subway, one local commented, "Good. Shorter lines at Maspero." Locals do indeed line up for burgers, deli sandwiches (including a veggie muffuletta!), seafood, and grilled marinated chicken. It's good food in large portions at low prices—it even has a decent wine, beer, and cocktail list. No wonder there are lines.

601 Decatur St. ✆ **504/523-6250.** Main courses $4.25–$9. No credit cards. Sun–Thurs 11am–10pm; Fri–Sat 11am–11pm.

Camellia Grill ★★ ☺ DINER/HAMBURGERS/LIGHT FARE We'll miss riding the St. Charles streetcar to get there, but it's awfully convenient having a near-perfect replica (in style, service, and menu) of the Uptown original right smack in the French Quarter. See review of the Uptown branch on p. 152.

520 Chartres St. ✆ **504/522-1800.** www.camelliagrill.net. All entrees under $10. AE, DISC, MC, V. Daily 8am–1am.

Clover Grill ★ DINER/HAMBURGERS/COFFEE We go to the teensy Clover Grill when we need a pick-me-up. Not a cocktail, just a good laugh. The irreverent menu ("We're here to serve people and make them feel prettier than they are") isn't quite as joke-filled as it once was, but the charmingly sassy staff is still on their game, at least for most of the 24 hours that they're open; the burgers are still juicy and cooked under a hubcap (seals in the juices, they say); and if they're not too busy, they'll whir you up a big ole chocolate malt. Breakfast is served round-the-clock, and drag queens still hang out at the tables or counters. Snaps to the Clover.

900 Bourbon St. ✆ **504/598-1010.** www.clovergrill.com. All items under $8. AE, MC, V. Daily 24 hr.

Felix's Restaurant & Oyster Bar ★★ ☺ SEAFOOD/CREOLE Like its neighbor the Acme Oyster House, Felix's is a down-home place, full of locals and tourists standing at the bar having oysters on the half-shell. Both places have the same oyster supplier, yet each has its die-hard fans. At the tables, order your bivalves a multitude of ways: in stew, soup, pasta, or omelet; broiled or baked. The fried, grilled, or blackened fish, chicken, steaks, spaghetti, and Creole dishes are just fine, and an inexpensive kid's menu includes fried catfish, fried shrimp, or chicken tenders. Look for boiled crawfish in season. The place could use a good scrubbing, though (like much in the Quarter). *Tip:* On Wednesdays from 5pm to 10pm, a beer is free with a dozen raw oysters.

739 Iberville St. ✆ **504/522-4440.** www.felixs.com. Dozen raw oysters $11; po' boys under $15; other main courses $11–$20. AE, DISC. Mon–Thurs 10am–10pm; Fri–Sat 10am–1am; Sun 10am–11pm.

Johnny's Po-Boys ★ LIGHT FARE For location (right near a busy part of the Quarter) and menu simplicity (po' boys and more po' boys), you can't ask for much more than Johnny's (well, they *could* stay open later). They put anything you could possibly imagine (and some things you couldn't) on huge hunks of French bread, including the archetypal fried seafood (add some Tabasco, we strongly advise), deli meats, cheese omelets, ham and eggs, and the starch-o-rama that is a french-fry po' boy. Johnny boasts that "even my failures are edible," and that says it all. And they deliver within the Quarter!

511 St. Louis St. ✆ **504/524-8129.** www.johnnyspoboy.com. Most items under $13; specials may be more. No credit cards. Mon–Thurs 8am–3pm; Fri–Sun 8am–4:30pm.

Louisiana Pizza Kitchen PIZZA This local favorite features individual, wood-fired pies with standard and some regional toppings (try it with shrimp and roasted garlic). Crusts are thin and puffy, and toppings don't get lost in an over-abundance of cheese and sauce. The menu also includes pastas and mains, a good Caesar salad, and a yummy fire-roasted artichoke appetizer. Aficionados might find better pizza out in the 'hoods, but this location is conveniently next to the French Market. What puts LPK over the top for a pizza place is the extensive list of wines by the glass, dispensed from a nitrogen preservation system.

95 French Market Place. ✆ **504/522-9500.** www.louisianapizzakitchen.com. Pizzas $9–$15; pastas $12–$22. AE, DISC, MC, V. Daily 11am–10pm. Also at 615 S. Carrollton Ave. (✆ **504/866-5900**).

Napoleon House ★ CREOLE/ITALIAN Folklore has it that the name of this place was derived from a plot hatched here to snatch the Little Corporal from his island exile and bring him to live on the third floor of this building. Alas, it probably isn't true: The building dates from a couple of years after Napoleon's death. Shucks. But we'll still hang out in the atmospheric environs or on the pretty patio and sip the signature Pimm's Cup, a delightful cucumber-y gin remedy. Somewhere between tourist-geared and local-friendly, the Napoleon House serves large portions of adequate traditional New Orleans food (po' boys, jambalaya), plus wild cards like salads with goat cheese, pita and hummus, and, most significantly, a heated muffuletta.

500 Chartres St. ✆ **504/524-9752.** www.napoleonhouse.com. Main courses $7–$10. AE, DISC, MC, V. Mon 11am–5:30pm; Tues–Thurs 11am–10pm; Fri–Sat 11am–11pm.

Rémoulade ☺ CREOLE/CAJUN/AMERICAN An informal cafe offshoot of the venerable **Arnaud's** (p. 120), Rémoulade won't leave you rapturous, but it's better than the otherwise exceedingly tourist-trap restaurants on Bourbon Street (except Red Fish Grill and Bourbon House). It serves average, adequate local food at reasonable prices. The best items are the Arnaud's specialties, like shrimp rémoulade and the fine turtle soup. Parents can go for the oyster bar while kids can get burgers, hot dogs, and pizza. *Tip:* This is one of the few places in the Quarter that serves **Angelo Brocato's** dreamy Italian ice cream (p. 154).

309 Bourbon St. ✆ **504/523-0377.** www.remoulade.com. Main courses $9–$20. AE, DISC, MC, V. Daily 11:30am–midnight.

WHOLE LOTTA muffuletta GOIN' ON

Muffulettas are sandwiches of (pardon the expression) heroic proportions, enormous concoctions of round Italian bread, Italian cold cuts and cheeses, and olive salad. One person cannot (or should not) eat a whole one—at least not in one sitting. Instead, share; a half makes a good meal, and a quarter is a filling snack. They may not sound like much on paper, but once you try one, you'll be hooked. Vegetarians swear they're delicious done meatless.

Several places in town claim to have invented the muffuletta and also claim to make the best one. Decide for yourself: Muffuletta comparison-shopping can be a very rewarding pastime.

The lunchtime line can be daunting but it does moves fast at **Central Grocery ★★★**, 923 Decatur St. (✆ **504/523-1620**). There are a few seats at the back of this crowded, heavenly smelling Italian grocery, or you can order to go. Best of all, they ship, so once you're hooked—and you will be—you needn't wait to return for a muffuletta fix. Eat it across the street on the banks of the Mississippi for an inexpensive, romantic meal (about $14 for a whole sandwich). The staff at Central Grocery makes up their sandwiches early in the day, so they're ready for the rush. Don't worry about freshness; it actually helps when the olive flavors soak through the layers.

Are the heated muffulettas at **Napoleon House ★** (p. 131) better or blasphemy? It's a different taste sensation—judge for yourself. Feeling experimental? Go to **Nor-Joe's Importing Co. ★★**, 505 Friscoe, in Metairie (✆ **504/833-9240**), where the ginormous, outstanding muffulettas, constructed with such iconoclastic ingredients as prosciutto and mortadella, have their own cult following. Then there's **Cochon Butcher ★★★** (p. 145), whose house-cured meats form the basis of what may be our new favorite 'letta.

Somethin' Else Café ★ CAFE/LIGHT FARE This better-than-reliable cafe on an airy corner turns out surprisingly good fare morning till night, making it a good go-to spot whenever you need something easy and familiar. The mondo breakfast biscuits, with regular sausage gravy or localized with *boudin* balls, roast beef debris, or pulled pork, will start your day heartily (yes, do get a side of sweet potato hash). The cafe serves perfectly respectable omelets, requisite po' boys, and house-ground burgers that come on fluffy egg buns (as does the odd but oddly good shrimp burger). If you've hit that I-just-want-a-salad wall, try the Popeye (spinach, avocado, crab, and grilled shrimp), or choose your ingredients and they'll toss a salad to your specifications. It's small and there's often a wait on weekends, but it has free Wi-Fi and, like all good New Orleans cafes, a bar.

620 Conti St. ✆ **504/373-6439.** www.somethinelsecafe.com. Omelets, burgers, sandwiches $6–$14. DISC, MC, V. Sun–Wed 7am–10pm; Thurs 7am–midnight; Fri–Sat 7am–2am or 3am.

Stanley ★★ ☺ AMERICAN Right on the corner of Jackson Square, neat little Stanley, owned by the excellent chef/owner of Stella! (earlier) offers breakfast all day, cornmeal-crusted oyster po' boys, and drippy burgers (which some believe rival Port of Call's naked mammoths). Kids go for the genuine soda fountain featuring homemade ice cream and design-your-own ice cream sandwiches. A coffee and pastry-service bar next door sells a few grab-and-go lunch items.

457 St. Ann St. (corner of Jackson Sq. and St. Ann). ✆ **504/587-0093.** www.stanleyrestaurant.com. Everything under $15. AE, DISC, MC, V. Daily 7am–10pm.

THE FAUBOURG MARIGNY & BYWATER

For the restaurants in this section, see the "New Orleans Restaurants" map on p. 116. Also see **Mimi's in the Marigny** and **Three Muses,** listed under bars, p. 292 and 282.

Moderate

Feelings Café ★ AMERICAN/CREOLE This modest neighborhood spot is friendly and pretty and serves tasty, solid (if not spectacular) food. It feels like a true local find—because it is—and can be a welcome break from the Quarter or from more intense dining. Try to get a table in the plant-filled courtyard or on the balcony overlooking it (particularly delightful on a balmy night), though the dining rooms are perfectly pleasant. The ambience is even better when the piano bar is up and running (call ahead to see). A typical visit produces oysters *en brochette, pâté de maison,* seafood-stuffed eggplant (shrimp, crabmeat, and crawfish tails in a casserole with spicy sausage and crisp fried eggplant), and a chocolate-mousse/peanut-butter pie for dessert.

2600 Chartres St. ✆ **504/945-2222.** www.feelingscafe.com. Main courses $17–$26. AE, DC, DISC, MC, V. Thurs–Fri and Sun 6–9:30pm; Sat 6–10pm, Sun brunch 11am–2pm. Bar opens at 5pm.

Yuki ★★★ 🍴 JAPANESE It's tempting to walk by the inconspicuous sign amid the Frenchmen frenzy. Don't. Yuki Yamaguchi hews closely to the Japanese *izakaya* (neighborhood pub/noshery) tradition, offering an impressive array of imported sakes and *shochu* (a light distilled liquor) and serving traditional Japanese bar snacks and small plates of home-style dishes from her grandmother's recipes. She has an exceptional touch behind the stove. The crab *shumai* dumplings and delicately fried squid legs rocked us. Sushi is not on the menu, but a tuna sashimi salad is sweet and lively. The udon soups will rejuvenate carbo-spent clubbers, and more adventurous eaters will appreciate the offal specials and crispy, lemony beef tongue. This tiny, hip tavern veers closer to a club as night deepens, with eclectic live music (accordionist Norbert Slama hung with Piaf) or DJs spinning to vintage Japanese films projected above the bar.

525 Frenchmen St. ℓ **504/943-1122.** www.facebook.com/yukiizakaya. Small plates $4–$15. AE, MC, V. Mon–Thurs 6–11:30pm; Fri–Sat 6pm–2am (or later); Sun 6–10:30pm.

Inexpensive

Cake Café & Bakery ★ LIGHT FARE/DESSERT This sweet cafe (about a 10-min. walk from the Esplanade end of the Quarter) should fit the bill for an interesting but humble breakfast (with sides like organic yellow grits) or lunch, like a Reuben with homemade kraut, a big salad, or grilled tuna with wasabi. Both breakfast and lunch are served all day, with breads, enormous biscuits (served with homemade jam), and bagels baked on-site. And, of course, it sells cakes and cupcakes of simple and exotic flavors (Sazerac!). Better yet, a dollar extra gets you a cupcake at lunch!

2440 Chartres St. ℓ **504/943-0010.** www.nolacakes.com. Everything under $11. AE, DC, DISC, MC, V. Daily 7am–3pm.

Elizabeth's ★★★ CREOLE The average tourist may never get to the Bywater; it's a little out of the way, after all. That's too bad—they'll miss a true N'Awlins neighbahood, and experiences like Elizabeth's, with "Real Food, Done Real Good," as they say. Like Creole rice *calas* (sweet rice fritters), a classic breakfast dish that is nearly extinct; the infamous praline bacon, topped with sugar and pecans (aka "pork candy"), which you must not miss (it's served only at breakfast); or stuffed French toast—*pain perdu* piled high with cream cheese flavored with strawberries. We could go on, but the menu changes daily, so you might want to call ahead to see what's cooking. We tout breakfast, but lunch and dinner also rock, with specials like pan-seared salmon with Dijon beurre blanc sauce or Southern fried chicken livers with pepper jelly. Out of the way or not, this is one of the city's best restaurants, which is why it's very crowded on weekends. We'll meet you there—and let's walk back to the Quarter together. Yes, it's a hike, but doable, and we can justify that extra order of praline bacon.

601 Gallier St. ℓ **504/944-9272.** www.elizabeths-restaurant.com. Breakfast and lunch everything under $15; dinner $8.50–$17, specials higher. MC, V. Tues–Sun 8am–2:30pm; Tues–Sat 6–10pm.

La Peniche Restaurant ★ CREOLE A short walk into the Marigny brings you to this homey (as opposed to "homely") dive. Open nearly 24 hours (except from midday Tues till 8am Thurs; use caution late at night), it serves fried fish, po' boys, burgers, and even quiche. It's got a good brunch menu, which is why it's packed during that time. Come for specials such as bronzed (with Cajun spices) pork, and get the homemade chocolate layer cake or peanut butter–chocolate chip pie for dessert.

1940 Dauphine St. ℓ **504/943-1460.** www.facebook.com/LaPeniche24Hours. Everything under $16 except seafood platter (under $20). AE, MC, V. Open 24 hr. Thurs–Tues 8am–2pm.

Mona's Café & Deli ★★ MIDDLE EASTERN The various locations of Mona's all do credible versions of basic Middle Eastern fare (hummus, kabobs, and so forth). The Frenchmen and Magazine streets locations are the most convenient for the average tourist (especially vegetarians and vegans). We particularly like the marinated chicken with basmati rice. Last order is taken 15 minutes before closing.

504 Frenchmen St. ✆ **504/949-4115.** Sandwiches $4–$5.95; main courses $4.50–$19. AE, DC, DISC, MC, V. Mon–Thurs 11am–10pm; Fri–Sat 11am–11pm; Sun noon–9pm. Additional locations at 3901 Banks St.; Uptown, at 1120 S. Carrollton Ave.; and at 4126 Magazine St.

Praline Connection ★ 🍴 CREOLE/SOUL FOOD The quality has dipped a bit in recent years, which means solid, reliable Creole and soul food, anchored by superior fried chicken. It doesn't mean excellent, as their reputation (which rides a bit on sentiment and tradition) sometimes indicates. The fried pickles and the fried chicken livers with pepper jelly still always hit our table; after that if we're too fried for the chicken, the best entrees are often whatever's on the daily blackboard. And the servers still wear cute bowler hats.

542 Frenchmen St. ✆ **504/943-3934.** www.pralineconnection.com. Main courses $12–$20. AE, DC, DISC, MC, V. Mon–Sat 11am–10pm; Sun 11am–9pm.

MID-CITY/ESPLANADE

For a map of the restaurants in this section, see the "Mid-City Hotels & Restaurants" map on p. 95.

Expensive

Ralph's on the Park ★★ BISTRO You'd be hard-pressed to find a better setting for a New Orleans restaurant, with its iconic view of the Spanish moss–draped giant oaks across the street in City Park. It's just as likable on the inside, albeit a bit more high-style than expected. It's well placed and well priced for lunch after a visit to the park and museum, and easily reachable from the City Park streetcar line—which makes it an excellent alternative to the Quarter or Uptown dining choices.

The reliable food is Creole inflected with a bit of dash, and the menu changes seasonally. The signature "disgruntled" shrimp (tempura shrimp fried with chili crème fraîche) and crispy speckled trout are surefire winners; lately we're fond of the moist duck breast in a veal and cane syrup reduction. Desserts are stylish and playful, which, sadly, is a bit unusual in this city. The $28 three-course brunch is lovely and popular (bourbon soup with banana fritters!). Lately we've taken to hitting up the happy hour, as much for the small plates (*boudin* balls, mushroom Gruyère tart) as for Joe Krown's superb piano accompaniment.

900 City Park Ave. ✆ **504/488-1000.** www.ralphsonthepark.com. Reservations recommended. Main courses $12–$22 lunch, $23–$46 dinner, $15–$19 brunch. AE, MC, V. Daily 5:30–9pm; Wed–Fri 11:30am–2pm; Sun 11am–2pm.

Moderate

Café Degas ★★ BISTRO/FRENCH Café Degas is just an adorable, friendly, charming French bistro—a delightful, no-fuss neighborhood restaurant, ideal when you just want a nice meal and nice atmosphere. There's a big tree in the close-set, semi-outdoor dining room (the clear plastic "walls" roll up, making for a lovely sidewalk cafe feel). The cafe has daily dinner and lunch specials—think quiches and real, live salads (always a happy find in this town). Classics like onion soup and a salad Niçoise with yellowfin tuna are all done well; and the straightforward but flavorful fish and meat dishes are presented in generous portions—like the hanger steak or perfectly crisped Parmesan-crusted veal medallions. Though it's French, this is not France, and the bistro is informal enough for jeans. Sunday brunch is popular, so reserve ahead.

3127 Esplanade Ave. ✆ **504/945-5635.** www.cafedegas.com. Reservations recommended. Main courses lunch $10–$18, dinner $18–$25. AE, DC, DISC, MC, V. Wed–Sun 11am–3pm; Wed–Sat 6–10pm; Sun 6–9:30pm.

Dooky Chase ★★ SOUL FOOD/CREOLE For decades, Leah and husband Dooky Chase have served prominent African-American politicians, musicians, and businesspeople Chef Leah's classic soul food as gloriously influenced by the city's French, Sicilian, and Italian traditions. This was the place people like Ray Charles (who wrote "Early in the Morning" about it) would come to after local shows and stay up eating gumbo. The Chases lived in a FEMA trailer across from the restaurant during its extensive rebuild. It's back, serving a lunch buffet and entrees (with exquisite fried chicken, sautéed veal, and chicken Creole leading the way) in the art-filled dining room (though be aware that the neighborhood isn't the best). The charming Chases are everything that is New Orleans (nonagenarian Leah was the model for two characters in Disney's delightful film *The Princess and the Frog*) and so is their cuisine. Grandson Edgar "Dook" Chase IV, a Le Cordon Bleu grad, now helms the stove alongside Leah (she still cooks!); he seems to have inherited the tasty gene. Long may they cook.

2301 Orleans Ave. ✆ **504/821-0600.** Main courses $9–$20. Tues–Fri 11am–3pm dine-in or take-out.

Liuzza's ★★ 🍴 CREOLE/ITALIAN Actual moment from a Liuzza's visit: The crusty waitress hands a menu to a customer ("Here you go, Bay-bee") and then abruptly closes it. "Bay-bee," she instructs, gesticulating with a finger, "Numba One, or Numba Two—but *definitely* Numba One." Naturally, the Number One special was ordered (a seafood lasagna, dripping with a white cream sauce) and devoured, despite its enormous size.

Yep, this is a neighborhood institution (open since 1947 and surviving 8 feet of flood water); it's humble, small, and crowded with regulars. So when the waitress talks, you betcha you listen. There's nothing subtle about the hearty, saucy Italian and Creole comfort food, including the famous deep-fried dill pickle slices ("You people will batter and deep-fry anything that isn't nailed down!" said yet another astonished visitor) and po' boys. Top off any meal with an Abita Amber in Liuzza's massive frosted mugs.

3636 Bienville St. ✆ **504/482-9120.** www.liuzzas.com. Main courses $9.50–$20. No credit cards. Tues–Sat 11am–10pm.

Lola's ★★ INTERNATIONAL/SPANISH This small, neighborhood place doesn't take reservations, and there can be a wait for the tasty Spanish fare, from various paellas to garlic shrimp tapas and a heck of a garlic soup (one of several good vegetarian options). If there's a wait, relax with a carafe of red or white sangria; once you're seated, service is attentive and food comes quickly.

3312 Esplanade Ave. ✆ **504/488-6946.** www.lolasneworleans.com. Main courses $16–$28. Sun–Thurs 5:30–9:30pm; Fri–Sat 5:30–10pm.

Mandina's ★★ CREOLE/ITALIAN In a city renowned for its funky, local joints as well as its fine-dining establishments, dis is da ultimate neighbahood N'Awlins restaurant. Tommy Mandina's family has owned and operated this restaurant and bar since the late 1800s, and neither the menu nor much of the staff has changed much in the last 50 years or so—even after rebuilding from their post-Katrina hammering. This is a good thing.

The daily specials are worth considering, but the tangy shrimp rémoulade and crawfish cakes make standout appetizers. Go for the greasy but yummy fried onion rings and buttery, garlicky bread for the table, and the seafood gumbo and turtle soup au sherry are always fine. The red beans and rice with Italian sausage is wonderful. We'd get that or the sweet Italian sausage and spaghetti combo, a favorite comfort food, if we could resist the brown-buttery trout meunière. But we often can't. Hardly innovative gourmet, but it's exactly the way we remember it from childhood. Bring a sweater; they're A/C enthusiasts.

3800 Canal St. ✆ **504/482-9179.** www.mandinasrestaurant.com. Main courses $10–$25. No credit cards. Mon–Thurs 11am–9:30pm; Fri–Sat 11am–10pm; Sun noon–9pm.

Inexpensive

Lil' Dizzy's ★★ CREOLE/SOUL FOOD Good food, lively scene: It's more Treme than Mid-City, but it's another quintessential neighborhood restaurant, and understandably so; the owner grew up behind his family's legendary soul food/Creole restaurant. Locals pack the place for the lunch buffet, where the staples include terrific fried chicken and red beans and rice (you run the risk of them running out of certain things if you dine late). Other menu items include a decent T-bone steak. But the standout is the trout Baquet (fish topped with garlic-butter sauce and sometimes fresh crabmeat). Breakfast brings biscuits; crabmeat and shrimp omelets and pretty much anything else you can whip up with eggs; grits; homemade hot sausages; and the very popular calves' liver in brown gravy. If you're near the Central Business District, there's also a branch in the Wyndham Whitney Hotel on Poydras Street, where prices are a bit higher, but the space is considerably bigger.

1500 Esplanade Ave. ✆ **504/569-8997.** Everything under $13 except the $14 Fri seafood buffet and $16 Sun brunch. AE, DC, DISC, MC, V. Daily 8am–2pm; Sun brunch menu 9am–2pm.

Liuzza's by the Track ★★ CREOLE/LIGHT FARE Not to be confused with Liuzza's, above, and not to be overlooked, this is a near-flawless example of a corner neighborhood hole in the wall. In one visit, you will either get the point or not; by the second visit, the staff will know your name. It's not just the fact that they serve what may be the best gumbo and red beans 'n' rice in the city, it's the monster perfect po' boys, the addictive garlic fried oyster (our favorite), the drippy garlic-stuffed roast beef (with a pinch of horseradish in the mayo), and their signature astounding barbecued-shrimp po' boy (about three dozen shrimp in a hollowed-out po' boy loaf, soaked in spicy butter). It's also the surprise of serious daily specials such as "grilled crab cheese" and shish kabobs. It's the salads as well, huge and full of leafy greens (we like to negate the healthy aspects by topping ours with fried crawfish and green-onion dressing); vegetarians will be thrilled with the portobello mushroom version. Space is at a premium, so avoid noon-to-1pm-ish—lunchtime is especially popular with locals. Or sip a frigid schooner of beer while you wait.

1518 N. Lopez St. ✆ **504/218-7888.** Everything under $14. AE, DISC, MC, V. Mon–Sat 11am–7pm.

Parkway Bakery and Tavern ★★ LIGHT FARE A block or so off Bayou St. John, some enterprising, appreciative folks lovingly resurrected this long-boarded-up and once-much-beloved po' boy shop (circa-1922), and bakery. The bright interior and framed mementos still elicit flashbacks from old customers and deep pleasure in just about everyone. No innovations here, just classic po' boys (the falling-apart roast beef, which many believe to be the best in the city; the *sine non qua* fried oyster; and our go-to, the hot sausage and cheese topped with roast beef debris) and great sweet potato fries. The bar is a good hang as well, and you can walk off a meal strolling the pretty bayou after lunch. ***Note:*** Oysters were off the menu due to price spikes following the Gulf oil spill; we're told they'll be back in 2012, along with an expanded kitchen.

538 Hagan St. ✆ **504/482-3047.** www.parkwaybakeryandtavernnola.com. Everything under $13. AE, DISC, MC, V. Wed–Mon 11am–10pm. Closed Tues.

Willie Mae's Scotch House ★★ SOUL FOOD This is as much a fairy tale as a restaurant review. Once upon a time, not that many people outside her humble 6th Ward neighborhood thought much about Miss Willie Mae and the chicken shack attached to her home. Until 2005, that is, when the octogenarian and her secret-recipe fried chicken were designated an "American classic" by the James Beard Foundation. Weeks later, her home and restaurant were under 8 feet of water. Weeks after that, a dedicated group of volunteers, including local and regional restaurateurs, banded together to bring back Willie Mae's. (Their Herculean efforts are chronicled at www.southernfoodways.com.) Now fully restored, the place reminds us of how big a role the patina of time plays in the appeal of New Orleans, and how much sentiment plays into one's list of favorites. So—the most sublime fried chicken ever? When it's at its best, it's hard to figure out how to improve upon it (other than making it come out of the kitchen sooner—plan on a long wait). But of late it's been inconsistent and occasionally dry. Our backup plan is to also order the pork chops. There is no menu—just let your server recite the day's offerings, order at least one side of creamy butter beans, and wait as Miss Willie Mae's great-granddaughter, now in charge of the secret recipes, fries you up something. It's a reward for a beautiful effort of community, and hopefully for your stomach.

2401 St. Ann St. ✆ **504/822-9503.** Everything under $15. AE, DISC, MC. Mon–Fri 11am–3pm.

Ye Olde College Inn ★★ CREOLE/LIGHT FARE This is a 1930s hangout renovated into a nice, comfortable space, with a pretty, if simple, interior, smack between casual and classy. Murals and store signs from classic New Orleans haunts adorn the walls, and up front is an excellent, clean bar. The mammoth fried oyster or shrimp po' boy topped with bacon and havarti cheese is obscene (in a good way). We like the classic appetizer of fried oysters topped with blue cheese dressing. Seafood specials are usually quite fine, including a seasonal fried soft-shell-crab special on a crouton with sautéed spinach, a green onion aioli, and lump crabmeat. Other fave entrees include a comforting (and enormous) veal cutlet and a bacon-wrapped filet topped with sautéed mushrooms. And yes, the onion rings are as good as they look. ***Tip:*** Diners get $5 off the cover charge at Rock 'n' Bowl next door when visited on the same day. Ask your server. The normally attentive (and occasionally entertaining) service can be stretched when they're busy.

3016 Carrollton Ave. ✆ **504/866-3683.** www.collegeinn1933.com. Main courses $10–$20. DISC, MC, V. Tues–Sat 4–11pm.

CENTRAL BUSINESS DISTRICT & WAREHOUSE

For restaurants in this section, see the "New Orleans Restaurants" map on p. 116. *Note:* Lil' Dizzy's, reviewed above, has a branch in this area.

Very Expensive

Emeril's ★★★ CREOLE/NEW AMERICAN Emeril may be ubiquitous, but we can vouch for his first namesake restaurant. Although it may no longer be trendsetting, it certainly isn't resting on its laurels in terms of quality, a remarkable feat given how long the place has been around. Emeril's commitment to locally sourced and organic ingredients is firmly evident, the wine list is intelligent and broad, and this is still popular and exciting dining.

The menu changes often, but you can rely on, and should try, the barbecued shrimp, which comes with a heavier sauce than the classic versions of this local dish and is paired with charming little rosemary biscuits. The amusingly named "salad" of Abita root beer–glazed pork belly consists mostly of large slabs of the soft rich meat and is a must for carnivores in the crowd. Recent entree standouts include andouille-crusted redfish, a short-rib shepherd's pie, and panéed veal with mushrooms and sautéed sweetbreads. There can be some incredible specials on any given evening as well. Try to save part of your generously portioned meal for leftovers, so that you have room for the notable banana cream pie, a behemoth whose fat content doesn't bear thinking about, or perhaps more sanely, some delicate homemade sorbets.

800 Tchoupitoulas St. ☎ 504/528-9393. www.emerils.com. Reservations highly recommended at dinner. Main courses $15–$21 lunch, $26–$45 dinner; degustation by advance arrangement. AE, DC, DISC, MC, V. Daily 6–10pm; Mon–Fri 11:30am–2pm.

Emeril's Delmonico Restaurant and Bar ★★ CREOLE In theory this is Emeril's more traditionally Creole restaurant, but in reality it's a beautifully renovated space where we've had some mighty fine meals, and where you may or may not eat anything even remotely Creole, but you can get a beautiful dry aged strip steak. But as with Emeril's flagship restaurant (above), such interesting work is going on right now that you will find it hard to care. The menu changes regularly, but be sure to get a charcuterie plate to start; it comes beautifully laden with all sorts of house-made hams, salamis, and pâté. Small, medium, and large plates can consist of a duo of Moroccan-spiced lamb chops with *merquez* sausage, tarragon rabbit crepes, or a confit of duck leg. Like the rest of the menu, desserts are handsome and interesting.

1300 St. Charles Ave. ☎ 504/525-4937. www.emerils.com. Reservations highly recommended. Main courses $25–$45. AE, DC, DISC, MC, V. Sun–Thurs 6–9pm; Fri–Sat 6–10pm.

Restaurant August ★ FRENCH So there's chef John Besh, feeding streetloads of people in the dark post-Katrina days, helping to revive the venerable Willie Mae's Scotch House, planting, farming, and swearing not to source any ingredients from beyond 100 miles (well, 200 after the oil spill). Thus proving he's as much about local indigenous cooking as he is about fancy-pants frivolity. He wins a James Beard "Best Chef: Southeast" award, gets scads of other gourmet praise, garners near-ubiquity on the Food Network and in bookstores . . . and we still can't get too excited by August. We've tried, but we just don't get it. A little too foamy/gimmicky, perhaps, or too dainty/fussy, or too ingredient-intensive. Too *everything*, except flavor. In truth, we haven't had a bad meal here; we've just been underwhelmed. Still, reliable foodie friends dreamily recall a degustation menu (chef's choice that he varies from table to table) as a highlight of their dining lives, and others say the place is the best the city has to offer. We haven't given up—we'll try again, starting with the $20 prix-fixe lunch.

> ## Impressions
>
> *New Orleans is one place you can eat and drink the most, and suffer the least.*
> —**William Makepeace Thackeray**

301 Tchoupitoulas St. ☎ **504/299-9777.** www.restaurantaugust.com. Reservations recommended. 3-course lunch $20; main courses $27–$52; 4-course tasting menu $60 (wine pairing, add $30); 3-hr. degustation menu $95 per person, $145 with wine (whole table must participate). AE, DC, MC, V. Daily 5:30–10pm; Mon–Fri 11am–2pm.

Expensive

Café Adelaide ★★★ CONTEMPORARY CREOLE From the same branch of the Brennan family that brings you Commander's Palace, Café Adelaide doesn't seem to get the attention it deserves (perhaps because it's in a hotel?). But the talented chef consistently puts out playful menus with both substance and ingenuity. Small and shared plates allow the indecisive or groups to have sampling fun. The menu changes frequently but possibilities include shrimp and tasso "corn dogs," blue-crab pound cake with Port Salut icing, and *foie poutin* (potato-crusted onion rings with salted ricotta and black pepper foie gras gravy). But don't overlook the entrees, which are a bit more straightforward but rarely disappointing (ditto the white chocolate biscuit dessert). At breakfast they serve *pain perdu,* New Orleans's version of French toast. The **Swizzle Stick bar** is one of the better in town. As if all that isn't enough to lure you in, they usually have great lunch and dinner multicourse meal deals. We are fans.

300 Poydras St. (in the Loews Hotel). ☎ **504/595-3305.** www.cafeadelaide.com. Reservations suggested. Main courses $16–$19 lunch, $22–$38 dinner. AE, DC, DISC, MC, V. Mon–Fri 6:30–10:30am; Sat–Sun 6:30am–1:30pm; Mon–Thurs 11:30am–2pm; Fri 11:30am–2:30pm; Sun–Thurs 5:30–9pm; Fri–Sat 5:30–10pm. "Off hours" menu available at bar 11:30am–10:30pm.

Herbsaint ★★★ BISTRO Herbsaint has earned accolades and popularity contests since it opened its doors, including scooping up a 2007 James Beard "Best Chef: Southeast" award for chef Donald Link. It's understandable: Their gumbos and soups are consistent standouts that send us into rhapsodies, and the fresh, beautiful salads come delectably decorated with seasonal ingredients or lush extras like *burrata* cheese. Carnivores might weep over the splendor of the meticulous pork-belly preparation, roasted for 7 hours, or the pasta with *guanciale* and a fried poached egg. The desserts are often simple but of equally fine quality. All this keeps the small, window-lined room consistently jumping. A bistro menu served from 1:30 to 5pm features light entrees from both the lunch and dinner menus.

701 St. Charles Ave. ☎ **504/524-4114.** www.herbsaint.com. Reservations suggested for lunch and for 2 or more for dinner. Main courses $15–$18 lunch, $26–$34 dinner. AE, DC, DISC, MC, V. Mon–Fri 11:30am–1:30pm; Mon–Sat 5:30–10pm.

La Boca ★★★ STEAK Nobody goes to New Orleans for steak, but perhaps they should (this town gave us Ruth's Chris, after all). The intimate, cavernlike

La Boca is noted chef Adolfo Garcia's take on the Argentine steakhouse. You choose your weapon—first from the menu, then from an impressive array of knives proffered by the personable, helpful servers. Nothing went wrong here for us, and most things went very, very right. The *entraña fina* skirt steak, buttery American Kobe *terras* major, and *centra de entraña* 12-ounce hanger steak were standouts, each done to simple, charred perfection and bursting with beefiness. The fries, which undergo 3 days of preparation, are transcendent. The menu has other items, and they're probably fine, but steak and fries are all you need to know.

857 Fulton St. ✆ **504/525-8205.** www.labocasteaks.com. Reservations essential. Appetizers $8–$20; main courses $20–$36. AE, DISC, MC, V. Mon–Wed 6–10pm; Thurs–Sat 6pm–midnight.

LaCôte Brasserie ★ BISTRO The best feature of this restaurant in the Renaissance Arts Hotel is the whole-fish presentation. Almost no other place in town dares to serve an entire fish (local pompano, pan-roasted in a sweet ponzu sauce), head intact. For that matter, all fish options seem to fare pretty well here (many of them Cajun-inflected), as do the oysters. The second best thing is that it's somewhat sprawling, which means a table or seat at the oyster bar is almost always available.

In the Renaissance Arts Hotel, 700 Tchoupitoulas St. ✆ **504/613-2330.** www.lacotebrasserie. com. Reservations suggested. Lunch entrees $15–$22; dinner $24–$32. AE, DC, DISC, MC, V. Daily 6:30–11am; Mon–Sat 11:30am–2:30pm; Sun–Thurs 5:30–10:30pm; Fri–Sat 6–11pm; Sun brunch noon–2:30pm.

Le Foret ★★★ CONTEMPORARY FRENCH You'll find serious fine dining here, with New Orleans's traditional French influences as a launching pad for an ambitious updating. It largely succeeds, elegant on both the palate and the plate (meats more so than the seafood dishes, which were sometimes *too* subtle). The milky, window-laden room in a renovated 1800s building sets a traditional tone, although some diners were affected by unnervingly direct streetlight glare (it should be fixed by now). The winking *amuses-bouches* (plural—there were three!) reveal proprietor Danny Millan's local familiarity, having fronted some of the city's finest restaurants. In the fanciful Le Foret champignons appetizer, wild mushroom caps formed the "treetops" atop "trunks" of sliced foie gras pâté in a "forest" of greens. A roast loin of rabbit au jus dressed with herbs and white raisins worked marvelously. A lovely, caramelized milk soufflé was overpowered by the chocolate sauce—pour sparingly and eat the rest with a spoon, or opt for the intense rhubarb balsamic crisp. Service on one visit was either overly intrusive or not enough, but just fine another night.

129 Camp St. ✆ **504/553-6738.** www.leforetneworleans.com. Reservations suggested. Appetizers $11–$16; main courses $28–$33; 5-course tasting menu $60, $100 with wine. AE, DISC, MC, V. Sun–Thurs 5:30–10pm; Fri–Sat 5:30–10:30pm.

Meson 923 ★★★ MODERN INTERNATIONAL Barely a year after its opening, an upheaval saw the original chef leaving this notable startup and the sous chef stepping up. The fact that it's hardly skipped a beat speaks well for all involved, those here and gone. The refined cooking combines a thesaurus of pan-Continental, ultrafresh ingredients. It's distinctive, graceful, pricey—and often very good, as in the bliss-inspiring lobster hamachi *crudo,* sweet and spicy with pineapple and chili. The filet of beef *sous vide* with truffle sauce makes fine use of the trick, and the lush veal cheeks with mushrooms and jus on pappardelle were as comforting as a cashmere sweater—which we needed in the sleekly restored 1800s town house, dominated by a metallic chef's booth and glassed-in kitchen (the upstairs room is warmer and more subdued). Desserts are simpler but equally refined, like the signature, a silky coconut flan. There may be some overreaching here (though not in the wine list, which takes some surprising but ultimately rewarding leaps), but we'll take that over the opposite.

923 S. Peters St. ✆ **504/523-9200.** www.meson923.com. Reservations suggested. Appetizers and *crudo* $8–$16; main courses $19–$38. AE, DISC, MC, V. Tues–Thurs 5:30–9pm; Fri–Sat 5:30–10pm. Closed Sun–Mon.

MiLa ★ NOUVEAU SOUTHERN MiLa is a tad undersung: The cuisine is fresh in attitude and flavor, and while not head-bashingly bold, it's certainly skillful enough to garner more attention than it seems to get. Run by a married chef couple (the name reflects their Mississippi and Louisiana roots, respectively), the restaurant serves a daily menu largely dependent on what's available from a farm that grows exclusively for them. Recently, trigger-fish with saffron-infused couscous in a Meyer lemon reduction was quite gorgeous, an asparagus velouté was cloud-light, and black grouper was porcini dusted and coffee glazed. The service is better when it's busy—otherwise it can be distracted—and the room is slightly anachronistic. Located in the Renaissance Pere Marquette hotel, it's a bit cool. Things get busier at lunch—perhaps because it's in the business district or because of the $20 three-course deal. That's a good time to go.

817 Common St. (in the Renaissance Pere Marquette hotel). ✆ **504/412-2580.** www.milanew orleans.com. Reservations suggested. Main courses $17–$20 lunch, $19–$36 dinner; seasonal tasting menu $65, $100 with wine pairings. AE, DC, DISC, MC, V. Mon–Fri 11:30am–2:30pm and 5:30–10pm; Sat 6:30am–12pm and 5:30–10pm; Sun 6:30am–midnight.

Palace Café ★★ CONTEMPORARY CREOLE This is where to go for accessible, low-key, and nonintimidating dining that's still reasonably interesting. Housed attractively in the historic Werlein's for Music building, this popular Brennan-family restaurant has sidewalk dining on Canal, a treat on balmy nights, even if you just opt for the sweet 5 After 5 deal ($5 small plates and drinks). The menu focuses on evolving Creole cuisine and seasonal availability. The crabmeat cheesecake appetizer (a table-poundingly good dish) is a must-have. As for main courses, they do fish especially well (the andouille-crusted fish is always spot-on) and anything with the house-made duck pastrami will probably rock. The pork debris potpie is adorable comfort food. For dessert, they invented the by-now-ubiquitous white-chocolate bread pudding, and no matter what others may claim, they have the best, and they've finally brought back the Mississippi mud pie: five layers of chocolate mousse, from lightest to darkest, on a chocolate cookie-crumb crust. Lawdy.

605 Canal St. ✆ **504/523-1661.** www.palacecafe.com. Reservations recommended. Main courses $13–$18 lunch, $23–$34 dinner, $13–$20 brunch; 3-course meal before 7pm $28. AE, DC, DISC, MC, V. Mon–Sat 11:30am–2:30pm and 5:30–10pm; Sun brunch 10:30am–2:30pm.

Moderate

A Mano ★★ ITALIAN This is not "yo mama 'n dems'" Italian. That is, you won't find the traditional Creole Italian red gravy here (aka old-school tomato sauce—not that there's anything wrong with that). This is James Beard "Best Chef" nominee Adolfo Garcia's Italian. He and his talented partner Joshua Smith show their ingenuity and dedication to the freshest of fresh with ingredients plucked from their own plot at nearby Hollygrove farm. The result: lovely pastas, like *buccatini all'Amatriciana* with a hint of heat and kissably tender; sweet pork jowls; and a succulent roast rabbit with olives. The salumi is surely one of the best in a town of some mighty fine meat curers (the duck prosciutto is not to be missed). The house mixologists and *vino* list are equally inventive (showing some surprisingly affordable yet still vibrant Southern Italian options). We've found the service in the lively brick room a bit inconsistent, never bad per se, but sometimes fine, sometimes lackluster.

830 Tchoupitoulas St. ✆ **504/208-9280.** www.amanonola.com. Reservations recommended. Main courses $16–$24. AE, DC, DISC, MC, V. Fri 11:30am–2:30pm; Mon–Sat 6–10pm.

American Sector ★★ ☺ AMERICAN Two words: Corn. Dog. We're serious. The single best corn dog in America, at least in our experience, is housemade here. Taking his cue from the restaurant's locale inside the National WWII Museum, chef John Besh puts an updated riff on retro comfort foods. The generous chicken-fried steak and the truly messy sloppy joe sandwich—the latter loaded with shredded short ribs and fried onions—are both hearty winners, the overstuffed house-cured bologna sandwich, less so. Presentation is equally playful. Goods arrive in mason jars, cast-iron kettles, tin cans, and lunch pails, garnished with toy soldiers. Kids small and large will love the quart-size spritzer bottle of soda, mixed to order from homemade syrups, but there are fine adult beverages, too. Opt for the bananas Foster malted milk (hubba hubba) in lieu of so-so desserts. Given the prices, it's a downright reasonable way to experience the Besh touch, albeit his less serious side.

945 Magazine St. (in the National WWII Museum). ✆ **504/528-1940.** http://nationalww2 museum.org/american-sector. Sandwiches $10–$13; main courses $14–$26; sides and desserts $2.50–$7. AE, DISC, MC, V. Sun–Thurs 11am–9pm; Fri–Sat 11am–11pm. Museum admission not required for restaurant access.

Cochon ★★ CAJUN All hail Cochon chef Stephen Stryjewski, 2011 James Beard "Best Chef: South" award winner. We do believe he fires on porcine synapses, as he has an effortless way with all things pork. Those seeking a nouveau-Cajun experience will, like us, want more dishes like the garlicky *cochon* (pork that is pulled, then pan seared) with cracklins, the pork *rillette,* the ribs with watermelon pickle, and okay, the rabbit and dumplings. We also want bigger portions (yes, even the "small plates"), because the mouthfuls you get are so darn good. Then again, it's good to have room left for the lemon-buttermilk pie or its banana cream sibling. Ordering a mix-and-match slew of small plates here might just make you squeal with delight. We recommend it.

930 Tchoupitoulas St. ✆ **504/588-2123.** www.cochonrestaurant.com. Reservations strongly recommended. Small plates $8–$11; main courses $14–$24. AE, DISC, MC, V. Mon–Fri 11am–10pm; Sat 5:30–10pm.

Domenica ★★ 🗲 ITALIAN Walls the color of bittersweet chocolate, soaring ceilings, glossy glass surfaces, and even a communal table make up the atmosphere at this keen but over-the-top John Besh eatery in the Roosevelt Hotel. It's a good thing the pizzas are near perfection, with just-crisp-enough crusts, creamery mozzarella, and toppings farmed or cured with love. We want to marry these pizzas, but we'd cheat on them with the house-cured salumi (the smoky speck! the luscious lardo!) or pastas, some as wide as a tie. Antipasti and primi come small or large, so you can get the goat cheese–stuffed squash blossoms, the citrusy-sweet octopus carpaccio, and the puffy wonders of gnocchi, and still have room for the simple, moist whole roasted redfish (all seasonal items). The reasonable prices belie chef Alon Shaya's quality cuisine: His studies in Italy are our gain, down to the silken hazelnut chocolate *budino*. The small bar only fuels the noise level, serving well-crafted cocktails, well-priced boutique Italian wines, and homemade cellos that have drawn their own following. Service can be inconsistent, ranging from knowledgeable to perfunctory to disorderly.

123 Baronne St. (in the Roosevelt Hotel). ⓒ **504/648-6020.** www.domenicarestaurant.com. Reservations recommended. Pizza $13; antipasti $6–$16; lunch panini $10–$14; main courses $9–$30 dinner, $10–$12 lunch. AE, DISC, MC, V. Daily 11am–11pm.

Drago's ★★ SEAFOOD Drago's is located in the utterly unatmospheric, cavernous lobby of the Hilton Convention Center. But you come here for one thing, and it ain't ambience. It's charbroiled oysters, the eighth wonder of the modern world. Buttery, garlicky, Parmesan-y, and charred over an open flame, they're now served all over town, but as the originator, Drago's still does them best. We suppose the inexpensive Maine lobsters are also worth mentioning. Okay, we mentioned them. Now back to the oysters. The sprawling space manages to fill up, and they don't take reservations, so a wait is possible. Just don't arrive too hungry—the scent of oysters on the grill might just drive you to drink. Fortunately, there's a bar.

2 Poydras St. (in the Hilton Riverside). ⓒ **504/584-3911.** Also 3232 N. Arnoult Rd., Metairie. ⓒ **504/888-9254.** www.dragosrestaurant.com. No reservations. Charbroiled oysters $18 per dozen; dinner appetizers $7–$14; main courses $17–$26. AE, DISC, MC, V. Mon–Sat 11am–10pm.

Lüke ★★ ⓕ BISTRO This bistro from much-lauded chef John Besh, the local locavore, serves hearty, authentic, but not stodgy French and German brasserie fare. The quality on our last visit had slipped from our first ones, but there's still much to recommend. For a splurge, get the stunning grande plateau du mer, a multitiered riot of raw seafood ($85), and keep the wine flowing. *Flamen küche* is a swoony Alsatian tort topped with chunks of bacon and caramelized onions. The *choucroûte garnie* includes house-made sausages, bratwurst, and slow-cooked Berkshire pork shin, plus an optional *cochon de lait* (suckling pig) for $4 more. We're awfully fond of the big, juicy cheeseburger, with caramelized onions and thick-cut bacon on an onion roll. The shrimp and (organic) grits demolishes other, drier versions around town. The handsome bistro is quite popular at lunch, where a $15 express lunch special includes a hearty entree of the day plus a cup of soup. Desserts aren't much (hey, more room for pig). Service on our last visit was a bit spotty, but we'll put up with that for the quality and reasonable costs.

333 St. Charles Ave. ⓒ **504/378-2840.** www.lukeneworleans.com. Reservations strongly suggested at lunch and dinner. Main courses $11–$25; express dinner menu $23; express lunch menu $15. AE, DC, DISC, MC, V. Daily 7am–11pm.

Tommy's Cuisine ★★ FRENCH/ITALIAN Tommy's garnered an immediate following after breaking away from the legendary Irene's in the Quarter, as it served many of the same revered Creole Italian dishes. It still does, including the fantastic chicken Rosemarino, marinated in olive oil, garlic, and rosemary, and the duck Tchoupitoulas, which some consider the best duck dish in New Orleans. But Tommy also brought with him some traditional ideas (and some heavy sauces) from his prior days in some fine local kitchens (the Sazerac Restaurant, Galatoire's). The simplest ones fare best, like veal Marsala, and a shrimp linguine that was glorious thanks to the stellar local crustacean. We like to retire to the hopping wine bar next door for an after-dinner glass on weekends, when the piano holds sway.

746 Tchoupitoulas St. ✆ **504/581-1103.** www.tommyscuisine.com. Reservations preferred. Business casual. Main courses $20–$29. AE, DISC, MC, V. Sun–Thurs 5:30-10pm; Fri–Sat 5:30-11pm.

Inexpensive

Cochon Butcher ★★★ 🔥 CONTEMPORARY CAJUN If Donald Link and Stephen Stryjewski's Cochon are the head cheerleaders of updated Cajun cuisine, Butcher is the cooler little sister with the punk haircut. And we're its BFF. The deli-style storefront has just a few bar-height tables but plenty of excellent house-smoked meats and sausages, served as small plates or in sandwiches, and a few choice wines by the glass. You can't go wrong with a charcuterie plate and a selection of cheeses or their killer version of a muffuletta, which combines some of those ingredients. A pretty authentic *boudin* sausage link, a side of pancetta mac 'n' cheese, and some vinegary marinated Brussels sprouts make for an ideal quick bite before visiting the nearby museums (or after, to take advantage of happy-hour specials).

930 Tchoupitoulas St. ✆ **504/588-PORK** (588-7675). www.cochonbutcher.com. Sandwiches $7–$12; charcuterie plate $14; sides and bar food $3–$6. AE, DISC, MC, V. Mon–Thurs 10am–10pm; Fri–Sat 10am–11pm; Sun 10am–4pm.

Ernst Café AMERICAN The same family has owned this old brick building since 1902. Located right next to Harrah's casino and featuring live blues music some weekend nights, it draws a local scene, understandable given how late they stay open. It's good for drinks and sandwiches, salads, hamburgers, fried fish, red beans and rice, and the like.

600 S. Peters St. ✆ **504/525-8544.** www.ernstcafe.net. Main courses $8–$18. AE, DC, DISC, MC, V. Mon 3–10pm; Tues 11am–10pm; Wed–Sat 11am–4am; Sun 11am–10pm.

Mother's ★★ CREOLE/LIGHT FARE When the cardiologists hold their annual convention in New Orleans, they come to pay homage to Mother's. Their overstuffed, mountain-size po' boys have surely supported their livelihoods. Mother's has long lines (that move quickly) and a most typically humble New Orleans atmosphere, but who cares when faced with a Famous Ferdi Special—a giant roll filled with baked ham (the homemade house specialty), roast beef, gravy, and debris. There's homemade sausage, traditional Creole dishes, and really good breakfasts, but the po' boys are what you go for. Mother's is within walking distance of the Louisiana Superdome and a number of major hotels.

401 Poydras St. ✆ **504/523-9656.** www.mothersrestaurant.net. Menu items $4–$25. AE, DISC, MC, V. Mon–Sat 7:30am–10pm.

UPTOWN/THE GARDEN DISTRICT

For a map of restaurants in this section, see either the "New Orleans Restaurants" map on p. 116 or the "Uptown Hotels & Restaurants" map on p. 107.

Expensive

Brigtsen's ★ CAJUN/CREOLE Nestled in a converted 19th-century house at the Riverbend, Brigtsen's is warm, intimate, and romantic. The individual dining rooms are small and cozy, each sweetly painted with murals, and the menu changes daily. It's not cutting-edge local cuisine, just consistently good. Generous portions make appetizers superfluous, but the seasonal salads (produce, like much of everything, is local) and the BBQ shrimp with shrimp *calas* are hard to pass up. Brigtsen has a special touch with rabbit: The appetizer of rabbit tenderloin on a tasso-Parmesan grits cake with sautéed spinach and Creole mustard sauce is mouthwatering. You can't miss with any of the soups, and a broiled Gulf fish with crabmeat Parmesan crust and béarnaise sauce is a great piece of seafood. Roast duck with dried cherry sauce is always reliable, with the skin of the duck done to a cracklin' just-rightness. A perennial favorite.

723 Dante St. ✆ **504/861-7610.** www.brigtsens.com. Reservations recommended. Main courses $26–$38. AE, DC, DISC, MC, V. Tues–Sat 5:30–10pm.

Clancy's ★ CREOLE Your friendly cabdriver may insist that Clancy's is "out of town" because this local favorite is so far uptown; he'll also be impressed that you know about it. It's worth the trip to get a bit off the tourist path. The locals who cram into the smallish, oh-so–New Orleans room nightly are a loyal bunch, but our last meal at Clancy's was only average and quite forgettable. We may have hit it on a bad night, or failed to follow the locals' lead and order the night's specials (though the duck dish on the menu is as good as duck gets). You could try the fried oysters with brie appetizer; the smoked, fried soft-shell Louisiana lake-raised crab topped with crabmeat (smoke flavor not overpowering, crab perfectly fried without a drop of grease to taint the dish); or veal topped with crabmeat and béarnaise sauce. Food too heavy? What the heck—you might as well get the lemon icebox pie. Better than grandma's!

6100 Annunciation St. ✆ **504/895-1111.** Reservations recommended. Main courses $25–$32. AE, DC, DISC, MC, V. Mon–Sat 5:30–10:30pm; Thurs–Fri 11:30am–2pm.

 Anythin' Flamin'

Once upon a time, while waiting for Casamento's doors to open and just moments from an oyster loaf, three youngish tourist gals struck up a chat (as happens nearly automatically in New Orleans) with three Uptown ladies-of-a-certain-age ahead of them. They were St. Charles–born and –bred, dined at Casamento's weekly, and offered us NOLA newbies some well-tested tips. This one still sticks (and sounds best when read with a high-pitched, breathy lilt): "You simply *must* go to any of the fine, old French restaurants, and when you do, why you just order anythin' flamin'." Meaning, go to Antoine's, Arnaud's, Commander's Palace, or Galatoire's, and get the bananas Foster, *café brûlot,* cherries jubilee, or anything prepared tableside and involving conflagration. Naturally we bought the ladies a round, and to this day we're still following their fine advice and living by the "anythin' flamin'" mantra: Indulge a bit, relish fun, and while there's no need to embrace drama in all aspects of life, when it comes to dessert, by all means do.

Commander's Palace ★★★ CREOLE The much-beloved Commander's is perhaps *the* symbol of the New Orleans dining scene, and for good reason. The building has been a restaurant for a century, it's at the top of the multibranched Brennan family restaurant tree, and its chefs have gone on to their own fame (Prudhomme and Emeril ring any bells?), plus they mentor their own outstanding local staff to keep the tradition going. Its decor is a subtle wonder—check out the hand-embroidered wallpaper in the entry hall, the display of painted wooden birds in the main dining room, and the excellent chandeliers—exemplifying the elegant but whimsical atmosphere that inevitably flavor an evening here. Dinner is always good, and it's often superlative, as is the wine list (not to mention lunch and brunch, lower-priced options well worth considering—if only for the 25¢ martinis!). The current menu reflects chef Tory McPhail's constantly working imagination and his commitment to locally grown and sourced ingredients. To really experience his talents, spring for the seven-course "Chef's Playground" tasting menu. The James Beard nominee turns out favorites like the pecan-crusted Gulf fish and the tasso shrimp in pepper jelly appetizer, along with all sorts of new culinary fun. A standout appetizer is the foie gras "Du Monde," seared foie gras atop a berry-flavored beignet paired with a chicory-flavored foie gras *café,* a rich salute to the venerable Café du Monde. It's ridiculous and delicious. The traditional gumbo can be a titch salty for our palate, but the daily gumbo variation often features delightfully unexpected ingredients. The menu changes frequently, but the fresh seafood and seasonal specialties never disappoint; on our last visit we were bowled over by the Creole mustard-crusted sliced rack of lamb. Your waitperson will tell you to order the bread pudding soufflé. Do so. And the Creole cream cheesecake, too, though the signature crème brûlée is a thin sheath of burnt yummy. Then again, bananas Foster flambéed tableside will put an exclamation point on your evening.

1403 Washington Ave. ☏ **504/899-8221.** www.commanderspalace.com. Reservations essential. No shorts or T-shirts; jackets preferred for men at dinner. Main courses $30–$42; tasting menu $80, $122 with wine; 3-course dinner $34–$44. 25¢ martinis Mon–Fri lunch only. AE, DISC, MC, V. Mon–Fri 11:30am–1:30pm; daily 6–9:30pm; brunch Sat 11:30am–1pm and Sun 10:30am–1:30pm. Summer hours June 1–Sept 1, dinner begins at 6:30pm and brunch ends at 1pm. Closed Dec 25 and Mardi Gras Day.

Coquette ★★★ BISTRO Things to love about Coquette: the cocktail menu, one of the best in a city that knows its drinks; upstairs, Bill Hemmerling's lovely folk paintings; the $20 three-course lunch, an almost ridiculously good deal (with options like tangy oysters roasted with fennel and bacon or buttery crawfish tails and asparagus over pasta); the $40 four-course dinner, ibid; the little kick delivered by the peppery, crispy, fried quail salad; understated seasonings—not bland, just mellow, the better to savor the super-fresh ingredients; chilling with the locals dining at the mahogany bar; the crab and asparagus soup, which we make at home but nothing like this oh-so-nuanced version; being enveloped in brick, wood, and tin; a perfect hanger steak; that the scallop preparation differs every time we're here (the entire menu is pretty fluid, actually). So very much to love. The main room is small and tables are set close, so do make reservations and bring your loud restaurant voice.

2800 Magazine St. ☏ **504/265-0421.** www.coquette-nola.com. Reservations recommended. 3-course lunch $20; lunch entrees $15–$22; 4-course dinner $40; dinner entrees $23–$27. AE, DC, DISC, MC, V. Wed–Sat 11:30am–3pm; daily 5:30–10pm.

Gautreau's ★★ FRENCH Tucked away in a residential Uptown neighborhood, with no signage to speak of, is this favorite local hideaway. Here you'll enjoy the star-level offerings of chef Sue Zemanick (*Top Chef Masters* contestant; named one of 2008's "Top 10 Chefs in America" by *Food & Wine* magazine). Popular for its elegant, understated decor and unimposing service, it's once again bringing in customers through its food. The richly restored apothecary shelves, original to the location and stocked with a classic wine and aperitif selection, surround the trompe l'oeil walls by well-known French muralist Grahame Ménage.

The talented chef changes the menu regularly, and not everything is a hit. But winning recent options included sea scallops with parsley oil, veal *glacé*, and crisp tender cauliflower (local, as are other veggies). Macadamia-crusted halibut with spaetzle, English peas, and champagne beurre blanc finds four different culinary cultures working harmoniously together, which speaks to the skill of this young chef. The bacon-wrapped pork tenderloin with tomato confit and arugula warmly satisfies, while a special of blood orange–glazed duck breast with honey-thyme jus was rich and sultry without being too heavy. A welcome departure from the usual New Orleans dessert offerings is a silky cheesecake flan with balsamic and basil-macerated strawberries.

1728 Soniat St. ✆ **504/899-7397.** www.gautreausrestaurant.com. Reservations advised. Main courses $25–$35. AE, MC, V. Mon–Sat 6–10pm.

Martinique Bistro ★ FRENCH This place is just far enough uptown to be off the regular tourist radar. Because it has only 44 seats when the romantic, jasmine-scented courtyard is not open (100 with), make reservations. It's a sweet little bistro, a local favorite, turning out bright, lovely French/Mediterranean–influenced dishes like sautéed escargot in a Roquefort gratiné, and light-handed scallops with pea shoots and bowfin caviar. A flank steak had the tenderness and robust flavor of venison, so much so that a diner wondered if it might really be so. It makes a lovely girlfriends' lunch spot, too.

5908 Magazine St. ✆ **504/891-8495.** www.martiniquebistro.com. Reservations recommended. Main courses $11–$18 lunch; dinner $20–$28. AE, DISC, MC, V. Nov–May Fri–Sun 11am–2:30pm, Tues–Thurs 5:30–9:30pm, Fri–Sat 5:30–10pm, Sun 5:30–9:30pm; June–Oct open for dinner half an hour later.

Patois ★ CONTEMPORARY CREOLE A very sweet setting in an old house on a residential street, and equally sweet, if not culinarily head-spinning food make this just a fine choice for a delightful Uptown meal or brunch, highlighting local seafood, produce, and cheese sources. Braised pork belly comes with scallops, while seasonal tuna carpaccio is topped with a ginger and orange-blossom vinaigrette. The grilled hanger steak, in a rich red-wine bone marrow reduction, is really quite excellent, while the roasted duck breast with a bacon-potato-apple hash is precisely done. Desserts show twists on standard local offerings; sample one or two.

6078 Laurel St. ✆ **504/895-9441.** http://patoisnola.com. Reservations recommended. Main courses $21–$27 dinner, $12–$22 lunch. AE, MC, V. Wed–Thurs 5:30–10pm; Fri 11:30am–2pm and 5:30–10:30pm; Sat 5:30–10:30pm; Sun 10:30am–2:30pm.

Upperline ★★★ CONTEMPORARY CREOLE In a small, charming house in a largely residential area, Upperline eschews the high-profile route (unless you count appearances on *Treme* and *The Best Thing I Ever Ate*), but it's a great place to try imaginative food at reasonable (by fancy-restaurant standards) prices, and we're excited to see what a new chef (on board in mid-2011) brings to the table. The friendly attitude of owner JoAnn Clevenger and staff helps make an Upperline dinner such a pleasant one: They actually—gasp!—recommend dishes at *other* restaurants (you can be so generous when your own offerings are so strong). Standout appetizers include fried green tomatoes with shrimp rémoulade sauce (they invented this oft-copied dish), spicy shrimp on jalapeño corn bread, seasonal duck confit, and fried sweetbreads. For entrees, there's moist roast duck with a tingly sauce (the aforementioned "Best Thing"—either ginger peach or port wine), Cane River Country shrimp, and a fall-off-the-bone lamb shank. For dessert, it's the warm honey-pecan bread pudding. June and July bring the all-garlic menu, in which even desserts contain garlic. The award-winning wine list focuses primarily on California selections.

1413 Upperline St. ✆ **504/891-9822.** www.upperline.com. Reservations suggested. Main courses $20–$30; 3-course prix-fixe menu $40. AE, DC, MC, V. Wed–Sun 5:30–9:30pm.

Moderate

Boucherie ★★★ 🍴 CONTEMPORARY SOUTHERN If you're on the way to a show at the Maple Leaf or Carrollton Station, consider this sweet neighborhood bistro in your preclub plans. Even if you're not going to a show, it's still well worth the detour. Chef Nathan Zimet's purple catering truck used to nourish Tipitina's throngs with mobile munchies exceeding all expectations. At Boucherie, they've parlayed that success into so much goodness that you could essentially close your eyes, point at the food or cocktail menus, and be thrilled with whatever's presented (and since the menu changes frequently, you might as well). But if the perfectly seared, sliced praline foie gras with a sweet-potato biscuit is on the menu, do not skip it, nor should you miss the duck confit with Steen's cane syrup and blue cheese. Oddly, we think their signature *boudin* balls *are* skippable; the pulled pork cake is a better piggy option (they cure and smoke all their meats). The Krispy Kreme bread pudding shames Paula Dean's, and the bacon brownie is, well, a BACON BROWNIE!

8115 Jeannette St. ✆ **504/862-5514.** www.boucherie-nola.com. Reservations recommended. Dinner small plates $6–$12; large plates $11–$15. AE, DISC, MC, V. Tues–Sat 11am–3pm and 5:30–9:30pm.

Dante's Kitchen ★★ CONTEMPORARY CREOLE Dante's is too easily overlooked, thanks to its left-of-center location and relatively low profile, but locals give it steady business (and really, it's just at the end of the St. Charles streetcar line). With its lively take on New Orleans cuisine, careful eye toward seasonal and local products, and cheerful "this old house" interior and enthusiastic staff, it's worthy of greater fame. At dinner, look for redfish "on the half shell" and a house-made charcuterie plate that might include goose *rillette* with caper berries. Brunch is a strong alternative, especially given the kitchen's splendid way with eggs Benedict: Tender rosemary-crusted pork takes the place of the traditional Canadian bacon, a hint of honey adds sweetness to the hollandaise sauce, and a caramelized biscuit supports it all. A fat ham-and-runny-brie sandwich is much better than any generic deli version of same, and the grits are perfect. So, too, are the drinks, in particular the seasonal fruit rum punch during watermelon season. Not just another standard-issue New Orleans restaurant.

736 Dante St. ✆ **504/861-3121.** http://danteskitchen.com. Dinner reservations recommended (not accepted for lunch). Main courses $10–$16 brunch, $20–$26 dinner. AE, DISC, MC, V. Mon and Wed–Sun 5:30–10pm; Sat–Sun brunch 10:30am–2pm. Closed Tues.

Dick & Jenny's ★★ CREOLE The room is small, and the wait may be long (especially before a show at neighbor Tipitina's), but this casual boho-atmosphere restaurant is a good choice on any night, despite its out-of-the-way location. The menu changes often, but recent examples include an excellent summer fruit soup; solidly good spinach, mushroom, and mascarpone ravioli; blackened red-fish with crawfish rice; and pan-seared scallops with shrimp and sausage pie and smoked tomato beurre. Portions are generous but each dish is a little busy—just one less layer on everything would help. Desserts include clever variations on classics; lunch brings sandwiches, salads, and lower prices.

4501 Tchoupitoulas St. ℂ **504/894-9880.** http://dickandjennys.com. Reservations for parties of 5 or more. Main courses $9–$18 lunch, $16–$28 dinner. AE, DISC, MC, V. Mon–Thurs 5:30–10pm; Fri–Sat 5:30–10:30pm; Tues–Fri 11am–2pm.

Dominique's on Magazine ★★★ BISTRO/INTERNATIONAL Magazine Street exudes character-infused bistros in converted cottages where you can dine on well-constructed, locally sourced contemporary cuisine (woe to us who must choose). Worldliness makes this newcomer shine: The mature yet adventurous cuisine yields gently surprising flavor profiles, attesting to Dominique's years in some of the city's best kitchens and his African-French-Louisiana roots, respectively. Fennel-cured pork belly comes stacked atop spiked watermelon cubes, small but splendid; a crab and mango salad is generous and bright. The lamb and leek roulade is seasoned to perfection (so we forgive its slight toughness); the dreamy duck breast, with an ultracreamy parsnip purée, shows off its maple-y goodness beneath a blood orange jus. Skip the style-over-substance "chocolate bar" for the tangy, silken lemon grass pannacotta or goat cheesecake (with table-side honeycomb service!). You want to settle in to the soft warmth of this smart, uncluttered room, watch the candles burn down, and let the evening flow over you—the superb bar and wine programs don't hurt.

4729 Magazine St. ℂ **504/894-8881.** www.dominiquesonmag.com. Reservations suggested. Main courses $23–$26. AE, DISC, MC, V. Tues–Sat 5:30–10:30pm.

Jacques-Imo's ★ CREOLE/SOUL FOOD We used to be really big fans of this local favorite, a funky, colorful neighborhood joint next door to the **Maple Leaf** (p. 287) that the natives love. But the last few times we ate here, the food wasn't worth the wait, which can be absurdly long. So stick to the fried chicken (from a recipe from the late Austin Leslie, of Chez Helene and *Frank's Place* fame), or the catfish stuffed with crabmeat, or the solidly good shrimp Creole. Proceed with caution when it comes to the shrimp and alligator-sausage "cheese-cake" (more like a quiche), which has both its fans and detractors, while lovers of chicken livers will certainly want this version, on toast in a dark brown sauce. Try the three-layer chocolate (white, milk, and dark) mousse pie for dessert. Get there early to avoid the line.

8324 Oak St. ℂ **504/861-0886.** www.jacquesimoscafe.com. Reservations for 5 or more required. Main courses $19–$37. AE, DC, DISC, MC, V. Mon–Thurs 5–10pm; Fri–Sat 5–10:30pm.

La Crêpe Nanou ★ FRENCH La Crêpe Nanou is another not-so-secret local secret. The always-crowded, romantic spot (windows angled into the ceiling let you gaze at the stars) is simultaneously 19th century and quite modern. You can order crepes wrapped around a variety of stuffings, including crawfish. But you might want to save your crepe consumption for dessert (big and messy, full of chocolate and whipped cream) and concentrate instead on the robust salads;

moist, flaky whole grilled fish with herbs; or garlicky mussels (get extra bread to sop up the white-wine sauce). Meat dishes come with your choice of sauce (garlic or cognac, for example).

1410 Robert St. ℂ **504/899-2670.** www.lacrepenanou.com. Main courses $10–$24. MC, V. Mon–Thurs 6–10pm; Fri–Sat 6–11pm. Closed New Year's Day.

La Petite Grocery ★★ BISTRO Among the many bistros along Magazine Street, this way-Uptown standard-bearer found its footing long ago, settling into a reliably good, comfortably welcoming groove. It's just consistently lovely. Local ingredients and keen technique hold sway at La Petite Grocery, French more in name than in menu (though the excellent wine list leans that way). Like a sheep's milk gnudi in a rustic pork cheek ragout, or the tangy crab and roast beet salad. Steak tartare fans should try the version here, perhaps the best in the city; ditto the beautifully bronzed, crisp panéed rabbit. Best, perhaps, are the specials, like a plush turnip and radish soup, fragrant with truffle oil, or a softly savory crawfish pirogi. Desserts may be a bit overly sweet, but sometimes that's just right for lingering over a tawny port. Take time to check out the photos of the original grocery, and savor the room. It's not showy, just secure and stylish—like any proper Frenchwoman.

4238 Magazine St. ℂ **504/891-3377.** www.lapetitegrocery.com. Reservations highly recommended on weekends. Main courses $9–$14 lunch, $15–$28 dinner. AE, DC, MC, V. Tues–Sat 11:30am–2:30pm and 6–10:30pm.

Lilette ★★ BISTRO Lilette's chef-owner John Harris, a 2009 James Beard "Best Chef: South" nominee, trained locally under Bayona's Susan Spicer, who sent him to work in France with Michelin-starred chefs. The result is a menu of arty playfulness, which wears its Frenchiness on its sleeve. Filled with locals, the fashionable, high-ceilinged space would not look out of place in Tribeca. The business crowd knows the lunch menu is the best deal going. A simple roasted chicken breast with caramelized, balsamic-marinated onions topped with velvety mushroom sauce succeeded handily, but braised pork belly was heavy rather than satisfyingly rich. Braciola with cheesy polenta and the classic bouillabaisse were just right. Don't miss the curious signature dessert, little rounds of goat-cheese crème fraîche delicately paired with pears poached in vanilla-bean and raisin-flavored liquid, and topped with pistachios and lavender honey—a marriage made on Mount Olympus.

3637 Magazine St. ℂ **504/895-1636.** www.liletterestaurant.com. Reservations suggested. Main courses $10–$24 lunch, $22–$37 dinner. AE, DISC, MC, V. Tues–Sat 11:30am–2pm; Tues–Thurs 5:30–9:30pm; Fri–Sat 5:30–10:30pm.

Pascal's Manale ★ ITALIAN/STEAK/SEAFOOD Barbecued shrimp: This restaurant has built its reputation on that one dish, and you should come here if only to marvel at the colossal buttery crustaceans. Not to mention the oyster shuckers, whose repartee is as skilled as their shucking (and the bivalves are top-notch, too). The place is crowded, noisy, verging on expensive—but it's real hearty, traditional N'Awlins fare, in a hearty, traditional N'Awlins setting. Which is all good—as long as you don't expect anything more. Do top your turtle soup with sherry, and skip the dull and even possibly icky desserts. Instead, get another order of shrimp, don't think about your arteries, and vow to walk your socks off tomorrow.

1838 Napoleon Ave. ℂ **504/895-4877.** Reservations recommended. Main courses $17–$34. AE, DC, DISC, MC, V. Mon–Fri 11:30am–2pm; Mon–Sat 5pm–"until."

Inexpensive

Camellia Grill ★★ ☺ DINER/HAMBURGERS/LIGHT FARE Even though it's *only* been a part of the city's food culture since 1946, the Camellia Grill seems to have always been there. Consequently, when it was closed after the floods, locals plastered the front door with notes begging the place to return. It did, with a new owner who rehired all the same white-jacketed waiters (some there for decades), still calling their orders to the line as they regale you with banter. And just because you're sitting on a stool at a counter doesn't mean you can't dine on white linen. There's often a (worth it) wait for these perfect, simple burgers (try the patty melt) and Camellia's famously huge omelets, which are simultaneously heavy and fluffy. Don't forget the pecan waffle, a work of art. Wash it all down with one of the famous chocolate freezes and then contemplate a slice of the to-die-for pecan pie for dessert. And those notes stuck to the front door? Look closely at the framed flower artwork on the right-hand wall.

626 S. Carrollton Ave. ✆ **504/309-2679.** All items under $10. AE, DISC, MC, V. Sun–Thurs 8am–midnight; Fri–Sat 8am–2am. Also see p. 130 for French Quarter location.

Casamento's ★★ SEAFOOD Probably the best "erster" joint in the city, this family restaurant takes oysters so seriously that it simply closes down when they're not in season. The oysters are scrubbed clean and well selected. You might also take the plunge and order an oyster loaf: a big, fat loaf of bread fried in butter, filled with oysters (or shrimp), and fried again to seal it. Casamento's has terrific gumbo as well.

4330 Magazine St. ✆ **504/895-9761.** www.casamentosrestaurant.com. Main courses $4.95–$15, market price on some items. No credit cards. Wed–Sun 11am–2pm; Thurs–Sat 5:30–9pm. Closed June to mid-Sept.

Franky & Johnny's ★ SEAFOOD This is a favorite local hole-in-the-wall neighborhood joint with either zero or off-the-charts atmosphere, depending on how you view these things. And by "things" we mean plastic checked tablecloths, a ratty but friendly bar, and locals eating enormous soft-shell-crab po' boys with the crab legs hanging out of the bread and their mouths. You got your po' boys, your boiled or fried (local) seafood platters with two kinds of salad, and, goodness knows, you got your beer. Try that po' boy or the excellent red beans and rice with smoky sausage and other down-home dishes and know you are somewhere that isn't for tourists—and enjoy it all the more.

321 Arabella St. (at Tchoupitoulas St.). ✆ **504/899-9146.** www.frankyandjohnnys.com. Main courses $6.95–$20, market price on some seafood items. AE, DISC, MC, V. Mon–Sat 11am–9pm.

Joey K's ★ CREOLE/SEAFOOD/DINER/HAMBURGERS Savvy visitors are hip to this corner hangout. Indeed, it was a tourist who told us to order the trout Tchoupitoulas, and boy, were we happy—lovely pan-fried trout topped with grilled veggies and shrimp. Daily blackboard specials such as brisket, lamb shank, white beans with pork chops, and Creole jambalaya won't fail to please. Order it all to go, and you'll be dining like a real Uptown local.

3001 Magazine St. ✆ **504/891-0997.** www.joeyksrestaurant.com. Main courses $6.95–$14. DC, MC, V. Mon–Fri 11am–3pm; Sat 11am–4pm; Mon–Sat 5–9pm.

Slim Goodies Diner ★ DINER/HAMBURGERS We were already partial to this place, but when they busted out some heroic culinary moves practically

road trip EATS

You can snag plenty of good eats out in the suburbs and parishes in and around New Orleans. If you have a car (or a friend with one), these local favorites are well worth the 10- to 30-minute drives.

- **Charlie's Seafood:** Noted chef Frank Brigtsen's neighborhood seafood joint. Just like when he was a kid, only better (8311 Jefferson Hwy., Harahan; ✆ 504/737-3700; $8–$22; Mon–Sat 9am–4pm, Sun 10am–3pm).

- **The Crab Trap:** Down a remote narrow lane and on the edge of Lake Pontchartrain, the freshest crabs, shrimp, and crawfish might be found (Peavine Rd. off Hwy. 51, Frenier; ✆ 985/651-2345; $8–$22; Feb–Mar Fri–Sun 11am–7pm, Apr–Oct Fri–Sun 11am–8pm; closed Nov–Jan).

- **Deanie's:** This well-respected seafood joint is the very model of a neighborhood restaurant. There's one in the French Quarter now but we prefer the original (1713 Lake Ave., Metairie; ✆ 504/831-4141; $10–$35 or market price; Tues–Sun 11am–10pm).

- **The Galley:** The folks who do the soft-shell crab po' boys at Jazz Fest do other things just as well, and they're nearby in pretty Old Metairie (2534 Metairie Rd.; ✆ 504/832-0955; $11–$27; Tues–Sat 11am–9pm).

- **The Joint BBQ:** A funky, ah, joint with stellar dry-rubbed and slo-o-o-o-w smoked barbecue, plus homemade sauces, sides, and pies (801 Poland Ave., Bywater; ✆ 504/949-3232; $7–$22; Mon–Sat 11:30am–9pm).

- **Martin Wine Cellar:** Just great deli sandwiches, good salads, plus a daily soup and hot food option. Counter service (714 Elmeer at Veterans, Metairie; ✆ 504/896-7350; everything under $14; Mon–Sat 9am–4pm, Sun 10am–3pm).

- **Middendorf's:** A classic, on-the-water joint that fries up the crispiest, thinnest, freshest catfish imaginable (30160 Hwy. 51 South, Akers; ✆ 985/386-6666; $12–$19; Wed–Sun 10:30am–9pm).

- **Mondo:** Bayona chef Susan Spicer's popular, casual place in the suburb of Lakeview (900 Harrison Ave., Lakeview; ✆ 504/224-2633; $6.50–$12 lunch, $12–$21 dinner; Wed–Fri 11:30am–2:30pm, Mon–Thurs 5:30–10pm, Fri–Sat 5:30–10:30pm, Sun brunch 11am–2pm).

- **Mosca's:** Generations of New Orleanians make the drive and wait the wait for killer old-school Italian (4137 U.S. Hwy. 90, Avondale; ✆ 504/436-8950; $11–$34; Tues–Sat 5:30–9:30pm).

- **R&O's:** Thoroughly unpretentious old-school neighborhood joint serving the usual classics: po' boys, fried seafood, Italian essentials (216 Hammond Hwy., Metairie; ✆ 504/831-1248; most items under $15, crab $24; Mon–Sat 11am–3pm, Wed–Sat 5:30–9pm, Sun 11:30–3pm and 5–9pm).

- **Walker's:** Another Fest favorite. The *cochon de lait* po' boy comes from right here, along with really good barbecue (10828 Hayne Blvd., Lakefront; ✆ 504/241-8227; $6–$18; Tues–Fri 10:30am–2pm, Sat 10:30am–6pm).

days after Katrina, they won our hearts forever. (They dodged anxious health inspectors by serving only fried eggs and other easy-cleanup items on plastic dinnerware.) The comeback pioneers quickly became a meeting place for stressed-out locals (as shown on HBO's *Treme*). Come for classic diner food with clever modern-diner names like "Low Carbonator" and burgers named after famous folks, though we aren't sure why the Robert Johnson has bacon and blue cheese. The menu features large salads, omelets, and even sweet-potato pancakes and a biscuit topped with étouffée. It's a fine, fun stop for breakfast while you're shopping Uptown.

3322 Magazine St. ✆ **504/891-3447.** Everything under $12. No credit cards. Daily 6am–2pm.

COFFEE, BAKERIES & DESSERTS

For other sweet treats, see the section on "Candies, Pralines & Pastries" in the "Shopping" chapter, p. 257.

Angelo Brocato's Ice Cream & Confectionery ★★★ ☺ ICE CREAM/DESSERT Though this sweet, genuine ice-cream parlor celebrated its 100th birthday under 5 feet of water, it's long since back—and ostensibly not a thing has changed. Run by the same family since 1905, Angelo Brocato makes rich Italian ice cream and ices daily, cookies, and pastries amid a wonderful throwback atmosphere. Standards like chocolate and *stracciatella* (chocolate chip) are capital-P Perfect; the fresh lemon ice is legendary (don't try to decide between that and seasonal fresh fruit ices, like Ponchatoula strawberry and blood orange; just get both), while the pana cotta custard has brought us to our knees. After that we get a fresh cannoli. Heck yeah, we do.

214 N. Carrollton Ave. ✆ **504/486-0078.** www.angelobrocatoicecream.com. Everything under $10. AE, DC, DISC, MC, V. Tues–Thurs 10am–10pm; Fri–Sat 10am–10:30pm; Sun 10am–9pm. Closed Mon.

Buttermilk Drop Bakery and Cafe ★ BAKERY/DESSERT Dear Donut People (and you know who you are): After you've done Café du Monde, you need to see Henry the Donut Whisperer for the $20 dozen: around $6 for a dozen donuts, the rest for the cab from the Quarter and back. It's about what you'd pay for a ride to the Maple Leaf, and equally worth it. Have the cab wait, hope the line is short, stick to the drops and classic glazed.

1718 N. Dorgenois St., 7th Ward. ✆ **504/252-04538.** A dozen donuts around $6. No credit cards. Mon–Sat 6am–6pm; Sun 6am–1pm.

Café du Monde ★★★ ☺ 📷 COFFEE/DESSERT Excuse us while we wax rhapsodic. Since 1862, Café du Monde has been selling café au lait and beignets (and nothing but) on the edge of Jackson Square. A New Orleans landmark, it's a must-stop, and *the* place for people-watching, 24 hours a day. A beignet (ben-*yay*) is a square French doughnut–type object, steaming-hot and covered in powdered sugar. You might be tempted to shake off some of the sugar. Don't. Trust us. Pour more on, even. At three to an order for about $2.35, they're a hell of a deal. Wash them down with chicory café au lait or really good hot chocolate. Feeling guilty? The fresh orange juice is excellent, too, and presumably has vitamins.

In the French Market, 800 Decatur St. ✆ **504/525-4544.** www.cafedumonde.com. 3 beignets for $2.35. No credit cards. Daily 24 hr. Closed Christmas. Additional location at Riverwalk Mall.

Café EnVie COFFEE/BAKERY/LIGHT FARE This is a Euro-style coffee-house, very handsome, with a nice selection of drinks and pastries, some bagels and cream cheese, and even free Wi-Fi access. The location is excellent if you are waiting for the clubs on Frenchmen to get cranking.

1241 Decatur St. ✆ **504/524-3689.** www.cafeenvienola.com. Everything under $10. AE, DISC, MC, V. Daily 7am–midnight.

Creole Creamery ★★★ ICE CREAM/DESSERT Their loyal following is mad about the thick, luscious ice cream with a rotating list of flavors, from laven-der-honey to red velvet cake, with stops at tiramisu, chocolate with hot pepper, and more along the way. Completely refreshing, maybe even mandatory on a hot day, with late enough hours to make it an option for a snack on the way to or from an Uptown club or bar.

4924 Prytania St. ✆ **504/894-8680.** www.creolecreamery.com. Everything under $10 except 8-scoop "Eating Challenge" and whole cakes. No credit cards. Sun–Thurs noon–10pm; Fri–Sat noon–11pm.

Croissant D'Or ★ COFFEE/BAKERY A quiet and calm place with the same snacks you might find in a French-leaning coffeehouse, and you can almost al-ways find an open table. Are the croissants made of gold? The prices feel like it sometimes, but they are credibly French.

617 Ursulines St. ✆ **504/524-4663.** Pastries under $7. AE, MC, V. Wed–Mon 6am–2pm.

La Boulangerie ★★★ BAKERY This bakery would be a jewel even if it were in a major bread city. It sells perhaps the only authentic, crusty baguettes in the city (the owners are from France, so they are particular about their bread, as you might guess). But still, we often opt for the heavily studded olive bread, just slightly greasy (in a good way) with olive oil. Heaven. They also do marvelous croissants, chocolate-filled croissants, and other pastries, and even have savory sandwiches. No coffee, though.

4600 Magazine St. (Uptown). ✆ **504/269-3777.** Loaf of bread $3–$8. No credit cards. Mon–Sat 6:30am–5pm; Sun 7am–1pm.

La Divina Gelateria ★★ ICE CREAM/DESSERT This superb gelato place has a great selection of standard and exotic ice-cream flavors, but its interior needs work to make it a more inviting place to dawdle. Look for seasonal fruit and flavors and daily options like dark chocolate with cayenne gelato, fruit and herb sorbets, or a sorbet made with local Abita Turbodog beer—and the dairy is from Louisiana cows. They also have nice light lunches and excellent coffee, and they serve breakfast on the weekends (French Quarter location only).

621 St. Peter St. (French Quarter). ✆ **504/302-2692.** www.ladivinagelateria.com. Scoops $2–$5.95. AE, MC, V. Mon–Thurs 11am–10pm; Fri–Sat 8:30am–11pm; Sun 8:30am–10pm. Also at 3005 Magazine St. ✆ **504/342-2634.** Daily 11am–11pm.

La Madeleine ★ BAKERY/COFFEE One of a chain of French bakeries, it has a wood-burning brick oven that turns out a wide variety of breads, croissants, and brioches—and claims that the skills for making these treats come right from France, so it's all authentic. We like their thick-chunk chocolate chip cookie, even if they don't serve milk to wash it down with. Skip the main dishes and stick with the wonderful baked goods.

601 S. Carrollton Ave. ✆ **504/861-8662.** www.lamadeleine.com. Pastries $1.50–$4; main courses $4–$12. AE, DISC, MC, V. Daily 7am–9pm.

Meltdown Ice Pops ★★ 🍴 DESSERT/ICE CREAM We still don't understand why there isn't a decent snoball stand in the French Quarter, but Meltdown fills the icy void very well, thanks. Another food-truck-to-retail success story, this teensy shop proffers fresh-daily frozen yumminess on a stick, made from ingredients so local that co-owner Michelle Weaver actually hand-picks some of them from the vine. But these ain't yo' mama's pop. The daily flavors range from Vietnamese coffee and salted caramel (our personal favorites) to herb-inflected concoctions like pineapple basil and Ponchatoula strawberry basil, some with chunks of fruit. The straightforward fudgsicles (watermelon or peanut butter) are kid-pleasers.

508 Dumaine St. ℰ **504/301-0905.** $3 each. No credit cards. Daily noon–6pm.

A snoball's CHANCE

We all scream for ice cream (New Orleans is no exception), but New Orleans has another popular iced dessert: the snoball. Lest you think it's just a snow cone or shaved ice clone, let us assure you: It's no such thing. These mouthwatering concoctions are made with only the best-quality shaved ice, ice so fine that skiers envy the powder. And the flavors—including exotic ones such as wedding cake (almond, mostly), nectar (think cream soda, only much better), and even orchid cream vanilla (bright purple and must be seen to be believed)—are absolutely delectable (the better proprietors make their own flavored syrups). Order them with condensed or evaporated milk if you prefer your refreshing drinks on the more decadently creamy side, or go further—some shops have started spiking them with booze. At any time on a hot day, lines can be out the door, and like so many other local specialties, loyalties are fierce. You should stop in at any snoball stand you see, but the following locations are worth seeking out. Be sure to call for hours because they vary, especially during the winter when a stand might be closed entirely. Go with a sweet tooth and get plenty of napkins.

Hansen's Sno-Bliz ★★★, 4801 Tchoupitoulas St. (ℰ **504/891-9788;** www.snobliz.com), is a city tradition after decades of service, still provided with a smile by the third-generation owner Ashley Hansen, who officially took over after her grandparents died in the months after Katrina. Hansen's grandparents invented the particular shaved-ice machine in use here and their own special syrups, and the snoballs come in a souvenir cup. Try the bubble gum–flavored Sno-bliz. **Plum St. Snoballs** ★★,

1300 Burdette St. (ℰ **504/866-7996;** www.plumstreetsnoball.com), has been cooling New Orleanians for more than 70 years, serving favorites in Chinese food containers. Fans of **Pandora's** ★★, 901 S. Carrollton Ave. (ℰ **504/289-0765**), say its ice is the softest anywhere, and the flavor list is so long it's taking over the neighborhood. You'll have to fight the hordes of school kids in line, even, it often seems, during school hours. But clearly they've learned where to get a good snoball.

P.J.'s Coffee & Tea Company ★ COFFEE P.J.'s is a local institution, with lots of locations around town. It offers a great variety of teas, coffees, and espressos, and it roasts its own coffee beans. The iced coffee is made by a cold-water process that requires 12 hours of preparation. The granita is prepared with P.J.'s Espresso Dolce iced coffee concentrate, frozen with milk and sugar, and served as a coffee "slushee"—great on hot, muggy days.

5432 Magazine St. ℭ **504/895-2202.** www.pjscoffee.com. Drinks and pastries 95¢–$4. AE, DC, MC, V. Daily 6am–9pm (sometimes later on weekends). P.J.'s has branches at Tulane University (ℭ **504/865-5705**); 644 Camp St. (ℭ **504/529-3658**); and 7624 Maple St. (ℭ **504/866-7031**), among other locations.

Royal Blend Coffee & Tea House ★ COFFEE/LIGHT FARE This place is set back off the street; to reach it, you walk through a courtyard. Order a sandwich, quiche, or salad and take it out into the courtyard. If you're just in the mood for coffee and pastry, they have plenty of that, too, and the pastry menu changes daily.

621 Royal St. ℭ **504/523-2716.** www.royalblendcoffee.com. Drinks and pastries 85¢–$2.95; lunch items $5.25–$10. AE, MC, V. Daily 8am–6pm. Royal Blend has a branch at 204 Metairie Rd. in Metairie (ℭ **504/835-7779**).

Rue de la Course ★ COFFEE This is your basic comfy boho coffeehouse: cavernous in appearance, thanks to a very tall ceiling; manned by cool, friendly college kids; and full of locals seeking a quick pick-me-up, lingering over the paper, or poring over their journals. They have decent sandwiches, and newspapers and local magazines, too.

3121 Magazine St. ℭ **504/899-0242.** Coffee $2–$4; pastries $2–$4; sandwiches under $10. No credit cards. Mon–Fri 6:30am–11pm; Sat–Sun 7am–11pm. Also at 1140 S. Carrollton Ave., ℭ **504/861-4343.**

Sucré ★ DESSERT/ICE CREAM See the listing for this high-end confectionery under "Candies, Pralines, & Pastries," on p. 258.

3025 Magazine St. ℭ **504/520-8311.** www.shopsucre.com. All desserts under $10, except full cakes. AE, DC, MC, V. Sun–Thurs 9am–10pm; Fri–Sat 9am–midnight.

RESTAURANTS BY CUISINE

AMERICAN, NEW AMERICAN & REGIONAL AMERICAN

American Sector ★★ ($$, p. 143)
Emeril's ★★★ ($$$$, p. 139)
Ernst Café ($, p. 145)
Feelings Café ★ ($$, p. 133)
Nola ★ ($$$, p. 125)
The Pelican Club ★ ($$$, p. 125)
Rémoulade ($, p. 132)
Stanley ★★ ($, p. 133)

BAKERY

Buttermilk Drop Bakery and Cafe ★ ($, p. 154)
Café EnVie ($, p. 155)
Croissant D'Or ★ ($, p. 155)
La Boulangerie ★★★ ($, p. 155)
La Madeleine ★ ($, p. 155)

KEY TO ABBREVIATIONS:
$$$$** = Very Expensive   **$$$** = Expensive   **$$** = Moderate   **$ = Inexpensive

BARBECUE

BISTRO

CAFES/COFFEE

CAJUN/CONTEMPORARY CAJUN

CREOLE/CONTEMPORARY CREOLE/LOUISIANA

DESSERT

La Divina Gelateria ★★ ($, p. 155)
Meltdown Ice Pops ★★ ($, p. 156)
Sucré ★ ($, p. 258)

DINER

Camellia Grill ★★ ($, p. 130 and
  p. 152)
Clover Grill ★ ($, p. 131)
Joey K's ★ ($, p. 152)
Slim Goodies Diner ★ ($, p. 152)

FRENCH

Brennan's ★ ($$$, p. 122)
Café Degas ★★ ($$, p. 135)
Galatoire's ★ ($$$, p. 123)
Gautreau's ★★ ($$$, p. 148)
Irene's Cuisine ★★ ($$, p. 127)
La Crêpe Nanou ★ ($$, p. 150)
Le Foret ★★★ ($$$, p. 141)
Martinique Bistro ★ ($$$, p. 148)
Restaurant August ★ ($$$$, p. 139)
Tommy's Cuisine ★★ ($$, p. 144)

HAMBURGERS

Camellia Grill ★★ ($, p. 130 and
  p. 152)
Clover Grill ★ ($, p. 131)
Joey K's ★ ($, p. 152)
Port of Call ★★ ($$, p. 128)
Slim Goodies Diner ★ ($, p. 152)

ICE CREAM

Angelo Brocato's Ice Cream &
  Confectionery ★★★ ($, p. 154)
Creole Creamery ★★★ ($, p. 155)
La Divina Gelateria ★★ ($, p. 155)
Meltdown Ice Pops ★★ ($, p. 156)
Sucré ★ ($, p. 258)

INTERNATIONAL

Angeli on Decatur ★ ($, p. 130)
Bayona ★★ ($$$, p. 120)
Dominique's on Magazine ★★★
  ($$, p. 150)
Lola's ★★ ($$, p. 136)
Meson 923 ★★★ ($$$, p. 141)
Mondo ($$, p. 153)
Stella! ★★ ($$$, p. 126)

ITALIAN

A Mano ★★ ($$, p. 142)
Angeli on Decatur ★ ($, p. 130)
Domenica ★★ ($$, p. 143)
Irene's Cuisine ★★ ($$, p. 127)
Liuzza's ★★ ($$, p. 136)
Mandina's ★★ ($$, p. 137)
Mosca's ($$–$$$, p. 153)
Napoleon House ★ ($, p. 131)
Pascal's Manale ★ ($$, p. 151)
Tommy's Cuisine ★★ ($$, p. 144)

JAPANESE

Yuki ★★★ ($$, p. 133)

LIGHT FARE

Acme Oyster House ★★ ($, p. 129)
Angeli on Decatur ★ ($, p. 130)
Antoine's Annex ★ ($, p. 130)
Café Maspero ★ ($, p. 130)
Cake Café & Bakery ★ ($, p. 134)
Camellia Grill ★★ ($, p. 130 and
  p. 152)
Café EnVie ($, p. 155)
Johnny's Po-Boys ★ ($, p. 131)
Liuzza's by the Track ★★ ($, p. 137)
Martin Wine Cellar ($, p. 153)
Mother's ★★ ($, p. 145)
Parkway Bakery and Tavern ★★ ($,
  p. 138)
Royal Blend Coffee & Tea House ★
  ($, p. 157)
Somethin' Else Café ★ ($, p. 133)
Ye Olde College Inn ★★ ($, p. 138)

MIDDLE EASTERN

Mona's Café & Deli ★★ ($, p. 134)

PIZZA

Louisiana Pizza Kitchen ($, p. 131)

SEAFOOD

Acme Oyster House ★★ ($, p. 129)
Café Maspero ★ ($, p. 130)
Casamento's ★★ ($, p. 152)
Charlie's Seafood ($–$$, p. 153)
Deanie's ($$, p. 153)
Dickie Brennan's Bourbon House
  Seafood ★★ ($$$, p. 123)

Drago's ★★ ($$, p. 144)
Felix's Restaurant & Oyster Bar ★★
($, p. 131)
Franky & Johnny's ★ ($, p. 152)
The Galley ($$, p. 153)
Joey K's ★ ($, p. 152)
Middendorf's ($–$$, p. 153)
Pascal's Manale ★ ($$, p. 151)
R&O's ($–$$, p. 153)
Red Fish Grill ★ ($$, p. 129)
Rib Room ★ ($$$, p. 126)

SOUL FOOD

Dooky Chase ★★ ($$, p. 136)
Jacques-Imo's ★ ($$, p. 150)
Lil' Dizzy's ★★ ($, p. 137)
Praline Connection ★ ($, p. 135)
Willie Mae's Scotch House ★★ ($, p. 138)

SOUTHERN, CONTEMPORARY SOUTHERN & NOUVEAU SOUTHERN

Boucherie ★★★ ($$, p. 149)
Café Amelie ★ ($$, p. 126)
Le Meritage ★★ ($$$, p. 124)
MiLa ★ ($$$, p. 142)
R&O's ($, p. 153)
Walker's ($, p. 153)

SPANISH

Lola's ★★ ($$, p. 136)

STEAK

Dickie Brennan's Steakhouse ★★
($$$, p. 123)
La Boca ★★★ ($$$, p. 140)
Pascal's Manale ★ ($$, p. 151)
Rib Room ★ ($$$, p. 126)

SIGHTS TO SEE & PLACES TO BE

We've made no secret of our favorite New Orleans activities: walking, eating, listening to music, dancing, and eating again. If, instead of sightseeing, that's all you do while you're visiting the town, we won't complain. But New Orleans is a vibrant, visual city with a rich history and gobs of culture worthy of your time—some of which is indoors and blessedly air-conditioned. That's likely to be handy when you'll need to escape the rain or heat!

Frankly, New Orleans itself is one big sight—it's one of the most unusual-looking cities in America. It's nice and flat, just made for exploring on foot. (See the walking tours in chapter 8, "City Strolls," if you'd like some structure.)

While the French Quarter certainly is a seductive place, to go to New Orleans and never leave the Quarter is like visiting Greenwich Village and believing you've seen New York. Stroll the lush Garden District, marvel at the oaks in City Park, ride the streetcar on St. Charles Avenue and gape at the gorgeous homes, or go visit some gators on a swamp tour. And yes, if you like, make a pilgrimage to the still-recovering neighborhoods. You'll no longer see utter devastation, but you will be witnessing history.

THE FRENCH QUARTER

Those who have been to Disneyland might be forgiven if they experience some déjà vu upon first seeing the French Quarter. It's somewhat more worn, of course, and, in spots, a whole lot smellier. But despite the fact that Walt actually did replicate a French Quarter street in Disneyland's New Orleans Square, it's an actual neighborhood—over 200 years old—and one of the most visually interesting in America. (Some of the people living in the Quarter are the fifth generation of their family to do so.) That it was spared any flooding and suffered relatively little storm damage after Hurricane Katrina was a tremendous gift to the city.

There's a great deal to the French Quarter—history, architecture, cultural oddities—and to overlook all that in favor of T-shirt shops and the ubiquitous bars is a darn shame (though we certainly enjoy the lure of an occasional venture to tacky, outlandish Bourbon Street—the operative word being "occasional"). And regardless of where you go in the Quarter, remember that you are walking by people's homes. Please afford French Quarter dwellers the same courtesy you would expect in your own neighborhood: Be courteous, quiet, and clean, folks.

A French engineer named Adrien de Pauger laid out the Quarter in 1718, and today it's a great anomaly in America. Many other American cities have torn down or gutted their historic centers, but thanks to a strict preservation policy, the area looks much as it always has and is still the center of town.

PREVIOUS PAGE: **New Orleans loves a parade.**

Jackson Square bustles with musicians, artists, fortune-tellers, jugglers, and those peculiar "living statue" performance artists entertaining for change. Pay attention to that seeming ad-hoc jazz band that plays right in front of the Cabildo—their jazz music

is about as good as you will hear, and notable locals occasionally sit in. **Royal Street** is home to stellar street musicians, numerous antiques shops, and galleries; with other interesting stores on **Chartres and Decatur streets** and the cross streets between.

The closer you get to **Esplanade Avenue** and toward **Rampart Street,** the more residential the Quarter becomes, and buildings are entirely homes (in the business sections, the ground floors are commercial and the stories above apartments). Peep in through any open gate; surprises await in the form of graceful brick- and flagstone-lined courtyards filled with foliage and bubbling fountains.

The Vieux Carré Commission is ever vigilant about balancing contemporary economic interests in the Quarter with historical preservation. There's not a traffic light in the whole interior of the French Quarter—they're relegated to fringe streets—and streetlights are of the old gaslight style. Large city buses are banned, and during part of each day, Royal and Bourbon streets are pedestrian malls. No vehicles are *ever* allowed around Jackson Square. We also applaud the exclusion of most generic chain stores.

The Quarter streets are laid out in an almost perfect rectangular grid so it's easily navigable. It's also so well traveled that it is nearly always safe. Again, as you get toward the fringes (especially near Rampart) and as night falls, you should exercise caution; stay in the more bustling parts and try not to walk alone.

The French Quarter walking tour in chapter 8 will give you the best overview of the historic structures in the area and of the area's (and city's) history. Many other attractions that aren't in the walking tour are listed in this chapter (and mapped on p. 167), so make sure to cross-reference as you go along.

Major Attractions

Audubon Aquarium of the Americas ★★★ ☺ The world-class Audubon Institute's Aquarium of the Americas' joyful, post-Katrina reopening in May 2006 made worldwide news when the aquarium's penguin evacuees made a triumphant return home from exile via a specially designated FedEx flight, and waddled down the (FedEx) purple carpet.

More recently, the aquarium has been rescuing and rehabilitating sea turtles suffering the effects of the Gulf oil spill. Several rescued turtles and an informative exhibit are now on display. Kids love this stellar aquarium—it's highly entertaining and painlessly educational with beautifully constructed exhibits—even those too impatient to read the graphics. But adults shouldn't overlook it, and it's a handy refuge from the heat or rain. The aquarium straddles the banks of the Mississippi River, an easy walk from the Quarter action. It showcases a veritable ocean of aquatic life, with a strong focus on the Mississippi and the Gulf of Mexico. We particularly like to wander in the rainforests (complete with birds and piranhas) and see what goes on below the surface of swamps. Not to be missed are a fine exhibit on frogs, the impossibly cute giant sea otters, and the

New Orleans Attractions

Southern Baptist Hospital

BROADMOOR

New Orleans Arena

Union Passenger Terminal (Amtrak)

UPTOWN

Simon Bolivar

GARDEN DISTRICT

Lee Circle

Ferry Service to Algiers Point

Riverfront streetcar route/stops

St. Charles streetcar route/stops

Vieux Carre loop route/stops

Canal St. streetcar route/stops

See also "Uptown Hotels & Restaurants" map.

0   1/4 mi
0   0.25 km

MID-CITY

N. Rocheblave
N. Tonti
N. Miro
N. Galvez
N. Johnson
N. Prieur
N. Roman
Derbigny

LaFitte Ave.
Orleans Ave.
St. Ann
Dumaine
St. Phillip
Ursulines Ave.
Bayou Rd.

8

9

St. Bernard Ave.

12

See "Mid-City Hotels & Restaurants" map.

N. Claiborne Ave.

10

11

N. Villere

16

See "French Quarter Hotels" map.

Superdome

10

La Salle St.
Poydras
Duncan Plaza

Gravier
Common
Canal

Basin St.
Univ. Pl.
Conti
St. Louis
Toulouse

N. Rampart
St. Ann
Dumaine
Burgundy

St. Claude Ave.

31

13

14

LOUIS ARMSTRONG PARK

15   **17**

Barracks

FAUBOURG MARIGNY

Loyola Ave.
S. Rampart
O'Keefe St.
Union
Perdido

Iberville
Bienville

THE FRENCH QUARTER

Dauphine
Bourbon
Royal

Ursulines
Gov. Nichols
Esplanade

Touro
Frenchmen
Elysian

CENTRAL BUSINESS DISTRICT

Carondelet
St. Charles Ave.
Loyola
Poydras

Chartres

Marigny
Chartres St.

18

Lafayette Square

Decatur

French Market

19 Camp   **21**

20

Magazine St.
Girod
Julia
S. Peters
Commerce
Tchoupitoulas
Fulton

30

Woldenburg Riverfront Park

St. Joseph
Howard Ave.

92

28

29

27

Conv. Ctr. Blvd.

23 RIVERFRONT

24

26 World Trade Center

Canal St. Ferry (Toll)

Mississippi River

25

ALGIERS

Morgan
Delaronde
Bermuda
Verret
Seguin
Bouny

Lake Pontchartrain

CITY PARK

10   **610**

Area of detail

Superdome

10

rare albino gator. The aquarium also features an excellent interactive play zone for kids, a manta ray touch tank, and Parakeet Pointe, where birds alight right on you (especially if you buy the $1 feed sticks).

The **IMAX theater ★★** shows two or three films at regular intervals, including an astonishing Katrina documentary, *Hurricane on the Bayou.* **Combination tickets** for the aquarium, the IMAX theater, the Insectarium, and Audubon Zoo are $40 for adults and $25 for seniors and children, and tickets are good for 5 days (excluding Mon, when the attractions are closed). These are the best admission deals, even if you only make three out of the four attractions. The St. Charles streetcar will get you to Audubon Park; you can catch the free shuttle from there to the zoo. Various other discount ticket combinations are available for all the Audubon attractions.

1 Canal St., at the river. ✆ **800/774-7394** or 504/581-4629. www.auduboninstitute.org. Aquarium $20 adults, $15 seniors, $16 children 2-12. IMAX $10 adults, $9 seniors, $7 children. Aquarium and IMAX Tues–Sun 10am–5pm. Call for showtimes; advance tickets recommended. Closed Mardi Gras and Christmas.

Audubon Insectarium ★★ ☺ This fascinating museum is dedicated to all things bug and arachnid, specifically 900,000 species of critters that creep, crawl, and flutter. Located in the old U.S. Customs House, it's the largest free-standing museum in the world dedicated to its multilegged, winged subjects.

The journey through ickiness (kidding! Bugs are great!) begins in the Prehistoric hallway with 30-inch insect replicas. A gallery that simulates the experience of being underground exposes the tiny world living in our soil. In the **Tiny Termite Café,** each glass-topped table has an insect colony living in it (watch silkworms spin their fibers while you dine), and it even serves a few creepy-crawler-based snacks. Finally, the Japanese-inspired butterfly gallery, full of living, fluttering beauty, is a peaceful departure from the hustle outside.

423 Canal St. ✆ **800/774-7394** or 504/581-4629. www.auduboninstitute.org. Admission $19 adults, $13 seniors, $11 children 2-12. Insectarium, Aquarium, and IMAX tickets $40 adults, $28 seniors, $21 children. Tues–Sun 10am–5pm (last entry at 4pm).

The Historic French Market ★★ ☺ Legend has it that the site of the French Market was originally used by Native Americans as a bartering market. It grew

Millicent the Penguin entertains a visitor at the Audubon Aquarium of the Americas.

The Historic French Market has plenty of tacky souvenirs, but it's also got a farmers' market with fresh produce, nuts, and dried fruits.

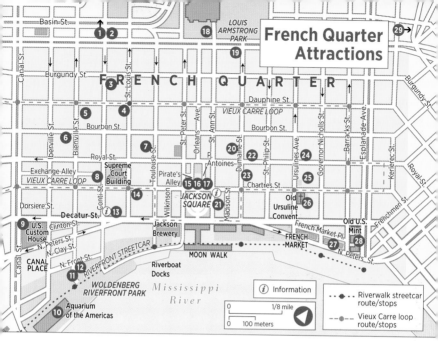

LOUIS ARMSTRONG PARK

FRENCH QUARTER

Basin St.

Canal St.

Burgundy St.

St. Louis St.

Dauphine St.

VIEUX CARRE LOOP

Bourbon St.

Bourbon St.

Iberville St.

Bienville St.

Royal St.

Exchange Alley
VIEUX CARRE LOOP

Supreme Court Building

Pirate's Alley

Antoines.

St. Peter St.

Orleans Ave.

St. Ann St.

Dumaine St.

St. Philip St.

Ursulines Ave.

Governor Nicholls St.

Barracks St.

Esplanade Ave.

Burgundy St.

Royal St.

Kerlerec St.

Toulouse St.

Wilkinson

JACKSON SQUARE

Madison St.

Chartres St.

Old Ursuline Convent

French Market Pl.

Frenchmen St.

Dorsiere St.

Conti St.

Decatur St.

Jackson Brewery

FRENCH MARKET

Old U.S. Mint

N. Peters St.

U.S. Custom House

Clinton St.

N. Peters St.

N. Clay St.

N. Front St.

RIVERFRONT STREETCAR

MOON WALK

CANAL PLACE

WOLDENBERG RIVERFRONT PARK

Riverboat Docks

Mississippi River

Aquarium of the Americas

(i) Information

0   1/8 mile
0   100 meters

- - ● - - Riverwalk streetcar route/stops

- - ● - - Vieux Carre loop route/stops

into an official market in 1812. From around 1840 to 1870, it was part of Gallatin Street, an impossibly rough area full of bars, drunken sailors, and criminals. Today it's a mixed bag, and not nearly as colorful as its past (but we're quite glad to have its clean public bathrooms following an extensive recent renovation). The farmers' market makes a fun amble as you admire everything from fresh produce and fish to more tourist-oriented items like hot sauces and Cajun and Creole mixes. (*Tip:* If you can, get someone to take you to a proper supermarket for that stuff, where it costs way less.) Snacks like gator on a stick will amuse the kids. The flea market, a bit farther down from the farmers' market, is considered a must-shop place, but the reality is that many of the goods are kind of junky: T-shirts, jewelry, hats, cheap sunglasses, and so on. Still, some good deals can be had and they're willing to bargain a bit, plus there's no state sales tax on flea market items. It's convenient for souvenir shopping and great for buying New Orleans–related jewelry, especially silver—you'll find a vast array of inexpensive fleur-de-lis and water-meter-shaped items (though we can't vouch for the quality of the metal). If you've outshopped your luggage, you can pick up a duffle bag or small suitcase here.

On Decatur St., toward Esplanade Ave. from Jackson Sq. www.frenchmarket.org. 🕾 **504/522-2621.** Mon–Fri roughly 9am–5pm (tends to start shutting down about an hour before closing).

St. Louis Cathedral ★★ The St. Louis Cathedral prides itself on being the oldest continuously active cathedral in the United States. What usually doesn't get mentioned is that it is also

A look inside St. Louis Cathedral.

one of the ugliest. The outside is all right, but the rather grim interior wouldn't give even a minor European church a run for its money.

Still, its history is impressive and somewhat dramatic. The cathedral formed the center of the original settlement, and it is still the major landmark of the French Quarter. This is the third building to stand on this spot. A hurricane destroyed the first in 1722. On Good Friday 1788, the bells of its replacement were kept silent for religious reasons rather than ringing out the alarm for a fire—which eventually raged out of control and burned down more than 850 buildings, including the cathedral itself.

Rebuilt in 1794, the structure was remodeled and enlarged between 1845 and 1851 by J. N. B. de Pouilly. The brick used in its construction was taken from the original town cemetery and was covered with stucco to protect the mortar from dampness. And just when you think nothing else can go wrong, along comes Katrina. The roof leaked, ruining the $1-million organ (it's been rebuilt and returned). Outside, two magnificent, ancient live oaks fell down, narrowly missing the statue of Jesus that stood between them. Jesus's thumbs were amputated, and Archbishop Hughes, in his first post-Katrina sermon in the cathedral, vowed not to replace them until all of New Orleans is healed. The dramatically lit statue makes a resplendent, if somewhat eerie, nighttime silhouette; do make a point to walk by at night. It's worth going inside for a look, and you may catch a choir practice, if you're lucky; the knowledgeable guides are full of fun facts about the windows and murals and how the building nearly collapsed once from water-table sinkage. Take a look at the slope of the floor: Clever architectural design somehow keeps the building upright even as it continues to sink. Outside is a plaque marking the visit by Pope John Paul II in 1987. An additional large commemorative marker is set into the flagstones of Jackson Square, renaming that area for the late pontiff.

615 Pere Antoine Alley. 🕾 **504/525-9585.** www.stlouiscathedral.org. Free admission; docents available. Mon–Sat 9am–4pm; Sun 9am–2pm. Cafe and gift shop Mon–Sat 10am–3pm; Sun 1–4pm.

Historic Buildings

Beauregard-Keyes House ★ This "raised cottage," with its Doric columns and handsome twin staircases, was built as a residence by a wealthy New Orleans auctioneer, Joseph LeCarpentier, in 1826. Confederate General P. G. T. Beauregard lived in the house with several members of his family for 18 months between 1865 and 1867, and from 1944 until 1970, it was the residence of Frances Parkinson Keyes (pronounced *Cause*), who wrote many novels about the region. One of them, *Madame Castel's Lodger,* concerns the general's stay in this house. *Dinner at Antoine's,* perhaps her most famous novel, was also written here. Mrs. Keyes left her home to a foundation, and the house, rear buildings, and garden are open to the public. The gift shop has a wide selection of her novels.

1113 Chartres St., at Ursulines St. ✆ **504/523-7257.** www.bkhouse.org. Admission $10 adults; $9 seniors, students, and AAA members; $4 children 6–12; free for children 5 and under. Mon–Sat 10am–3pm. Tours on the hour. Closed Sun and holidays.

The 1850 House ★ James Gallier, Sr., and his son designed the historic Pontalba Buildings for the Baroness Micaela Almonester de Pontalba (see box below), who had them built in 1849 (see stop no. 32 of "Walking Tour 1: The French Quarter" in chapter 8, "City Strolls") in an effort to combat the deterioration of the older part of the city. The rows of town houses on either side of Jackson Square were the largest private buildings in the country at the time. Legend has it that the baroness, miffed that her friend Andrew Jackson wouldn't tip his hat to her, had his statue erected in the square, where to this day he continues to doff his chapeau toward her top-floor apartment. It's probably not true, but we never stand in the way of a good story.

Here, the **Louisiana State Museum** presents a demonstration of life in 1850, when the buildings opened for residential use. The self-guided tour uses

a fact-filled sheet that explains in detail the history of the interior. Period furnishings are arranged to show how the rooms were typically used. It vividly illustrates the difference between the "upstairs" portion of the house, where the upper-middle-class family lived in comfort (and the children were largely confined to a nursery and raised by servants), and the "downstairs," where the staff toiled in considerable drudgery to make their bosses comfortable. It's a surprisingly enjoyable look at life in the good, or not so good, old days.

Lower Pontalba Bldg., 523 St. Ann St., Jackson Sq. ✆ **800/568-6968** or 504/568-6968. http://lsm.crt.state.la.us/1850ex.htm. Admission $3; $2 students, seniors, and active military; free for children 12 and under. Tues–Sun 10am–4pm. Closed all legal holidays.

The courtyard at the Beauregard-Keyes House.

Old Absinthe House The Old Absinthe House was built in 1806 and now houses the Old Absinthe House bar and two restaurants. The drink for which the building and bar were named was once outlawed in this country (certain chemical additives, not the actual wormwood used to flavor the drink, caused blindness and madness). Now you can legally sip the infamous libation in the bar and feel at one with the famous types who came before you, listed on a plaque outside: William Thackeray, Oscar Wilde, Sarah Bernhardt, and Walt Whitman. Andrew Jackson and the Lafitte brothers plotted their desperate defense of New Orleans here in 1815.

The house was a speak-easy during Prohibition, and when federal officers closed it in 1924, the interior was mysteriously stripped of its antique fixtures—including the long marble-topped bar and the old water dripper that was used to infuse water into the absinthe. Just as mysteriously, it all reappeared down the street at a corner establishment called, oddly enough, the Old Absinthe House Bar (400 Bourbon St.). The latter has closed, and a neon-bedecked daiquiri shack opened in its stead. The fixtures have since turned up in one of the restaurants on this site! The bar is covered with business cards (and drunks), so don't come here looking to recapture old-timey and classy atmosphere, but it's still a genuinely fun hangout.

240 Bourbon St., btw. Iberville and Bienville sts. ℂ **504/523-3181.** Free admission. Sun–Thurs 9am–2am; Fri–Sat 9am–4am.

Old Ursuline Convent ★★ Forget tales of America being founded by brawny, brave, tough guys in buckskin and beards. The real pioneers—at least, in Louisiana—were well-educated Frenchwomen clad in 40 pounds of black wool robes. That's right; you don't know tough until you know the Ursuline nuns, and this city would have been a very different place without them.

The Sisters of Ursula came to the mudhole that was New Orleans in 1727 after a journey that several times nearly saw them lost at sea or succumbing to

pirates or disease. Here, they provided the first decent medical care (saving countless lives) and later founded the first local school and orphanage for girls. They also helped raise girls shipped over from France as marriage material for local men, teaching them everything from languages to homemaking of the most exacting sort (laying the foundation for who knows how many local families).

The convent dates from 1752 (the sisters themselves moved uptown in 1824, where they remain to this day), and it is the oldest building in the Mississippi River valley and the only surviving building from the French colonial period in the United States. It also houses Catholic archives dating back to 1718.

1100 Chartres St., at Ursulines St. ℂ **877/529-2242.** Admission $5 adults, $4 seniors, $3 students, children 6 and under free. Mon–Sat 10am–4pm. (Last tour begins at 4pm.)

The Old Ursuline Convent, which dates from 1752, is the oldest building in the Mississippi River valley.

The Old U.S. Mint ★★ ☺ The exterior of the Old U.S. Mint (the only building in America to have served as both a U.S. and a Confederate mint) got hammered by Katrina, but that gave them the opportunity to audit their collection, design new exhibits, and renovate pretty much everything. It has since reopened to display worthwhile exhibits showcasing Louisiana-related art and artifacts. Numismatists will also find much to see here (like O-minted coins, struck right here). *Fun fact:* Ghost hunters believe William Mumford, who met the noose here in 1862, still hangs around. The big news is that the entire building will house a serious, comprehensive jazz history museum and nightclub, projected for 2013. Very cool. Swingin', in fact.

400 Esplanade Ave., at N. Peters St. (enter on Esplanade Ave. or Barracks St.). © **800/568-6968** or 504/568-6968. http://lsm.crt.state.la.us/mintex.htm. Admission $6 adults; $5 students, seniors, and active military; children 6 and under free. Tues–Sun 10am–5pm. Closed all legal holidays.

Our Lady of Guadalupe Chapel—International Shrine of St. Jude ★ This "funeral chapel" was erected in 1826 conveniently near St. Louis Cemetery No. 1, specifically for funeral services, so as not to spread disease through the Quarter. We like it for three reasons: the catacomb-like devotional chapel with plaques thanking the Virgin Mary for favors granted, the gift shop full of religious medals including a number of obscure saints, and the statue of St. Expedite. The saint got his name, according to legend, when his crate arrived with no identification other than the word EXPEDITE stamped on the outside. Now he's the "saint" you pray to when you want things in a hurry. (We are not making this up.) Expedite has his cults in France and Spain and is also popular among the voodoo

lady bountiful: **BARONESS DE PONTALBA**

New Orleans owes a great debt to Baroness Micaela Almonester de Pontalba and her family—without them, Jackson Square would be a mudhole. Her father, Don Almonester, used his money and influence to have the St. Louis Cathedral, Cabildo, and Presbytère built. The baroness was responsible for the two long brick apartment buildings that flank Jackson Square and for the renovation that turned the center of the square into what it is today.

Born in 1795 into the most influential family in New Orleans, the baroness married her cousin, who subsequently stole her inheritance. When she wanted a separation at a time when such things were unheard of, her father-in-law shot her several times and then shot himself. She survived, though some of her fingers did not. In subsequent portraits, she would hide the wounded hand in her dress. In the end, she got her money back—she used it for those French Quarter improvements—and also ended up taking care of her (eventually) slightly nutty husband for the rest of his life. She died in Paris in 1874; her home there is now the residence of the American ambassador. The book *Intimate Enemies,* by Christina Vella (Louisiana State University Press, 1997), has all the details about this remarkable woman.

folks. He's just inside the door on the right. The chapel also has a pretty great religious gift shop in case you want to pick up an Expedite prayer card. For those interested in some extra prayer power for lost causes, the St. Jude solemn novena runs quarterly for 9 days at a time—call for the exact start dates.

411 N. Rampart St., at Conti St. parish office. ℭ **504/525-1551.** Gift shop Mon–Sat 9am–5pm. Masses daily starting at 7am.

Museums

In addition to the destinations listed here, you might be interested in the **Germaine Wells Mardi Gras Museum** at 813 Bienville St., on the second floor of Arnaud's restaurant (p. 120; ℭ **504/523-5433**), where you'll find a private collection of Mardi Gras costumes and ball gowns dating from around 1910 to 1960. Admission is free, and the museum is open from 4:30pm until the restaurant closes.

The Cabildo ★★★ Constructed from 1795 to 1799 as the Spanish government seat in New Orleans, the Cabildo was the site of the signing of the Louisiana Purchase transfer. It was severely damaged by fire in 1988 and closed for 5 years for reconstruction, which included total restoration of the roof by French artisans using 600-year-old timber-framing techniques. It is now the center of the Louisiana State Museum's facilities in the French Quarter.

The Cabildo is located right on Jackson Square and is quite worth your time. A multiroom exhibition informatively, entertainingly, and exhaustively traces the history of Louisiana from exploration through Reconstruction from a multicultural perspective. It covers everything from slavery and statehood to topics like antebellum music, mourning and burial customs (a big deal when much of your population is succumbing to yellow fever), immigrants and how they fared here, and the changing roles of women in the South. It's a dense collection, but each room seems more interesting than the last. Throughout are portraits of nearly all the prominent figures from Louisiana history plus other fabulous artifacts, including Napoleon's death mask.

Equally detailed but covering another end of Louisiana's historical spectrum is *Unsung Heroes: The Secret History of Rock 'n Roll.* Highlighting Louisianans—some known, some not—who influenced rock music locally and beyond, it's packed with cool rock arcana, mostly from the awesome collection of the Ponderosa Stomp (p. 33) folks.

701 Chartres St. ℭ **800/568-6968** or 504/568-6968. http://lsm.crt.state.la.us/cabildo/cabildo.htm. Admission $6 adults; $5 students, seniors, and military; free for children 12 and under. Tues–Sun 10am–5pm.

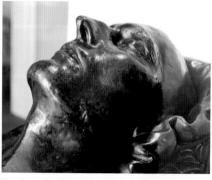

Napoleon's Death Mask is on display at the Cabildo.

Gallier House Museum ★ James Gallier, Jr. (it's pronounced *Gaul*-ee-er, by the way; he was Irish, not French), designed and built the Gallier House Museum as his residence in 1857. Anne Rice fans will want to at least walk

Period furnishings are on display inside the Gallier House Museum.

by—this is the house she was thinking of when she described Louis and
Lestat's New Orleans residence in
Interview with the Vampire. Gallier and
his father were leading New Orleans
architects—they also designed the
old French Opera House, the original St. Charles Exchange Hotel,
Municipality Hall (now Gallier Hall),
and the Pontalba Buildings. This carefully restored town house contains an
early working bathroom, a passive ven-
tilation system, and furnishings of the
period. Leaders of local ghost tours
swear that Gallier haunts the place.
Inquire about seasonal special programs. Combination tickets with the
Hermann-Grima House are available
for an additional $8.

The Hermann-Grima House has been
meticulously restored.

1118 and 1132 Royal St., btw. Gov. Nicholls and
Ursulines sts. ✆ **504/525-5661.** www.hgghh.
org. Admission $10 adults; $8 seniors, students, AAA members, and children 8–18; free for children 7 and under. Open for tours Mon and Fri at 10am, 11am, noon, 1pm, and 2pm; Sat at noon,
1pm, 2pm, and 3pm.

Hermann-Grima House ★ The Hermann-Grima House is a symmetrical
Federal-style building (perhaps the first in the Quarter) that's very different from
its French surroundings. The knowledgeable docents who give the regular tours
make this a satisfactory stop at any time, but keep an eye out for the frequent
special tours. At Halloween, for example, the house is draped in typical 1800s
mourning, and the docents explain mourning customs (Historic New Orleans

Tours, p. 204, offers a year-round, interactive specialty tour of the Hermann-Grima House focusing on mourning customs). The house, which stretches from St. Louis Street to Conti Street, passed through two different families before becoming a boardinghouse in the 1920s. It has been meticulously restored and researched, and the tour is one of the city's more historically accurate offerings. On Thursdays from October through May, cooking demonstrations are scheduled to take place in the authentic 1830s kitchen, using methods of the era. (Alas, health rules prevent those on the tour from sampling the results.) The house also contains one of the Quarter's last surviving stables, complete with stalls. Combination tickets with the Gallier House are available for an additional $8.

820 St. Louis St. © **504/525-5661.** www.hgghh.org. Admission $10 adults; $8 seniors, students, AAA members, and children 8–18; free for children 7 and under. Open for tours Mon–Tues and Thurs–Fri 10am, 11am, noon, 1pm, and 2pm; Sat tours noon–3pm on the hour.

Historic New Orleans Collection—Museum/Research Center ★★ The Historic New Orleans Collection's museum of local and regional history is almost hidden away within a complex of historic French Quarter buildings. The oldest, constructed in the late 18th century, was one of the few structures to escape the disastrous fire of 1794. These buildings were owned by the collection's founders, General and Mrs. L. Kemper Williams. Their former residence, behind the courtyard, is open for tours. There are also excellent tours of the Louisiana history galleries, which feature choice items from the collection—expertly preserved and displayed art, maps, and original documents like the transfer papers for the Louisiana Purchase (1803). It also offers an architecture and courtyards tour, as well as seasonal history tours (like a history of Mardi Gras tour during Carnival season). The collection is owned and managed by a private foundation, not a governmental organization, and therefore offers more historical perspective and artifacts than boosterism. The Williams Gallery, also on the site, is free to the public and presents changing exhibitions that focus on Louisiana's history and culture; an upcoming exhibit in 2012 will focus on the state of Louisiana's bicentennial. It also has the best gift shop in town.

If you want to see another grandly restored French Quarter building (and a researcher's dream), visit the **Williams Research Center,** 410 Chartres St., near Conti Street (© **504/598-7171**), which houses and displays the bulk of the collection's many thousands of items. Admission is free.

533 Royal St., btw. St. Louis and Toulouse sts. © **504/523-4662.** www.hnoc.org. Free admission; tours $5. Tues–Sat 9:30am–4:30pm; Sun 10:30am–4:30pm. Tours Tues–Sat 10am, 11am, 2pm, and 3pm; Sun 11am, 2pm, and 3pm. Closed major holidays and Mardi Gras.

Madame John's Legacy ★ This is the second-oldest building in the Mississippi Valley (after the Ursuline Convent) and a rare example of Creole architecture that miraculously survived the 1794 fire.

Built around 1788 on the foundations of an earlier home that was destroyed in the fire of that year, the house has had a number of owners and renters (including the son of Governor Claiborne), but none of them were named John (or even Madame!). It acquired its moniker courtesy of author George Washington Cable, who used the house as a setting for his short story "'Tite Poulette." The protagonist was a quadroon named Madame John after her lover, who willed this house to her. Unfortunately the house is not open to the public except on rare occasions, but it's worth a walk-by for history and architecture buffs.

632 Dumaine St. © **504/568-6968.** http://lsm.crt.state.la.us.

7

The French Quarter

SIGHTS TO SEE & PLACES TO BE

Musée Conti Wax Museum ★ ☺ You might wonder about the advisability of a wax museum in a place as hot as New Orleans, but the Musée Conti holds up fine. This place is pretty neat—and downright spooky in spots. A large section is devoted to a sketch of Louisiana legends (Andrew Jackson, Napoleon, Jean Lafitte, Marie Laveau, Huey Long, a Mardi Gras Indian, Louis Armstrong, and Pete Fountain) and historical episodes. Whether or not these figures are the exact reproductions touted and prized by so many other wax museums is highly dubious, but the descriptions, especially of the historical scenes, are surprisingly informative and witty.

917 Conti St. ℂ **504/525-2605.** www.neworleanswaxmuseum.com. Admission $7 adults, $6.25 seniors, $6 children 4–17, children 3 and under free. Mon and Fri-Sat 10am–4pm, or by appointment.

New Orleans Historical Pharmacy Museum ★ Founded in 1950, the New Orleans Historical Pharmacy Museum is just what the name implies. In 1823, the first licensed pharmacist in the United States, Louis J. Dufilho, Jr., opened an apothecary shop here. The Creole-style town house doubled as his home, and he cultivated the herbs he needed for his medicines in the interior courtyard. Inside you'll find old apothecary bottles, voodoo potions, pill tiles, and suppository molds as well as the old glass cosmetics counter (pharmacists of the 1800s also manufactured makeup and perfumes), plus 19th-century surgical instruments and questionable medical devices such as blood-letting gizmos, and a whole slew of opium products. As alternative medicine gains acceptance, it's fascinating to look back at a time when all medicine was barely more than snake-oil potions.

514 Chartres St., at St. Louis St. ℂ **504/565-8027.** www.pharmacymuseum.org. Admission $5 adults, $4 students and seniors, children 5 and under free. Wed–Thurs 10am–1pm; Fri–Sat 10am–5pm.

New Orleans Historic Voodoo Museum Some of the hard-core voodoo practitioners in town might scoff at the Voodoo Museum, and perhaps rightly so. It is largely designed for tourists, but it is also really the only opportunity for tourists to get acquainted with the history and culture of voodoo. Don't expect high-quality, comprehensive exhibits—the place is dark, dusty, and musty. It's such a wasted opportunity, given the potential. There are occult objects from all over the globe plus some articles that allegedly belonged to the legendary Marie Laveau. Unless someone on staff talks you through it (which they will, if you ask), you might come away with more confusion than facts. Still, it's an adequate introduction. Who wouldn't want to bring home a voodoo doll from here? The people who run the museum are involved in voodoo, and there is generally a voodoo priest or priestess on-site, giving readings and making personal gris-gris bags. Again, it's voodoo for tourists, but for most tourists, it's probably the right amount. (Don't confuse this place with the Marie Laveau House of Voodoo on Bourbon St.)

A relic from the New Orleans Historical Pharmacy Museum.

724 Dumaine St., at Bourbon St. ℂ **504/680-0128.** www.voodoomuseum.com. Admission $7 adults; $5.50 students, seniors, and military; $4.50 high-school students; $3.50 children 11 and under; check website for discounts. Cemetery tour $19 adults, $10 children 12 and under. Daily 10am–6pm.

The Presbytère ★★★ The Presbytère was planned as housing for clergy but was never used for that purpose. It's now a museum with two terrific exhibits, one of which is a smashing Mardi Gras museum that does an excellent job of summing up the complex history of the city's major holiday, which is so much more than just rowdies displaying nekkid body parts. Five major themes trace the history of this high-profile but frankly little-understood (outside of New Orleans) annual event. The attention to detail covers everything from elaborate Mardi Gras Indian costumes to antique Rex Queen jewelry, and a re-creation of a float allows you to pretend you are throwing beads to a crowd (float aficionados should also check out Blaine Kern's Mardi Gras World, p. 181, where the floats are designed and built).

The first floor houses the multimedia exhibit *Living with Hurricanes: Katrina and Beyond* on the history and human drama of superstorms. Accessible rather than scholarly, the audio and video pieces are most effective at telling individual tales with appropriate shock, heartbreak, humor, and optimism. A replica attic with a crude hole in the ceiling displays the actual axe used by one woman to escape through her own roof; her recorded voice recounts the event. Hands-on scientific exhibits explain what happened with levees, wetlands, and storm-tracking—and what actually *should* happen. On one wall hangs a man's blue jeans, on which he inscribed his name, blood type, and next of kin's phone number in bold marker down the left leg, should he need to be I.D.'d. The moving exhibit stops short of being overwhelming (and just scratches the surface of some relevant sociopolitical topics) and provides a solid foundation for understanding New Orleans in both its pre- and post-Katrina contexts.

Allow a couple of hours to take it all in properly.

751 Chartres St., Jackson Sq. ℂ **800/568-6968** or 504/568-6968. http://lsm.crt.state.la.us. Admission $6 adults, $5 seniors and students, free for children 12 and under. Tues–Sun 10am–5pm.

Woldenberg Riverfront Park ★ This 20-acre park along the river serves as promenade and public art gallery, with numerous works by popular local artists amid green lawns and hundreds of trees. Seek out the kinetic Holocaust memorial sculpture by noted Israeli sculptor Yaacov Agam, and make a slow circle around it to get the full effect of its changing perspectives, which use a rainbow to unexpected symbolic effect.

A wonderful Mardi Gras museum, which includes exhibits featuring costumes, jewelry, and even a float, is housed within the Presbytère.

The nearby **Moonwalk** ★★★ is a paved pedestrian thoroughfare along the river, a wonderful walk on a pretty New Orleans day but really a must-do for any weather other than pouring rain. It has steps that allow you to get right down to Old Muddy—on foggy nights, you feel as if you are floating above the water. There are many benches from which to view the city's busy port—perhaps while enjoying a muffuletta to a street musician's song. To your right, you'll see the Greater New Orleans Bridge and the World Trade Center of New Orleans (formerly the International Trade Mart) skyscraper as well as the Toulouse Street wharf, the departure point for excursion steamboats. This is also an excellent spot to watch full moons rise over the river.

Along the Mississippi from the Moonwalk at the old Governor Nicholls St. wharf to the Aquarium of the Americas at Canal St. ℰ **504/861-2537.** Daily dawn–dusk.

OUTSIDE THE FRENCH QUARTER
Uptown & the Garden District

If you can see just one thing outside the French Quarter, make it the Garden District. These two neighborhoods are the first places that come to mind when one hears the words "New Orleans." It has no significant historic buildings or important museums—it's simply beautiful. In some ways, even more so than the Quarter, this is New Orleans. Authors as diverse as Truman Capote and Anne Rice have been enchanted by its spell. Gorgeous homes stand quietly amid lush foliage, elegant but ever so slightly (or more) decayed. You can see why this is the setting for so many novels; it's hard to imagine that anything real actually happens here.

But it does. Like the Quarter, this is a neighborhood, so please be courteous as you wander around. Seeing the sights consists mostly of looking at the exteriors of nice houses, so we suggest that you see "Walking Tour 2: The Garden District" (see chapter 8, "City Strolls"), which will help guide you to the Garden District's treasures and explain a little of its history. Use the listings in chapter 9, "Shopping," to find the best shops, galleries, and bookstores on **Magazine Street,** the main shopping strip that bounds the Garden District.

Meanwhile, a little background: Across Canal Street from the Quarter, "American" New Orleans begins. After the Louisiana Purchase of 1803, an essentially French-Creole city came under the auspices of a government determined to develop it as an American city. Tensions between Creole society and the encroaching American newcomers began to increase. Some historians lay this at the feet of Creole snobbery; others blame the naive and uncultured Americans. In any case, Creole society succeeded in maintaining a relatively distinct social world, deflecting American settlement upriver of Canal Street (Uptown); the Americans in turn came to dominate the city with sheer numbers of immigrants. Newcomers bought up land in what had been the old Gravier Plantation (now the Uptown area) and began to build a parallel city. Very soon, Americans came to dominate the local business scene, centered along Canal Street. In 1833 the American enclave that we now know as the Garden District was incorporated as Lafayette City, and—thanks in large part to the New Orleans–Carrollton Railroad, which covered the route of today's St. Charles Avenue streetcar—the Americans kept right on expanding until they reached the tiny resort town of Carrollton. It wasn't until 1852 that the various sections came together officially as a united New Orleans.

Again, as with the Quarter, it was great good fortune for the crucial economy generated by tourism that the Garden District was largely undamaged by Katrina and Rita, and its beauty remains as intoxicating as ever.

Trolling St. John's Bayou & Lake Pontchartrain ★★★

St. John's Bayou is a body of water that originally extended from the outskirts of New Orleans to Lake Pontchartrain, and it's one of the key reasons New Orleans is where it is today. Jean-Baptiste Le Moyne, Sieur de Bienville, was commissioned to establish a settlement in Louisiana that would both make money and protect French holdings in the New World from British expansion. Bienville chose the spot where New Orleans now sits because he recognized the strategic importance of the bayou's "back-door" access to the lake, and ultimately to the Gulf of Mexico. Boats could enter the lake from the Gulf and then follow the bayou until they were within easy portage distance of the mouth of the Mississippi River. Native Americans had used this route for years.

The early path from the city to the bayou is today's Bayou Road, an extension of Governor Nicholls Street in the French Quarter. Modern-day Gentilly Boulevard, which crosses the bayou, was another Native American trail—it led around the lake and on to settlements in Florida.

As New Orleans grew and prospered, the bayou became a suburb as planters moved out along its shores. In the early 1800s, a canal was dug to connect the waterway with the city, reaching a basin at the edge of Congo Square. The bayou became a popular recreation area with fine restaurants and dance halls (and meeting places for voodoo practitioners, who held secret ceremonies along its shores). Gradually, New Orleans reached beyond the French Quarter and enveloped the whole area—overtaking farmland, plantation homes, and resorts.

The canal was filled in long ago, and the bayou is a meek re-creation of itself. It is no longer navigable (even if it were, bridges were built too low to permit the passage of watercraft other than kayaks), but residents still prize their

Residents of Bayou St. John take advantage of the water.

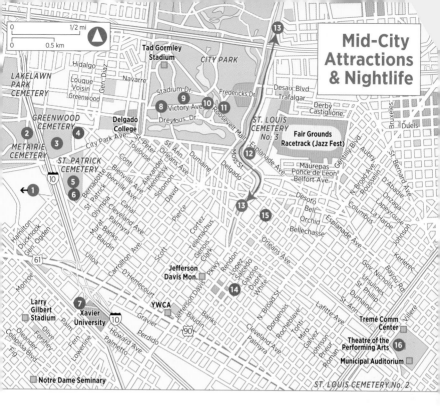

waterfront sites, and rowboats and sailboats sometimes make use of the bayou's surface. This is one of the prettiest areas of New Orleans—full of the old houses tourists love to marvel at without the hustle, bustle, and confusion of more high-profile locations. A stroll along the banks and through the nearby neighborhoods is one of our favorite things to do on a nice afternoon.

GETTING THERE The simplest way to reach St. John's Bayou from the French Quarter is to drive straight up Esplanade Avenue about 20 blocks (you can also grab the bus that says ESPLANADE at any of the bus stops along the avenue). Or take the Esplanade Ridge walking tour in chapter 8, "City Strolls." Right before you reach the bayou, you'll pass **St. Louis Cemetery No. 3** (just past Leda St.). It's the final resting place of many prominent New Orleanians, among them Father Adrien Rouquette, who lived and worked among the Choctaw; Storyville photographer E. J. Bellocq; and Thomy Lafon, the black philanthropist who bought the old Orleans Ballroom as an orphanage for African-American children and put an end to its infamous "quadroon balls," where well-bred women of mixed color would socialize with and become the mistresses of white men. Walking just past the cemetery, turn left onto Moss Street, which runs along the banks of St. John's Bayou. If you want to see an example of an 18th-century West Indies–style plantation house, stop at the **Pitot House,** 1440 Moss St. (p. 189).

To continue, drive along Wisner Boulevard, on the opposite bank of St. John's Bayou from Moss Street, and you'll pass some of New Orleans's grandest modern homes—a sharp contrast to those on Moss Street. Stay on Wisner to Robert E. Lee Boulevard, turn right, drive to Elysian Fields Avenue, and then turn left. That's the University of New Orleans campus on your left. Turn left onto the broad concrete highway, Lake Shore Drive. It runs for 5½ miles along the lake, and normally in the summer, the parkway alongside its sea wall is swarming with swimmers and picnickers. On the other side are more luxurious, modern residences. About 2 miles down the road to the west is the fishing-oriented Bucktown neighborhood. If you haven't already noticed some leftover Katrina desolation along this drive, you'll probably see it here. This area, home to commercial fishing since the late 1800s, was totally devastated by the 17th Street Canal breech, including the marina, where the storm piled boats atop each other. The beloved Sid-Mar's restaurant is gone for good from its decades-old Lakeview home—but locals were thrilled to see it come back a few miles farther afield in Metairie. There's a thriving restaurant hub along Harrison Avenue, something to think of before you head home. You may want a snack after this drive.

As you return, you can drive through the Lakeview neighborhood, south of Robert E. Lee, between Canal and City Park. This area suffered greatly in the storm (sitting in up to 12 ft. of water), but was also one of the first to come back in earnest.

Lake Pontchartrain is some 40 miles long and 25 miles wide. You can drive across it over the 24-mile Greater New Orleans Causeway, the longest bridge in the world.

Museums & Galleries

Backstreet Cultural Museum ★ Part private obsession, part cultural jewel, this small facility is off the beaten path but a must-stop for anyone interested in the true history and culture of New Orleans. The city would be nothing without the rhythms of such rituals as brass bands, second lines, social clubs, jazz funerals, and the wholly unique Mardi Gras Indians, and this collection gathers remarkable examples and explanations for all of them in one place. It's not as slick as similar efforts at the Presbytère, but it contains even more special examples of such art as the feathered and sequined wonders that are the Mardi Gras Indians' handmade suits. It's also located right in the heart of the Treme, the neighborhood that spawned so much of what is celebrated here. The owner, Sylvester, is an eccentric trip, but not only has he carefully documented this vital culture, he's also the real New Orleans, so spend some time with him. *Note:* Be forewarned, the posted hours can be a little loose.

1116 St. Claude Ave. ✆ **504/522-4806.** www.backstreetmuseum.org. Admission $8. Tues–Sat 10am–5pm.

A few familiar faces at Blaine Kern's Mardi Gras World.

Blaine Kern's Mardi Gras World ★★ ☺ Few cities can boast a thriving float-making industry. New Orleans can, and despite recent family scandals, no float makers thrive more than the Kerns, who make more than three-quarters of the floats used by the various krewes every Carnival season (and now they're made with energy-saving hybrid chassis). Mardi Gras World offers tours of its collection of float sculptures and its studios, where you can see floats being made year-round. Visitors may see sculptors at work, making small "sketches" of the figures or the enormous sculptures that adorn the floats. You can even try on some heavily bejeweled and dazzling costumes (definitely bring your camera!). Although they could do more with this tour, the entire package does add up to a most enjoyable experience, and it is rather nifty to see the floats up close—and tours include King Cake and coffee.

1380 Port of New Orleans Place. ✆ **504/361-7821.** www.mardigrasworld.com. Admission $19 adults, $15 students and seniors (66 and over), $12 children 3–11, free for children 2 and under. Daily 9am–4:30pm. Last tour at 4:10pm. Closed Mardi Gras, Easter, Thanksgiving, and Christmas.

Confederate Memorial Hall Museum ★★ Not far from the French Quarter is the Confederate Museum, the oldest surviving museum in Louisiana (established in 1891, and surviving a takeover bid for its lovely brick facility by next door's Ogden Museum of Southern Art). It currently houses the second-largest collection of Confederate memorabilia in the country, many items in excellent condition, having been donated soon after the war. Among these are guns, swords, photographs, oil paintings, 125 battle flags, and Confederate uniforms. You'll see the personal effects of Confederate General P. G. T. Beauregard, Confederate President Jefferson Davis, and Robert E. Lee, as well as portraits and artifacts that were standard issue for the troops. It's heaven for Civil War buffs.

929 Camp St., at St. Joseph's. ✆ **504/523-4522.** www.confederatemuseum.com. Admission $7 adults; $5 students, active military, and seniors; $2 children 12 and under. Tues–Sat 10am–4pm.

Relics from the Civil War are on display at the Confederate Memorial Hall Museum.

The Contemporary Arts Center exhibits work by regional, national, and international artists.

Contemporary Arts Center ★★ Redesigned in the early 1990s to much critical applause, the Contemporary Arts Center (CAC) is a main anchor of the city's young arts district, now home to a plethora of leading local galleries. Over the past 2 decades, the center has consistently exhibited influential and ground-breaking work by regional, national, and international artists in various mediums. The CAC staggers its shows, so there should always be something worth see-ing hanging on the walls; it also presents theater, performance art, and music concerts. Individual exhibitions hang for 6 to 8 weeks, and performances are weekly.

900 Camp St. © **504/528-3805.** www.cacno.org. Gallery admission $5, $3 students and se-niors, free for members. (Sometimes exhibits are free, even for nonmembers!) Performance and event tickets $5–$15. Galleries Thurs–Sun 11am–4pm.

National World War II Museum ★★★ Opened in 2000 on the anniversary of D-Day, to tell the story of Normandy and the 18 other U.S. amphibious opera-tions worldwide on that fateful day, it has since expanded tremendously in size and scope. This creation of the late best-selling author (and *Saving Private Ryan* consultant) Stephen Ambrose with major support from Tom Hanks has become a New Orleans highlight and true world-class facility, due to its rich collection of artifacts (including some British Spitfire airplanes) and top-of-the-line edu-cational materials (check out the fascinating oral-history station). Perhaps most affecting are the many exhibits emphasizing personal stories, including audio and video of civilians and soldiers recounting their experiences. Artifacts from both home and former soldiers provide the sort of personal details that pull history off the pages of books. A panorama allows visitors to see just what it was like on those notorious beaches; a short, shocking film on the atomic bomb is aptly silent but for carefully chosen classical music (it may be too gruesome and intense for children). There is also a copy of Eisenhower's contingency speech, in which he planned to apologize to the country for the failure of D-Day—thankfully, it was a speech that was neither needed nor delivered. Opening in 2012, the Freedom Pavilion will showcase an actual Boeing B-17 and an interactive submarine where visitors can "man the controls."

To lighten the mood (if not the belly), the **Stage Door Canteen** has live, 1940s-era USO-style shows. The talented cast swings and croons with aplomb, and dinner or brunch shows make this a good, old-fashioned outing (adults $50–$60; children $45–$50; $30 show only). Showing in the **Solomon Victory Theater,** *Beyond All Boundaries,* billed as having "4D technology," is a brief, widescreen film that summarizes the Allied war effort with multisensory effects (seats shake, lights flash, and jungle steam and winter snow make appearances). It's moderately successful at engaging kids (though not for the very young) in the war story, but James Cameron can relax. Tickets are adults $10 ($23 with museum admission), seniors $8 ($18), and kids $9 ($12). Lastly, celeb chef John Besh helms the museum's fun **American Sector** restaurant (p. 143), serving modern comfort food that harkens back to the war era.

Volunteers who served in the war are often around, ready to tell their own history in vivid and riveting detail. This is the only museum of its kind in the country, and the entire place is deeply moving, even for those with only minimal interest in matters military.

945 Magazine St., in the Historic Warehouse District. ✆ **504/527-6012.** www.ddaymuseum.org. Admission for museum only $18 adults, $14 seniors, $9 active or retired military with ID and children 5–17, WWII veterans free. Other discounts apply for combination tickets and military in uniform. Daily 9am–5pm. Closed holidays.

The National World War II Museum houses a rich collection of artifacts from World War II.

Opened in 1911, the New Orleans Museum of Art (NOMA) is located in City Park.

New Orleans Museum of Art ★★ Often called NOMA, this museum is located in an idyllic section of City Park. The front portion of the museum is the original large, imposing neoclassical building ("sufficiently modified to give a subtropical appearance," said the architect Samuel Marx); the rear portion is a striking contrast of contemporary curves and materials. The museum opened in 1911 with seed money gifted by Isaac Delgado, a sugar broker and Jamaican immigrant. Today it houses a 40,000-piece collection including pre-Columbian and Native American ethnographic art; 16th- through 20th-century European paintings, drawings, sculptures, and prints; early American art; Asian art; a gallery entirely devoted to Fabergé; and one of the six largest decorative glass collections in the United States. **Ralph Brennan's Courtyard Café** offers light lunch fare, wine, and picture windows during museum hours.

Next door is the superb **Besthoff Sculpture Garden** ★★★, 5 serene, landscaped acres spotlighting 50 modern sculptures by artists such as Henry Moore, Gaston Lachaise, Elisabeth Frink, George Segal, and others, including a version of Indiana's famous pop-art *LOVE* sculpture. Admission is free to this New Orleans cultural highlight. Consider grabbing a po' boy at nearby Parkway Bakery and picnicking among the stellar garden collection.

1 Collins Diboll Circle, at City Park and Esplanade. ✆ **504/658-4100.** www.noma.org. Admission $10 adults, $8 seniors (65 and over) and students, $6 children 7–17, kids 6 and under and local students free. Free admission Wed. Tues–Sun 10am–5pm (Fri to 9pm). Closed Mon and most major holidays. Sculpture Garden daily 10am–4:45pm (Fri to 8:45pm).

The Ogden Museum of Southern Art ★★★ This is the premier collection of Southern art in the United States. Though the building is dazzling, it is built around an atrium that takes up a great deal of space that could be devoted to still more displays. It does make for a dramatic interior, but given such a marvelous collection, one is greedy for more art rather than more architecture. But the facility is wonderful, the artists are impressive, and the graphics are well designed,

informative, and often humorous. Just the permanent exhibit of self-taught/outsider art alone makes this worth a visit. Special exhibits are thoughtfully constructed, often containing enriching details.

Consider coming during Thursdays' delightful **Ogden After Hours,** which includes a live band (anything from 1930s country to old Delta blues guys to the New Orleans Philharmonic and all manner of jazz) playing in the atrium, adding a soundtrack to your visit. These evenings are among the special delights of New Orleans. We're also keen on the well-curated gift shop, which has consistently covetable souvenirs with a local spin.

A sculpture sits in the courtyard at the Ogden Museum of Southern Art.

925 Camp St. ☎ **504/539-9600.** www. ogdenmuseum.org. Admission $10 adults, $8 seniors and students, $5 children 5–17. Wed–Mon 10am–5pm; Thurs 6–8pm for evening shows featuring live music.

Southern Food and Beverage Museum & Museum of the American Cocktail The South's first food-and-beverage museum is an informative assemblage of Southern food and drink history, from farmers to cooks and everything in between, represented by all kinds of goodies. Ultimately, this is probably more for food or history buffs than a general audience, however. The location is in the far west end of the Riverwalk Marketplace—be prepared for a potentially long walk, but enjoy the river views along the way. The main hall houses a comprehensive collection of artifacts illustrating how different ethnic groups (the usual French, Spanish, and African suspects, but also Germans, Italians, and Irish), geography, and time have contributed to the local cuisine. Exhibits rotate, but we enjoyed one that explored the various aspects of White House culinaria and customs through photos, menus, tableware, and even a sneak peek into the refrigerator of the official capital kitchens. An installation on all things absinthe is promised for 2012, and interesting special events and tastings are fairly frequent. Behind the scenes are scholarly research and extensive cookbook and menu archives. Enticing scents from the nearby food court—a little eau de red beans 'n' rice and crawfish étouffée—only adds to the atmosphere.

The **Museum of the American Cocktail** is a stumble through 200 years of cocktail history and New Orleans's own vital role in same. (So the Sazerac was only *one* of the first cocktails!) Curator Ted "Dr. Cocktail" Haigh is passionate about his impressive collection and offers an original and lively glimpse into the colorful history of our favorite "poison." Historical artifacts include defunct product packaging and Prohibition-era photos. (We love the bottles of commercially sold gin, rye, and bourbon flavoring that would go into whatever rotgut you made at home to make it palatable.) Like the main SOFAB, exhibits rotate, and the museum has regular seminars, demonstrations, and tastings.

1 Poydras St. (in the Riverwalk Marketplace Mall). ℂ **504/569-0405.** http://southernfood.org and www.museumoftheamericancocktail.org. Admission to both museums: $10 adults; $8 AAA members; $5 seniors, active military, and students with ID. Mon–Sat 10am–7pm; Sun noon–6pm.

Historic New Orleans Churches

Church and religion are not likely to be the first things that jump to mind in a city known for its debauchery. But New Orleans remains a very Catholic city—don't forget that Mardi Gras is a pre-Lenten celebration. In fact, religion of one form or another directed much of the city's early history and molded its culture in countless ways.

For a detailed review of the St. Louis Cathedral, see "Major Attractions," earlier in this chapter.

St. Alphonsus Church ★ The interior of this church is probably the most beautiful of any church in the city, right up there with some of the lusher ones in Italy. The Irish built St. Alphonsus Church in 1855 because they refused to worship at St. Mary's (see below) with their German-speaking neighbors. The gallery, columns, and sharply curving staircases lead to spooky, atmospheric balconies where the paint and plaster are peeling off in chunks.

The church no longer holds Mass. Ironically, when St. Mary's was restored, St. Alphonsus was closed, and the congregation moved across the street. Hopes for similar restoration here are high but it's no small undertaking. The downriver bell tower was blown dramatically across the street when Katrina hit, while the upriver one was moved 15 degrees. It also lost several stained-glass windows (since repaired) and ultimately incurred over half a million dollars in damage.

Currently, the church operates an Arts and Cultural Center, which includes a small Irish art and history museum. You can tour the still fabulous-looking interior and the museum or take the free (but donations gratefully accepted and much needed) tour conducted by Anne Rice's raconteur cousin Billy Murphy, an option we highly recommend. Informal tour times are Tuesdays, Thursdays, and Saturdays 10am to 2pm or by advance arrangement; calling ahead to check is recommended.

2030 Constance St., at St. Andrew St. ℂ **504/524-8116.** For information, call the Friends of St. Alphonsus at ℂ **504/482-0008.**

St. Augustine Church ★★ One of the great cultural landmarks of New Orleans's black history, St. Augustine has been a center of community life in the troubled but striving Treme neighborhood since the mid-1800s. This church was founded by "free people of color," who also purchased pews to be used exclusively by slaves (frustrating their white masters!). This was a first in the history of slavery in the U.S., and resulted in one of the most integrated churches in the country. In the modern era, under the direction of its visionary and charismatic then-pastor, Father Jerome LeDoux, St. Augustine continued to celebrate its history by integrating traditional African and New Orleans elements into its services. Homer Plessy, Sidney Bechet, and Big Chief Tootie Montana all called this their home church. In late 2005 the archdiocese decided to close St. Augustine due to diminished membership, but a major public outcry bought it a reprieve and it is going strong again. Services here remain remarkable, especially when the jazzy 10am Sunday Mass features a guest performer like Troy Andrews or John Boutté—this can be one of the best free concerts in town.

St. Augustine's was founded by "free people of color."

Frequent art exhibits celebrating the neighborhood, and the deeply moving Tomb of the Unknown Slave outside, make this worth a stop any time (though you should call ahead to make sure it's open). Combine it with a trip to the Backstreet Cultural Museum across the street. And please leave a donation; let's try to keep St. Augustine going another couple centuries.

1210 Governor Nicholls St. ✆ **504/525-5934.** www.staugustinecatholicchurch-neworleans.org.

St. Mary's Assumption ★ Built in 1860 by the German Catholics, this is an even more baroque and grand church than its Irish neighbor across the street (see St. Alphonsus Church, above), complete with dozens of life-size saints' statues. The two churches make an interesting contrast to one another. Also inside the church is the national shrine to the hero of the 1867 yellow-fever epidemic, Blessed Father Francis Xavier Seelos, who was beatified (one step away from sainthood) in 2000. Here you can see his original coffin, some of his personal belongings, a display containing recently discovered locks of his hair, and the centerpiece of the shrine, a reliquary containing his bodily remains. Should Father Seelos become a saint, expect this shrine to be an even bigger deal and place of pilgrimage than it already is.

2030 Constance St., at Josephine St. ✆ **504/522-6748.** Open during Mass, Mon–Fri 8am; Fri-Sat 4pm; Sun 10:30am; otherwise by appointment only. Call the number above or ✆ **504/525-2495.**

St. Patrick's Church The original St. Patrick's was a tiny wooden building founded to serve the spiritual needs of Irish Catholics. The present building, begun in 1838, was constructed around the old one, which was then dismantled. The distinguished architect James Gallier, Sr., designed much of the interior, including the altar. It opened in 1840, proudly proclaiming itself as the "American" Catholics' answer to the St. Louis Cathedral in the French Quarter (where, according to the Americans, God spoke only in French).

724 Camp St., at Girod St. ✆ **504/525-4413.** www.oldstpatricks.org.

St. Roch and the Campo Santo

★★ 🎁 Saint Roch is the patron saint of plague victims; a local priest prayed to him to keep his flock safe during an epidemic in 1867. When everyone came through all right, the priest made good on his promise to build Saint Roch a chapel. The Gothic result is fine enough, but what is best is the small room just off the altar, where successful supplicants to Saint Roch leave gifts, usually in the form of plaster anatomical parts or medical supplies, to represent what the saint healed for them. The resulting collection of bizarre artifacts (everything from eyeballs and crutches to organs and false limbs) is either deeply moving or the greatest creepy spontaneous folk-art installation you've ever seen. The chapel, located on the cemetery grounds, isn't always open despite the posted hours, so hope for the best.

A small room off the altar in St. Roch's chapel contains a collection of bizarre gifts.

1725 St. Roch Ave., at N. Derbigny St. Daily 10am–5pm.

A Few More Interesting New Orleans Buildings

Degas House ★ Legendary French Impressionist Edgar Degas had a tender spot in his heart for New Orleans; his mother and grandmother were born here, and he spent several months in 1872 and 1873 visiting his brother at this house. It was a trip that resulted in a number of paintings, and this is the only residence or studio associated with Degas anywhere in the world that is open to the public. One of the artist's paintings showed the garden of the house behind his brother's. His brother liked that view, too; he later ran off with the wife of the judge who lived there. His brother's wife and children later took back her maiden name, Musson. The Musson home, as it is formally known, was erected in 1854 and has since been sliced in two and redone in an Italianate manner and restored as a B&B. It's also open to the public for tours, brunch events, and painting parties, all by appointment only.

2306 Esplanade Ave., north of the Quarter, before you reach N. Broad Ave. ☏ **504/821-5009.** www.degashouse.com. Admission $15 adults; $13 seniors, students, and active military; $8 for children 12 and under. Breakfast, mimosas, and tours $35, reservations required. Daily 10:30am–noon, or by appointment.

Gallier Hall This impressive Greek Revival building was the inspiration of James Gallier, Sr. Erected between 1845 and 1853, it served as City Hall for just over a century and has been the site of many important events in the city's history —especially during the Reconstruction and Huey Long eras. Several important figures in Louisiana history lay in state in Gallier Hall, including Jefferson Davis and General Beauregard. Of late, it was local music legends Ernie K-Doe and Earl King who were so honored. Five thousand mourners paid respects to K-Doe,

Pitot House is a typical West Indies–style plantation home.

who was laid out in a white costume with a silver crown and scepter before being delivered to his final resting place accompanied by a big, brassy jazz procession. King, wearing a vivid purple suit, also was honored with a jazz funeral, with twirling umbrellas and rock royalty in attendance at his 2003 service.

545 St. Charles Ave. Not usually open to the public.

Pitot House ★ Set along pretty Bayou St. John (p. 178), the Pitot House is a typical West Indies–style plantation home, restored and furnished with early-19th-century Louisiana and American antiques. Dating from 1799, it originally stood where the nearby modern Catholic school is. In 1810 it became the home of James Pitot, the first mayor of incorporated New Orleans (he served 1804–05). Tours here are usually given by a most knowledgeable docent or an equally knowledgeable architecture student, and are surprisingly interesting and informative.

1440 Moss St., near Esplanade Ave. ✆ **504/482-0312.** www.pitothouse.org. Admission $7 adults, $5 seniors and students, free for children 6 and under, parties of 10 or more $5 each. Wed–Sat 10am–3pm (last tour at 2:15pm), or by appointment.

The Superdome ★ Completed in 1975, the Superdome is a landmark civic structure that took on a new worldwide image when it was used as a shelter during Katrina. Intended only as a locale of last resort for those who simply had no other evacuation choice (and with no adequate assistance plans in place), the Superdome quickly turned into hell on earth when tens of thousands of refugees came or were brought there. Along with the Convention Center, it became a symbol of suffering, neglect, and despair, as people were trapped without sufficient food, water, medical care, or, it seemed, hope.

As it happened, the New Orleans Saints reopened the Superdome in 2006 with much hoopla for their first home game (and halftime featuring Green Day and U2), and went on to the playoffs. The following year they won their first Super Bowl ever, to ridiculous rejoicing far beyond the city boundaries. Capping the gleaming success of the team and the Dome's $118-million renovation (new seats, suites, and so on), the entire building was then "re-skinned" in glittery gold tone, a shining beacon of what can arise from the darkest Katrina days. Do join us locals in a chant of "WHO DAT?!"

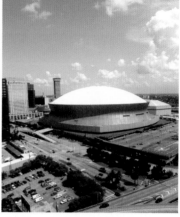

All eyes were focused on the Superdome in the days after Hurricane Katrina, when it housed thousands of refugees from the storm.

Here are the Superdome's stats: It's the largest fixed-dome structure in the world (680 ft. diameter, covering 13 acres), a 27-story windowless building with a seating capacity of 76,000 and a computerized climate-control system that uses more than 9,000 tons of equipment. Inside, no posts obstruct the spectator's view of any sporting event while movable partitions and seats allow the building to be vastly configured. Besides sports events (the Super Bowl is slated again for 2014, and the Sugar Bowl is back annually), this flying saucer of a building plays host to conventions, balls, concerts, and other productions, as does its sister Arena next door. **Champions Square,** a new outdoor and indoor plaza, has become pre- and post-game central, and official Saints and Hornets gear is available year-round in the Dome store.

1500 block of Poydras St., near Rampart St. ℂ **504/587-3663.** www.superdome.com.

Floating Across the River to Algiers Point

Algiers, annexed by New Orleans in 1870, is about a quarter-mile across the Mississippi River from New Orleans. Generally ignored because of its location, it became a sort of God's country after the hurricane because it did not flood at all, and many services, such as mail delivery, were restored quite quickly. It still has the feel of an undisturbed turn-of-the-20th-century suburb, and strolling around here is a delightfully low-key way to spend an hour or two. It is easily accessible via the free **Canal Street ferry** that runs from the base of Canal Street. *Tip:* This unfancy ferry is one of New Orleans's best-kept secrets—it's a great way to get out onto the river and see the skyline (and it's perfectly timed for kids' attention spans). A ferry leaves New Orleans at 15 and 45 minutes past the hour from 6:15am to 12:15am, and departs Algiers on the half-hour. The last ferry returns at around midnight, but be sure to check the schedule before you set out, just in case.

PARKS & GARDENS

One of the many unsettling details following weeks of Katrina flooding was how normally verdant New Orleans had turned to shades of gray and brown. The vegetation had drowned. Regular rainfall has restored New Orleans's lushness, though the loss of some centuries-old oaks is hard to get past. With enough funds and TLC, all but the most badly damaged buildings can be repaired, but a massive old oak cannot be replaced in our lifetime.

Parks

Audubon Park ★★ ☺ Across from Loyola and Tulane universities, Audubon Park and the adjacent Audubon Zoo (see "A Day at the Zoo," below) sprawl over 340 acres, extending from St. Charles Avenue all the way to the Mississippi River. This tract once belonged to city founder Jean-Baptiste Le Moyne and later was part of the Etienne de Boré plantation, where sugar was granulated for the first time in 1794. Although John James Audubon, the country's best-known ornithologist, lived only briefly in New Orleans (in a cottage on Dauphine St. in the French Quarter), the city has honored him by naming the park, the zoo, and even a golf course after him.

The huge trees with black bark are live oaks; some go back to plantation days, and more than 200 additional ones were recently planted here to replace the many that did not survive Hurricane Katrina. Other than the trees, it's not the most visually arresting park in the world—it's just pretty and a nice place to be. Visitors can enjoy a shaded picnic among statuary, fountains, and gazebos; feed ducks in a lagoon; and pretend they're Thoreau. Or they can look with envy at the lovely old houses whose backyards literally bump up against the park. The most utilized feature of the park is the 1¾-mile paved, traffic-free walking, running, skating, and biking road that loops around the lagoon and golf course. Along the track are 18 exercise stations; tennis courts and horseback-riding facilities can be found elsewhere in the park. Audubon Zoo is toward the back of the park, across Magazine Street. Behind the zoo, check out the pavilion and green space on the riverbank; this popular area, called the **Fly,** has pleasant views of Frisbee players and the Mississippi.

6500 Magazine St., btw. Broadway and Exposition Blvd. ℂ **504/581-4629.** www.audubon institute.org. Daily 5am–10pm.

Chalmette Battlefield/Jean Lafitte National Historical Park & Preserve
★★ On the grounds of what is now Chalmette National Historical Park, the bloody **Battle of New Orleans** was waged on January 14, 1815. Ironically, the battle should never have been fought: A treaty signed 2 weeks before in Ghent, Belgium, had ended the War of 1812. But word had not yet reached Congress, the commander of the British forces, or Andrew Jackson, who stood with American forces to defend New Orleans and the mouth of the Mississippi River. The battle did, however, succeed in uniting Americans and Creoles in New Orleans and in making Jackson a hero in this city.

Markers on the battlefield allow you to follow the course of the battle (or you can just watch the film in the visitor center). Inside the park is a national cemetery, established in 1864. It holds only two American veterans from the Battle of New Orleans and some 14,000 Union soldiers who fell in the Civil War. For a terrific view of the

Audubon Park is a favorite place for locals to bike, run, skate, and walk, among other outdoor activities.

The peaceful and scenic lagoons in City Park make for a quiet place to fish, ride pedal boats, or just sit for a spell.

Mississippi River, climb the levee in back of the Beauregard House. To reach the park, take St. Claude Avenue southeast from the French Quarter until it becomes St. Bernard Highway, in approximately 7 miles. **Note:** This drive will take you through the hard-hit Lower 9th Ward and the similarly recovering towns of Arabi and Chalmette.

8606 W. St. Bernard Hwy. ✆ **504/589-3882.** www.nps.gov/jela. Free admission. Grounds and restrooms daily 9am–4:30pm. Closed Mardi Gras and Dec 25.

City Park ★★★ ☺ Once part of the Louis Allard plantation and recently named one of America's "Coolest Parks," City Park has been here a long time and has seen it all—including that favorite pastime among 18th-century New Orleans gentry: dueling. At the entrance, you'll see a statue of General P. G. T. Beauregard, whose order to fire on Fort Sumter kicked off the Civil War. The extensive, beautifully landscaped grounds were Katrina-ized, enduring serious flooding, though you'd never know it now. This enormous treasure (1,300 acres) looks terrific, and it's a charming spot for a walk and bird-watching, golf, tennis, and gazing at the moss-dripping live oaks (the largest collection in the world!). It holds botanical gardens and a conservatory, picnic areas, lagoons for boating and fishing, pedal boats, a brand-spanking-new tennis center, a bandstand with summertime concerts, two stadiums, playing fields, two miniature trains, and **Children's Storyland,** an amusement area, including fairy-tale figures upon which one can climb and carouse, an antique carousel (see "Especially for Kids," later in this chapter), and rides. At Christmastime, the mighty oaks are strung with lights—quite a magical sight—and during Halloween the park hosts the massive Voodoo Experience music festival (p. 56).

You'll also find the **New Orleans Museum of Art** (p. 184) at Collins Diboll Circle, on Lelong Avenue, in a building that is itself a work of art. Tucked away here is one of the oddest and most charming attractions in this odd and charming city, the **Train Garden.** Imagine a massive train set, the kind every 9-year-old kid (or kid at heart) would kill for. Now imagine that it's located in Dr. Seuss's basement, if Dr. Seuss was obsessed with both New Orleans and organic materials. Along 1,300 feet of track are replicas of 1890s streetcars and ornately detailed, bizarrely beautiful representations of actual New Orleans neighborhoods and landmarks—all made from organic plant material! In a town of must-see attractions, this is just one more. The Botanical and Train Gardens are open year-round Tuesday to Sunday from 10am to 4:30pm, but the trains only run on Saturday and Sunday from 10am to 4pm, weather permitting. Admission to the gardens is $6 adults, $3 children 5 to 12, and free for children 4 and under. The gardens are located in the Pavilions of Two Sisters on Victory Avenue in the park. Storyland admission is $3. The Carousel Gardens Amusement Park admission is $3 and rides are $3 each; a $17 bracelet allows you unlimited rides.

1 Palm Dr. ☏ **504/482-4888.** www.neworleanscitypark.com. Free admission to park. Park daily sunrise–10pm. Each attraction has its own hours that vary by season, so call or check website.

Gardens

Longue Vue House & Gardens ★★ ☺ One of many remarkable things about New Orleans is all the little pockets of the unexpected. Sure, this relatively big city has its share of typical big-city landscapes, but it also has the Garden District, the Marigny, and the Longue Vue mansion. Just 20 minutes from the city center, near the more interesting end of suburban Metairie, is a unique expression of Greek Revival architecture set on an 8-acre estate, constructed from 1939 to 1942 and listed on the National Register of Historic Places. It's like stumbling across a British country-house estate, and while it was never a plantation, it may just satisfy your Tara-esque cravings while keeping you within 5 minutes of a Home Depot. So add it to your list of "nice places to ramble on a pretty day."

The mansion was designed to foster a close rapport between indoors and outdoors, with vistas of formal terraces and pastoral woods. Sometimes if you've seen one big, fancy house you've seen them all, so you may not want to bother timing your visit with one of the house tours. The charming gardens were partly inspired by the Generalife, the former summerhouse of the sultans in Granada, Spain; look also for fountains and a colonnaded loggia.

The Longue Vue House, near Metairie, is an example of Greek Revival architecture.

193

It goes without saying that this is a must for garden enthusiasts, but others may also become smitten with the delightful **Discovery Garden,** where kids can play (and maybe even learn) from various clever and amusing exhibits. It costs more than a public park, and there is nothing that goes beep (though there might be buzzing exhibits on insects!), but do keep it in mind for an alternate kid-friendly activity.

7 Bamboo Rd., New Orleans, near Metairie. ℂ **504/488-5488.** www.longuevue.com. Admission $10 adults; $9 children, seniors, active military, and students. Tues–Sat 10am–5pm; Sun 1–5pm. Hourly tours start at 10am Tues–Sat and at 1pm on Sun; last tour 4pm. Closed Jan 1, Mardi Gras, Easter Sunday, July 4th, Labor Day, Thanksgiving, and Dec 24–25.

A Day at the Zoo

Audubon Zoo ★★★ ☺ It's been about 30 years since the Audubon Zoo underwent a total renovation that turned it from one of the worst zoos in the country into one of the best. The notable achievement resulted in a place of justifiable civic pride that delights even non–zoo fans. While a terrific destination for visitors with children, this small and sweet attraction offers a good change of pace for anyone. **Note:** On hot and humid days, you should plan your visit for early or late in the day; otherwise, the animals will be sleeping off the heat (there are misters and shady oaks for the humans, but hot is hot).

Here, some 1,800 animals (including rare and endangered species) live in natural habitats in a setting of subtropical plants, waterfalls, lagoons, and a Louisiana swamp replica complete with rare white gators.

A memorable way to visit the zoo is to take the St. Charles Avenue streetcar to Audubon Park, where a free shuttle at the park, departing every 20 to 30 minutes, will take you to the zoo. You can also stroll through the park to the zoo. See a funny-looking mound near the river? That's **Monkey Hill,** constructed so that the children of this flatlands city could see what a hill looked like. The hill also

Around 1,800 animals live in natural habitats, including a Louisiana swamp, at the Audubon Zoo.

has a wading pond suitable for younger kids, while all ages will appreciate the Cool Zoo splash park. So bring swimsuits and towels if the weather is apt.

6500 Magazine St. ℭ **504/581-4629.** www.auduboninstitute.org. Admission $15 adults, $12 seniors (65 and over), $11 children 2-12. Add $5 for Cool Zoo access. Aquarium/IMAX/Zoo combo tickets available. Mar through Labor Day Tues–Sun 10am–5pm; Labor Day through 1st Tues in Mar Tues–Sun 10am–4pm. Last ticket sold 1 hr. before closing. Closed Mardi Gras Day, 1st Fri in May, Thanksgiving, and Christmas.

NEW ORLEANS CEMETERIES ★★★

Along with Spanish moss and lacy iron balconies, the cities of the dead are part of the indelible landscape of New Orleans. Their ghostly and inscrutable presence enthralls visitors, who are used to traditional methods of burial—in the ground or in mausoleums.

Why are bodies here buried aboveground? Well, it rains in New Orleans—a lot—sometimes to flooding. Soon after New Orleans was settled, it became apparent that Uncle Etienne had an unpleasant habit of bobbing back to the surface (doubtless no longer looking his best). Add to that cholera and yellow-fever epidemics, which helped increase the number of bodies and also the infection possibility. Given that the cemetery of the time was *inside* the Vieux Carré, it's all pretty disgusting to think about.

So in 1789 the city opened St. Louis Cemetery No. 1, right outside the city walls (which no longer exist) on what is now Rampart Street. The "condo crypt" look—the dead are placed in vaults that look like miniature buildings—was inspired to a certain extent by the famous Père Lachaise cemetery in Paris. Crypts were laid out haphazardly in St. Louis No. 1, which quickly filled up. Other cemeteries soon followed and eventually were incorporated into the city proper. Each has designated lanes, making for a more orderly appearance. The rows of tombs look something like a city, where the dead inhabitants peer over the shoulders of the living.

There are two types of these functional crypts: the aforementioned "family vaults" and the "oven crypts"—so called because of their resemblance to bread ovens in a wall. A coffin is slid inside, and the combination of heat and humidity acts like a slow form of cremation. In a year or so, the occupant's bones are pushed to the back, coffin pieces are removed, and another coffin can be inserted. In the larger family vaults (made of whitewashed brick), there are a couple of

 A tomb **OF ONE'S OWN**

For a singular souvenir or gift, artist **Michael Clement** sculpts miniature tombs (and shotgun houses) in rough-hewn terra cotta, finished in aged gold, bronze, and gunmetal gray. You're not going to find these in San Francisco. Not in Bali. Only in New Orleans. They're available at the **Historic New Orleans Collection gift shop** (p. 174) or directly from the artist (ℭ **504/899-1804;** www.michaeljclement.com). Prices start around $95 (and remember, no tax is charged on original works of art in many parts of the city). It's not everyone who wants a gilt crypt on their coffee table, but we do.

7

New Orleans Cemeteries

SIGHTS TO SEE & PLACES TO BE

Aboveground tombs are, along with Spanish moss and lacy iron balconies, part of the landscape of New Orleans.

shelves and the same thing happens. As family members die, the bones are swept into a pit below, and everyone eventually lies jumbled together. The result is sometimes dozens of names, going back generations, on a single spot. It's a very efficient use of cemetery space, far more so than conventional sweeping expanses of graveyard landscaping.

For many years, New Orleans cemeteries were in shambles. Crypts lay open, exposing their pitiful contents—if they weren't robbed of them—bricks, shattered marble tablets, even bones, lay strewn around. Several of the worst eyesores have been cleaned up, though others still remain in deplorable shape. Most of the restoration and cleanup efforts are spearheaded by the nonprofit **Save Our Cemeteries** (www.saveourcemeteries.org). Consider throwing a few, um, bones their way, especially since cemetery access is usually free. The website accepts online donations.

Safety First

You may be warned against going to the cemeteries alone and urged to go with a scheduled tour group (see "Organized Tours," later in this chapter). Thanks to the cemeteries' location and layout—some are in dicey neighborhoods, and the crypts obscure threats to your safety—visitors have historically been prime pickings for muggers and so forth. Cemeteries with better security and in better neighborhoods (or accessible to cars) are probably fine.

Ironically, two of the most hazardous, St. Louis No. 1 and Lafayette No. 1, are often so full of tour groups that they're fairly safe. So although this is no longer such a serious issue, a good tour is fun and informative, so why not take the precaution? If you're going to make a day of the cemeteries, think about renting a car. You won't be driving through horrendous downtown traffic, you can visit tombs farther away and at your own pace, and you'll feel safer.

196

A faux voodoo practice continues in some of the St. Louis cemeteries, where visitors scrawl Xs on the tombs. Please don't do this; not only is it a made-up voodoo ritual, but it also destroys the fragile tombs.

Concerns were high for the fate of the iconic cemeteries during the disaster days, but "the system worked": The tombs survived unscathed, except for some high-water marks much like those borne by any other flooded structure.

For more information, we highly recommend Robert Florence's **New Orleans Cemeteries: Life in the Cities of the Dead** (Batture Press, 1997). It's full of photos, facts, and human-interest stories and is available at bookstores throughout the city.

Three Cemeteries You Should See with a Tour

Lafayette Cemetery No. 1 Right across the street from Commander's Palace restaurant, this is the lush uptown cemetery. Once in horrible condition, it's been mostly restored. Anne Rice's Mayfair witches have their family tomb here.

1427 Sixth St.

St. Louis Cemetery No. 1 This is the oldest extant cemetery (1789) and the most iconic. Here lie Marie Laveau, Bernard Marigny, and assorted other New Orleans characters. Also, the acid-dropping scene from *Easy Rider* was shot here.

Basin St. btw. Conti and St. Louis sts.

St. Louis Cemetery No. 2 Established in 1823, the city's next-oldest cemetery, unfortunately, is in such a terrible neighborhood (next to the so-called Storyville Projects) that regular cemetery tours don't usually bother with it. If there is a tour running when you are in town, go—it's worth it. The Emperor of the Universe, R&B legend Ernie K-Doe, was laid to rest here in 2001, with bluesman extraordinaire Earl King joining him in the same tomb in 2003, and K-Doe's widow, Empress Antoinette, followed in 2009.

Note: As of this writing, there is no regular tour of St. Louis No. 2, which is unsafe and should be avoided.

N. Claiborne Ave. btw. Iberville and St. Louis sts.

Some Cemeteries You Could See on Your Own

If you decide to visit the cemeteries below on your own, please exercise caution. Most of these cemeteries (such as St. Louis No. 3 and Metairie) have offices that can sometimes provide maps; if they run out, they will give you directions to any grave location you like. All have sort-of-regular hours—figure from 9am to 4pm as a safe bet.

Cypress Grove and Greenwood Cemeteries Located across the street from each other, both were founded in the mid-1800s by the Firemen's Charitable and Benevolent Association. Each has some highly original tombs; keep your eyes open for the ones made entirely of iron. These two cemeteries are an easy street-car ride up Canal Street from the Quarter.

120 City Park Ave. and 5242 Canal Blvd. By car, take Esplanade north to City Park Ave., turn left until it becomes Metairie Ave.

Hurricane Katrina Memorial On the former site of Charity Hospital's pauper's field, the ominous but oddly affecting circle of tombs holds the bodies of

A tomb in St. Louis Cemetery No. 1.

Iron tombs can be found in Cypress Grove and Greenwood cemeteries.

85 unclaimed victims of the 2005 levee failures and the names of others who perished. It's an unfussy place that's easily missed, the better for contemplative solitude, perhaps. Surrounded by a storm-shaped series of pathways, the memorial does its duty to give one enormous pause.

5056 Canal St. ℂ **504/568-3201.** Take the Canal St. streetcar to City Park Ave.

Metairie Cemetery Don't be fooled by the slightly more modern look—some of the most amazing tombs in New Orleans are here. Don't miss the pyramid-and-sphinx Brunswig mausoleum, the "ruined castle" Egan family tomb, and the former resting place of Storyville madam Josie Arlington. Her mortified family had her body moved when her crypt became a tourist attraction, but the tomb remains exactly the same, including the statue of a young woman knocking on the door. Legend had it that it was Josie herself, being turned away from her father's house, or a virgin being denied entrance to Josie's brothel—she claimed never to despoil anyone. The reality is that it's just a copy of a statue Josie liked. Other famous residents include Confederate General P. G. T. Beauregard, jazz greats Louis Prima and Al Hirt, and Ruth of Ruth's Chris Steakhouse (in a marble edifice that oddly resembles one of her famous pieces of beef).

5100 Pontchartrain Blvd. ℂ **504/486-6331.** Daily 8:30am–5pm. By car, take Esplanade north to City Park Ave., turn left until it becomes Metairie Ave.

St. Louis Cemetery No. 3 Conveniently located next to the Fair Grounds racetrack (home of the Jazz Fest), St. Louis No. 3 was built on top of a former graveyard for lepers. Storyville photographer E. J. Bellocq lies here. Take the Esplanade Avenue bus to get here.

3421 Esplanade Ave.

VOODOO

Voodoo's mystical presence is one of the most common motifs in New Orleans—though the presence is mostly reduced to a tourist gimmick. Between the voodoo dolls for sale, the **Voodoo Museum** (p. 175), and the mythology surrounding voodoo queen Marie Laveau, a very real religion with a serious past and considerable cultural importance gets lost amid the kitsch.

Voodoo's roots can be traced in part back to the African **Yoruba** religion, which incorporates the worship of several different spiritual forces that include a supreme being, deities, and the spirits of ancestors. When Africans were kidnapped, enslaved, and brought to Brazil—and, ultimately, Haiti—beginning in the 1500s, they brought their religion with them.

Later, other African religions met and melded, and when slaves were forced to convert to Catholicism, they found it easy to merge and practice both religions and rituals. Rituals involved participants dancing in a frenzy to wild drumbeats and eventually falling into a trancelike state, during which a *loa* (a spirit and/or lower-level deity intermediary between humans and gods) would take possession of them.

Voodoo was banned in Louisiana until the Louisiana Purchase in 1803. The next year, the Haitian slaves overthrew their government, and new immigrants came to New Orleans, bringing along a fresh infusion of voodoo.

Napoleonic law (which still holds sway in Louisiana) forced slave owners to give their slaves Sundays off and to provide them with a gathering place: **Congo Square** on Rampart Street, part of what is now Louis Armstrong Park. Voodoo practice there, including dancing and drumming rituals, gave slaves a way to have their own community and a certain amount of freedom. These gatherings naturally attracted white onlookers, as did the rituals held (often by free people of color) along St. John's Bayou. The local papers of the 1800s are full of lurid accounts of voodoo "orgies" and of spirits possessing both whites and blacks. The Congo Square gatherings became more like performance pieces rather than religious rituals, and legend has it that nearby madams would come down to the Sunday gatherings and hire some of the performers to entertain at their houses.

During the 1800s, the famous voodoo priestesses came to some prominence. Mostly free women of color, they were devout religious practitioners, very good businesswomen with a steady clientele of whites who secretly came to them for help in love or money matters. During the 1900s, voodoo largely went back underground.

It is estimated that today as much as 15% of the population of New Orleans practices voodoo, though the public perception—casting spells or sticking pins in voodoo dolls—is largely Hollywood nonsense.

Most of the stores and places in New Orleans that advertise voodoo are set up strictly for tourism. This is not to say that some facts can't be found there or that you shouldn't buy a mass-produced souvenir. For an introduction to voodoo, check out the **New Orleans Historic Voodoo Museum** (p. 175) or **Voodoo Authentica** (p. 200). For true voodoo, however, seek out real voodoo temples or practitioners. You can find them at the temples listed below or by calling **Ava Kay,** who works on her own. She is available for readings, gris-gris bags (packets of meaning-infused herbs, stones, and other such bits), and other items of interest by appointment only, call her at ✆ **504/412-0202**. Also, check out Robert Tallant's book ***Voodoo in New Orleans*** (Pelican Pocket, 1983).

Voodoo Temples ★★

There are three authentic voodoo temples and botanicas selling everything you might need for potions and spells. The public is welcome, and employees are happy to educate the honestly inquisitive.

The **Island of Salvation Botanica** in the New Orleans Healing Center, 2372 St. Claude Ave. (in the Marigny), and the **Temple Simbi-sen Jak,** 835 Piety St. (✆ **504/948-9961**), are run by Sallie Glassman, voodoo priestess and author of a deck of voodoo tarot cards. The botanica is open Wednesday through Saturday from 10:30am to 5pm, but call first to make sure they are not closed for readings (or to schedule one).

Located right in the French Quarter, the **Voodoo Spiritual Temple,** 828 N. Rampart St. (✆ **504/522-9627**), is the real McCoy—interested tourists are welcome, but please be respectful. Priestess Miriam belonged to the Spiritual Church in Chicago before setting up this spiritual house, a temple with a store attached. There are both personal and open rituals, and the sincerely interested are quite welcome. Of interest is a haunting CD of Priestess Miriam's voodoo chants and rituals. It's open but keeps irregular hours. Primarily a store, **Voodoo Authentica,** 612 Dumaine St. (✆ **504/522-2111**), also has working altars. Mama Lola, subject of the sociological voodoo study *Mama Lola: Haitian Voodou Priestess in Brooklyn,* is often in attendance, reading cards and performing cleansings.

Visiting Marie Laveau

Marie Laveau is the most famous New Orleans voodoo queen. Though she was a real woman, her life has been so mythologized that it is nearly impossible to separate fact from fiction. But who really wants to? Certainly we know that she was born a free woman of color in 1794.

Items for sale at the New Orleans Historic Voodoo Museum.

Marie Laveau's tomb in St. Louis No. 1.

A hairdresser by trade, Marie became known for her psychic abilities and powerful gris-gris. Her day job allowed her into the best houses, where she heard all the good gossip and could apply it to her other clientele. In one famous story, a young woman about to be forced into a marriage with a much older, wealthy man approached Marie. She wanted to marry her young lover instead. Marie counseled patience. The marriage went forward, and the happy groom died from a heart attack while dancing with his bride at the reception. After a respectable time, the wealthy widow was free to marry her lover.

Marie wholeheartedly believed in voodoo—and business. Her home at what is now 1020 St. Ann St. was purportedly a gift from a grateful client. A devout Catholic, Marie continued to attend daily Mass and was publicly noted for her charity work.

Her death in 1881 was noted by the *Times-Picayune*. Her look-alike daughter, Marie II, took over her work, leading some to believe (mistakenly) that Marie I lived a very long time, looking quite well indeed—which only added to her legend. But Marie II allegedly worked more for the darker side than her mother. Her eventual reward, the story goes, was death by poison (delivered by whom is unknown). Today visitors bring Marie tokens (candles, Mardi Gras beads, change) and ask her for favors—she's buried in **St. Louis Cemetery No. 1.**

ANNE RICE'S NEW ORLEANS ★

Long before Sookie Stackhouse, before anyone cared whether you were Team Edward or Team Jacob, there was Lestat—and the originator of the modern vampire era, author Anne Rice. Love her or loathe her, Anne Rice has been one of New Orleans's biggest boosters. Though her popularity may have peaked, visitors still come here because they have read her books, or simply because they're obsessed Twihards mining the eerie ore. Rice writes seductive descriptions of her hometown that are actually quite accurate—minus the vampires, witches, and ghosts, of course—and cites many real locales.

Anne Rice (née O'Brien) was born on October 4, 1941, in New Orleans to Irish parents. When she was 16, her family moved to Texas, where she met her husband, the late poet Stan Rice. They married in 1961 and moved to the San Francisco area, resettling in New Orleans in the 1980s after *Interview with the Vampire* exploded (she has since moved to California). Rice remains something of a legendary doyenne of fang fiction. You can find signed copies of her books at the **Garden District Book Shop,** 2727 Prytania St. (p. 257).

Anne Rice in the French Quarter

The romance of the French Quarter seems to attract vampires, who found easy pickin's in its dark corners in the days before electricity.

St. Louis Cemetery No. 1, 400 Basin St.: A tomb (empty, of course) with Louis the vampire's name is located here in the Vampire Chronicle books, and Louis occasionally goes to sit on it and brood. Rumor has it that Rice has purchased a tomb here for her eventual use. See p. 209 for more on cemetery tours.

Gallier House, 1132 Royal St.: This famously preserved museum is said by Rice scholars to be the model for the house on Rue Royal that was home to vampires Lestat and Louis in *Interview with the Vampire*. Also see p. 172.

Madame John's Legacy.

The stretch of 700 to 900 Royal St.: Quite a few of the exteriors for the *Interview with the Vampire* movie were filmed along this stretch—though the set decorators had to labor long to erase all traces of the 20th century, covering the streets in mud. Imagine how folks who live around here felt about it.

Madame John's Legacy, 632 Dumaine St.: In the *Interview with the Vampire* movie, this is the house from which the caskets are being carried as Brad Pitt's voice-over describes Lestat and the little vampire Claudia going out on the town: "An infant prodigy with a lust for killing that matched his own. Together, they finished off whole families." Also see p. 174.

Café du Monde, 800 Decatur St.: Lestat visits this restaurant in *The Tale of the Body Thief,* and Michael and Rowan snack here in *The Witching Hour.* Also see p. 154.

Court of Two Sisters, 613 Royal St.: Characters in *The Witching Hour* dine here. Also see p. 122.

Galatoire's, 209 Bourbon St.: Characters from several books, including *The Witching Hour,* dine here as well. Also see p. 123.

Hotel Monteleone, 214 Royal St.: This was Aaron Lightner's house in *The Witching Hour.* Also see p. 87.

Marsoudet-Caruso House, 1519 Esplanade Ave.: A few blocks north of the French Quarter at the intersection of Esplanade and Claiborne avenues, this is the house where Louis smells the scent of old death in the *Interview with the Vampire* movie and finds the moldering Lestat shrinking from helicopters in a musty chair.

Anne Rice in the Garden District

Rice's books have also featured the Garden District and the area around it, where she and her family used to live in and own properties.

Coliseum Theater, 1233 Coliseum St.: In the film version of *Interview with the Vampire,* this is the theater where Louis sees *Tequila Sunrise.*

For many years Anne Rice's primary New Orleans residence was at 1239 First St.

Pontchartrain Hotel, 2031 St. Charles St.: This upscale hotel and its restaurant, the Caribbean Room (now closed), appear in *The Witching Hour*.

The old Mercedes dealership (now a different property), 2001 St. Charles Ave.: This building was at the center of an amusing local dispute. The vampire Lestat disappeared from this world through an image of himself in the window of this building. Lestat (wink, wink—could it be Copeland himself?) then mysteriously returned to this realm and bought an ad of his own, congratulating Copeland for his "stroke of genius."

St. Alphonsus Church, 2030 Constance St.: This small (now deconsecrated) church with a stunning interior (p. 186) was where Anne's parents married and she was baptized and received communion. She also took Alphonsus as her confirmation name. It is a setting in *The Witching Hour*.

1239 First St.: This historic property (see "Walking Tour 2: The Garden District" in chapter 8, "City Strolls") was for many years Anne Rice's primary residence. The Mayfair house in *The Witching Hour* matches her home in almost every detail, including address.

2301 and 2524 St. Charles Ave.: Rice's childhood homes.

Commander's Palace, 1403 Washington Ave.: Rice readers will recognize this restaurant as a favorite of the Mayfair family (p. 147).

Lafayette Cemetery No. 1: This centerpiece of the Garden District is also a frequent setting in Rice's work, especially as a roaming ground for Lestat and Claudia in *Interview with the Vampire* and as the graveyard for the Mayfairs in *The Witching Hour*.

ORGANIZED TOURS

There are some advantages to taking tours. Though many are touristy (by definition), someone else does the planning, it's an easy way to get to outlying areas, and if the tour guide is good, you should learn a lot in an entertaining way. For tours to the swamps and plantation homes, you'll be saving the earth a bit by carpooling (well, buspooling). It's also comforting to know that New Orleans tour guides must be licensed, a process that involves rigorous study and testing. So at least in theory, not just anyone can load you on a bus and take you for a (literal or figurative) ride.

Be warned: Though we can't vouch for the accuracy of this information, we have heard reports that some hotel concierges and storefront tour offices take kickbacks from the tour companies they recommend—a widespread practice around the world. Obviously, not every concierge is on the take, and some may have honest opinions about the merits of one company over another. Avoid this problem by doing the research yourself (if you're looking for a particular type of tour) and cut out the middleman; no matter how you learned about it, pay the fee directly to the company, not to your concierge. No reputable firm will insist you pay someone else first. In addition, except for the consistently outstanding **Historic New Orleans Tours,** most tour companies seem to be hit-or-miss, depending on the guide you get.

For information on organized and self-guided tours of the plantation houses outside New Orleans, see chapter 11, "Side Trips from New Orleans."

In the French Quarter

Note: Chapter 8, "City Strolls," includes a French Quarter walking tour you can do on your own.

Historic New Orleans Tours ★★★ (© **800/979-3370** or 504/947-2120; www.tourneworleans.com) is the place to go for authenticity rather than sensationalism. The guides are carefully chosen for their combination of knowledge and entertaining manner, and we cannot recommend them enough. The daily French Quarter tours are the best straightforward, nonspecialized walking tours of this neighborhood. They also offer tours themed around voodoo, jazz, and haunted buildings, plus a combo Hurricane/City Rebirth tour and the terrific, adults-only Scandalous Cocktail tour, which strings a series of fascinating

Taking an organized tour through the French Quarter is a great way to get to know the historic neighborhood.

tales around local bars and cocktails. It delves into historic brothels, organized crime, and the JFK assassination. The colorful bartenders, when not too busy, also tell their own tales (do pace your drinking, though!). The majority of tours are $20 for adults, $15 students and seniors with ID, $7 children 6 to 12, free for 5 and under. The Scandalous Cocktail and Creole Mourning tours are $25 per person. The 3-hour Hurricane/Rebirth tour requires reservations; the cost is $40 for adults and $20 for children 12 and under.

The nonprofit volunteer group **Friends of the Cabildo** (⟨℡ 504/524-9118;** www.friendsofthecabildo.org) also offers an excellent 2-hour walking tour of the Quarter. It leaves from in front of the 1850 House Museum Store, at 523 St. Ann St., on Jackson Square. The fee is $15 per adult; it's free for children 12 and under accompanied by an adult. Tours leave Tuesday through Sunday at 10am and 1:30pm, except holidays. Reservations aren't necessary—just show up about 15 minutes early.

Stop by the **Jean Lafitte National Park and Preserve's Folklife and Visitor Center,** 419 Decatur St., near Conti Street (℡ **504/589-2636;** www. nps.gov/jela), for details on its excellent free walking tour conducted by National Park Service rangers. The History of New Orleans tour covers about a mile in the French Quarter along the riverfront and brings to life the city's history and the ethnic roots of its unique cultural mix. No reservations are required, but only 25 people are taken in a group. The tour starts at 9:30am daily (except for Mardi Gras and Christmas); the office opens at 9am, and it's strongly suggested that you get there then to ensure that you get a ticket.

Roberts Batson offers a **Gay Heritage Tour,** by appointment only. These last roughly 2½ hours and generally cost $20 per person (℡ **504/945-6789;** info@southerndecadence.net; www.southerndecadence.net).

For 25 years, Inez Douglas has guided **Heritage Literary Tours ★★** (℡ **504/451-1082).** Originated by the esteemed author and professor Kenneth Holditch, the tours stop at spots where the greats and the pretty-goods lived, played, wrote, and caroused. Tours can be designed around a specific author such as John Kennedy Toole or Tennessee Williams and nonliterary topics as well. Group tours (2½-hr. walking tour, $20 per person for adults, three people minimum) are scheduled by appointment only.

Le Monde Creole ★★★ (℡ **504/568-1801;** www.mondecreole.com) offers a unique tour that uses the dramatic lives of one classic Creole family as a microcosm of the Creole world of the 19th century. This is the sister operation of **Laura Plantation** (p. 310). At the city location, you can learn about Creole city life and the extraordinary story of Laura's family, off the plantation and in the Vieux Carré, while viewing French Quarter courtyards associated with the family. This is probably the only operation that also offers tours in French. Currently, tours (which include a visit to St. Louis Cemetery No. 1 and the voodoo temple on Rampart) depart daily at 10:30am (English) and 10am (French) daily. All tours by advance reservation only, so call in advance. Prices are $22 adults, $16 students and active military, $10 children 4 to 10, and free for kids 3 and under.

Beyond the French Quarter

Author Robert Florence (who has written two excellent books about New Orleans cemeteries as well as our Garden District walking tour in chapter 8, "City Strolls") loves his work, and his **Historic New Orleans Tours ★★★** (℡ **800/979-3370** or 504/947-2120; www.tourneworleans.com) are full of

Destruction after Hurrican Katrina, in 2005.

meticulously researched facts and more than a few good stories. A very thorough tour of the Garden District and Lafayette Cemetery (a section of town not many of the other companies go into) leaves daily at 11am and 1:45pm from the Garden District Book Shop (in the Rink, corner of Washington Ave. and Prytania St.); arrive about 15 minutes before departure. Rates are $20 adults, $15 students with ID and seniors, $7 children 6 to 12, and free children 5 and under. The same company also offers a 2½-hour walking tour of the historic Treme neighborhood for $30 per person (as does the African American Museum; see below). All tours require reservations; contact them for times and meeting places.

Tours by Isabelle ★★ (℃ 504/398-0365; www.toursbyisabelle.com) offers eight different tours for small groups in passenger vans, the majority of which are plantation and swamp tours. They also do an extensive Post-Katrina Tour ($65 per person). It is 70 miles long and takes 3½ hours. It shows the French Quarter, City Park, and other important places in the city's early history, as well as post-Katrina damage and sights. The tour departs at 8:30am and 1pm. Make reservations as far in advance as possible. Isabelle's 4-hour New Orleans Combo-City Tour ($70 per person) adds Longue Vue House and Gardens to a tour of the French Quarter, St. Louis Cemetery No. 3, Bayou St. John, the shores of Lake Pontchartrain, and the Uptown and Downtown neighborhoods; the tour departs at 8:30am and 1pm. Plantation, bayou, and many other tours are also available; contact them for more information.

Gray Line ★★, 2 Canal St., Ste. 1300 (℃ 800/535-7786 or 504/569-1401; www.graylineneworleans.com), also runs combination city and post-Katrina disaster tours. They were one of the first to do so, back when it was controversial and seen as exploitative, but it's handled with the proper respect. A portion of the ticket price still goes to relief causes. Gray Line also offers city, swamp, and plantation-home tours in comfortable coaches; a 2-hour cruise on the steamboat *Natchez* (www.steamboatnatchez.com); plus French Quarter walking tours for those who wish to see ghosts and gardens or explore the city's cocktail heritage.

The **New Orleans African American Museum** (see box, below) now offers a 2-hour walking tour of key points within the Faubourg Treme, at 10:30am each Saturday (weather permitting). The year 2012 is the Treme's bicentennial, an ideal time to tour this historic neighborhood. The tour includes museum admission and costs $23 adults, $19 students and seniors, $12 kids 2 to 12.

TREME, true & false

In 2010, HBO launched the drama *Treme* to stellar reviews, intense local curiosity, and a predictable dollop of cynicism. But mostly (given the producers' widely publicized intent to "get it right"), New Orleans collectively tuned in to see itself portrayed to the nation and debate whether the show in fact nailed the authenticity.

Not surprisingly, opinions differed. But all agreed on two things: 1) It did a better job than *The Big Easy;* and 2) the show's location manager had been awfully busy.

Treme revolves around a collection of musicians and others finding their footing in the gritty months following Katrina. Many of them are from the historic Faubourg Treme neighborhood. This complex community just north of the French Quarter, considered the oldest African-American neighborhood in America, was the 19th-century home to the city's free people of color and has for generations been a massively productive musical enclave. It remains a leading incubator of talent and a remarkable keeper of cultural flames. The show was filmed in many locations both in and outside the real Treme. These are a few worth visiting:

TREME, THE NEIGHBORHOOD

St. Augustine Church Considered the first Catholic church to integrate African-Americans and whites, it was and remains the beating heart of the Treme neighborhood. See p. 186.

Backstreet Cultural Museum
A modest but essential collection of the cultural traditions unique to its neighborhood: brass bands, Mardi Gras Indians, jazz funerals, social aid and pleasure clubs, and so on. See p. 180.

New Orleans African American Museum of Art, Culture and History Protecting and promoting African-American history, it's set in a lovely 1820s Creole villa (1418 Governor Nicholls St.; ✆ **504/566-1136;** www.neworleansmuseums.com; Wed–Sat 11am–4pm [subject to change; call ahead]; $7 adults, $5 students and seniors, $3 children 2–12).

Lil' Dizzy's This local diner is a gathering place for movers, shakers, neighbors, and nobodies, as much for the neighborhood lowdown as for the divine trout Baquet. See p. 137.

Congo Square Slaves and free people of color gathered here to drum, dance, and practice voodoo rituals and eventually, many believe, give birth to jazz. See p. 199.

TREME, THE SHOW

Bayona The show's Jeanette Desautel is roughly modeled on Bayona's famed chef/owner Susan Spicer. Restaurant Patois is the actual stand-in for the fictional "Desautel's." See p. 120.

Vaughan's Already a character, Kermit Ruffins plays himself on the series. He plays his trumpet at Vaughan's most Thursdays. See p. 283.

Angelo Brocato's Ice Cream & Confectionery Creighton Bernette, played by John Goodman, expresses his longing for the post-storm return of the lemon ice at this beloved 100-year-old institution. See p. 154.

Bacchanal Jeannette's pop-up restaurant at Bacchanal gets rained out, but the scruffy wine bar with the killer food and lushly unkempt garden lives on, thankfully (600 Poland Ave., Bywater; ✆ **504/948-9111;** www.bacchanalwine.com).

Tee-Eva's The pie and praline queen whose shop has been a fixture on Magazine Street for years had a cameo on *Treme* as a bus passenger (5201 Magazine St.; ✆ **504/899-8350;** www.tee-evapralines.com).

Swamp Tours

In addition to the tour providers listed below, Isabelle, Historic New Orleans Tours, and Gray Line (see above) all offer **swamp tours,** which can be a hoot, particularly if you get a guide who calls alligators to your boat for a little snack of chicken (please keep your hands inside the boat—they tend to look a lot like chicken to a gator). On all of the following tours, you're likely to see alligators, bald eagles, waterfowl, egrets, owls, herons, ospreys, feral hogs, otters, beavers, frogs, turtles, raccoons, deer, and nutria (maybe even a black bear or a mink)— and a morning spent floating on the bayou can be mighty pleasant.

Dr. Wagner's Honey Island Swamp Tours ★★ (✆ **985/641-1769** or 504/242-5877; www.honeyislandswamp.com), at 41490 Crawford Landing Rd. in Slidell about 30 miles outside of New Orleans, takes you by boat into the interior of Honey Island Swamp to view wildlife with native professional naturalist guides (captains Charlie and Brian both grew up plying these waters). The guides provide a solid educational experience to go with the purer swamp excitement. Tours last approximately 2 hours. Prices are $23 for adults and $15 for children 11 and under if you drive to the launch site yourself; rates are $45 for adults and $32 for children if you want a hotel pickup in New Orleans.

Jean Lafitte Swamp Tours (✆ **800/445-4109;** www.jeanlafitteswamp tour.com) in Marerro offers "native Cajun" tour guides replete with lore about the flora, fauna, and legends on a swamp boat cruise through their privately owned bayou area—as well as proximity to New Orleans. Speedy airboat tours are also available for the more adventurous. Tours last 1 hour, 45 minutes and include transportation from most downtown hotels for an additional fee. Prices are $25 for adults and $13 for children 3 to 12 for drive-ups; with transportation, prices are $49 for adults and $24 for children. Kids 2 and under are free with paid adult.

Pearl River Eco-Tours ★★, 55050 Hwy. 90, Slidell (✆ **866/59-SWAMP** [597-9267] or 504/581-3395; www.pearlriverecotours.com), is built on Southern

LEFT: Alligators are common sights on swamp tours. RIGHT: Swamp tours are a wonderful opportunity to see all manner of wildlife in their wetlands home.

7

SIGHTS TO SEE & PLACES TO BE | Organized Tours

hospitality. Captain Neil has been doing tours of Honey Island Swamp for over 10 years, and the other captains also know their stuff. The swamp is beautiful, even during the cooler months when the gators are less frisky. If you have a car, you can drive there and tour for $23 ($15 children 4–12). If transportation is provided from New Orleans, the cost is $49 for adults and $33 for children ages 4 to 12. Tours run at 10am and 2:30pm.

They're a little farther out and you'll need to provide your own transportation, but we'd be remiss if we didn't add two other excellent guides. **Annie Miller's Son's Swamp and Marsh Tours ★★**, 3718 Southdown Mandalay Rd., Houma (ⓒ **800/341-5441** or 985/868-4758; www.annie-miller.com), and **A Cajun Man's Swamp Cruise**, 3109 Southdown Mandalay Rd., Houma (ⓒ **985/868-4625**; www.cajunman.com). These neighbors are both so utterly authentic you'd swear that swamp water runs in their veins. Jimmy Miller, son of the legendary Alligator Annie, is carrying on in her down-home tradition and knows every inch of these swamps. Self-proclaimed Cajun Man Ron "Black" Guidry is an equally well-informed naturalist, and usually brings his guitar and accordion along on the boat. Both require reservations; call for schedules. Annie Miller's Sons: $15 adults, $12 children 4 to 12, free 3 and under. Tours run 2 to 2½ hours. A Cajun Man: $25 adults and $15 children under 12; tours run about 2 hours.

Mystical & Mysterious Tours

Interest in the supernatural, ghostly side of New Orleans—let's go right ahead and blame Anne Rice and subsequent stories of sparkly vampires—has meant an increased number of tours catering to the vampire set. It has also resulted in some rather humorous infighting as rival tour operators have accused each other of stealing their shtick—and customers. We enjoy a good nighttime ghost tour of the Quarter as much as anyone, but we also have to admit that what's available is really hit-or-miss in presentation (it depends on who conducts your particular tour) and more miss than hit with regard to facts. Go for the entertainment value, not for the education (with some exceptions—see below). But just remember this: There was no New Orleans vampire tradition until Ms. Rice created one.

While most of the ghost tours are a bunch of loud, showy hokum, we are pleased that there is one we can send you to with a clear conscience: The Cemetery and Voodoo Tour offered by **Historic New Orleans Tours ★★★** (ⓒ **800/979-3370** or 504/947-2120; www.tourneworleans.com) is consistently fact- and not sensation-based, though no less entertaining. The trip goes through St. Louis Cemetery No. 1 and Congo Square and visits an active voodoo temple. It leaves Monday through Saturday at 10am and 1pm (Sun at 10am only) from the courtyard at 334-B Royal St. Rates are $20 adults, $15 students and seniors, and free children 11 and under. They also offer a nighttime haunted tour, perhaps the only one in town where well-researched guides provide genuine thrills and chills. It leaves at 7:30pm from Bourbon-Oh! at the corner of Bourbon and Orleans streets. Finally, their fascinating Creole Mourning Tour incorporates visits to the Hermann-Grima House and St. Louis Cemetery No. 1. It's $25 and departs Monday to Saturday at 11am and 1pm (Sun at 9:30am and 11:30am) from 820 St. Louis St.; reservations are required.

Let's be perfectly clear. Vampires—they're not real. But if they were real, they'd hang out in the French Quarter. Both are spooky. Both are centuries old. Both are sexy. It makes sense. Personally, we prefer our history with a bit of, well, history—but if high drama is what you seek, the 1½-hour New Orleans Vampire tour given by **Haunted History Tours ★**, 97 Fontainebleau Dr. (📞 **888/6-GHOSTS** [644-6787] or 504/861-2727; www.hauntedhistorytours. com), dishes it out, complete with fake snakes, blood, and costumes. The tour departs daily at 8:30pm from outside St. Louis Cathedral (just look for the hordes). It costs $20 for adults, $17 students/seniors, $10 kids under 12, free kids under 6. Haunted History Tours also offers a range of vampire, cemetery, and nighttime French Quarter tours.

Boat & Kayak Tours

For those interested in doing the Mark Twain thing, a few operators offer ways to get out on the rolling Mississippi. They're touristy, but they can be fun if you're in the right mood, and they're good for families. Docks are at the foot of Toulouse and Canal streets, and there's ample parking. Call for reservations (required) and to confirm prices and schedules. We think it best to skip the food—too much time spent at the buffet is time better spent enjoying the river, and besides, you can find better food all over town.

The steamboat *Natchez,* 2 Canal St., Ste. 1300 (📞 **800/233-BOAT** [233-2628] or 504/586-8777; www.steamboatnatchez.com), a marvelous three-deck stern-wheeler docked at the wharf behind the Jackson Brewery, offers at least two 2-hour daytime cruises Wednesday through Sunday, and a jazz dinner cruise Tuesday through Sunday. The narration is by professional guides, and the boat has a cocktail bar, live jazz, an engine room tour, an optional lunch on the first cruise of the day ($10 extra for ages 5 and up; the meal is $8 for kids 4 and under), and a gift shop. Daytime fares are $25 for adults and $13 for children; evening cruises without dinner are $42 for adults and $21 for children; kids 6 and under ride free with paid adult. Dinner cruises cost $68 for adults, $34 for children 6 to 12, and $13 for children 2 to 5. Times may change seasonally, so call ahead.

The paddle-wheeler *Creole Queen,* Riverwalk Dock (📞 **800/445-4109** or 504/529-4567; www.neworleanspaddlewheels.com), departs from the Poydras Street Wharf adjacent to the Riverwalk on Friday and Saturday afternoon for a

 Creole Cooking Vacations

Visitors can take their New Orleans culinary experience one big, tasty step further at the **New Orleans Cooking Experience** (📞 **504/945-9104;** www. neworleanscookingexperience.com), which offers personalized cooking classes, from half-day courses (10 people max) to multiday complete vacations. The latter includes classes, dining out, and most meals. Classes are taught at the House on Bayou Road (p. 94), a charming 18th-century inn. Celebrated New Orleans Chef Frank Brigtsen has created the yummy course curriculum, which features classic New Orleans Creole dishes, taught by Brigtsen, Gerard Maras, and other high-profile local chefs. It's fun, informative, and likely to be fattening. *C'est la vie.* **Single half-day classes** are $150 per person and include recipes, a multicourse meal, and wines. **Complete vacation classes** are $290 and $385 for 2 and 4 days. Private classes, group rates, and multiple class rates are available by reservation.

The steamboat *Natchez* heads out for a cruise on the Mississippi.

1½-hour narrated excursion to the port and to the historic site of the Battle of New Orleans. There is also a 7pm jazz dinner cruise. The boat has a covered promenade deck and a snack bar, and its inner lounges are air-conditioned or heated as needed. Daytime fares are $20 for adults and $10 for children. The evening cruise is $40 for adults, $15 for children 6 to 12, and free for children 5 and under. Dinner adds $25 to the adult ticket and $20 to the 6- to 12-year-olds; dinner for kids 3 to 5 is $10.

Kayak-iti-Yat (*©* **985-778-5034;** http://kayakitiyat.com) explains city lore from the unique perspective of a kayak along Bayou St. John. When the weather's right, it's a sublime way to explore some historic neighborhoods, City Park, and even Lake Pontchartrain (and at 4 hr., it's a good upper-body workout—the better to justify last night's indulgent dinner). Guided kayak tours run daily at 9am and 2pm; costs are $60. Call for reservations and meeting spot directions. All equipment is provided, but bathroom stops are scant, so plan ahead. (Be sure to ask about their new Lazy Twilight Tour for sunset kayaking.)

Also see "Swamp Tours" on p. 208.

Bicycle Tours

Confederacy of Cruisers (*©* **504/400-5468;** www.confederacyofcruisers. com) offers a terrific way to explore some lesser-seen parts of this flat city up close and in depth. The pace is outright leisurely, so you needn't be a serious rider, but bike familiarity and a healthy dose of pluck will help you handle the hazards of potholes and traffic (including a stretch along busy Esplanade Ave.). Do opt-in to the optional helmets. The comfortable, well-maintained single-gear cruisers have baskets for your stuff, and a bottle of water is included (there's a restroom stop halfway through, but you'd be wise to take care of that before departure, too). The guide-led group (eight-person maximum) pulls over about every 10 minutes at such diverse stops as the New Orleans Center for Creative Arts (NOCCA), St. Roch Cemetery, the Mother-in-Law Lounge, and St. Augustine Church, where guides offer up well-informed insights on history, culture, and architecture. They're full of restaurant recommendations, too (at press time, a culinary-themed bike tour was in development). Tours are $45 for 3 hours and depart twice daily from Washington Square Park on Frenchmen and Royal streets, on the outskirts of the French Quarter.

Carriage rides are popular in the French Quarter.

Carriage Tours

Corny it may be, but there is a sheepish romantic lure to an old horse-drawn carriage tour of the Quarter or beyond. (They're actually mules—they handle heat and humidity better.) The mules are decked out with ribbons, flowers, and even hats, and the drivers seem to be in a fierce competition to win the "most entertaining" award. They share history and "unusual city" anecdotes of dubious authenticity, and will customize itineraries on request. Carriages wait on Decatur Street in front of Jackson Square from 8:30am to midnight (except in heavy rain). Private carriages are $75 per half-hour for up to four people; share with other tourists for $15 per person per half-hour. A 1½-hour Garden District tour runs $225 for one to four people. Call ✆ **504/943-8820** for custom tours and hotel pickups. *Tip:* Check www.royalcarriages.com for discount coupons.

Antiquing Tours

Antiquing in New Orleans can be an exhilarating if overwhelming experience. For expert guidance, Macon Riddle of **Let's Go Antiquing!** (✆ **504/899-3027;** www.neworleansantiquing.com) will organize and customize antiques-shopping tours to fit your needs. Hotel pickup is included, and she will even make lunch reservations for you and arrange shipping of any purchases. Prices vary.

ESPECIALLY FOR KIDS

If you plan to give the kids a lifelong complex for confining you to your hotel room when you *know* all that big clubbing and fooding is going on mere blocks away, then perhaps New Orleans is better done *sans enfants.* But the truth is, despite its reputation, it's a terrific family destination, with oodles of conventional and unconventional only-in-New-Orleans activities to entertain them (and you). **Mardi Gras** (p. 38) and **Jazz Fest** (p. 52) are both doable and enjoyable with kids, as are many of the organized tours (p. 203)—those above spooking age love to tour the **cemeteries** and haunted places, and the **plantation homes** (p. 304) can be eye-opening to the Nintendo set.

The **French Quarter** in and of itself is fascinating to children over 7. You can while away a pleasant morning on a Quarter walkabout, seeing the architecture and peeking into shops, with a rest stop for beignets at **Café du Monde** (p. 154). Continue (or begin) your progeny's roots-music education with a visit to the **Presbytère** (p. 176) for some colorful Mardi Gras history and later to **Preservation Hall** (p. 280) for a live show. For those kids who aren't terrifically self-conscious, a **horse-and-buggy ride** (see "Carriage Tours," above) around the Quarter is very appealing—especially when they're getting tired or hot and you need a tiny bribe to keep them going (or a way to rock the little ones to sleep—it works pretty well). If you happen to be in New Orleans in December, take a ride through City Park, when thousands of lights turn the landscape and trees into fairy-tale scenery. The free **Canal Street ferry** (p. 190) crosses the Mississippi River and ends just preboredom (and makes a great intro to reading *Huckleberry Finn* together). Add a clackety-clacking **streetcar ride** (p. 348), and you've hit the trifecta of ever-fascinating transportation options.

The **Musée Conti Wax Museum** (p. 175), which features effigies of local historical figures, is an acceptable pick, though you need to call in advance to tour it. **Riverwalk Marketplace** (p. 249), the glass-enclosed shopping center on the edge of the Quarter on Canal Street, also appeals to kids with its relaxed atmosphere and food vendors, though for adults it's a rather basic and (apart from the river views) dull mall. (But if you can sneak away, the **Museum of the American Cocktail** is inside!)

Returning to Canal Street, you'll find the **Audubon Aquarium of the Americas** (p. 163), with lots of jellyfish, sea horses, and other creatures from the deep and the not so deep. Only the most squeamish should skip the **Insectarium,** because it's swell. The *John James Audubon* riverboat chugs from the aquarium to lovely, oak-filled **Audubon Park** (p. 191) and the highly regarded **Audubon Zoo** comes complete with a seasonal splash park for the pool-deprived (see "A Day at the Zoo," earlier in this chapter). A **swamp tour** (p. 208) doesn't guarantee you'll see gators, but it's a pretty good bet, and if not, hey, you're on a boat in a swamp. Many also offer speedier airboats for young adrenaline junkies.

Amusement Park and Children's Storyland ★★ ☺ The under-8 set will be delighted with this playground (rated one of the 10 best in the country by *Child* magazine), where well-known children's stories and rhymes have inspired

the charming decor. It offers plenty of characters to slide down and climb on and generally get juvenile ya-yas out.

Kids and adults will enjoy the carousel, Ferris wheels, bumper cars, miniature trains, tilt-a-whirl, the lady-bug-shaped roller coaster, and other rides at the **Carousel Gardens,** also in City Park. Delighting local families since 1906, the carousel (or "da flying horses," as real locals call it) is one of only 100 all-wood merry-go-rounds in the country, and the only one in the state (more on p. 192).

Recognizable characters and images from children's stories will charm kids and adults alike at Children's Storyland in City Park.

Pedal boating in City Park.

City Park at Victory Ave. ℰ **504/483-9432.** www.neworleanscitypark.com/carouself_gardens. html. Admission $3, rides $3 each, unlimited rides with $17 armband. Carousel Gardens amusement park mid-Mar to mid-Nov Fri–Sun 11am–6pm with extended hours June–Aug. Storyland daily but hours vary by season. Check website for specifics.

City Park Pedal Boats ★ ☺ Big Lake in City Park is a pretty spot for a boat ride, and the kids might spot egrets and turtles. The pedaling action can be a workout, which means you can justify a visit to nearby Angelo Brocato's ice cream parlor afterward. Boats hold three people, at least one of whom must be 21 or older. Life jackets (provided) are required.

City Park Big Lake, at Esplanade Ave. ℰ **504/224-2601.** $10 per half-hour. Nov–Feb Sat–Sun 11am–5pm; 1st weekend in Mar through end of Oct 11am–6pm. Weather permitting.

Louisiana Children's Museum ★★★ ☺ This interactive museum is really a playground in disguise that will keep kids occupied for a good couple of hours. Along with changing exhibits, the museum offers an art shop with regularly scheduled projects, a mini grocery store, a chance to "build" a New Orleans–style home, and lots of activities exploring music, fitness, water, and life itself. If you belong to your local science museum, check for reciprocal entry privileges. *Note:* Children 15 and under must be accompanied by a parent.

420 Julia St., at Tchoupitoulas St. ℰ **504/523-1357.** www.lcm.org. Admission $8, children under 1 free. Children 15 and under must be accompanied by an adult. Sept–May Tues–Sat 9:30am–4:30pm, Sun noon–4:30pm; June–Aug Mon–Sat 9:30am–5pm, Sun noon–5pm.

SPORTING EVENTS

Big Easy Rollergirls ★ Okay, it's a total goof, but a hoot of a goof. By definition, roller derby is going to be a bit wild (though the athleticism can't be denied). Mix in New Orleans and the resulting outcome is pure wack. The Big Easy babes play it up for all it's worth, and the crowd action is equally rowdy. More of a hipster scene than a family scene, it's all in fun, and worth the modest ticket price just to check out the fluff-punk outfits.

University of New Orleans's Human Performance Center, Elysian Fields and Leon C. Simon Dr. www.bigeasyrollergirls.com. Adults $12–$15, kids $6.

The Big Easy Rollergirls in action.

New Orleans Hornets ★★ Playing in the renovated Arena, the Hornets now command an exclusive area on the sidelines called "Hollywood" where seats can command serious green. A few years ago that was not a possibility. Then Chris Paul came along to change everything by leading the team to the 2008 NBA semis and playoffs in 2009 and 2011. Now, even though the franchise ownership was in doubt at press time, the Hornets remain a major attraction.
1501 Girod St. Ticket info ✆ **504/525-HOOP** [525-4667]. www.hornets.com. Tickets $113–$1,260.

New Orleans Jesters ☺ This minor-league soccer team with the big plans brings family-friendly action to City Park. Since changing hands in 2008, the team has amped up their profile and their play, making it good, clean fun for soccer fans.

GAMBLING

Harrah's Casino is quite like a Vegas casino (115,000 sq. ft., 2,100 slot machines, over 100 tables, Besh Steakhouse restaurant, and the Masquerade Lounge). It's located on Canal Street at the river (✆ **504/533-6000**; www.harrahs.com). *Tip:* Locals know the voluminous buffet can satisfy the most serious munchies for $20 Mon–Wed; $30 Thurs–Sun. There's also riverboat gambling in the area. Outside the city, you can find the **Boomtown Casino** (✆ **504/366-7711** for information and directions; www.boomtownneworleans.com) on the West Bank and the **Treasure Chest Casino** (✆ **504/443-8000**; www.boomtownneworleans.com) docked on Lake Pontchartrain in Kenner. **Slot machines** can be found in every imaginable locale in the city, from bars to laundromats to riverboats, often separated from the main room by a door or curtain.

Pan American Stadium, Wisner Blvd. and Zachary Taylor Blvd., City Park, New Orleans. ℂ **504/312-3979.** www.nola jesters.com. Tickets $5–$10.

New Orleans Saints ★★ Who dat won the Super Bowl? The Saints' incredible 2010 Super Bowl victory was the culmination of the city's 43-year collective dream (to say nothing of the end of 43 years of frustration), in which the beloved 'Aints finally won the big one, becoming a worldwide phenomenon and a metaphor for the city's own comeback. The rousing fourth-quarter victory brought a frenzy of pride to the city not seen since, well, ever, and effectively sealed New Orleans's post-Katrina revival. If there's a downside, it's the increased demand for tickets. Your best bet is the **NFL Ticket Exchange** (www.ticketexchangebyticketmaster.com). Otherwise, the pregame party at **Champions Square,** outside the Superdome (or any sports bar, really), is an excellent place to be on game days.

The New Orleans Saints play at the Superdome.

Superdome, 1500 block of Poydras St. Saints home office: 5800 Airline Dr., Metairie. ℂ **504/733-0255.** Ticket info: ℂ **504/731-1700.** www.neworleanssaints.com. Tickets $40–$500 and up depending on the game.

New Orleans Zephyrs ★★ ☺ There may be no better entertainment value in pro sports than minor-league baseball. An afternoon or evening at Zephyr Field out near the airport affirms that. Mascots Boudreaux D. and Clotile Nutria do their enthusiastic best to ensure that family fun is foremost, with various promotions and fan-participation activities. There's a pool area behind right field (rentable for groups or parties), and a general-admission grass "levee" behind center field.

Zephyr Field, 6000 Airline Dr., Metairie. ℂ **504/734-5155.** www.zephyrsbaseball.com. Tickets $6–$12.

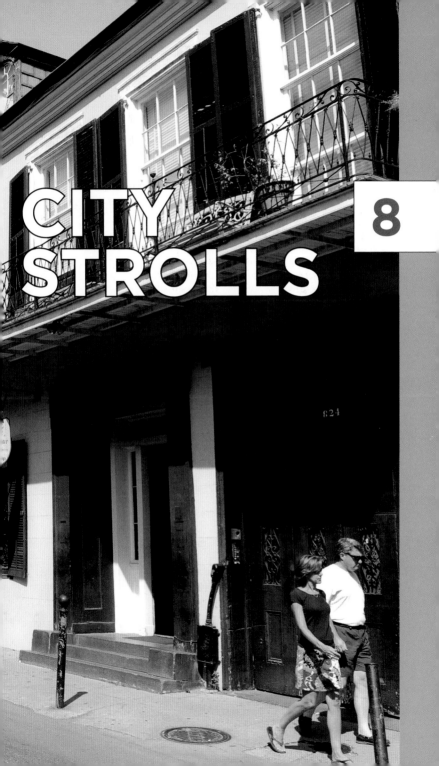

CITY STROLLS

8

We've said it before, and we will keep saying it: This town was made for walking. Except maybe at the height of the summer months when heat and humidity—especially humidity—make you not want to do much of anything except sit gasping in the nearest shade, sipping cool drinks, fanning yourself.

New Orleans is simply one of the most beautiful and unique cities anywhere—it is made to stroll through and marvel at. Each gorgeous building is more interesting than the last. Colorful characters abound. The French Quarter and the Garden District have their own distinct appearances, and both are easily manageable on foot.

You'll be hard-pressed to see any remaining Katrina damage in these parts (or most parts, thankfully, although there's still plenty, but you'll need to seek it out if that's your intent; see p. 206)—it largely bypassed the Garden District and French Quarter. So put on some good walking shoes, breathe in that tropical breeze, and mosey. Go slow, take it (big) easy. Admire the varying iron lacework patterns. Peek through French Quarter gateways, where simple facades hide exquisite courtyards with fountains, brickwork, and thick foliage. Gawk at the mighty oaks, some dripping with swaying Spanish moss.

Stroll along St. John's Bayou, turning at any corner that strikes your fancy. If you're lucky you might have a street to yourself (or share it with a fleeting ghost?). Imagine it 100 years ago; it would have looked almost as it does now.

Our personalized walking tours of the French Quarter, Garden District, and the less-traveled Esplanade Ridge will give you a nice overview and answer most "That looks interesting—what the heck *is* it?" kinds of queries. Formal professional walking tours cover more ground and considerably more detail (p. 204).

WALKING TOUR 1: THE FRENCH QUARTER

START:	**The intersection of Royal and Bienville streets.**
FINISH:	**Jackson Square.**
TIME:	**Allow approximately 1½ hours, not including time spent in shops or historic homes.**
BEST TIMES:	**Any day between 8am and 10am (the quiet hours).**
WORST TIME:	**At night. Some attractions won't be open, and you won't be able to get a good look at the architecture.**

If you only spend a few hours in New Orleans, do it in the exquisitely picturesque French Quarter. In these 80 city blocks, the colonial empires of France, Spain, and, to a lesser extent, Britain, intersected with the emerging American

PREVIOUS PAGE: The Dejan House, in the French Quarter.

nation. It's called the Vieux Carré or "old square," but somehow it's timeless—recognizably old while vibrantly alive. Today's residents and merchants are stewards of a rich tradition of individuality, creativity, and disregard for many of the concerns of the world beyond. This tour will introduce you to its style, history, and landmarks.

From the corner of Royal and Bienville streets, head into the Quarter (away from Canal St.). That streetcar named Desire rattled along Royal Street until 1948. (It was replaced by the bus named Desire. Really.) Imagine how noisy these narrow streets were when the streetcars were in place. Your first stop is:

1 339–343 Royal St., Rillieux-Waldhorn House

Now the home of Waldhorn and Adler Antiques (est. 1881), the building was built between 1795 and 1800 for Vincent Rillieux, the great-grandfather of the French Impressionist artist Edgar Degas. Offices of the (second) Bank of the United States occupied the building from 1820 until 1836 when, thanks to President Andrew Jackson's famous veto, its charter expired. Note the wrought-iron balconies—an example of excellent Spanish colonial workmanship.

2 333 Royal St., The Bank of Louisiana

Across the street, this old bank was erected in 1826, its Greek Revival edifice followed in the early 1860s, and the bank was liquidated in 1867. The building suffered fires in 1840, 1861, and 1931, and has served as the Louisiana State Capitol, an auction exchange, a criminal court, a juvenile court, and an American Legion social hall. It now houses the Vieux Carré police station.

The wrought-iron work at 339–343 Royal St. is an example of Spanish colonial workmanship.

Cross Conti Street to:

3 403 Royal St., Latrobe's

Benjamin H. B. Latrobe died of yellow fever shortly after completing designs for the Louisiana State Bank, which opened here in 1821. Latrobe was one of the nation's most eminent architects, having designed the Bank of Pennsylvania in Philadelphia (1796) and contributed to the design of the U.S. Capitol and White House. Note the monogram "LSB" on the Creole-style iron balcony railing. It's now a banquet hall named for the architect.

4 417 Royal St., Brennan's Restaurant

The iron balcony at 403 Royal St. contains the initials "LSB," which stand for Lousiana State Bank.

Brennan's (p. 122) opened in this building, also built by Vincent Rillieux, in 1855. The structure was erected after the fire of 1794 destroyed more than 200 of the original buildings along this street. It has been home to the Banque de la Louisiane, the world-famous chess champion Paul Charles Morphy, and the parents of Edgar Degas.

5 437 Royal St., Peychaud's Drug Store

When Masons held lodge meetings here in the early 1800s, proprietor and druggist Antoine A. Peychaud served after-meeting drinks of bitters and cognac to lodge members in small egg cups, called coquetier—later Americanized to "cocktails." And so it began (the cocktail and the legend).

6 400 Royal St., New Orleans Court Building

Built in 1909, this was and still is a courthouse, covering the length of the block. The baroque edifice made of Georgia marble seems out of place in the French Quarter—especially considering that many Spanish-era structures were demolished to make way for it. The building was laboriously renovated and now houses the Louisiana Supreme Court and the Fourth Circuit Court of Appeals.

Cross St. Louis Street to:

7 520 Royal St., The Brulatour Court

This structure was built in 1816 as a home for François Seignouret, a furniture maker and wine importer from Bordeaux—his furniture, with a signature "S" carved into each piece, still commands the respect of collectors. During business hours you should ask to walk into the exotic courtyard—it's

Walking Tour: French Quarter

- - - • - - - Riverwalk streetcar route/stops
- - - ● - - - Vieux Carre loop route/stops

1 339–343 Royal St., Rilleux-Waldhorn House
2 333 Royal St., The Bank of Louisiana
3 403 Royal St., Latrobe's
4 417 Royal St., Brennan's Restaurant
5 437 Royal St., Peychaud's Drug Store
6 400 Royal St., New Orleans Court Building
7 520 Royal St., The Brulatour Court
8 533 Royal St., The Merieult House
9 613 Royal St., The Court of Two Sisters
10 627 Royal St., Horizon Gallery
11 640 Royal St., Le Monnier Mansion
12 700 Royal St., The LaBranche House
13 714 St. Peter St., Lacoul House
14 718 St. Peter St., Pat O'Brien's
15 726 St. Peter St., Preservation Hall

16 730 St. Peter St., Plique-LaBranche House
17 623 Bourbon St., Lindy Boggs Home
18 717 Orleans St., Bourbon Orleans Hotel
19 716 Dauphine St., Le Pretre Mansion
20 707 Dumaine St., Spanish Colonial Cottage
21 632 Dumaine St., Madame John's Legacy
22 941 Bourbon St., Lafitte's Blacksmith Shop
23 721 Governor Nicholls St., The Thierry House
24 1140 Royal St., The Lalaurie Home
25 1132 Royal St., Gallier House Museum
26 617 Ursulines Ave., Croissant D'Or ☕
27 1113 Chartres St., Beauregard-Keyes House

28 The Old U.S. Mint
29 The Historic French Market
30 Decatur Street
31 923 Decatur St., Central Grocery ☕
32 The Pontalba Buildings
33 751 Chartres St., The Presbytère
34 St. Louis Cathedral
35 The Cabildo
36 624 Pirates Alley, Faulkner House Books
37 632 St. Peter St., Tennessee Williams House
38 813 Decatur St., Café du Monde ☕

one of the few four-walled courtyards in the French Quarter. From the street, notice the elaborate, fan-shaped guard screen (*garde de frise*) on the right end of the third-floor balcony—look for Seignouret's "S" carved into the screen.

8 533 Royal St., The Merieult House

Built for the merchant Jean François Merieult in 1792, this house was the only building in the area left standing after the fire of 1794. Legend has it that Napoleon repeatedly offered Madame Merieult great riches in exchange for her hair. (He wanted it for a wig to present to a Turkish sultan.) She refused. Nowadays, it's home to the Historic New Orleans Collection Museum and Research Center. (See p. 174 for tour times and more information.)

Cross Toulouse Street to:

9 613 Royal St., The Court of Two Sisters

This structure was built in 1832 for a local bank president on the site of the 18th-century home of a French governor. The two sisters were Emma and Bertha Camors, whose father owned the building; from 1886 to 1906, they ran a curio store here.

10 627 Royal St., Horizon Gallery

Walk through the entrance to the back to see another magnificent

Inside the Historic New Orleans Collection, located at 533 Royal St.

courtyard. This 1777 building is where 17-year-old opera singer Adelina Patti first visited and then lived after becoming a local heroine in 1860. As a last-minute stand-in lead soprano in *Lucia di Lammermoor*, she saved the local opera company from financial ruin.

11 640 Royal St., Le Monnier Mansion

The city's first "skyscraper" was all of three stories high when it was built in 1811. A fourth story was added in 1876. Sieru George, fictional hero in George W. Cable's *Old Creole Days*, "lived" here.

Cross St. Peter Street to:

12 700 Royal St., The LaBranche House

This building is probably the most photographed building in the Quarter—and no wonder. The lacy cast-iron grillwork, with its delicate oak leaf and acorn design, fairly drips from all three floors. There are actually 11 LaBranche buildings (three-story brick row houses built 1835–1840 for the widow of wealthy sugar planter Jean Baptiste LaBranche). Eight face St. Peter Street, one faces Royal, and two face Pirates Alley.

Turn left at St. Peter Street and continue to:

13 714 St. Peter St., Lacoul House

Built in 1829 by prominent physician Dr. Yves LeMonnier, this was a boardinghouse run by Antoine Alciatore during the 1860s. His cooking became so popular with the locals that he eventually gave up catering to open the famous Antoine's restaurant (p. 120), still operated today by his descendants.

The acorns and oak leaves are visible in the cast-iron grillwork at the LaBranche House.

14 718 St. Peter St., Pat O'Brien's

Now the de facto home to the famed Hurricane cocktail (p. 8), this building was completed in 1790 for a wealthy planter. Later, Louis Tabary put on popular plays here including, purportedly, the first grand opera in America. The popular courtyard is well worth a look, maybe even a refreshment.

15 726 St. Peter St., Preservation Hall

Scores of people descend on this spot nightly to hear traditional New Orleans jazz (p. 280). A daytime stop affords a glimpse, through the big, ornate iron gate, of a lush tropical courtyard in back. Erle Stanley Gardner, the author who brought us Perry Mason, lived upstairs.

16 730 St. Peter St., Plique-LaBranche House

Built in 1825, this is believed to be the site of New Orleans's first theater, which burned in the fire of 1816. But that is the subject of some debate.

Continue up St. Peter Street until you reach Bourbon Street. Turn left onto Bourbon Street.

A peak through the gates into the courtyard at Preservation Hall.

223

17 623 Bourbon St., Lindy Boggs Home

Tennessee Williams and Truman Capote stayed in this house (no, not together). It's owned by Lindy Boggs, a much-beloved local politician, philanthropist (and mother of NPR and ABC commentator Cokie Roberts), who took over her husband's congressional seat after his death.

Turn around and head the other way down Bourbon Street. At the corner of Bourbon and Orleans streets, look down Orleans Street, toward the river, at:

18 717 Orleans St., Bourbon Orleans Hotel

This was the site of the famous quadroon balls, where wealthy white men would come to form alliances (read: acquire a mistress) with free women of color,

Tennessee Williams and Truman Capote once stayed in this house, but it's now home to Lindy Boggs, a local politician.

who were one-eighth to one-fourth black. Look at the balcony and imagine the assignations that went on there while the balls were in session. The building later became a convent, home to the Sisters of the Holy Family, the second-oldest order of black nuns in the country. Their founder (whose mother was a quadroon mistress!), Henriette Delille, has been presented to the Vatican for consideration for sainthood.

Turn left onto Orleans and follow it a block to Dauphine (pronounced Daw-**feen**) Street. On the corner is:

19 716 Dauphine St., Le Pretre Mansion

In 1839 Jean Baptiste Le Pretre bought this 1836 Greek Revival house and added the romantic cast-iron galleries. The house is the subject of a real-life horror story: In the 19th century, a Turk, supposedly the brother of a sultan, arrived in New Orleans and rented the house. He was conspicuously wealthy, with an entourage of servants and beautiful young girls—all thought to have been stolen from the sultan.

Rumors quickly spread about the situation, even as the home became the scene of lavish high-society parties. One night screams came from inside; the next morning, neighbors entered to find the tenant and the young beauties lying dead in a pool of blood. The mystery remains unsolved. Local ghost experts say you can sometimes hear exotic music and piercing shrieks.

The lobby of the Bourbon Orleans Hotel.

Turn right on Dauphine Street and go 2 blocks to Dumaine Street and then turn right. You'll find an interesting little cottage at:

20 707 Dumaine St., Spanish Colonial Cottage

After the 1794 fire, all houses in the French Quarter were required by law to have flat tile roofs. Most have since been covered with conventional roofs, but this Spanish colonial cottage is still in compliance with the flat-roof rule.

21 632 Dumaine St., Madame John's Legacy

This structure was once thought to be the oldest building on the Mississippi River, originally erected in 1726, 8 years after the founding of New Orleans. Recent research suggests, however, that only a few parts of the original building survived the 1788 fire and were used in its reconstruction. Its first owner was a ship captain who died in the 1729 Natchez Massacre; upon his death, the house passed to the captain of a Lafitte-era smuggling ship—and 21 owners subsequently. The present structure is a fine example of a French "raised cottage." The above-ground basement is of brick-between-posts construction (locally made bricks were too soft to be the primary building material), covered with boards laid horizontally. The hipped, dormered roof extends out over the veranda. Its name comes from George W. Cable's fictional character who was bequeathed the house in the short story "'Tite Poulette." Part of the Louisiana State Museum complex, it is currently not open for tours.

Take a left at the corner of Dumaine and Chartres streets and follow Chartres to the next corner; make a left onto St. Philip Street and continue to the corner of St. Philip and Bourbon streets to:

22 941 Bourbon St., Lafitte's Blacksmith Shop

For many years, this structure has been a bar (for the full story, see p. 292), but the legend is that Jean Lafitte and his pirates posed as blacksmiths here while using it as headquarters for selling goods they'd plundered on the high seas. It has survived in its original condition, reflecting

Lafitte's Blacksmith Shop.

the architectural influence of French colonials who escaped St. Domingue in the late 1700s.

It may be the oldest building in the Mississippi Valley, but that has not been documented. Unfortunately, the exterior has been redone to replicate the original brick and plaster, which makes it look fake (it's actually not). Thankfully the owners haven't chromed or plasticized the interior—it's an excellent place to imagine life in the Quarter in the 19th century.

Turn right onto Bourbon Street and follow it 2 blocks to Governor Nicholls Street. Turn right to:

23 721 Governor Nicholls St., The Thierry House

This structure was built in 1814 and announced the arrival of the Greek Revival style of architecture in New Orleans. It was designed in part by 19-year-old architect Henry S. Boneval Latrobe, son of noted architect Benjamin H. B. Latrobe.

Backtrack to the corner of Royal and Governor Nicholls streets. Take a left onto Royal and look for:

24 1140 Royal St., The Lalaurie Home

When Madame Delphine Macarty de Lopez Blanque wed Dr. Louis Lalaurie, it was her third marriage—she'd already been widowed twice. The Lalauries moved into this residence in 1832, and were soon impressing the city with extravagant parties. One night in 1834, however, fire broke out and neighbors crashed through a locked door to find seven starving slaves chained in painful positions, unable to move. The sight, combined with Delphine's stories of past slaves having "committed suicide," enraged her neighbors. Madame Lalaurie and her family escaped a mob's wrath and fled to Paris. Several years later she died in Europe. Her body was returned to New Orleans—and even then she had to be buried in secrecy.

Through the years, stories have circulated of ghosts inhabiting the building, especially that of one young slave child who fell from the roof trying to escape Delphine's cruelties.

Gallier House Museum.

The building was a Union headquarters during the Civil War, a gambling house, and more recently home to actor Nicolas Cage. Haunted by his own financial difficulties, Cage turned the house over to the bank in 2009.

25 1132 Royal St., Gallier House Museum

James Gallier, Jr., built this house in 1857 as his residence. He and his father were two of the city's leading architects (p. 172). Anne Rice considered this house when she described Lestat and Louis's home in *Interview with the Vampire*.

Turn left onto Ursulines Street, toward the river.

26 617 Ursulines Ave., Croissant D'Or ☕

If you need a little rest or sustenance at this point, you can stop in the popular Croissant D'Or, 617 Ursulines St. (✆ **504/524-4663;** p. 155). The croissants and pastries here are very good, and the ambience—inside or out on the patio—even better.

At the corner of Ursulines and Chartres streets is:

27 1113 Chartres St., Beauregard-Keyes House

This "raised cottage" was built as a residence in 1826 by Joseph Le Carpentier, though it has several other claims to fame (p. 169). Notice the Doric columns and handsome twin staircases.

Turn left onto Chartres Street and continue walking until you get to Esplanade (pronounced Es-pla-*nade*) Avenue, which served as the parade ground for troops quartered on Barracks Street. Along with St. Charles Avenue, it is one of the city's most picturesque historic thoroughfares. Some of the grandest town houses built in the late 1800s grace this wide, tree-lined avenue. (If you're interested in viewing some of these houses, Walking Tour 3, later in this chapter, concentrates on the architecture of Esplanade Ridge.) The entire 400 block of Esplanade is occupied by:

28 The Old U.S. Mint

This was once the site of Fort St. Charles, one of the defenses built to protect New Orleans in 1792. Andrew Jackson reviewed the "troops" here—pirates, volunteers, and a nucleus of trained soldiers—whom he later led in the Battle of New Orleans (p. 20). Now home to the Louisiana State Museum, it is soon to house a comprehensive Jazz Museum.

Follow Esplanade toward the river and turn right at the corner of North Peters Street. Follow North Peters until it intersects with Decatur Street. This is the back end of:

29 The Historic French Market

This European-style market (p. 166) has been here for well over 200 years, and today it has a farmers' market and stalls featuring everything from gator on a stick to tacky trinkets (that is, jewelry, T-shirts, and knockoff purses) though some excellent souvenirs and bargains have been found therein.

When you leave the French Market, exit on the side away from the river onto:

30 Decatur Street

Not long ago, this section of Decatur—from Jackson Square all the way over to Esplanade—was a seedy, run-down area of wild bars and cheap rooming

Fresh produce for sale at the Historic French Market.

houses. Fortunately, few of either remain. Instead, it has fallen into step with the rest of the Quarter, sporting a number of restaurants and noisy bars. (The stretch of Decatur between Ursulines and Esplanade has retained more of the run-down aesthetic, including Goth and punk shops, dank bars, and a few secondhand shops worth browsing.)

As you walk toward St. Ann Street along Decatur, you'll pass 923 and 919 Decatur St., where the Café de Refugies and Hôtel de la Marine, respectively, were located in the 1700s and early 1800s. These were reputed to be gathering places for pirates, smugglers, European refugees, and outlaws.

31 923 Decatur St., Central Grocery 🍴

If you're walking in the area of 923 Decatur St. around lunchtime, pop into the Central Grocery (ⓒ **504/523-1620;** p. 132), and pick up a famed muffuletta sandwich. Eat inside at little tables, or take your food and sit outside, maybe right on the riverbank.

Decatur Street will take you to Jackson Square. Turn right onto St. Ann Street; the twin four-story, red-brick buildings here and on the St. Peter Street side of the square are:

32 The Pontalba Buildings

These buildings sport some of the most impressive cast-iron balcony railings in the French Quarter. They also represent early French Quarter urban revitalization In the mid-1800s, Baroness Micaela Almonester de Pontalba inherited rows of buildings along both sides of the Place d'Armes from her father, Don Almonester (who rebuilt St. Louis Cathedral; p. 168). In

The Pontalba Buildings, lining Jackson Square, display impressive iron balcony railings.

an effort to counteract the emerging preeminence of the American sector across Canal Street, she razed the structures and built high-end apartments and commercial space.

The Pontalba Buildings were begun in 1849 under her direct supervision; you can see her mark today in the entwined initials "A.P." in the ironwork. The buildings were designed in a traditional Creole-European style, with commercial space on the street level, housing above, and a courtyard in the rear. The row houses on St. Ann Street, now owned by the state of Louisiana, were completed in 1851.

Baroness Pontalba was also responsible for the current design of Jackson Square, including the cast-iron fence and the equestrian statue of Andrew Jackson. (See p. 169 and 171 for more on the statue and Baroness Pontalba, respectively.)

At the corner of St. Ann and Chartres streets, turn left and continue around Jackson Square; you will see:

33 751 Chartres St., The Presbytère

This, the Cabildo, and the St. Louis Cathedral (read on for descriptions of the latter two buildings)—all designed by Gilberto Guillemard—were the first major public buildings in the Louisiana Territory. The Presbytère was originally designed as the cathedral's rectory. Baroness Pontalba's father financed the building's beginnings, but he died in 1798, leaving only the first floor done. It was finally completed in 1813. It was never used as a rectory, but was rented and then purchased (in 1853) by the city to be used as a courthouse. It now houses wonderful exhibits on the history of Mardi Gras (p. 176).

Next you'll come to:

34 St. Louis Cathedral

Although it is the oldest Catholic cathedral in the U.S., this is actually the third building erected on this spot—the first was destroyed by a hurricane in 1722, the second by fire in 1788. The cathedral was rebuilt in 1794; the central tower was later designed by Henry S. Boneval Latrobe, and the building was remodeled and enlarged between 1845 and 1851 under Baroness Pontalba's direction. The bell and stately clock (note the nonstandard Roman numeral four) were imported from France (p. 168).

On the other side of the cathedral, you'll come to Pirates Alley. Go right down Pirates Alley to:

35 The Cabildo

In the 1750s, this was the site of a French police station and guardhouse. Part of that building was incorporated into the original Cabildo, statehouse of the Spanish governing body (known as the "Very Illustrious Cabildo"). It was still under reconstruction when the transfer papers for the Louisiana Purchase were signed in a room on the second floor in 1803. Since then, it has served as New Orleans's City Hall, the Louisiana State Supreme Court, and, since 1911, a facility of the Louisiana State Museum (p. 172).

Think those old Civil War cannons out front look pitifully obsolete? Think again. In 1921, in a near-deadly prank, one was loaded and fired. That missile traveled across the wide expanse of the Mississippi and 6

blocks inland, landing in a house in Algiers and narrowly missing its occupants.

36 624 Pirates Alley, Faulkner House Books

In 1925, William Faulkner lived here. He contributed to the Times-Picayune and worked on his first novels, Mosquitoes and Soldiers' Pay, making this lovely bookstore a requisite stop for Faulkner lovers and collectors of both new and classic literature (p. 256).

To the left of the bookstore is a small alley that takes you to St. Peter Street, which is behind and parallel to Pirates Alley.

TOP: **A cannon in front of the Cabildo.** ABOVE: **A colorful home in the French Quarter.**

37 632 St. Peter St., Tennessee Williams House

Have a sudden urge to scream "Stella!!!" at that second-story wrought-iron balcony at 632 St. Peter St.? No wonder. This is where Tennessee Williams wrote *A Streetcar Named Desire,* one of the greatest pieces of American theater. He said he could hear "that rattle trap streetcar named Desire running along Royal and the one named Cemeteries running along Canal and it seemed the perfect metaphor for the human condition."

Return to Jackson Square. On the left side of the cathedral on the corner of Chartres and St. Peter streets (with your back to the Mississippi River and Jackson Square) is:

38 813 Decatur St., Café du Monde ☕

You've finished! Now go back across Jackson Square and Decatur Street to Café du Monde (✆ **504/525-4544;** p. 154)—no trip to New Orleans is complete without a leisurely stop here for beignets and coffee. Be sure to hike up the levee and relax on a bench, and watch the river roll.

WALKING TOUR 2: **THE GARDEN DISTRICT**

START:	**Prytania Street and Washington Avenue.**
FINISH:	**Lafayette Cemetery.**
TIME:	**45 minutes to 1½ hours.**
BEST TIME:	**Daylight.**
WORST TIME:	**Night, when you won't be able to get a good look at the architecture.**

Walking through the architecturally phenomenal Garden District, you could get the impression that you've entered an entirely separate city—or time period—from the French Quarter of New Orleans. Although the Garden District was indeed once a separate city (Lafayette) from the Vieux Carré and was established in a later period, their development by two different groups most profoundly distinguishes the two.

The French Quarter was initially established by Creoles during the French and Spanish colonial periods, and the Garden District was created by Americans after the 1803 Louisiana Purchase. Antebellum New Orleans's lucrative combination of Mississippi River commerce, regional abundance of cash crops, slave trade, and national banks fueled the local economy, resulting in a remarkable building boom that extended for several square miles through Uptown.

Very few people from the United States lived in New Orleans during its colonial era. Thousands of Americans moved here after the Louisiana Purchase. Friction arose between them and the Creoles due to mutual snobbery, language barriers, religious division, and competition over burgeoning commerce. Americans were arriving at the brink of a boom time to make fortunes. With inferior business experience, education, and organizational skills, the Creoles worried that les Americains would work them out of business. Americans were thus barred from the already overcrowded French Quarter. The snubbed Americans moved upriver and created a residential district of astounding opulence: the Garden District. It is, therefore, a cultural clash reflected through architecture, with Americans creating an identity by boldly introducing styles and forms familiar to them but previously unknown here.

Note: The houses described on this tour are not open to the public.

To reach the Garden District, take the St. Charles streetcar to Washington Avenue (stop no. 16) and walk 1 block toward the river to:

1 2727 Prytania St., The Garden District Book Shop

This bookshop's (p. 257) stellar collection of regional titles is an appropriate kickoff for a Garden District tour. Owner Britton Trice schedules readings by many locally and nationally acclaimed authors, and stocks many signed editions. The historic property known as the Rink was built in 1884 as the Crescent City Skating Rink, and subsequently acted as a livery stable, mortuary, grocery store, and gas station.

The Rink also offers a coffee shop, restrooms, and air-conditioning (crucial in the summer).

Across Prytania Street, you'll find:

TOP: **The cornstalk fence out front of Colonel Short's Villa, at 1448 Fourth St.** ABOVE: **The Garden District Book Shop.**

2 1448 Fourth St., Colonel Short's Villa

This house was built by architect Henry Howard for Kentucky Colonel Robert Short. The story goes that Short's wife complained of missing the cornfields in her native Iowa, so he bought her the cornstalk fence. But a recent owner's revisionist explanation is that the wife requested it because it was the most expensive fence in the building catalog. Second Civil War occupational governor Nathaniel Banks was quartered here.

Continuing down Prytania, you'll find:

3 2605 Prytania St., Briggs-Staub House

This is the Garden District's only example of Gothic Revival architecture (unpopular among Protestant Americans because it reminded them of their Roman Catholic Creole antagonists). Original owner Charles Briggs did not hold African slaves but did employ Irish servants, for whom he built the relatively large adjacent servant quarters. Irish immigration was then starting to create the Irish Channel neighborhood across Magazine Street from the Garden District.

4 2523 Prytania St., Our Mother of Perpetual Help

Once an active Catholic chapel, this site was one of several in the area owned by Anne Rice and the setting for her novel *Violin*. The author's childhood home is down the street at 2301 St. Charles Ave.

5 2504 Prytania St., Women's Opera Guild Home

Some of the Garden District's most memorable homes incorporate more than one style. Designed by William Freret in 1858, this building combines Greek Revival and Queen Anne styles. Now owned by the Women's Opera Guild, the home can be toured on Mondays from 10am to noon and 1 to 4pm for $7, or by advance arrangements for groups (𝄐 **504/899-1945**).

6 2340 Prytania St., Toby's Corner

The Garden District's oldest known home dates to at least 1838. Built for Philadelphia wheelwright Thomas Toby, it is in the then-popular Greek Revival style. Although it represents an Anglicized attempt at non-Creole identity, this style required Creole building techniques such as raising the house up on brick piers to combat flooding and encourage air circulation.

8

The Garden District

CITY STROLLS

The Women's Opera Guild features Greek Revival and Queen Anne styles of architecture.

Bradish Johnson House.

Walking Tour: The Garden District

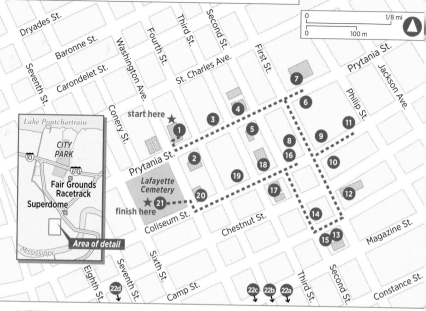

1 2727 Prytania St., The Garden District Book Shop
2 1448 Fourth St., Colonel Short's Villa
3 2605 Prytania St., Briggs-Staub House
4 2523 Prytania St., Our Mother of Perpetual Help
5 2504 Prytania St., Women's Opera Guild Home
6 2340 Prytania St., Toby's Corner
7 2343 Prytania St., Bradish Johnson House and
  Louise S. McGehee School
8 1420 First St., Archie Manning House
9 1407 First St., Pritchard-Pigott House
10 1331 First St., Morris-Israel House
11 2329-2305 Coliseum St., The Seven Sisters
12 1239 First St., Brevard-Mahat-Rice House

13 1134 First St., Payne-Strachan House
14 2427 Camp St., Warwick Manor
15 1137 Second St.
16 2425 Coliseum St., Joseph Merrick Jones House
17 1331 Third St., Musson-Bell House
18 1415 Third St., Robinson House
19 2627 Coliseum St., Koch-Mays House
20 1403 Washington Ave., Commander's Palace
21 1400 Washington Ave., Lafayette Cemetery
22a Tracey's
22b Coquette
22c Still Perkin'
22d Sucré

7 2343 Prytania St., Bradish Johnson House & Louise S. McGehee School

Paris-trained architect James Freret designed this French Second Empire–style mansion, built for sugar factor Bradish Johnson in 1872 at a cost of $100,000 ($1.6-plus million today). Contrast this house's awesome detail with the stark classical simplicity of Toby's Corner (see above) across the street—a visual indication of the effect that one generation of outrageous fortune had on Garden District architecture. Since 1929 it has been the private Louise S. McGehee School for girls.

Turn down First Street (away from St. Charles) and it's less than a block to:

235

8 1420 First St., Archie Manning House

Home of former New Orleans Saints superstar quarterback Archie Manning and the childhood home of his sons, also familiar to football fans: Peyton, quarterback for the Indianapolis Colts, and Eli, New York Giants quarterback.

9 1407 First St., Pritchard-Pigott House

This Greek Revival double-galleried town house shows how, as fortunes grew, so did Garden District home sizes. Americans introduced two house forms: the cottage (as in Toby's Corner; see above) and this grander town house.

10 1331 First St., Morris-Israel House

As time passed, the simplicity of Greek Revival style moved toward more playful design styles. By the 1860s, Italianate was popular, as seen in this (reputedly haunted) double-galleried town house. Architect Samuel Jamison designed this house and the Carroll-Crawford House on the next corner (1315 First St.); note the identical ornate cast-iron galleries.

Follow Coliseum Street to the left less than half a block to:

11 2329–2305 Coliseum St., The Seven Sisters

This row of "shotgun" houses gets its nickname from a (false) story that a 19th-century Garden District resident built these homes as wedding gifts for his seven daughters. Actually, there are eight "Seven Sisters," and they were built on speculation.

"Shotgun" style homes are so named because, theoretically, if one fired a gun through the front door, the bullet would pass unhindered out the back. Also, a West African word for this native African house form sounds like "shotgun." The shotgun house effectively circulates air and is commonly

An example of a typical shotgun house.

found in hot climates. The relatively small shotguns are rare along the imposing Garden District streets, but they are extremely popular throughout the rest of New Orleans.

Now turn around and go back to First Street and turn left. At the corner of First and Chestnut, you'll see:

12 1239 First St., Brevard-Mahat-Rice House

Designed in 1857 as a Greek Revival town house and later augmented with an Italianate bay, this house is a fine

The diamond pattern on the fence at 1239 First St. is believed to be a precursor to the chain-link fence.

example of "transitional" architecture. It was called Rosegate for the rosette pattern on the fence. (The fence's woven diamond pattern is believed to be the precursor to the chain-link fence.) This was the home of novelist Anne Rice and the setting for her Witching Hour novels.

13 1134 First St., Payne-Strachan House

As the stone marker in front of the house notes, Jefferson Davis, president of the Confederate States of America, died in this classic Greek Revival antebellum home, that of his friend Judge Charles Fenner. Davis was bur-

ied in magnificent Metairie Cemetery for 2 years and then was disinterred and moved to Virginia. Note the sky-blue ceiling of the gallery—the color is believed to keep winged insects from nesting there and to ward off evil spirits. Many local homes adhere to this tradition.

Turn right on Camp and go less than a block to:

14 2427 Camp St., Warwick Manor

An example of Georgian architecture, this house is a rare (for the vicinity) multifamily residence. Note the buzzers, which indicate rented apartments.

Jefferson Davis died at 1134 First St., the Payne-Strachan House.

15 1137 Second St.

This house exemplifies the type of Victorian architecture popularized in uptown New Orleans toward the end of the 19th century. Many who built such homes were from the Northeast and left New Orleans in the summer; otherwise, it would be odd to see this "cool climate" style of claustrophobic house in New Orleans. Note the exquisite stained glass and rounded railing on the gallery.

Turn right onto Second Street and go 2 blocks to the corner of Coliseum, where you'll see:

16 2425 Coliseum St., Joseph Merrick Jones House

This house, now home to actor John Goodman, was previously owned by Nine Inch Nails singer Trent Reznor. When he moved in, more anti-noise ordinances were introduced into city council proceedings. His next-door neighbor was City Councilwoman Peggy Wilson. Coincidence?

Turn left onto Coliseum Street and go 1 block to Third Street. Turn left to get to:

17 1331 Third St., Musson-Bell House

This is the 1853 home of Michel Musson, one of the few French Creoles then living in the Garden District and the uncle of artist Edgar Degas, who lived with Musson on Esplanade Avenue during a visit to New Orleans. On the Coliseum Street side of the house is the foundation of a cistern. These water tanks were so common in the Garden District that Mark Twain once commented that it looked as if everybody in the neighborhood had a private brewery. Cisterns were destroyed at the turn of the 20th century when mosquitoes, which breed in standing water, were found to be carriers of yellow fever and malaria.

Turn around and cross Coliseum to see:

18 1415 Third St., Robinson House

This striking unusual home was built between 1859 and 1865 by architect Henry Howard for tobacco grower and merchant Walter Robinson. Walk past the house to appreciate its scale—the outbuildings, visible from the front, are actually connected to the side of the main house. The entire roof is a large vat that once collected water. Add gravity and water pressure, and thus begat the Garden District's earliest indoor plumbing.

Continue down Coliseum Street 2 blocks to the corner of Washington Avenue. There you'll find:

19 2627 Coliseum St., Koch-Mays House

This picturesque chalet-style dollhouse (well, for a large family of dolls) was built in 1876 by noted architect William Freret for James Eustis, a U.S. senator and ambassador to France. Along with four other spec homes he built on the block, it was referred to as Freret's Folly. No detail was left unfrilled, from the ironwork to the gables and finials. Actress Sandra Bullock and her adopted baby Louis (a native New Orleanian) moved here in 2010; wonder if he rides a Big Wheel around the full-size ballroom. Please enjoy the elaborate design, and respect the tenant's privacy.

20 1403 Washington Ave., Commander's Palace

Established in 1883 by Emile Commander, this turreted Victorian structure (a bordello back in the 1920s) is now the pride of the Brennan family, the most visible and successful restaurateurs in New Orleans, and one of the city's top restaurants (p. 147). Rain damage after Katrina demanded a to-the-studs stripping inside and out, but the iconic turquoise and white manse looks as it always did!

Detailed ironwork at the Koch-Mays House, at 2627 Coliseum St..

21 1400 Washington Ave., Lafayette Cemetery

Established in 1833, this "city of the dead" is one of New Orleans's oldest cemeteries and a popular film location. It has examples of all the classic aboveground, multiple-burial techniques. These tombs typically house numerous corpses—one here lists 37 entrants, while several others are designated for members of specific fire departments. It's often active with visitors (Commander's Palace diners walking off the bread pudding soufflé?), and thus safe, but unfortunately there is much disrepair here. (The website www.SaveOurCemeteries.org accepts donations toward restoration and preservation efforts.)

Walk to St. Charles Avenue to pick up the streetcar (there is a stop right there) or flag down a cab to return to the French Quarter.

22 Wind Down at Still Perkin', Tracey's, Coquette, or Sucré ☕

Now go back to your first stop, the Rink, where you can enjoy a cup of coffee and some light refreshments at Still Perkin'. Or head south on Washington to Magazine Street, where a po' boy at Tracey's, lunch at Coquette, or a sweet from Sucré (p. 157) will satisfy other appetites.

WALKING TOUR 3: **ESPLANADE RIDGE**

START:	**Esplanade Avenue and Johnson Street.**
FINISH:	**City Park.**
TIME:	**Allow approximately 1½ hours, not including museum, cemetery, and shopping stops.**
BEST TIMES:	**Monday through Saturday, early or late morning.**
WORST TIMES:	**Sunday, when attractions are closed. Also, you certainly don't want to walk in this area after dark; if you decide to stay in City Park or in the upper Esplanade area until early evening, plan to return on the bus or by taxi.**

If you're heading to City Park, the New Orleans Museum of Art, or the Jazz & Heritage Festival, consider strolling this overlooked region, or leaving enough time for sightseeing from your car. We particularly enjoy the stretch along St. John's Bayou—mostly as slow and quiet as the sluggish water itself. Historically, the Esplanade Ridge area was Creole society's answer to St. Charles Avenue— it's an equally lush boulevard with stately homes and seemingly ancient trees stretching overhead. Originally home to the descendants of the earliest settlers, the avenue had its finest days toward the end of the 19th century, and some of the neighborhoods along its path, especially the Faubourg Treme, are visibly suffering. Esplanade is a little worn compared to St. Charles Avenue, but it's closer to the soul of the city (read: Regular people live here, whereas St. Charles always was and still is for the well-heeled).

You can catch a bus on Esplanade Avenue at the French Quarter, headed toward the park to your starting point. Otherwise, stroll (about 15 min.) up Esplanade Avenue to:

1 2023 Esplanade Ave., Charpentier House

Originally a plantation home, this house was designed in 1861 for A. B. Charpentier and now operates as Ashtons Bed & Breakfast (p. 96).

2 2033–2035 Esplanade Ave., Widow Castanedo's House

Juan Rodriguez purchased this land in the 1780s, and his granddaughter, Widow Castanedo, lived here until her death in 1861 (when it was a smaller, Spanish colonial–style plantation home). Before Esplanade Avenue extended this far from the river, the house was located in what is now the middle of the street. The widow tried and failed to block the extension of the street. The late-Italianate house was moved to its present site and enlarged sometime around the 1890s. It is split down the middle and inhabited today by two sisters.

3 2139 Esplanade Ave.

A great example of the typical Esplanade Ridge style. Note the Ionic columns on the upper level.

On the opposite side of the street is:

4 2176 Esplanade Ave.

A simple, classic-style town house, this was the second Bayou Road home built by Hubert Gerard, who also built the 1861 at no. 2023 (see above).

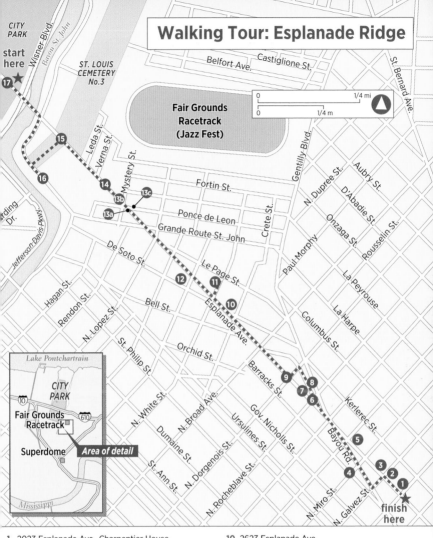

Walking Tour: Esplanade Ridge

1 2023 Esplanade Ave., Charpentier House

2 2033-2035 Esplanade Ave., Widow
   Castanedo's House

3 2139 Esplanade Ave.

4 2176 Esplanade Ave.

5 Goddess of History—Genius of Peace Statue

6 2306 Esplanade Ave., Degas House

7 2326 Esplanade Ave., Reuther House

8 2337 and 2341 Esplanade Ave.

9 2453 Esplanade Ave.

10 2623 Esplanade Ave.

11 2809 Esplanade Ave.

12 2936 Esplanade Ave.

13a Café Degas

13b Terranova's

13c Fair Grinds

14 3330 Esplanade Ave.

15 3421 Esplanade Ave., St. Louis Cemetery No. 3

16 1440 Moss St., Pitot House

17 Esplanade and City Park Aves., City Park

After you cross North Miro Street, Esplanade Avenue crosses the diagonal Bayou Road, which was the route to the French-Canadian settlements at St. John's Bayou in the late 17th century. Veer left at the fork to stay on Esplanade Avenue and look for:

5 Goddess of History—Genius of Peace Statue

In 1886, this triangular piece of land, called Gayarre Place, was given to the city by Charles Gayarre. George H. Dunbar donated the original terra-cotta statue, a victory monument, which was destroyed in 1938. The present one, made of cement and marble, is a replacement.

6 2306 Esplanade Ave., Degas House

The Musson family rented this house for many years. Estelle

TOP: The columns at 2139 Esplanade Ave. ABOVE: The *Goddess of History* statue.

Examples of Creole cottages can be seen at 2325, 2329, and 2331 Esplanade Ave.

Musson married René Degas, brother of Edgar Degas, the French Impressionist artist. (She and her descendants dropped his last name after he ran off with a neighbor's wife.) Degas is said to have painted the portrait of Estelle that is now in the New Orleans Museum of Art, among other works, during the brief time he spent living here.

The house was built in 1854, and the Italianate decorations were added later when it was split into two buildings. It's a B&B now, with studio tours available by appointment (p. 188).

7 2326 Esplanade Ave., Reuther House

The current resident of this house—a founder of the Contemporary Arts Center (p. 301) and a major figure in the city's arts community—has a collection of metal and cinder-block sculptures in his front yard, readily visible from the street.

In passing, take a look at nos. 2325, 2329, and 2331—all are interesting examples of Creole cottages. Then, continue to:

8 2337 & 2341 Esplanade Ave.

These houses were identical structures when they were built in 1862 for John Budd Slawson, owner of a horse-drawn-streetcar company that operated along Bayou Road in the 19th century. Back then, they were both single-story shotgun-style houses. Notice the unusual ironwork underneath the front roof overhang.

8

CITY STROLLS   Esplanade Ridge

243

Cross North Dorgenois Street to:

9 2453 Esplanade Ave.

Until the other was demolished, this house was one of a pair at the corner of Dorgenois Street. Though its architecture has been changed extensively, it's one of the few remaining mansard-roofed homes on Esplanade Ridge.

Cross North Broad Street to:

10 2623 Esplanade Ave.

Here is a classical revival Victorian home built in 1896 by Louis A. Jung. Note the Corinthian columns. The Jungs donated the triangular piece of land at Esplanade Avenue, Broad Street, and Crete Street to the city on the condition that it remain public property. Now called DeSoto Park, it is graced by an Art Nouveau fence.

11 2809 Esplanade Ave.

This is one of the more decorative Victorian Queen Anne center-hall houses on Esplanade Ridge.

12 2936 Esplanade Ave.

A nice example of what's known as a Gothic villa.

13 Take a Break at Café Degas, Terranova's, or Fair Grinds 🍴

At the intersection of Mystery Street and Esplanade Avenue, you'll find a little grouping of shops and restaurants. If you're in the area at lunchtime, you might want to stop at Café Degas (p. 135), for a leisurely meal—if the weather is nice, the semi-outdoor setting is exceedingly pleasant. If you just want a snack or some picnic food for City Park, you can get cold cuts, ice cream, and snacks at the family-run Terranova's Italian Grocery, 3308 Esplanade Ave. (✆ **504/482-4131**), across the street. Or opt for a break at the quirky Fair Grinds coffeehouse just off Esplanade at 3133 Ponce De Leon St. (✆ **504/913-9072**).

Continue to:

14 3330 Esplanade Ave.

A galleried frame home built in the Creole-cottage style.

On your right is:

15 3421 Esplanade Ave., St. Louis Cemetery No. 3

This was the site of the public Bayou Cemetery, established in 1835. It was purchased by the St. Louis diocese in 1856 and contains the burial monuments of many of the diocese's priests. If you've been putting off going into the cemeteries because of concerns over safety, you can explore this one on your own—though as always, you should still be alert.

From the cemetery, head back out to Esplanade Avenue and continue walking toward City Park. When you get to the bridge, go left, following the signs, along St. John's Bayou (one of the nicest and least touristy areas of the city), to:

A tomb for multiple people at St. Louis Cemetery No. 3.

16 1440 Moss St., Pitot House

This Creole country house overlooks historic Bayou St. John and is open for public viewing (p. 189). Knowledgeable docents offer a window onto life in the day when the bayou was the major trade route. Years later, this was home to the first mayor of New Orleans.

Head back to Esplanade Avenue, turn left, cross the bridge, and walk straight into:

17 Esplanade & City Park Avenues, City Park

Explore the sculpture garden, amphitheater, museum, botanical gardens, lakes, and much more in this glorious, expansive park (p. 192).

9

SHOPPING

Shopping in New Orleans is a highly evolved leisure activity, with a shop for every strategy and a fix for every shopaholic—and every budget. Those endless T-shirt shops on Bourbon Street and the swanky antiques stores on Royal Street aren't all that New Orleans has to offer. The range of shopping here is as good as it gets—many a clever person has come to New Orleans just to open up a quaint boutique filled with strange items gathered from all parts of the globe or produced by local, somewhat twisted, folk artists.

Want to totally redecorate your house? You can do that here whether your taste runs to Victorian or top-to-bottom folk art. Want to double your music collection? That's what this town is made for. Need the perfect souvenir? From an antique sofa that costs about as much as a college education to 50¢ Mardi Gras beads, you'll have plenty of options.

Searching for these treasures will contribute to your calorie-burning walks, as you stroll along Magazine Street or window shop in the Quarter. Antiques aficionados used to eschew exorbitant Royal Street to find buys on Magazine, but real bargains are now hard to come by in either locale. Still, there are deals to be made on both streets (and don't forget the Esplanade end of Decatur for real deals on less hoity goods). We also love Magazine for its adorable shops with trendy clothes and unique gifts. For more specific information on said shops, call ℂ **866/679-4764** or 504/342-4435, or try **www.magazinestreet.com**.

Over the past 20-plus years (uncoincidentally, about as long as the Contemporary Arts Center has been open), New Orleans has grown to be an important regional and national market for contemporary fine arts. The city's art galleries tend to be clustered near the C.A.C. on Julia Street, or on Royal Street.

We've listed store hours but they may change unexpectedly, so call ahead if you're on a tight schedule.

MAJOR HUNTING GROUNDS

CANAL PLACE At the foot of Canal Street (365 Canal St.) near the Mississippi River, this sophisticated shopping mall holds more than 50 shops, many of them branches of elegant retailers like Brooks Brothers, Saks Fifth Avenue, and Coach. There's also a two-story Anthropologie and a branch of local jeweler Mignon Faget (reviewed later in this chapter). Open Monday to Saturday 10am to 7pm, Sunday noon to 6pm. www.theshopsatcanalplace. com.

THE FRENCH MARKET Shops within the market begin on Decatur Street across from Jackson Square; offerings include candy, cookware, fashion, crafts, toys, New Orleans memorabilia, and jewelry. It's open from 10am to 6pm (and Café du Monde, next to the farmers' market, is open 24 hr.). You'll find a lot of junk here, but with some very good buys mixed in, and it's always fun

More than 150 shops line Magazine Street in the Garden District.

to stroll through and grab a nibble (there's a good juice bar . . . or gator on a stick!). Be sure to walk all the way to the "flea market" in the back (near Esplanade), where you can find jewelry; designer-knockoff sunglasses; pretty, flowing dresses; and more. The actual farmers' market portion has pretty fruit and veggies, and the stalls with foodstuffs—including local seafood, meats, and spices—can pack your purchases for travel or shipping. www.frenchmarket.org.

JAX BREWERY Just across from Jackson Square at 600–620 Decatur St., the old brewery building has been transformed into a jumble of shops, cafes, delicatessens, restaurants, and entertainment. **Save NOLA,** on the first floor, has a good selection of shirts, hats, bags, and other souvenirs from nonprofits that support New Orleans and the Gulf Coast, like Drew Brees's Dream Foundation and Brad Pitt's Make It Right Foundation. Open daily from 10am to 6pm.

JULIA STREET From Camp Street down to the river on Julia Street, you'll find some of the city's best contemporary-art galleries (many are listed below, under "Art Galleries"). Some of the works are a bit pricey, but there are good deals to be had if you're collecting and fine art to be seen if you're not.

MAGAZINE STREET This is the Garden District's premier shopping street. More than 150 shops line the street in 19th-century brick storefronts and quaint cottage–like buildings, offering antiques, art galleries, boutiques, and all manner of restaurants. You *could* shop the full 6 miles from Washington Street to Audubon Park, or hit prime sections from, roughly, the 3500 to 4200 blocks (from about Aline St. to Milan St., with the odd block or so of nothing); the 1900 to 2100; 2800 to 3300; and 5400 to 5700 blocks.

Definitely pick up a copy of *Magazine Street Shoppers' Guide,* a free store list and map available along the street. www.magazinestreet.com.

RIVERBEND & OAK STREET   To reach this district (in the Carrollton area), ride the St. Charles Avenue streetcar to stop no. 44, then walk down Maple Street 1 block to Dublin Park, the site of an old public market that was once lined with open stalls. Nowadays, a variety of renovated shops inhabit the old general store, a produce warehouse made of barge board, and the town surveyor's raised-cottage home. Walk 4 blocks down Dublin to recently renovated Oak Street, excellent for strolling, shopping, dining, and taking a snoball snack break.

RIVERWALK MARKETPLACE   A mall is a mall, unless it has picture windows offering a Mississippi River panorama. Thus, this one, at 1 Poydras St., is worth visiting. Stop by the Fudgery for their highly entertaining musical fudge-making demos. An uncrowded branch of Café du Monde (for easy beignet access) and the Southern Food and Beverage Museum (p. 185) are also located here, adding considerable motivation for a trip. Otherwise, it's the usual suspects and souvenir shops. Open daily from 10am to 7pm, Sunday noon to 6pm. Validated parking with $10 purchase is $5 for 4 hours. www.riverwalkmarketplace.com.

SHOPPING A TO Z
Antiques

Note: A majority of the listings below are true antiques shops, and in many cases, the sort of establishments that have objects in the six-figure range. For those of us without jet-set budgets, we have listed, and made note of, less stratospherically priced places.

Aesthetics & Antiques Retro Fun ★★   This self-named "Baby Boomer's Gumbo," carries all the stuff that's too good, quirky, or collectible to let go at a yard sale. Prices are already reasonable but they will bargain if you buy enough. Last visit, we bought old sheet music, a piece of Sputnik encased in Lucite, and a 1940s collie figurine, while passing up a menu from Antoine's 75th anniversary and a decanter shaped like the pope. Throw in some china, vintage postcards, local antique doorknobs, jewelry, and you get the idea. Tellingly, it's a haven for set decorators shooting locally. 3122 Magazine St. ✆ **504/895-9999.** Mon and Thurs–Sat 11am–6pm; Sun 1–5:30pm. Closed Tues–Wed.

Bush Antiques ★   There is serious stuff here, mostly of the European variety, and some not so serious. But the warren of rooms, some cunningly arranged according to theme, are giddy fun to browse whether or not you're in the market for a 19th-century French Empire settee or an elaborately embroidered priest's garment. 2109 Magazine St. ✆ **504/581-3518.** www.bushantiques.com. Mon–Sat 11am–5pm.

Collectible Antiques ★★   One of our favorites of the several little, dusty, crammed, and eclectic antiques/junk stores on the Esplanade end of Decatur, perhaps because we bought old Gibson-girl cartoons and a cookie jar shaped like a monk at prices that didn't deplete our meal budget. The large, jumbled shop includes lighting fixtures and stock runs from Art Deco to the 1960s. 1232 Decatur St. ✆ **504/566-0399.** Daily noon–6pm.

Greg's Antiques ★ 🖋 A funky mixed bag of serious antiques, junky used furniture, salvaged windows and ironwork, and original art on consignment—not necessarily pedigreed but at pretty decent prices—make this a personal favorite (and they're open late). Frequent shipments and sales mean goods move fast. 1209 Decatur St. 📞 **504/202-8577.** Daily 10am–8pm.

Ida Manheim Antiques At this gallery, you'll find an enormous collection of Continental and English furnishings along with porcelains, silver, and fine paintings, and sometimes attitude to match. 409 Royal St. 📞 **888/627-5969** or 504/620-4114. www.idamanheimantiques. com. Mon–Sat 9am–5pm.

Keil's Antiques ★★ Established in 1899 and currently run by the fourth generation of the founding family, Keil's has a considerable collection of 18th- and 19th-century French and English furniture, chandeliers, jewelry, and decorative items. Somewhere on

A number of antiques stores can be found on and around Royal Street.

their three crowded floors (and more in a warehouse), there is something for almost every budget. Try to talk to one of the members of the family, for tales of

Goblets for sale at Keil's Antiques.

the doorman who worked his spot for 78 years and whatever other stories you can coax out of them. 325 Royal St. ℂ **504/522-4552.** www.keilsantiques.com. Mon–Sat 9am–5pm.

Lucullus ★★★ An unusual shop, Lucullus has a wonderful collection of culinary antiques as well as 17th- through 19th-century furnishings to "complement the grand pursuits of cooking, dining, and imbibing." You'll find "anything for gracious dining," from china and Art Deco silverware to coffee grinders, even absinthe glasses and spoons. 610 Chartres St. ℂ **504/528-9620.** www.lucullusantiques. com. Mon–Sat 9am–5pm. Closed Mon in the summer.

Magazine Antique Mall ★★ Diggers will dig the superb browsing and many good deals found among the 50-plus stalls here, where home furnishings, vintage clothes, cookware, decorative gewgaws, card and coin collectibles, and the usual kitsch abound. 3017 Magazine St. ℂ **504/896-9994.** www.magazineantiquemall. com. Mon–Sat 10:30am–5:30pm; Sun noon–5:30pm.

M.S. Rau ★★★ The sheer scale and absurdity of the inventory makes Rau a must-see for everyone, and a destination for many serious buyers. Every opulent item that could possibly be crafted from fine metals, gems, crystal, wood, china, and marble, plus articles made by every name known to the antique world, are here for the ogling or the investing, filling room after jaw-dropping room. We particularly like the selection of walking canes and the life-size knight and steed, both in full armor. Most every item has a story to tell, and the knowledgeable sales reps pleasantly indulge your curiosity. 630 Royal St. ℂ **866/349-0705** or 504/523-5660. www.rauantiques.com. Mon–Sat 8:45am–5:15pm.

Rare Finds ★★ Unusual for a shop on Decatur Street, this establishment is beautifully organized by subject, theme, or sometimes color. It makes browsing among the vintage jewelry, dolls, books, dishware, and other collectibles so much easier. 1231 Decatur St. ℂ **504/568-1004.** www.rarefindsneworleans.com. Wed–Mon noon–6pm; summer Fri–Mon noon–6pm.

Rothschild's Antiques ★ Rothschild's is a fourth-generation furniture merchandiser with a dreamy display of antiques as well as estate and custom-made jewelry. There's a fine selection of antique silver, marble mantels, and English and French furnishings including chandeliers. 321 Royal St. ℂ **504/523-5816.** Mon–Sat 9:30am–5pm; Sun and any day by appointment.

Whisnant Galleries ★ The quantity and variety of merchandise in this shop is mind-boggling. You'll find all sorts of unique and unusual antique collectibles, including items from Ethiopia, Russia, Greece, South America, Morocco, and other parts of North Africa and the Middle East. 229 Royal St. ℂ **504/524-9766.** Mon–Sat 9:30am–5:30pm; Sun 10am–5pm.

Art Galleries

Galleries share the **Royal and Magazine street** landscapes with the aforementioned antiques shops, while in the Warehouse District, the blocks numbered 300 to 700 Julia Street house some 20 contemporary fine-arts galleries, anchored by the Contemporary Arts Center (p. 301) and Ogden Museum (p. 184). Monthly gallery crawls, with street music and flowing wine, are a fun, mostly locals scene (6–9pm the first Sat of each month; see www.neworleansartsdistrict. com). For the more intrepid, the St. Claude Arts District is a burgeoning lowbrow and outsider art movement around St. Claude Avenue, with monthly openings on the second Saturday (see www. scadnola.com for listings). We list only a few galleries here, but there's certainly no lack of fodder for the art enthusiast.

Angela King Gallery Angela King Gallery shows paintings and sculptures by significant con-

temporary artists such as Peter Max, Frederick Hart, Charles Thysell, Joanna Zjawinska, Mark Erickson, LeRoy Neiman, Andrew Baird, Richard Currier, and Michelle Gagliano. 241 Royal St. ✆ **504/524-8211.** www.angelakinggallery.com. Mon–Sat 10am–5pm; Sun 11am–5pm.

Arthur Roger Gallery ★★ Arthur Roger helped develop the city's fine art scene when he opened in New Orleans more than 30 years ago, tying the local community to the New York art world and pioneering the Warehouse District. Still blazing trails, Roger schedules shows that range from strongly regional to far-flung work. The gallery represents Francis Pavy, Ida Kohlmeyer, Douglas Bourgeois, Willie Birch, Gene Koss, and George Dureau. 432 Julia St. ✆ **504/522-1000.** www.arthurrogergallery.com. Tues–Sat 11am–5pm; 1st Sat of month till 9pm.

Berta's and Mina's Antiquities ★★ Once, this was just another place that bought and sold antiques, secondhand furniture, and art. That all ended in 1993 when the late Nilo Lanzas (Berta's husband and Mina's dad) began painting. His paint-on-wood folk art (much of which has since gone to collectors) depicts colorful scenes from life in New Orleans or his native Latin America, stories out of the Bible, or images sprung from his imagination. Mina's joyful celebrations

Colorful folk art works inside Berta's and Mina's Antiquities.

of local life, landscapes, and "dancing houses" have their own following. 4138 Magazine St. ☎ **504/895-6201.** Mon–Sat 10am–6pm; Sun noon–5pm.

Carol Robinson Gallery The grande dame of the local contemporary Southern arts scene, Robinson still shows accessible but surprisingly affordable works, including the stunning pastels of Sandra Burshell, Jere Allen's mysterious figures wafting in white, James King's haunting oils, and Christina Goodman's exquisite, minute tableaus. 840 Napoleon Ave. ☎ **504/895-6130.** Tues–Sat 10am–5pm.

Chris Roberts-Antieau We love her whimsical sewn works, which often riff on current events. If Bryan Cunningham's equally mad folk assemblages are also on exhibit, more's the better. 927 Royal St. ☎ **504/304-0849.** www.antieaugallery.com. Thurs–Mon 10am–8pm.

Cole Pratt Gallery, Ltd. ★ This gallery showcases the work of Southern artists whose creations include abstract and realist paintings, sculptures, and ceramics. The art is of the highest quality, the prices are surprisingly reasonable, and the staff is welcoming. 3800 Magazine St. ☎ **504/891-6789.** www.coleprattgallery.com. Tues–Sat 10am–5pm.

Davis Galleries ★★★ This world-class gallery may be the best place in the world for Central and West African traditional art. The owner makes regular trips to Africa, returning with sculpture, costuming, basketry, textiles, weapons, and/or jewelry. 904 Louisiana Ave. ☎ **504/895-5206.** www.davisafricanart.com. By appointment only.

Derby Pottery ★ One of Mark Derby's hand-pressed tiles, glazed in gleaming single hues, makes for a lovely keepsake. One hundred make for a stunning backsplash or fireplace surround. 2029 Magazine St. ☎ **504/586-9003.** www.derbypottery. com. Mon–Sat 10am–5pm.

A Gallery for Fine Photography ★★★ It would be a mistake to skip this incredibly well-stocked photography gallery, even if you aren't in the market. Owner Joshua Mann Pailet calls this "the only museum in the world that's for sale." The gallery emphasizes New Orleans and Southern history and contemporary culture (you can buy Ernest Bellocq's legendary Storyville photos) as well as black culture and music (including Herman Leonard's jazz images), but just about every period, style, and noted photographer is represented here. There's also a terrific collection of affordable photography books (including Pailet's own volume of images taken during and after Katrina). Ask for them to open the cabinets, where more art is cleverly hung inside. 241 Chartres St. ☎ **504/568-1313.** www.agallery.com. Tues noon–5pm; Thurs–Mon 10:30am–5:30pm; Wed by appointment.

Great Artists' Collective ★★ More than 40 local artists take turns manning this shop, which stocks their work. Filling half a Creole cottage is a colorful hodgepodge of paints, prints, ceramics, glasswork, earrings by "the Earring Lady," photos, hand-tinted clothing, and more. By going, you support local artists, the local economy, and the collective spirit! 815 Royal St. ☎ **504/525-8190.** www.great artistscollective.com. Mon–Tues 11am–7pm; Wed–Sun 11:30am–8pm.

Hemmerling Gallery ★★ Bill Hemmerling's paintings of spirituals, jazz musicians, and his muse, "Sweet Olive," have charmed collectors and curators alike with their dignified naiveté. His second career as a painter spanned just about 7 years, following his retirement from Sears and until his death in 2009. The gallery features giclees and a few rare originals, and works by several of his protégés. 733 Royal St. ☎ **504/524-0909.** Mon–Sat 11am–8pm; Sun noon–5pm.

Jonathan Ferrara Gallery ★★ Since 1998, Ferrara has been showing emerging cross-media artists. Exhibitions are typically accessible yet thought-provoking, with an eye toward playfulness and irony. We love Krista Jurisich's photographic collage quilts affixed with found items, and Brian Cunningham's large-scale reclaimed metal works. 409 Julia St. ✆ **504/522-5471.** www.jonathanferraragallery.com. Mon–Sat 11am–5pm.

Kurt E. Schon, Ltd. ★★ Here you'll find the country's largest inventory of 19th-century European paintings. Works include French and British Impressionist and post-Impressionist paintings as well as art from the Royal Academy and the French Salon. 510 St. Louis St. ✆ **504/524-5462.** www.kurteschonltd.com. Mon–Fri 10am–5pm; Sat 10am–3pm.

LeMieux Galleries ★ LeMieux represents contemporary artists and fine craftspeople from Louisiana and the Gulf Coast. They include works focusing on iconic local musicians, by Jon Langford and Leslie Staub; as well as Brice Bischoff's haunting black-and-white photography; Charles Barbier's dreamscapes; New Orleans's urban scenes by photorealist Shirley Rabe Masinter; Kate Samworth's luminous nature fantasies; and Paul Ninas's stunning cubist works on paper. 332 Julia St. ✆ **504/522-5988.** www.lemieuxgalleries.com. Mon–Sat 10am–6pm.

Martine Chaisson Gallery ★ Based on recent shows at Martine's newish gallery, we can't wait to see where she flings us next. Her stark space and gleaming floors scream for high-impact, highly saturated imagery, and so far she's delivered, particularly with photographic works by Aaron Ruell and Herman Mhire. 332 Julia St. ✆ **504/522-5988.** www.martinechaissongallery.com. Mon–Sat 10am–6pm.

New Orleans School of GlassWorks and Printmaking Studio ★★★ This institution, with 25,000 square feet of studio space, houses a 550-pound tank of hot molten glass and a pre–Civil War press. At this sister school to the Louvre Museum of Decorative Arts, established glasswork artists, bookbinders, and master printmakers display their work in the on-site gallery, demonstrate glass-blowing, and teach classes in their many crafts. Beginning in October, visitors may design their holiday ornaments. 727 Magazine St. ✆ **504/529-7277.** www.neworleans glassworks.com. Mon–Sat 10am–5pm.

Photo Works ★★ Photographer Louis Sahuc's family has been in New Orleans "since day one," so it's no wonder his life's work has been documenting his city. This gallery is devoted to his photos of iconic images (such as Jackson Square swathed in fog, or fragments of the ironwork and other architecture that give New Orleans its distinct look), in black-and-white and color. 521 St. Ann St. ✆ **504/593-9090.** www.photoworksneworleans.com. Thurs–Tues 10am–5:30pm, and by appointment.

Rodrigue Studio New Orleans Blue Dog is the Freddie Krueger of New Orleans; once you've seen Cajun artist George Rodrigue's creation, it invades your consciousness and torments your life. Available in every imaginable pose or setting, the ubiquitous, glaring, bordering-on-kitsch canine has its fans, but it creeps us out. This gallery is the source for all your Blue Dog needs. 730 Royal St. ✆ **504/581-4244.** www.georgerodrigue.com. Daily 10am–6pm.

Shadyside Pottery ★ Master potter Charlie Bohn, who apprenticed in Japan, can be seen at his wheel pretty much all the time (but do call to confirm if it's important that you see him). He specializes in the Japanese tradition of raku, a type of pottery with a "cracked" look. 3823 Magazine St. ✆ **504/897-1710.** www.shady-sidepottery.com. Mon–Sat 10am–5pm.

Studio Inferno ★★ A longtime seller at Jazz Fest, Studio Inferno is known for its clever, NOLA-related cast- and blown-glass designs, such as reproductions of the stylish local water meters; chili pepper necklaces; flaming hearts, torsos, and other "miraculous" *milagro* shapes. These, their stemware, and paperweights make excellent, unique, and affordable gifts. 3000 Royal St. in the Bywater area. ☎ **504/945-1878.** Mon-Sat 10am-4pm.

Taylor Bercier ★ This newish French Quarter space primarily features local and national painters, whose works are often as disturbing as they are profoundly beautiful. 233 Chartres St. ☎ **504/527-0072.** www.taylorbercier.com. Wed-Sat 11am-5pm; Sun 11am-4:30pm.

Bath & Beauty Products & Day Spas

Old-fashioned gentlemen should consider the barbershop at the Hotel Monteleone, where one can receive a proper hot towel, straight-razor shave. Call for an appointment at ☎ **504/523-6700.**

Aidan Gill for Men ★★ To be a sharp-dressed man, start here. This is old-fashioned men's grooming, from the days when a guy could be a dandy with no fear, and the barbershop was your local hangout. Look for old-fashioned shave brushes, hand-held razors, hot towels, and cigar smoke—all of it adding up to the blissful experience they call "the Shave at the End of the Galaxy" (no less authority than *Playboy* called it the "best shave in America"). Or, buy yourself or your man some fine accessories or good grooming implements from their fine selection, and for the love of mike, teach him to shave with the grain. 2026 Magazine St. ☎ **504/587-9090.** www.aidangillformen.com. Mon-Fri 10am-6pm; Sat 9am-5pm; Sun noon-6pm. Also at 550 Fulton St. ☎ **504/566-4903.** Mon, Wed and Fri-Sat 10am-6pm; Thurs 10am-7pm; Sun noon-6pm.

Belladonna Day Spa ★ A very nice, oasis-like, Asian/Zen-themed day spa in Uptown, offering a variety of spa services featuring fine natural and organic products. Not Guerlain or the Ritz, but a good bet for a detoxing, revivifying afternoon of relaxation. 2900 Magazine St. ☎ **504/891-4393.** www.belladonnadayspa.com. Mon-Tues and Fri-Sat 9am-6pm; Wed-Thurs 9am-8pm.

Guerlain Spa at the Roosevelt ★★★ There's pampering, and then there's the Guerlain Spa. One of just three hyperluxe Guerlain spas in the U.S., its sophisticated dark wood and white decor sets the hush-hush tone, and every type of body work and service is yours for the asking (and the paying—facials and massages start at $140; a full day of beauty runs more than $900. Still, waxing or a basic cut and style are about market rate). Rationalize the posh by making a day of it, starting in the excellent workout room next door and perhaps finishing with a Ramos Gin Fizz in the Sazerac Bar upstairs. 123 Baronne St. ☎ **504/335-3190.** www.therooseveltneworleans.com/guerlainSpa.php. Mon-Sat 9am-7pm; Sun 10am-6pm, or by appointment.

Hove ★★★ The oldest perfumery in the city, Hove features all-natural scents (except for the synthetic musk), and the selection would almost be overwhelming if strips with options for both men and women weren't laid out to help you. Original creations ("Kiss in the Dark") and Southern smells such as vetiver and tea olive, available in many forms, make lovely presents, even for you. An octogenarian, Hove is not too old to be moving to a new location at 434 Chartres St. soon after press time (we pray its character moves, too). Literature buffs will

...used by the letter from author Tom Robbins, confirming that the shop in ...s *Jitterbug Perfume* was roughly based on Hove. 434 Chartres St. ℂ **504/525-7827.** www.hoveparfumeur.com. Mon–Sat 10am–5pm.

Ritz-Carlton Spa ★★★ The Ritz spa is tranquil, majestic, classy, lush—and costly. But who cares? With this kind of atmosphere it's all about the pampering. After all, you stayed up late and danced hard last night. You earned this! In addition to a wide range of exotic scrubs, rubs, wraps, water treatments, and more, they have sauna and relaxation areas, a full-service beauty salon, and an apothecary bar where a specialist will help you blend your own proprietary scent. 921 Canal St. ℂ **504/524-1331.** www.ritzcarlton.com. Mon–Wed 9am–7pm; Thurs–Sun 8am–8pm.

Books

Acadian Books ★★ Bibliophiles will bask in these wondrous, dusty stacks, especially lovers of the classics (in English and Latin); the history (local and far beyond) inquisitive; and seekers of literature in French, German, or Russian. Proprietor Russell Desmond is ridiculously knowledgeable, nearly as personable, and knows every item in this gloriously decrepit grotto. 714 Orleans Ave. ℂ **504/523-4138.** www.crescentcitybooks.com. Mon–Sat 10am–7pm; Sun 10am–5pm.

Beckham's Bookshop ★ Beckham's has two entire floors of old editions, rare secondhand books, and thousands of classical LPs that will tie up your whole afternoon or morning if you don't tear yourself away. The owners also operate **Librairie Bookshop,** 823 Chartres St. (ℂ **504/525-4837**), which has a sizable collection of secondhand books. 228 Decatur St. ℂ **504/522-9875.** Daily 10am–5pm.

Crescent City Books ★ Explore two floors of dusty treasures (the emphasis is on history, local interest, literary criticism, philosophy, and art) and encounter a staff that ranges from nonchalant to quite sweet and helpful. 230 Chartres St. ℂ **800/546-4013** or 504/524-4997. www.crescentcitybooks.com. Mon–Sat 10am–7pm; Sun 10am–5pm.

FAB, Faubourg Marigny Art & Books ★ This well-stocked locally themed store also carries many LGBT titles. It has a used section, CDs, posters, cards, and gifts, all with a more-or-less gay or lesbian slant, and holds regular readings and signings. The staff actually makes this a fine resource center for local gay, lesbian, and neighborhood info. They're open quite late, and their Frenchmen Street locale provides an incongruous contrast to the surrounding club hopping. 600 Frenchmen St. ℂ **504/947-3700.** www.fabonfrenchmen.com. Daily 1pm–11pm.

Faulkner House Books ★★★ This shop is on a lot of walking tours of the French Quarter because it's where Nobel prize–winner William Faulkner lived while he was writing his early works *Mosquitoes* and *Soldiers' Pay*. Those who step inside instead of just snapping a photo will find a remarkable selection, with shelf after high shelf occupied by a book that's highly collectible and/or of literary value. The shop holds a large collection of Faulkner first editions and rare and first-edition classics by many other authors. It also has a particularly comprehensive collection of New Orleans–related work and a sampling of current bestsellers. Just one room and a hallway, Faulkner House feels like a portion of somebody's private home—which it is—but the gracious advice and selection here shows the art that is in bookselling. 624 Pirates Alley. ℂ **504/524-2940.** www.faulknerhouse.net. Mar–Oct daily 10am–6pm; Nov–Feb daily 10am–5pm.

Garden District Book Shop ★★★ Owner Britton Trice has stocked his medium-size shop with just about every New Orleans– or Louisiana-specific book you can think of, no matter what the exact focus (interiors, exteriors, food, Creoles, you name it). This is also where former neighbor Anne Rice did many a reading and signing, and other authors still do. They usually have a selection of autographed books by Rice, Tom Piazza, and other local authors and nonlocal authors (from Clive Barker to James Lee Burke). 2727 Prytania St. (in the Rink). ✆ **504/895-2266.** www.gardendistrictbookshop.com. Mon–Sat 10am–6pm; Sun 10am–4pm.

Kitchen Witch ★ In a town of foodies, chefs, cooks, and eaters of all interests and proficiency, this quirky used cookbook store is the rainbow's end. It stocks nearly 10,000 volumes, from the ultrarare to the just-released—and if they don't have it, they'll find it. Set the egg timer or you could spend way too much time browsing and chatting here. 631 Toulouse St. ✆ **504/528-8382.** www.kwcookbooks.com. Thurs–Mon 10am–6pm; Wed 10am–2pm. Closed Tues.

Maple Street Book Shop ★★ This is an unmissable uptown destination for bookworms seeking new, used, or children's books. 7523 and 7529 Maple St. ✆ **504/866-4916.** www.maplestreetbookshop.com. Mon–Sat 9am–7pm; Sun 11am–5pm.

Octavia Books ★ We do love our independent bookstores, and although this may be a bit far uptown, a sweet, tiny patio, complete with waterfall, is the customer's reward—what better way to linger over a purchase from stock that is chosen with obvious literary care? Book signings and other literary events are common. 513 Octavia St. (at Laurel St.). ✆ **504/899-7323.** www.octaviabooks.com. Mon–Sat 10am–6pm; Sun noon–5pm.

Candies, Pralines & Pastries

Aunt Sally's Praline Shop ★ At Aunt Sally's you can watch skilled workers perform the 150-year-old process of cooking the original Creole pecan pralines right before your eyes, so you'll know they're fresh. The large store also has a broad selection of regional cookbooks, Creole and Cajun foods, and local CDs and memorabilia. They'll ship any purchase. In the French Market, 810 Decatur St. ✆ **800/642-7257** or 504/944-6090. www.auntsallys.com. Sun–Mon 9am–7pm; Tues–Thurs 9am–6pm; Fri–Sat 8am–9pm.

Pralines make great gifts.

Blue Frog Chocolates ★★ If you've noticed our chocolate bias, you know how happy we are at this store, which has the finest chocolate and candy collection in the city. Just for starters, they carry Nancy's truffles, Norman Love chocolates, Michel Cluizel fresh butter creams (from France), Jordan almonds (good ones are difficult to find), *dulce de leche* (from Argentina) to serve over ice cream—or as Ann Streiffer, owner with husband Rick, suggested, "Eat it with a spoon from the jar." 5707 Magazine St. ✆ **504/269-5707.** www.bluefrogchocolates.com. Sept–June Mon–Fri 10am–6pm, Sat 10am–5pm, Sun noon–5pm; July–Aug Tues–Fri 11am–5:30pm, Sat 11am–4pm.

Laura's Candies ★ Laura's is said to be the city's oldest candy store, established in 1913. It has fabulous pralines, but it also has rich, delectable golf ball–size truffles—our personal favorite indulgence, although they've gotten a bit pricey as of late. 331 Chartres St. ✆ **504/525-3880.** www.laurascandies.com. Daily 10am–6pm.

Leah's Candy Kitchen ★★ If you've tried all of the city's Creole candies, you might conclude that Leah's tops the list. Everything here, from the candy fillings to the chocolate-covered pecan brittle, is made from scratch by second- and third-generation members of Leah Johnson's praline-cookin' family, who have been confecting confections since 1944. 714 St. Louis St. ✆ **888/523-5324** or 504/523-5662. www.leahspralines.com. Mon–Sat 10am–6pm.

Southern Candymakers ★★ Here is yet another place to taste-test pralines. Our group of experts found these a bit nontraditional (the usual suspects, plus coconut and sweet potato, among others!) but creamylicious. They're made daily, right in front of you: If the display doesn't reel you in, the aroma might. Their confections—like the pecan-laden *tortues*—send people into swoons, and the boxed chocolate crawfish and gator pops make fine little gifts. 334 Decatur St. ✆ **800/344-9773** or 504/523-5544. www.southerncandymakers.com. Daily 10am–7pm. Also at 1010 Decatur St. Daily 9am–6pm.

Sucré ★ The emphasis of this charming modern-stylish shop is on high-end confectionery and gorgeous chocolates, ideal for gifts or an afternoon indulgence. They're not overly sweet, so opinions vary from bland to brilliant. The popular sherbet-hued macaroons are undoubtedly pretty and the "Big Kid Shakes" (read: boozy) are great fun, but we think chef Tariq Hanna (winner of TLC's *Ultimate Cake Off*) shines brightest in his airy gelatos and minicakes, like the dark chocolate mousse and luscious "Tiffany." 3025 Magazine St. ✆ **504/520-8311.** www.shop sucre.com. Sun–Thurs 7am–10pm; Fri–Sat 7am–midnight.

Costumes & Masks

Costumery is big business in New Orleans, and not just in the days before Lent. In this city you never know *when* you're going to want or need a costume. A number of shops in New Orleans specialize in props for Mardi Gras, Halloween, and other occasions. *Tip:* New Orleanians often sell their costumes back to the shops after Ash Wednesday, and you can sometimes pick up an outfit that's only been worn once at a small fraction of its original cost.

Uptown Costume & Dance Company ★ The walls of this small store are covered with spooky monster masks, goofy arrow-through-the-head-type tricks, hats, wigs, makeup, and similar sorts of playfulness. It draws a steady, yearlong stream of loyal customers, but needless to say things really get cooking at Mardi Gras. 4326 Magazine St. ✆ **504/895-7969.** Tues–Wed 11am–6pm; Thurs–Fri 11am–7pm; Sat 10am–5pm. Extended hours during Halloween and Carnival season; closed Mardi Gras day.

Locals and visitors frequent Uptown Costume & Dance Company, where fun masks, wigs, and other accouterments can be picked up year-round, not just during Mardi Gras.

Fashion & Vintage Clothing

Fleur de Paris ★★★ Remember when a woman was simply not dressed unless she wore a hat? Help bring back those times by patronizing this shop, which makes hand-blocked, stylishly trimmed hats. Think you aren't a hat person? The experts here can take one look at any head and face and find the right style to fit it. Expensive, but works of art often are. They will also stay open late and even bring in champagne for special parties! Additionally, they have luscious stockings and an ever-changing collection of vintage gowns. The 1920s and 1930s elegance on display constantly brings us to our knees with covetousness. 523 Royal St. ℃ **504/525-1899.** Daily 10am–6pm.

Green Serene ★ The simple, stylish lines and soft touch of the clothes belie the fact that they're all eco-friendly—in fabric and fabrication. Who knew that a soybean could feel like cashmere? We love the tailored Deux FM dresses and Lara Miller bamboo/cotton blends, and Synergy Organics' appliquéd skirts. 2041 Magazine St. ℃ **504/252-9861.** www.greenserene.biz. Daily 11am–6pm.

House of Lounge ★★ If you want to be a couch potato, you might as well be a well-dressed one. Or do you want to treat your humble bedroom more like a boudoir? House of Lounge offers all sorts of silky robes and glamorous "hostess gowns," plus sexy lingerie (and admittedly, there isn't much difference between the categories). 2044 Magazine St. ℃ **504/671-8300.** www.houseoflounge.com. Mon–Sat 11am–6pm.

Muse ★★ Gentlemen, should the city and the spirit move you to finding you need an emergency infusion of a seersucker sport jacket, Muse will fix you right up in your choice of colorful stripes (seasonally, and for about $150). Cute, flirty party frocks for ladies range from about $85 to $175. A small but well-chosen selection of accessories includes the ultracool religious iconography of Virgin Saints and Angels jewelry. 532 St. Peter St. (on Jackson Sq.). ℃ **504/552-8738.** www.museinspiredfashion.com. Daily 10am–6pm.

Oh! ★★ 🎁 If you need a cocktail dress or ball gown, Sandy Thigpen is the guy with the eye. And if not, checking out his collection of vintage new and gently used finery is nonetheless an utter scream. From Halston disco pants to a Cher-esque Bob Mackie bling fest to last year's perfect Chanel suit to an authentic fringed flapper get-up to, well, you get the idea, and we haven't even started on the hats and lingerie yet. Buy now and figure out the occasion later. 330 Chartres St. and 829 Royal St. ℃ **504/525-8880.** Mon and Thurs–Sat 11am–6pm; Sun 11pm–6pm. Closed Tues–Wed.

Sessi ★ This small shop just off Jackson Square, plus an additional location in the Riverwalk Mall (1 Poydras St.; ℃ **504/525-1999**) enables power-shoppers to pick up a reasonably priced, perfectly cute dress or top in about 15 minutes—in spite of the indifferent sales help. You'll need to go elsewhere for accessories, though. 623 St. Peter St. ℃ **504/592-0070.** Mon–Sat 10am–7pm; Sun noon–6pm.

Tomato ★ Here's a kicky-cute women's store geared toward seasonal clothing fresh for the picking. Prices can be high, but there is a better-priced sales rack in the back. 3318 Magazine St. ℃ **504/895-0444.** Mon–Fri 11am–6pm; Sun noon–4pm.

Trashy Diva ★★ There is actually nothing trashy about the vintage-inspired clothes here. They are floaty, flirty, curve-flattering numbers in silks and velvets that will please everyone from the hat-and-gloves-wearing crowds to the inner flappers to the Goth teens. Check the sales rack in the back for good bargains. They also have vintage-inspired shoes, and va-voom corset and lingerie shops next door to the French Quarter location. 829 Chartres St. and 2048 Magazine St. ✆ **888/818-DIVA** (818-3482) or 504/299-8777. www.trashydiva.com. Mon–Fri noon–6pm; Sat 11am–6pm; Sun 1–6pm (Chartres) or 1–5pm (Magazine St.)

UAL ★★★ Destination One for local and visiting fashionistas, UAL offers incredible deals on discontinued and leftover goods from designers of all levels (Michael Kors, Marc Jacobs, Balenciaga handbags). The ridiculous markdowns and hourly sales can lead to a fiercely competitive but utterly satisfying shopping experience. Average sizes go fast, stock varies weekly, and there's often just one of anything: It's hit-or-miss, guerilla shopping. But when you do hit, you'll be the envy of bargain lovers everywhere. 518 Chartres St. ✆ **504/301-4437.** Mon–Wed 10am–6pm; Thurs–Sat 11am–8pm; Sun 11am–6pm.

Violet's ★★ This might be our greatest temptation among French Quarter shops, given how we feel about romantic, Edwardian, and '20s-inspired clothes in lush velvets and satins. There are some dazzling creations here with appropriate accessories (jewelry, hats, scarves), and contemporary wear as well, with the emphasis on bling. 808 Chartres St. ✆ **504/569-0088.** Sun–Thurs 11am–7pm; Fri–Sat 10am–9pm.

Voluptuous Vixens ★ Catering to "real-size women"—that would be figures from size 12 to size 24—this shop covers everything from dresses and pants to fancy T-shirts and intimate apparel. All of it is cute and/or elegant. 818 Chartres St. ✆ **504/529-3588.** Hours vary seasonally but hover around daily 11am–6pm. We recommend calling ahead.

Yvonne LaFleur—New Orleans ★ Yvonne LaFleur, a confessed incurable romantic, is the creator of beautifully feminine original designs. Her custom millinery, silk dresses, evening gowns, lingerie, and sportswear are surprisingly affordable, and all are enhanced by her signature perfume. Her store is in the Riverbend district. 8131 Hampson St. ✆ **504/866-9666.** www.yvonnelafleur.com. Mon–Wed and Fri–Sat 10am–6pm; Thurs 10am–8pm.

Food & Drink

Martin Wine Cellar If you're a wine lover or connoisseur—or if you want to become one—Martin Wine Cellar may be your most significant find in New Orleans. It carries an eye-popping selection of wines, beers, spirits, and champagnes at surprisingly reasonable prices. It's not rare to find a $10 wine recommended and described in baffling detail. The store has an extensive selection of imported, hard-to-find preserves, coffees, teas, crackers, biscotti, cookies, cheeses, and even cigars that are a perfect accompaniment to drinks. A bigger location is in the 1200 block of Veterans Memorial Boulevard in Metairie (✆ **888/407-7496** or 504/896-7300). 3500 Magazine St. ✆ **504/899-7411.** www.martinwine.com. Tues–Sat 10am–7pm.

Vieux Carré Wine and Spirits If you're looking for Herbsaint, absinthe, or Sazerac rye, are a serious wine buyer, or just want a bottle for your hotel room, this densely packed French Quarter shop should fit the bill. 422 Chartres St. ✆ **504/568-9463.** Mon–Sat 9am–9pm.

W.I.NO. ★ For those who believe in try before you buy (and who wouldn't when it comes to wine?), the Wine Institute of New Orleans's Enomatic system is your new best friend. Top up a debit card (do this first, it's easy to run up a jolt of a tab), order a charcuterie plate, and set to dispensing 1-, 2-, or 3-ounce pours of some 120 wines, covering many regions and varietals. See if you don't end up with a case or two in your hotel room. 610 Tchopitoulas St. ✆ **504/324-8000.** www.winoschool.com. Mon–Thurs 11am–10pm; Fri–Sat 11am–midnight; Sun 2–10pm.

Gifts & Home Decor

If you're in town on the third Saturday of any month, consider a trip to the **Bywater Art Market** (Royal St. at Piety; ✆ **504/944-7900;** www.art-restoration.com/bam; 10am–4pm). Similarly the fourth Saturday finds the **Palmer Park Arts Market** (S. Carrollton and S. Claiborne aves.; ✆ **504/523-1465;** www.artscouncilofneworleans.org; 10am–4pm). Paintings, pottery, glass mosaic, jewelry, handmade frames from old wood, and more, with the quality assured, as only juried artists are permitted to participate. It's free, all original, all local and regional, and much of it is surprisingly affordable.

The Artists' Market ★★ This collective is overseen by four local artists who display their own work alongside that of up to 65 others working on consignment. Local themes are reflected in the pottery, plates, paintings, photos, ironwork, and more. There are also glassworks and custom beads. The shop extends all the way through the block to the French Market behind, which makes for easy souvenir shopping. 1228 Decatur St. ✆ **504/561-0046.** Mon–Fri 10am–5pm; Sat–Sun 10am–6pm.

Aux Belles Choses ★★ This shop feels as though it could be located at a lonely crossroads in rural France. Maybe it's all the pretty dried plants and flowers. If you like creamy French soaps, especially with exotic scents, you'll probably leave with a handful—this place has many that are hard to find on this side of the Atlantic. The shop has everything from beautiful linens to old English pudding pots—terrific wedding and other special-occasion gifts. 3912 Magazine St. ✆ **504/891-1009.** www.abcneworleans.com. Wed–Sat 10am–5pm.

Belladonna Retail Therapy ★★ If you've booked a treatment at the day spa, be sure to allow extra time for browsing through the shop—you are going to need it. Between the jewelry lines, including those whose simple silver work is etched with wee inscriptions of quotes from Shakespeare and others, the selection of gorgeous homewares, sultry bed linens (including the Bella Notte washable embroidered satin line), the cute clothes, and the clever gift items, there is a lot to coo over. 2900 Magazine St. ✆ **504/891-4393.** www.belladonnadayspa.com. Mon–Tues and Fri–Sat 9am–6pm; Wed–Thurs 9am–8pm.

The Black Butterfly ★★ The Black Butterfly is a place for any collector or admirer of miniatures. This fourth-generation shop (in business since 1894) is filled with porcelain, brass, wood, and pewter figures as well as dollhouse furniture and accessories. 727 Royal St. ✆ **504/524-6464.** www.blackbutterfly.com. Mon–Fri 11am–5pm; Sat 11am–4pm.

Hazelnut ★ With one notable exception, most of the housewares and gifts here are cute but unremarkable. The exception is the line of toile items: Look closely and you'll notice the customized pattern of iconic New Orleans scenes—the St. Charles streetcar, a live oak tree, St. Louis Cathedral, and such. It's desperately darling and we want it all—the bedding, tote bag, and picture frame. Sigh. Fun fact: *Mad Men*'s Bryan Batt is part owner. 5515 Magazine St. ✆ **504/891-2424.** www.hazelnutneworleans.com. Mon–Sat 10am–6pm.

Hoi Polloi Boutique ★★ Feeling a little underdressed compared to those well-put-together Southern ladies? Forgot to pack that little extra something needed to pull your outfit together? Here's your solution. A feminine boutique with stylish quality hats, scarves, purses, jewelry, and more. It's fun to poke around in, because the products are all interesting and playful. 434 Chartres St. ✆ **504/561-7585.** www.hoipolloiboutique.com. Daily 10am–6pm.

perch ★★ Would owner Caroline Roberts please come make over my living room? Okay, just one corner of it . . . please? We love her clever eye. Although she offers complete interior design services, you can also pick up some modest contemporary or vintage home decor pieces here that will have you batting your eyes in the mirror as you flatter yourself for being so effortlessly eclectic and refined. Yeah, it's like that, all over the shop. 2844 Magazine St. (C) **504/899-2122.** www. perch-home.com. Mon–Sat 10am–6pm.

Scriptura ★★ This store has everything related to the elegant art of scribbling. You can get designer stationery, glass fountain pens, sealing wax, and all types of generic or specific (travel, cigar, wine, restaurant) journals. This is the kind of place where you can find a gift for that impossible-to-shop-for person in your life. They have a second location at 3301 Veterans Blvd., Ste. 137. 5423 Magazine St. (C) **504/897-1555.** www.scriptura.com. Mon–Sat 10am–5pm.

Simon of New Orleans/Antiques on Jackson ★★ Folk artist Simon, whose brightly painted signs are seen throughout New Orleans in homes and businesses, will paint-to-order your own personal sign and ship it to you. This gallery and shop is shared by Simon and his wife, Maria, who has particularly good taste in primitive furniture, antiques, and hodgepodgery. Visit them at this relatively new location in a larger space that shows off the eclectic collections. 1028 Jackson Ave. (C) **504/524-8201.** Mon by appointment; Tues–Sat 10am–5pm; Sun 11am–4pm.

Vintage 329 ★ The new location for this autograph hound's heaven is double the size, and it's packed with memorabilia signed by all manner of film, rock, and sports stars. There's also antique weaponry and shipwreck recoveries. It makes for fun browsing, though it may be a little pricey for impulse buys. 329 Royal St. (C) **866/846-8429** or 504/529-2288. www.vintage329.com. Daily 10am–5:30pm, or by appointment.

Hats

See also the superb Fleur de Paris millinery, p. 259.

Meyer the Hatter ★★★ Meyer's opened more than 100 years ago and has been in the same family ever since. Today the haberdashery has one of the largest selections of fine hats and caps in the South. Men will find distinguished international labels such as Stetson, Kangol, Akubra, Dobbs, and Borsalino (and there are some hats for women as well). Half the fun is having the owner and his son fuss over you—let them pick out the proper feather to go in your new chapeau! Go outfit yourself like a proper gentleman caller. 120 St. Charles Ave. (C) **800/882-4287** or 504/525-1048. www.meyerthehatter.com. Mon–Sat 10am–5:45pm.

Jewelry

Marion Cage ★★★ 🎁 Cage's ultrafine, exquisitely wrought work is known to collectors far and wide, but after living in Paris and New York, she opened her namesake shop in her native New Orleans. Clean lines of matte rose and yellow gold, rhodium, and hardwoods average $200 to $500 (and go up), making the teeny, perfectly detailed Chinese zodiac charms a tasty deal at $50. 3719 Magazine St. (C) **504/891-8848.** www.marioncage.com. Tues–Sat 10am–5pm.

Mignon Faget, Ltd. ★★ Mignon Faget is one of the biggest personalities in New Orleans's jewelry universe. The designer is a New Orleans native; her signature style is evident in gold, silver, and bronze d'oré fashioned into pendants, bracelets, rings, earrings, and cuff links. Their New Orleans–specific pieces make superb presents for anyone, including you, and sales of the silver redfish and pelican pins, set on black mourning ribbons, help support the Coalition to Restore Coastal Louisiana. There's an uptown location at 3801 Magazine St. (✆ **504/891-2005**). Canal Place, Level 1. ✆ **800/375-7557** or 504/524-2973. www.mignonfaget.com. Mon–Sat 10am–7pm; Sun noon–6pm.

Sabai Jewelry Gallery ★ This store offers a unique array of Asian and hand-crafted jewelry. The stones and settings are displayed on antique wooden block prints (some on flat stones embedded in rice). But the best part is when one discovers the lack of designer prices that usually tag along with incredible designs. 3115 Magazine St. ✆ **504/899-9555.** Mon–Sat 10:30am–6pm; Sun 11am–5pm. Also at 924 Royal St. ✆ **504/525-6211.** Daily 10:30am–6pm.

Thomas Mann Designs/Gallery I/O ★★ Local jewelry designer Thomas Mann is known for his "techno-romantic" work with metal and found objects, creating curious pieces of highly original jewelry and homewares that straddle a line between classic and contemporary. 1812 Magazine St. ✆ **504/581-2111.** Mon–Sat 11am–5pm.

Music

Beckham's Bookshop ★ It's better known for its fine collection of used books (see "Books," earlier in this chapter), but Beckham's also has a large selection of secondhand classical LPs. 228 Decatur St. ✆ **504/522-9875.** Daily 10am–5pm.

Euclid Records ★ If you love the smell of vinyl in the morning, or any time, Euclid will fire your pheromones. This younger-than-it-feels Bywater record store (little sistah of the iconic St. Louis shop) stocks vintage platters from every era, including gobs of locals. There are nominal CDs and occasional in-store performances, too. Look for the Pepto pink building, and let the bin diving begin. 3401 Chartres St. ✆ **504/947-4348.** www.jimrussellrecords.com. Mon–Sat 11am–7pm; Sun noon–6pm.

Jim Russell Records ★★ We can't imagine that this classic, family-owned, packed-to-the-rafters shop, well-known to collectors and DJs, won't have what you're looking for. 1837 Magazine St. ✆ **504/522-2602.** www.jimrussellrecords.com. Mon–Sat 10am–5pm.

Louisiana Music Factory ★★★ This popular and terrific store carries a large selection of regional music—including Cajun, zydeco, R&B, jazz, blues, and gospel—plus books, posters, and T-shirts. Vinyl miners, your quarry is upstairs. It also has frequent live music, and beer coupons for the bar across the street—shop while you bop! It's the place to get yourself informed about and stocked with New Orleans music. 210 Decatur St. ✆ **504/586-1094.** www.louisianamusicfactory.com. Mon–Sat 10am–7pm; Sun noon–6pm.

Peaches Records This family-owned indie shop moved boldly into the French Quarter space vacated by Tower Records and stocked the place with a broad swath of locally focused CDs, vinyl, books, DVDs, T-shirts, and art. Peaches' New Orleans roots go back to 1975 when their first store opened and became a stop-off for R&B royalty like Stevie Wonder; later they supported local hip-hop artists like Juvenile and Lil Wayne. The selection spans all genres including New Orleans tuneage. 408 N. Peters St. ✆ **504/282-3322.** www.peachesrecordsneworleans.com. Mon–Thurs 8am–9pm; Fri–Sat 8am–10pm; Sun 10am–9pm.

The Occult

Bottom of the Cup Tearoom ★ This place has been open since 1929 and bills itself as the "oldest tearoom in the United States." You can have a psychic consultation, and also purchase teas, books, jewelry, crystal balls, tarot cards, crystals, and healing wands. 327 Chartres. ✆ **504/524-1997.** www.bottomofthecup.com. Daily 10am–6pm.

Boutique du Vampyre Twihards and *True Blood* fans may go batty for the rings with hidden compartments (for poison, ostensibly), capes, and all manner of bloody goods here. Some of it's pretty cheesy, but they're a good source of info about vampire-related events, and they have the hook-up for custom-made fangs. 633 Toulouse St. ✆ **504/561-8267.** www.feelthebite.com. Daily noon–8pm.

Esoterica Occult Goods ★ The hip witch store for all your occult needs. Well, maybe not all, but they cover both pagan witch and voodoo rituals with their potions, herbs, gris-gris bags, and selection of related books plus similar magical and death-oriented jewelry. 541 Dumaine St. ✆ **504/581-7711.** www.onewitch. com. Daily noon–6pm.

Marie Laveau's House of Voodoo This is tourist voodoo, to be sure, but their voodoo dolls and gris-gris bags make great souvenirs for the right friends, and it's a fun store to poke around in. 739 Bourbon St. ✆ **504/581-3751.** Sun–Thurs 10am–11:30pm; Fri–Sat 10am–1:30am (sometimes slightly earlier or later).

Voodoo Authentica ★ This shop specializing in voodoo paraphernalia doesn't feel like someone's dusty shack, but like a real retail establishment. Two big rooms are filled with a range of locally made voodoo dolls, from cheap to costly, and range from an easy souvenir to serious works of art, plus a similar array of potions, spell candles, and daubs. 612 Dumaine St. ✆ **504/522-2111.** www.voodooshop. com. Daily 11am–7pm.

T-Shirts & More

If crass suits your style, by all means buy up the Bourbon Street goods. But if you seek a garment with local flavor that's also clever, and maybe even has a decent design aesthetic, there are a plethora of superior options. Shirts (and hats, hoodies, and so forth) in these shops will probably run $5 to $10 more than your average show-me-your-whatever tops, but they're softer as well as smarter.

Dirty Coast ★★ It's waaay uptown, but their eye-catching and original T-shirt designs (painted in the city) are utterly witty, like the "Crawfish Pi," with the Greek symbol composed of a tasty pile of mudbugs, and "504Ever." 5631 Magazine St. ✆ **504/324-3745.** www.dirtycoast.com. Mon–Sat 11am–6pm; Sun 11am–4pm.

Jeantherapy ★ Besides all manner of trendy denim (J Brand, Current/Elliot, AG, and so on), their small collection of soft cotton tees for men, women, and kids includes the primary color NOLA (à la the classic Indiana *LOVE* design), a "Who Dat" logo designed by Simon (p. 262), and other locally inspired tees. 5505 Magazine St. ✆ **504/897-5535.** www.jeantherapy.com. Mon–Sat 10am–6pm; Sun noon–5pm.

Skip N' Whistle This Oak Street shop's shirts include a double-trumpet *Treme* design, and a vintage Jax Beer logo. 8123 Oak St. ✆ **504/862-5909.** www.skipnwhistle. com. Mon–Sat 11am–7pm; Sun 11am–4pm.

Storyville ★★ You've heard it, now wear it: The "Yeah You Right!" tee is here, as are the ever-popular "Brad Pitt for Mayor" and water meter styles. 3029 Magazine St. ✆ **504/304-6209.** www.wearyourstory.com. Mon–Sat 10am–7pm; Sun noon–7pm.

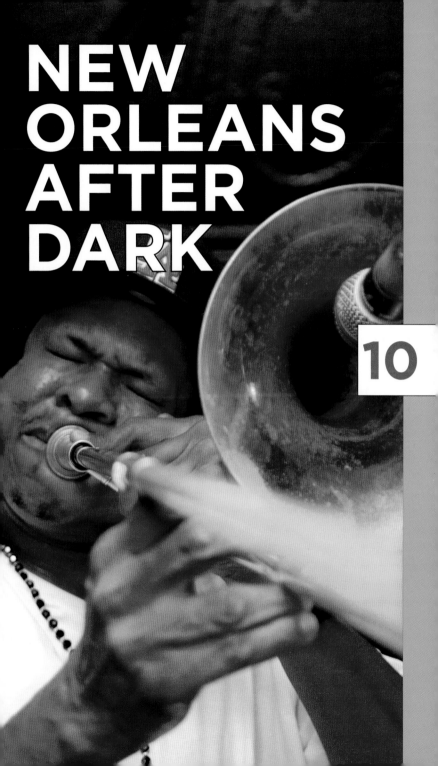

NEW ORLEANS AFTER DARK

10

New Orleans is one of the most beautiful cities in the United States, possibly the world, but we won't mind if you don't spend your days seeing the sights—provided, however, the omission is because you are spending the daylight hours recovering from the equally extraordinary nightlife.

This is a city of music and rhythm. It is impossible to imagine New Orleans without a soundtrack of jazz, brass bands, R&B, and even Cajun, zydeco, and now bounce, the nasty local hip-hop hybrid. Music streams from every doorway, and sometimes it seems people are dancing down the street. Sometimes they really are. (After all, this is the town that sends you to your grave with music and then dances back from the cemetery.) This is also the city of decadence and good times rolling. Not to mention really loose liquor laws and drinks in "go" cups (also known as "cruising crystal," plastic containers you can take with you). And all this increases at night. We aren't just talking about the open-air frat party that is Bourbon Street most evenings. In fact, we prefer not to talk about that at all.

Most important is that virtually every night, dozens of clubs all over town offer music that can range from average to extraordinary but is never less than danceable. In most places, cover prices vary from night to night and performer to performer, but rarely will you have to pay more than $20 (unless it's during Mardi Gras, Jazz Fest, or another big event)—and then only for more high-falutin' places such as the House of Blues.

When the clubs get too full, no matter: The crowd spills into the street, talking, drinking, and still dancing right there on the sidewalk (the music is often plenty audible out there). Sometimes the action outside is even more fun than inside, not to mention less hot and sweaty.

Club hopping is easy, though some of the better choices will require leaving the Quarter by vehicle. Don't worry—most are an easy taxi ride away, and many are within an additional, even easier, walk or cab ride of each other. We encourage you to leave the Quarter at night to visit some of the town's better joints, but it's not, however, required. There are great jazz and brass-band clubs right in the Quarter. And there are more just steps away at the excellent scene in the Frenchmen section of the Faubourg Marigny, where nearly a dozen clubs and bars are going at once within 3 blocks of each other. People wander from one to the other, sometimes never even going inside. If you do your evening right, those calories you consumed all day long will be gone by morning.

Or, yes, you could spend your night running from bar to bar. There is no lack of them. With such great music available, that seems a waste of time, however; if all you wanted to do was drink, you could have done that at home. Still, it is New Orleans, and some of these places are as convivial and atmospheric as you will ever find; ducking into a few isn't a bad idea at all. And, of course, everything only gets livelier and wilder as the evening goes on.

Speaking of which, don't be fooled by the times given in local listings for band performances. If it says 10pm, the band will probably go on, oh, 11pm or

PREVIOUS PAGE: **The Rebirth Brass Band is a crowd favorite.**

midnight, and keep playing until late. Really late. Still, once in a blue moon, an act will go on when billed and finish up rather early, but chances are good that if you come late, you will still catch quite a bit of the act you came to see.

However you decide to do it, don't miss it. New Orleans at night is a completely different animal. Just tell yourself you'll sleep when you get home.

For up-to-date information on what's happening around town, look for current editions of **Gambit, Offbeat,** and **Where Y'at,** all distributed free in many hotels and all record stores or online at www.bestofneworleans.com, www.offbeat.com, and www.whereyat.com. Other sources include the **Times-Picayune**'s daily entertainment calendar and Friday's **Lagniappe** section of the newspaper. Additionally, **WWOZ** (90.7 FM) broadcasts the local music schedule several times throughout the day.

For the nightlife listings in this chapter, see the "New Orleans Nightlife," "French Quarter Nightlife," or "Uptown Nightlife" maps in this chapter or the "Mid-City Attractions & Nightlife" map on p. 179 of chapter 7, "Sights to See & Places to Be."

THE RHYTHMS OF NEW ORLEANS

The late New Orleans R&B legend Ernie K-Doe was once quoted as saying, "I'm not sure, but I think all music came from New Orleans." What might be a more accurate account—and relatively hyperbole-free—is that all music came *to* New Orleans. Any style you can name, from African field hollers to industrial techno-rock, has found its way to the Crescent City, where it's been blended, shaken, and stirred into a new, distinctive, and usually frothy concoction that, it seems, could have come from nowhere else.

"Yeah," you scoff, "but what about classical music?" Well, maybe you've never heard how pianist James Booker, an eye-patched eccentric even by New Orleans standards, could make a Bach chorale strut like a second-line umbrella twirler. Or maybe you're forgetting that Wynton Marsalis has Grammy Awards for both jazz and classical recordings, not to mention a 1997 Pulitzer Prize for his slavery-themed jazz oratorio *Blood on the Fields.*

On the other side of the spectrum, don't forget that Trent Reznor, the man behind the brutal sounds and imagery of the industrial act Nine Inch Nails, chose to live and record in New Orleans (as rocker Lenny Kravitz does now).

Even more unusual are the Loose Marbles, a formerly itinerant group of stellar jazz musicians who've found a

Be sure to join a second line parade, if the opportunity arises during your visit.

home in the Crescent City clubs, where their shape-shifting membership only enhances their seductive, Victrola-meets-tattoo sound.

Or utter originals like singer, multi-instrumentalist, and YouTube sensation Theresa Andersson, whose innovative, self-looping technique creates a virtual live orchestra right in front of your eyes using nothing more than a row of foot pedals and sheer talent.

Of course, what you're most likely to experience is somewhere in the middle, music more truly rooted in the Crescent City—the Storyville jazz descended from Louis Armstrong and Jelly Roll Morton, the bubbly R&B transmitted via Fats Domino and Professor Longhair, the Mardi Gras Indians, and the brass bands of the second lines that recently added exuberant, youthful infusions of funk and hip-hop.

The Jazz Life of New Orleans

Adapted from a piece by George Hocutt
Jazz historian and executive producer of the Grammy Award–winning album *Doc Cheatham & Nicholas Payton*

New Orleans did not invent jazz, but the crescents in the Mississippi River became the crucible in which jazz evolved. The city's French Catholic background has always inspired a more tolerant attitude toward the simple pleasures of the world than did the Puritan fathers from Plymouth Rock. Melodic sounds of all kinds were one of those pleasures.

Music was of great importance to the Louisiana settlers and their Creole offspring, and the city early on had a fascination with marching bands and parades. As early as 1787, Governor Miro entertained a gathering of Indian leaders with a parade. Eventually, bands were required for nearly every occasion—Mardi Gras, dedications, religious holidays, cornerstone laying, weddings, funerals, ad infinitum.

The musicians of early New Orleans were considered tradesmen just like carpenters, shoemakers, and other skilled craftsmen. After an afternoon parade, they might be required to play at the opera and then possibly a late dance. Obviously, these 19th-century instrumentalists were quite accomplished and versatile.

In the early 19th century, slaves were allowed to congregate in the area known as **Congo Square** for dancing to the rhythms of their homelands' drums and other percussive instruments. With the passing of time, many slaves, former slaves, and free men of color became accomplished instrumentalists. There were even Negro marching bands in New Orleans before the Civil War. Some of these musicians, possibly graduates of the Congo Square gatherings, brought to their playing a native rhythm that was likely a primitive syncopation. In an evolutionary way, many of New Orleans's musicians began absorbing this amalgam of European and African influences. Then came the addition of the very personal statements of the blues, work songs, hollers, and spirituals. The music was changing and was taking on a certain American and distinctly New Orleanian aura.

In the 1870s two men were born who were to have a profound effect on the music. **"Papa" Jack Laine** was born in 1873 and **Charles "Buddy" Bolden** in 1878, both in New Orleans.

Bolden, a cornetist who would later be known as the First Man of Jazz, began playing dances and parties around 1895. By 1897 he had put together the

The tombstone of Buddy Bolden.

band that most old-timers remember. They also remember that Bolden's cornet could be heard for miles around. At approximately the same time, Papa Jack, primarily a drummer, formed several groups simultaneously, all called the Reliance Band. They played all over the Gulf Coast and in New Orleans and were extremely popular. Almost all the early white New Orleans jazzmen played in one of Laine's groups.

Concurrent with Bolden and Laine's contributions to the musical life of the city, another event that would affect the spread of jazz everywhere was unfolding. **Storyville,** the only prescribed district for legalized prostitution ever attempted in this country, was operating from 1897 to 1917. Most of the elegant houses had a piano player in the parlor. Among those entertainers were the immortal **Jelly Roll Morton,** the first true jazz composer and, next to Louis Armstrong, the most important figure in early jazz. His compositions were recorded well into the swing era and are still performed today.

There were many nighttime playing opportunities in the bars and clubs that dotted Storyville and the adjacent areas. During the day, the great musicians played in the multitude of brass bands that were always in demand. All the prominent names of early New Orleans jazz served this apprenticeship.

As early as 1916, some New Orleans bands that included many of Papa Jack's children decided to try the musical climate in Chicago. The most successful group was the **Original Dixieland Jazz Band,** led by Nick LaRocca. The ODJB moved on from Chicago to open at Reisenweber's Cafe in New York City in 1917. They were a smash. Everybody loved the new music from New Orleans. They cut the first jazz record ever, coupling "Livery Stable Blues" with "Dixie Jazz Band One Step," released by Victor Records on February 16, 1917, and it was an instant hit. The jazz flood had started.

In October 1917 the houses of Storyville were shut down, and a great many jobs for entertainers and musicians started drying up. The performers headed elsewhere for work: Kid Ory went to California, where he made the first black jazz record; King Oliver travelled to Chicago, California, and back to Chicago. In

Louis Armstrong.

Irvin Mayfield.

1922 he sent for **Louis Armstrong** to come up and join King Oliver's Creole Jazz Band—arguably the greatest collection of jazz musicians ever assembled (and all but one were natives of New Orleans). After leaving Oliver, Louis Armstrong, already the greatest soloist in jazz, went on to become one of the greatest, most identifiable entertainers we have ever known. He transcended New Orleans and became a national treasure.

Sidney Bechet settled in France after World War II and became a huge star performer and prolific composer. On his wedding day, a total holiday was declared in Antibes, and the entire city participated in a massive wedding party, dancing to music he had written.

New Orleans is still producing jazz greats. There is **Harry Connick, Jr.,** and **Ellis Marsalis,** father to a group of jazz-playing sons, including trumpeter Wynton, who won a 1997 Pulitzer Prize for his composition *Blood on the Fields,* the first such award for a jazz composer. **Nicholas Payton, Irvin Mayfield,** and **Terence Blanchard** (among many others) are pushing their horns to ever-adventurous distances—and we haven't even mentioned pianists, drummers, and so on. Obviously, the city still abounds with creativity.

Much remains in New Orleans for the adventurous jazz fan and explorer, from birthplaces to resting places, to former clubs and recording studios. They are well described in a series of free pamphlets detailing different jazz-history walking tours sponsored by the New Orleans Jazz Commission. They're available at the **New Orleans Jazz National Historical Park,** 916 N. Peters St. (© **504/589-4841;** www.nps.gov/jazz), or **Louisiana Music Factory** (p. 263). Alternatively, look at some of the books about music we've recommended on p. 25.

Music still resounds around the town, in the clubs listed in this chapter and beyond. So certainly there is life in the old gal yet. Whether it's in the water, the air, or that good Creole cooking, jazz continues to grow in the fertile soil that settles on the banks of the curves of the Mississippi River.

Brass Bands

Today, there's way more to New Orleans brass bands than the post-funeral "second line" parade of "When the Saints Go Marching In." In recent years, young African-American kids have picked up the tradition and given it new life while also stimulating renewed interest in some of the veteran practitioners. At its roots, it's primal jazz nonpareil, with group improvisations, unexpected turns, and spirit to burn.

The key acts of the current revival were the **Dirty Dozen Brass Band** and **Rebirth Brass Band.** Rebirth, as a gaggle of teens and preteens in the late 1980s and early 1990s, tossed pop-funk tunes like "Grazin' in the Grass" into their mix of New Orleans standards. They even had a local hit with "Do Whatcha Wanna." The group's still going strong, though trumpeter **Kermit Ruffins,** who as a preteen Louis Armstrong look- and sound-alike was the centerpiece, now fronts his own versatile jazz band, the **Barbecue Swingers.** Others in the same vein include **New Birth** and **Olympia,** while such newer arrivals as the **TBC** (To Be Continued), the **Stooges,** the **Soul Rebels** (perhaps the best of the new crop), and **Hot 8** have explored hip-hop, reggae, and funk styles in the brass context, often with terrific results. And brothers **Troy "Trombone Shorty"** and **James "Satchmo of the Ghetto" Andrews** demonstrate their knowledge of and reverence for the past as well as their intent for the future, as they fall between traditional jazz, brass bands (they both have and continue to play with various combos), and new directions with funk and jazz, such as Troy's own **Orleans Avenue.**

At the same time, older ensembles like the **Olympia Brass Band** have gained from the interest, as has **Treme Brass Band,** headed by the venerable and supremely dapper "Uncle" Lionel Batiste and recipient of a new crop of fans thanks to their appearances on the HBO TV show *Treme.* Look for brass bands at various venues around the city. Rebirth still plays every Tuesday night at the Maple Leaf, while the Soul Rebels have a regular Thursday gig at Le Bon Temps Roule and do regular weekend club gigs.

The Rebirth Brass Band can often be found playing at the Maple Leaf Bar.

Cajun & Zydeco

Two of the music styles often associated with New Orleans are technically not from here at all. Both Cajun and zydeco originated in the bayous of southwest Louisiana, a good 3 hours away. And while it's customary for the two to be named in the same breath, they are not the same thing—though they are arguably two sides of the same coin.

The foundations of the two styles lie in the arrival of two different French-speaking peoples in the swamp country: the white Acadians (French migrants who were booted out of Nova Scotia by the English in 1755) and the black Creole people (who were jettisoned by or escaped from the Caribbean slave trade of the same era). Both oppressed groups took to the button accordion, newly introduced from Germany and France, with its folksy, diatonic scale. It added a richness and

It's not uncommon to find street musicians playing all over New Orleans.

power to their fiddle and guitar music. Later, radio influenced the addition of drums, amplifiers, and steel guitars to fill out the sound.

In the post-WWII era, the styles began to separate, with the Cajuns gravitating toward country-and-western swing and Creole musicians being heavily influenced by the urban blues. Such figures as **D. L. Menard** (the Cajun Hank Williams) and **Clifton Chenier** (the King of Zydeco) pioneered exciting new strains in their respective directions. During the great folk-music boom of the early 1960s, such figures as the **Balfa Brothers** and fiddler **Dennis McGee** had the opportunity to perform at folk festivals. A turning point came when a Cajun group received a standing ovation at the 1964 Newport Festival. It was a real boost for the form and for Cajun pride, both of which seemed on the verge of extinction. Such younger musicians as **Marc Savoy,** who had begun producing fine homemade accordions, brought new energy and commitment, and Cajun music gained new life.

This spawned a new generation, proud of their Cajun musical legacy but also fueled by rock 'n' roll. Fiddler **Michael Doucet** and his band **BeauSoleil** lead the way, with **Steve Riley** close behind, both tireless ambassadors for their heritage. And Savoy's family continues his tradition: Son Wilson anchors the critically acclaimed and Grammy-nominated **Pine Leaf Boys,** which, along with young compatriots like **Feaufollet** and the **Lost Bayou Ramblers,** continues to inject raw verve and bring new fans to the genre.

In zydeco, Clifton Chenier led the way from the 1950s on, with a handful of others (the late Boozoo Chavis, John Delafose, Rockin' Sidney) adding their own embellishments. Chenier became internationally famous, even playing the esteemed Montreux Jazz Festival in Switzerland. Zydeco has, arguably, grown stronger than ever, even garnering a new Grammy category added in

2008, with Terrance Simien winning the first award. A new generation, including Chenier's son **C. J.,** Delafose's son **Geno,** various Dopsie kin (Rockin' Dopsie, Jr., and Dwayne Dopsie), and the riotous **Zydepunks** are updating the old traditions, while such senior figures as **Nathan Williams** and the late **Beau Jocque** added their own variations of blues, funk, and hip-hop.

Fats Domino.

Rhythm & Blues

Technically, the blues is not a New Orleans form, belonging more to the rural delta and, in its urban forms, Texas and Chicago. But rhythm and blues, with its gospel and African-Caribbean bloodlines, carries a Crescent City heartbeat. In the 1950s, **Fats Domino,** along with his great producer-collaborator Dave Bartholomew, fused those elements into such seminal songs as "Blueberry Hill" and "Walkin' to New Orleans"—music that still fuels much of the New Orleans R&B sound today. At the same time, such then-unheralded figures as **Professor Longhair** and **"Champion" Jack Dupree** developed earthier variations of the piano-based sound, contrasting mournful woe with party-time spirit.

 USING THE listings

Most clubs in New Orleans feature an eclectic lineup that reflects the town's music scene; the Rebirth Brass Band, for example, attracts as many rock fans as it does brass-band fans. Consequently, these listings' musical genres are somewhat misleading: The bulk of the club scene escapes categorization (and, of course, booking policies are often subject to change)—as many genres cross-pollinate the club scene.

Rock 'n' Bowl is listed under "Zydeco" but pretty much every kind of music gets played there, ditto for d.b.a. If you want a specific sound, you have to look at listings (in *Offbeat* and *Gambit* magazines, for example) night by night. Some places are generally good fun on their own regardless of who is playing; any night at the **Maple Leaf** is going to be a good one, while wandering from spot to spot in the Frenchmen section is a must-do evening. Be sure to check to see who is playing at the Ogden Museum of Southern Art (© **504/539-9600**) on Thursday nights, lest you think all the good music in the city happens only in humid bars. Also, many bars have music so check the bars listed below and chapter 1 as well. Really, in New Orleans, you can't go too wrong going just about anywhere simply to hang out. And in the process, you might get exposed to a new, wonderful genre of music or an incredible band.

The keepers of the flame today are the Neville Brothers, though some would argue the offshoot **Meters** have carried it further. And let's face it, the genre has broadly evolved into funk, jam, and hip-hop scenes (not to mention the only-in–New Orleans "sissy bounce" trend of transgender rappers) that would take chapters more to even adequately introduce. But under the R&B heading, we must include the Soul Queen of New Orleans, **Irma Thomas.** (The Rolling Stones' version of "Time Is on My Side" is note-for-note taken from Irma's!) Though she had only one national hit ("Wish Somebody Would Care"), her feel for a song and her magnanimous spirit still lead devotees to make regular pilgrimages to her performances. Go see her if you have the lucky opportunity.

JAZZ & BLUES CLUBS

This being New Orleans, jazz and blues are everywhere—though not all of it is worth hearing. Not that any of it is bad, per se. It's just that there is world-class stuff out there competing with tourist traps for your ears, so don't just settle for

 A NIGHT ON THE town

If you only have a night or two in New Orleans, you should try your best to hear some incredible live local music. How to choose? Here is a guide to some of the best regular performers doing their best to keep their city's musical traditions alive. Okay, it would take a whole bunch of nights to hear them all, but you can't go wrong with any one—or two, or three—of the following.

Bob French, a drummer and second-generation powerhouse, is the keeper of the flame of traditional New Orleans jazz both on the bandstand and on the air at WWOZ. Neo-traditionalists the Jazz Vipers, Loose Marbles, Cottonmouth Kings, Meschiya Lake and Dem Little Big Horns, and the New Orleans Moonshiners each bring their own flavor along with solid, speakeasy swing chops, while Panorama Jazz Band adds an Eastern European spin with their own flavor. **Hot 8** means nonstop booty shaking from one of the top of the current crop of brass bands. The **Soul Rebels** subtly integrate hip-hop energy into traditional brass band sound, while the **Stooges** guarantee solid jams and fun. **John Boutte** is one of *the* voices of New Orleans these days and a national treasure, now known for "Down in the Treme," the theme song to the HBO series *Treme,* but always

known for his ability to turn a wide range of old and new songs into topical, pointed missives. Boutte's one of the finest singers in the country, and not to be missed. **Rebirth Brass Band**'s Tuesday-night gigs at the Maple Leaf remain must-do marathons, as are Thursdays at Vaughan's, where trumpeter **Kermit Ruffins** holds forth on stage and behind the grill (that's his custom barbecue rig parked outside). Local boy turned national phenom **Troy ("Trombone Shorty") Andrews** brings on the funk constantly but if he's back home in New Orleans, don't miss him. His mentor and older brother **James ("12"),** also a leader on the scene, stays a bit more traditional. Cousin **Glen David Andrews** preaches high-energy funk that has to be seen to be believed. **Miss Sophie Lee** sings speak-easy sweet, while **Sasha Masakowski**'s jazz stylings are the first thing you hear. Seek out the really good stuff and you'll be rewarded. Opening and closing hours of New Orleans's clubs and bars are a bit loose: Bars can stay open constantly; clubs can open randomly; announced shows often (but not always) start later than posted; and some clubs never shut down.

The French Quarter & the Faubourg Marigny

Blue Nile ★ This medium-size venue is two-story—upstairs is generally reserved for smaller shows and DJs; the downstairs has decent sightlines despite some view-obscuring pillars. The mural on the left-hand wall was painted by a local artist on the plywood that covered the windows post-Katrina. Bookings feature a wide variety of locals, reggae, jam bands, plus late-night DJs. 532 Frenchmen St. ✆ **504/948-BLUE** (948-2583). www.bluenilelive.com. Cover varies.

The Famous Door As the oldest music club on Bourbon Street (it opened in 1934), many local jazz, pop, and rock musicians have passed through here. One of them, Harry Connick, Jr., played his first gigs here at the age of 13. The

swoony and feathery. **Tom McDermott** takes audiences on a tour of Caribbean, Southern, and South American piano styles that helped shape the music of Jelly Roll Morton and others. He's always a wonder, in particular in his shows with clarinetist **Evan Christopher. TBC Brass Band** is bringing raw new vigor and another generation into the brass-band fold. (If you can't find them in a club, check the corner of Bourbon and Canal sts.), while the well-established Treme Brass Band gained much deserved, wider recognition from their appearances on HBO's *Treme*. **Big Sam's Funky Nation:** Descended from Buddy Bolden, so he claims, trombonist Sam Williams ain't lying about the "funky" part. Formerly of popular party band Cowboy Mouth, **Paul Sanchez** may be the top singer-songwriter in town. Catch him solo, with his Rolling Road Show, or double-billed with breakout trumpeter **Shamarr Allen** or **Susan Cowsill**—yes, that Cowsill! Susan, now a superb singer-songwriter, covers a lot of ground in her terrific solo shows, especially her "Covered in Vinyl" nights when she and friends re-create entire classic albums by Springsteen, the Rolling Stones, U2, Fleetwood Mac, and others. Sax man **Donald Harrison, Jr.,** mixes his top-flight modern jazz with the spirit of his role as chief of the Congo Nation Mardi Gras Indian tribe, a role he inherited from his father.

Henry Butler is an heir to the piano crown of Professor Longhair (though he's not always in town). Butler can also bring in some modern styles with dazzling keyboard skills, as do **John Cleary** and **Joe Krown** on B3—and if piano royalty like **Dr. John** or **Allen Toussaint** happen to be playing, that's a gimme. **Bonerama** is a brass band, sure, but with funk-rock variations heard on versions of such songs as "Helter Skelter" and "Frankenstein." For deeper funking, catch **Galactic** or **Ivan Neville's Dumpstaphunk,** while any incarnation of superb songwriter **Alex McMurray** (he's in about six bands) is undoubtedly worthwhile. **Irvin Mayfield** has become a central educator and ambassador of a wide range of New Orleans jazz, on top of being a star trumpeter and leader of the superb **New Orleans Jazz Orchestra (NOJO).**

New Orleans Nightlife

Southern Baptist Hospital

BROADMOOR

New Orleans Arena

Union Passenger Terminal (Amtrak)

UPTOWN

Lee Circle

GARDEN DISTRICT

Ferry Service to Algiers Point

Riverfront streetcar route/stops

St. Charles streetcar route/stops

Vieux Carre loop route/stops

Canal St. streetcar route/stops

See also "Uptown Hotels & Restaurants" map.

MID-CITY

N. Rocheblave
N. Tonti
N. Miro
N. Galvez
N. Johnson
N. Prieur
N. Roman
Derbigny

See "Mid-City Hotels & Restaurants" map.

St. Ann

Dumaine
St. Phillip
Ursulines Ave.
Bayou Rd.

LaFitte Ave.
Orleans Ave.

N. Claiborne Ave.

St. Louis Cemetery No. 2

St. Louis Cemetery No. 1

Louis Armstrong Park

N. Villere

See "French Quarter Hotels" map.

Basin St.
Univ. Pl.

N. Rampart
Burgundy
Dauphine
Bourbon
Royal

Conti
St. Louis
Toulouse
St. Ann
Dumaine

Barracks
Esplanade

St. Claude Ave.

St. Bernard Ave.

FAUBOURG MARIGNY

THE FRENCH QUARTER

Iberville
Bienville

Ursulines
Gov. Nichols

Touro
Frenchmen
Elysian
Marigny

Chartres

Decatur

French Market

Chartres St.

Superdome

La Salle St.
Duncan Plaza

Poydras
Common
Gravier
Canal

Loyola Ave.
S. Rampart
O'Keefe St.
Lafayette
Union
Perdido

CENTRAL BUSINESS DISTRICT

St. Charles Ave.
Carondelet
Lafayette Square

Julia
St. Charles Ave.
Camp
Magazine St.
Tchoupitoulas
Commerce
S. Peters
Fulton
Conv. Ctr. Blvd.

St. Joseph
Howard Ave.

RIVERFRONT

World Trade Center

New Orleans Convention & Exhibition Center

Canal St. Ferry (Toll)

Mississippi River

ALGIERS

Morgan
Delaronde
Seguin
Verret
Bouny

Lake Pontchartrain

CITY PARK

Area of detail

Superdome

0   1/4 mi
0   0.25 km

In addition to regularly scheduled shows, Fritzel's European Jazz Pub often has late-night jam sessions.

current claims to fame are cheap drinks and a solid cover band. It's fratty fun, if that's what you're looking for, and there's no cover. 339 Bourbon St. ℭ **504/598-4334.** www.myspace.com/famousdoor. No cover.

Fritzel's European Jazz Pub ★★★ You might walk right past this small establishment, but that would be a big mistake, because the 1831 building brings some fine traditional jazz musicians to play on its tiny stage. Squishy bench seating and pushy servers are acceptable only because the music is that good, including occasional guests from Europe and late-night jam sessions when performers end their stints elsewhere and gather here. Sets are short, but if Tom McDermott or Tim Laughlin is on, don't miss them. The full bar stocks ice-cold schnapps and German beers. 733 Bourbon St. ℭ **504/586-4800.** www.fritzelsjazz.net. 1-drink minimum per set.

Funky Pirate Decorated to resemble a pirate's lair, the Funky Pirate lives up to the "funky" part of the name. It's perpetually full of loud beer drinkers, and can get jam-packed. Popular "Big" Al Carson (who lives up—and out—to his nickname) and the Blues Masters hold court here Tuesday through Saturday from 8:30pm on. **Note:** Sister bar **Tropical Isle** is next door. If "Drink from a plastic weapon" is on your bucket list, you can get one of their famously horrid hand grenades here. 727 Bourbon St. ℭ **504/523-1960.** www.tropicalisle.com. 1-drink minimum per set.

Irvin Mayfield's Jazz Playhouse ★★★ The draperied, midsize room in the venerable Royal Sonesta Hotel owned by hyphenated Mayfield (trumpeter-bandleader-composer–cultural ambassador) is the go-to spot for ambitious local jazz from established and on-the-rise artists. Wednesdays feature the New Orleans Jazz Orchestra; Friday midnight it's burlesque. It's swank but usually not stuffy, except when they hold tables for big spenders who never show. But there's rarely a cover, the drink prices aren't outrageous, and a small food menu makes it a fine retreat from Bourbon Street. 300 Bourbon St. ℭ **504/553-2299.** www.sonesta.com/RoyalNewOrleans. Usually no cover except for the burlesque show.

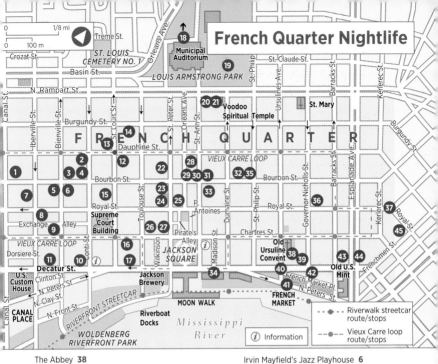

French Quarter Nightlife

Bourbon Street is famous for its rowdy nightlife.

Maison Bourbon ★★ Despite its location and the sign saying the building is "dedicated to the preservation of jazz" (which seems an attempt to confuse tourists into thinking this is the legendary Preservation Hall), Maison Bourbon is not a tourist trap. The music is authentic, and often superb, jazz, and the brick-lined room is a respite from the mayhem outside. From about midafternoon until the wee hours, hourly sets of Dixieland and traditional jazz hold forth, often at loud and lively volume. 641 Bourbon St. ⓒ **504/522-8818.** 1-drink minimum per set.

Palm Court Jazz Cafe ★★ This stylish jazz haunt/dinner club serves up top-notch jazz groups Wednesday through Sunday. It's generally traditional or classic jazz, but Saturday nights belong to trumpeter Lionel Ferbos—who turned 100 in 2011 (you read that right—and he's still gigging!). *Tip:* Make reservations—it's that kind of place. A small bar in the back can usually accommodate those who don't care to dine. 1204 Decatur St. ⓒ **504/525-0200.** www.palm courtjazzcafe.com. Cover $5 per person.

Preservation Hall ★★★ ☺ The gray, bombed-out building looks as if it were erected just shortly after the dawn of time, or at least the dawn of New Orleans—which it was. It doesn't seem like much, but it's an essential spot for traditional jazz fans and, well, everyone (U2's Edge and Robert Plant have sat in while in town). With no seats or much air, terrible sightlines, and constant crowds, the awesomeness is in

Musicians onstage at Palm Court Jazz Cafe.

Preservation Hall.

the ancient atmosphere and the superb musicianship. Even those uninterested in jazz become entranced. Plus, it's one of the few nightspots that kids can attend. Patrons start lining up around 6:15pm for the show starting around 8pm, another around 10pm, and midnight rock shows during Jazz Fest. A few VIP seats, sold online well in advance, guarantee a seat.

A sign on the wall gives prices for requests—$10 for "Saints Go Marchin' In," $5 for everything else. (Big-spender smart alecks toss in a $100 bill for 10 rounds of "Saints.") Do offer something (and maybe pick up a CD). Call ahead for current open hours. 726 St. Peter St. ✆ **888/946-JAZZ** (946-5299) or 504/522-2841. www.preservationhall.com. Cover $12; VIP $25.

Snug Harbor ★★ If your idea of jazz extends beyond Dixieland and if you prefer a sit-down, concert-style setting over a messy nightclub, get thee to Snug. In the heart of the Frenchmen Street action at the fringes of the French Quarter, it's the city's premier contemporary jazz showcase (elder piano statesman Ellis Marsalis holds court many Fridays). Here, jazz is presented as it should be: part entertainment, part art, and often, part intellectual stimulation.

The two-level seating provides generally good viewing of the bandstand (but beware the pillars upstairs if you don't get seats along the rail). Get tickets in advance, and hang out beforehand in the crowded, low-ceilinged (slightly claustrophobic) bar or the adjoining restaurant (which has great burgers). *Tip:* Tickets for the show aren't required to drink in the bar—where speakers and monitors convey the action inside. For the budget-minded, it's the next best thing to seeing it live. Doors open at 7pm; sets start at 8 and 10pm. 626 Frenchmen St. ✆ **504/949-0696.** www.snugjazz.com. Cover $15–$30, depending on performer.

The Spotted Cat Music Club ★★★ This might be our favorite live-music venue in the city. Our particular New Orleans aesthetic leans toward cramped rooms, little (or no) amplification, and scrappy bands with a fresh take on classic, big-band, gypsy, hot—well, any type of swinging jazz. If you're lucky there'll be a few frenetic-footed jitterbuggers in front of the teensy stage (often they're the instructors at Wed's free dance lessons, which start at 5pm).

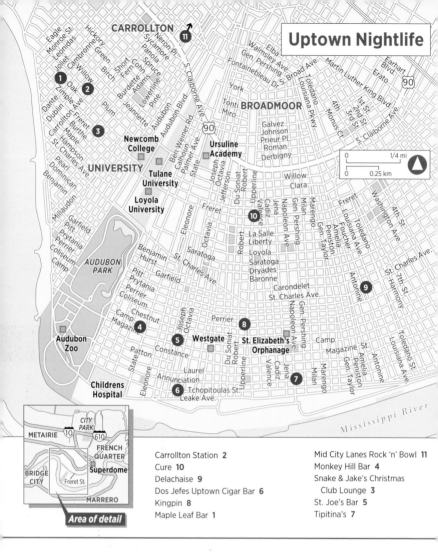

Uptown Nightlife

CARROLLTON

BROADMOOR

UNIVERSITY

Newcomb College

Tulane University

Loyola University

Ursuline Academy

AUDUBON PARK

Audubon Zoo

Childrens Hospital

Westgate

St. Elizabeth's Orphanage

Mississippi River

METAIRIE

CITY PARK

FRENCH QUARTER

Superdome

BRIDGE CITY

Freret St.

MARRERO

Area of detail

Carrollton Station **2**	Mid City Lanes Rock 'n' Bowl **11**
Cure **10**	Monkey Hill Bar **4**
Delachaise **9**	Snake & Jake's Christmas
Dos Jefes Uptown Cigar Bar **6**	Club Lounge **3**
Kingpin **8**	St. Joe's Bar **5**
Maple Leaf Bar **1**	Tipitina's **7**

This is some of the most reliable live music on Frenchmen. Seats are scarce and you may need to play dodge the dancers but this is the real deal. There's rarely a cover, which translates to tip the band and buy drinks (one per set minimum), and we love that the music starts by 4pm most afternoons. Mondays you'll find us hanging out with the Jazz Vipers, and any other time the Moonshiners or Smoking Time Club is there, so are we. Cash bar only. 623 Frenchmen St. www. spottedcatmusicclub.com.

Three Muses ★ The "three" are a pedigreed chef, a superb mixologist, and a spellbinding chanteuse. The result is the best addition to Frenchmen Street in years: a tidy, mellow room big on crooners and traditional jazz, well crafted cocktails, and bacon-wrapped oysters in jalapeno vinaigrette—among other killer bar snacks (though their small plates are indeed small, and the moola adds up. Feta fries are the best for value and sharing). With all that to recommend it, the scant tables and barstools fill up fast when the street is hopping. Open daily at 4pm except closed Tuesday. 536 Frenchmen St. ✆ **504/298-8746.** www.thethreemuses.com. No cover, tip the band.

Elsewhere Around the City

Candlelight Lounge ★★★ One of the last still-operating clubs in the Faubourg Treme, the big event here takes place Wednesday nights somewhere around 10pm, when the Treme Brass Band takes the small stage in their epony-mous neighborhood. Locally famous since the 1980s and newly nationally fa-mous thanks to the HBO series *Treme,* the rollicking brass band brings down the house. There's free red beans and rice, fast-flowing beer, friendly staff, and styling, 70-something "Uncle" Lionel Batiste strutting between the communal picnic tables, with or without his big bass drum strapped on. No one in the mixed crowd leaves this streamer-strewn room without smiling or sweating. No one. Take a cab, and get there early if you want a seat where you can see the band. 925 N. Robertson. ✆ **504/581-6689.** Cover $15.

Chickie Wah-Wah ★★ This Mid-City club has hit its stride, with the best of the local roots, rock, blues, and singer-songwriter acts drawing reverent crowds. The midsize, shotgun-style room (long and thin) is clean and smoke-free (smok-ers can hang on the patio), with cool old tin signs lending ambience. The small Taceaux Loceaux kitchen serves surprisingly good munchitos, and it's an easy streetcar ride from the Quarter. Try to catch Paul Sanchez, Tom McDermott, John Cleary, or the Nightcrawlers on their regular gigs here. 2828 Canal St. ✆ **504/304-4714.** www.chickiewahwah.com. Cover ranges $8–$20.

Irvin Mayfield's I Club At press time, Irvin Mayfield (see earlier) was set to open his second New Orleans nightclub, this one in the J.W. Marriott Hotel. Unlike his Jazz Playhouse (see earlier), this one will book other genres and have a cover charge, memberships, and valet parking. But if the Playhouse is any measure, we're excited to see what he'll bring to Canal Street. 614 Canal St. ✆ **504/527-6712.** Cover charges $10–$20.

Vaughan's Lounge ★ Deep in the Bywater section of New Orleans, Vaughan's Lounge is way down-home—as in, it's a rambling, shambling dive in a residential neighborhood. It's a taxi ride from the Quarter, but on Thursday nights when Kermit Ruffins is swing-ing, it's packed, loud, smoky, sweaty—and a requisite New Orleans scene. Go early for a chance to actually see the band, and to get some of the barbecued

Thursday night at Vaughn's features Kermit Ruffins.

turkey necks that Kermit grills up before the show. Most other nights, it's just a bar, but call to see if anything else is on. 4229 Dauphine St. ✆ **504/947-5562.** Cover varies, usually $10–$15.

CAJUN & ZYDECO JOINTS

Most of the so-called Cajun joints in New Orleans are really Cajun for tourists, in both sound and setting. If you want the real thing, you are better off going out to bayou or prairie country. Some mighty fine Cajun bands do play in New Orleans—but you are likely to find, say, the world-renowned BeauSoleil at Tipitina's, or the raucous Pine Leaf Boys at d.b.a., neither of which is a Cajun club. Terrific, authentic Cajun bands do play at the places listed below—but the quality is hit-or-miss. What these spots do offer, however, is a place to learn to Cajun dance, which is a dandy way to burn off calories—and it's also darn fun.

Mid City Lanes Rock 'n' Bowl ★★ The spiffy, spacious new Rock 'n' Bowl—still in Mid-City but now located a few blocks from the original locale—no longer has the rough-hewn, er, patina of its former (ca. 1941) locale. But if you like your lanes sans potholes and your dance floor big enough to seriously swing, you'll be happy as a split pickup here. The combination of bowling, dancing, a full bar, and stellar live music—from swing Wednesdays to zydeco Thursdays to rockabilly and beyond—is an utter hoot and an unbeatable experience that draws all ages and ranks (though most evening shows are for the 21-and-older crowd). If it's cool enough for Keith Richards, it's cool enough for us. Truth be told, on an uncrowded night, it can feel a bit *too* spacious, but with decent bar snacks, effective air-conditioning, and plenty of clean restrooms, that's just fine. We love the wood tables built from the old location's lanes, and we love it when legendary proprietor John Blancher breaks out his singular dance moves. Consider splurging on a custom-embroidered bowling shirt—a splendid souvenir. Open Monday

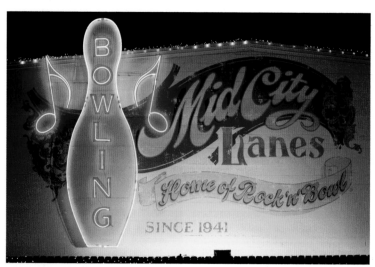

Zydeco music and bowling all in one spot—where else but New Orleans?

to Friday at 4pm and Saturday at 2pm until "the party closes down." *Tip:* Dine next door at Ye Olde College Inn (p. 138) and take $5 off admission. 3000 S. Carrollton Ave. © **504/861-1700.** www.rockandbowl.com. Private parties sometimes take it over; call ahead to be sure. Bowling $24 per hour per lane and a $1 shoe-rental fee; show admission $5–$25.

Mulate's ★ This is a likely place to find authentic good Cajun bands. The stage and dance area are relatively spacious, and the food isn't bad. During Jazz Fest 2006, when BeauSoleil played, none other than Bob Dylan dropped by to listen! 201 Julia St., at Convention Center Blvd. © **800/854-9149** or 504/522-1492. www.mulates. com. No cover.

RHYTHM, ROCK, BLUES & MORE
The French Quarter & the Faubourg Marigny

Balcony Music Club ★ Might as well start (or end) your Frenchmen Street club hopping here, since it's right on your way (if you are walking from the Quarter) at the corner of Esplanade and Decatur. The BMC's main room is well-sized, refreshingly clean, and has good sound; a sweet little back bar serves pizzas and fronts a teensy patio. Bookings include local acts and DJs. 1331 Decatur St. © **504/599-7770.** Cover varies.

d.b.a. ★★★ This place has aged into one of the best New Orleans bar/nightclubs. Their live bookings feature an occasional, on-the-cusp national or Louisiana act, and a wide variety of excellent local acts like magnificent crooner John Boutte, Walter Washington's tight blues, and Meschiya Lake's stunning vintage vocals. It helps that when they say an act goes on at 7pm, it usually does, and now it's strictly nonsmoking. Get there early if you want to see the band (earlier yet to snag a rare seat), because the stage is set fairly low and the talkers at the bar can be loud. The Scotch and beer lists (160 beers, none of them Bud Light) are the best in the city, with equally impressive selections of wines and other spirits. *Tip:* John Boutte's early Saturday shows now command a small cover charge, but most other nights these well-booked first acts are free. 618 Frenchmen St. © **504/942-3731.** www.drinkgoodstuff.com. Cover $5–$10, occasionally higher.

House of Blues ★ New Orleans was a natural place for this franchise to set up shop, but its French Quarter presence seems rather unnatural. With all the funky, authentic music clubs in town, why build one with ersatz *authenticity?* We suppose we should be glad that they've lined the walls with the works of many deserving Southern "primitive" artists, and the facility does have good sightlines and sound. Though it's lost the luster and muscle it had when it first opened, they still pull in first-rate bookings, from local legends the Neville Brothers to ace out-of-towners like Lady Gaga in her superstar-ascendant days. The restaurant's nouvelle Orleans menu is decent, from a piquant jambalaya to fancy-schmancy pizzas. Still, patronizing this club rather than the real thing, like Tipitina's, feels a bit like eating at McDonald's rather than Mother's. All that said, the smaller **Parish Room** has less forced-genuine decor, more value, and some interesting acts. 225 Decatur St. © **504/529-2583.** www.hob.com. Cover varies.

Jimmy Buffett's Margaritaville Cafe & Storyville Tavern Yeah, Jimmy Buffett might have played here a few times, and yeah, they serve cheeseburgers. We know Buffett means well (isn't that practically his whole shtick as an artist?), but he took over a perfectly nice little jazz club (the Storyville Tavern, which was

One Eyed Jacks has a bordello flavor, but its bookings favor indie songwriters and international alternative rock.

nowhere near Storyville) and made it part of the brand-name takeover of the Quarter. There's live, smooth rockin' music nightly and no cover (more to spend on the plentiful Parrothead paraphernalia), but it's easy, accessible, and the up-stairs patio is a nice spot for, yeah, a margarita. 1104 Decatur St. ✆ **504/592-2565.** www.margaritaville.com.

The Maison ★ This long, two-story room has plenty of dancing room, with a balcony overlooking the main floor and pool and air hockey tables upstairs. The booking policy is a bit disjointed, with early acts favoring traditional jazz (often with no cover) and main shows featuring hip-hop, DJs (Questlove took on the ta-bles last Mardi Gras), local rock, or something else. It's all part of the Frenchmen Street musical buffet—speaking of which, they do have a kitchen serving more than just snacks. 508 Frenchmen St. ✆ **504/371-5543.** www.maisonfrenchmen.com. Cover varies.

One Eyed Jacks ★★ With its bordello-flavored decor (red flocked wallpa-per, anyone?), Jack's is both a hip nightspot and funky club, with its tiered main level, proscenium stage, and crowded bar in the middle of the whole thing—all overlooked by a cozy balcony. The stepped setting and easy alcohol access pretty much invite people to fall on top of each other. Not that that's a bad thing. Bookings favor local and international alternative rock and indie songwriters, plus Saturday's ever-popular tough tender Fleur de Tease burlesque show. The three-ring psychodrama game show cabaret circus known as the New Orleans Bingo! Show makes occasional appearances here. If they do, so should you. You might like it, you might not, but you surely won't see anything else like it. 615 Toulouse St. ✆ **504/569-8361.** www.oneeyedjacks.net. Cover varies.

Elsewhere Around the City

Throughout this book, we keep nagging you to leave the Quarter. This advice is most important at night, when you can check out some of the many terrific clubs on the city's fringes. And not only do they feature some of the best music in town (if not, on some nights, in the country), but some aren't designed as tourist destinations, so your experience will be that much more legitimate. Rest assured, every cabdriver knows the way.

Carrollton Station ★★ Way uptown in the Riverbend area, Carrollton Station is a prime folk, acoustic, and local rock venue. A long, narrow space means that folks at the back won't get to see much of what's up onstage, but that puts them closer to the bar with its fine beer selection, so everyone wins. (Okay, not really. If you really want to see a band, come early to nab a spot near the front, where it can get sardinelike and airless. Hey, it's a trade-off—but the sound is good.) The crowd is a mix of college students, music aficionados, and fans of whatever act is appearing. If that's Susan Cowsill, you're in for a treat. The bar opens 3pm daily; shows usually start between 9:30 and 10:30pm. 8140 Willow St. © **504/865-9190.** www.carrolltonstation.com. Cover varies on weekends. No cover weekdays except during Jazz Fest.

The Howlin' Wolf ★ The popular Wolf outgrew their old Warehouse District site and now regularly fill their 10,000-square-foot space. The wide, shallow room has great sightlines from just about anywhere to see bands that range from leading local acts to midlevel national rock bands on tour. The latest addition is the Den, a smaller room next door serving decent food and presenting an eclectic mix of indie acts, from comedy to spoken word to funk (and brass on Sun). If you feel like a drive, there's a branch in Mandeville on the Northshore, at 1623 Montgomery St. Fun fact: The bar came from Al Capone's hotel in Chicago. Doors open at 9pm; shows start at 10pm. 907 S. Peters St., in the Warehouse District. © **504/522-WOLF** (522-9653). www.thehowlinwolf.com. Cover varies.

Maple Leaf Bar ★★★ This is what a New Orleans club is all about, and its reputation was only furthered when it became the first live music venue to reopen, just weeks after Katrina, with an emotional, generator-powered performance by Walter "Wolfman" Washington. It's medium-size but feels smaller when the crowds pack in, which they do by 11pm most nights. Personal space at times becomes something you can only wistfully remember, resulting in a whole new scene on the sidewalk and street, where the crowd spills out to escape the heat and sweat (which are prodigious despite many ceiling fans). A good bar, bad pool table, and a rather pretty patio out back (the other escape locale) make the Maple Leaf worth hanging out at even if you don't care about the music on a particular night. But if the Rebirth Brass Band is playing, do not miss it; go and dance until you drop. 8316 Oak St. © **504/866-9359.** www.mapleleafbar.com. Cover varies.

Republic Local indie bands and some of the hotter alternative bands coming through town play here, bringing, on occasion, new

HotTamales

Sometimes all you need is a quick, spicy food hit. Flirty **Holly Tamale** pedals her pink, tamale-toting tricycle around Frenchmen Street, the Marigny, and the St. Claude clubs. Find her and her traditional and offbeat creations (coconut chicken mushroom, anyone?) on Twitter @HollysTamales. Tamales are $3 each.

meaning to the words hideously overheated and overcrowded (when the band is itself blazingly popular). It's a former historic warehouse, a good thing if you're in the upstairs mezzanine or down front where the chandelier-laden ceiling is high overhead, but not so much if you're off to the back or sides, where headroom is compromised and the sightlines can be marred by archway pillars. Still, none of that matters when it's a band you *have* to see, say, Mumford & Sons, OK Go, Spoon, or Edward Sharpe & The Magnetic Zeros. 828 S. Peters St. © **504/528-8282.** www.republicnola.com. Cover varies.

Tipitina's ★★★ Dedicated to the late piano master Professor Longhair (that's him in bronze just inside the entrance; pat his head for luck) Tip's is, if not *the* New Orleans club, still a major musical touchstone, and a reliable place for top local and out-of-town roots, brass, jam, and rock bands from Wilco to Band of Horses. (A few years ago at Tip's we saw Michael Stipe of R.E.M. serenade Patti Smith with "Wichita Lineman.") If you can catch Troy "Trombone Shorty" Andrews, Galactic, or especially Dr. John here, it's a must.

Tipitina's, the iconic New Orleans nightclub.

Besides its pedigree as one of the city's premier live music venues, **Tipitina's** also actively supports and enhances the local scene through its foundation and educational activities. For example, at their Sunday afternoon music workshops, held from 1 to 3:30pm, music students can play and study with leading names such as Stanton Moore, Johnny Vidacovich, Kirk Joseph, and Theresa Andersson. This low-key scene, open to the public, offers a pretty cool opportunity to watch and listen as traditions are passed down.

It's nothing fancy: four walls, a wraparound balcony (often reserved for VIPs), and a stage (which, if you're under 6 feet, isn't easy to see from the back on busy nights). Oh, and a few bars, of course, including one that serves the atmospheric crowds milling outside the club. Big shows and their Jazz Fest bookings, including the brass-band blowout and Instruments a Comin' benefit, do sell out so buy advance tix. It's uptown and a bit out of the way (and food in the area is scant, so eat first), but it can make for a memorable experience that's definitely worth the cab ride on the right night. 501 Napoleon Ave. ✆ **504/895-8477** or 504/897-3943 for concert line. www.tipitinas.com. Cover varies.

12 Bar ★ This casual, brick-lined room with decent rock, roots, and blues music (and comedy, occasionally) books mostly locals, save for an occasional surprise like garage punkers the Fleshtones. Add good happy hour specials, and it's a solid addition to an underserved area (especially for conventioneers), tucked away on Fulton Street, in the downriver end of the Warehouse District. 608 Fulton St. ✆ **504/212-6476.** www.12barnola.com. Cover ranges $5–$25.

THE BAR SCENE

You won't have any trouble finding a place to drink in New Orleans. Heck, thanks to "go" (or *geaux*) cups, you won't have to spend a minute without a drink in your hand. (It's legal to drink in public as long as it's in a plastic cup. Sheesh, sometimes it almost seems illegal *not* to have such a cup in your hand.)

Bourbon Street comes off like a blocks-long bar—and smells like it. It's pointless to single out any one establishment there; ultimately they and their clientele vary little. If we sound a bit scornful, it's because so many seem to treat a visit to New Orleans as nothing more than a license to get blotto, and the streets

THE ST. CLAUDE scene

The scruffy local alternative types have carved out a pretty pulsing, punk-infused scene (well, with some garage rock, bluegrass, metal, and whatever else) along a stretch of St. Claude Avenue, where bars like the **Saturn Bar** (later in this chapter), the **Hi-Ho Lounge** (later in this chapter), the **AllWays Lounge,** and **Siberia** book music most nights. Hours, shows, and covers vary so do call ahead. If this sounds like your thing, do take a cab and don't wander in this transitional area. AllWays Lounge, 240 Saint Claude Ave. (✆ **504/218-5778;** www.theallwayslounge.com); Siberia, 2227 St. Claude Ave. (✆ **504/265-8855**).

as one big place to regurgitate. Not only is this obnoxious, but there's just so much more to this town.

Which is not at all to dismiss drinking as a recreational activity (or as a sociological study). Certainly, New Orleans provides some of the most convivial, quaint, or downright eccentric spots to do so; many places are worth going to even if you just quaff a soda. Also note that many of the clubs listed above are terrific spots to hoist a few, while some of the bars below also provide music. Many bars stay open constantly, or vary their hours depending upon day, season, or demand. If you have your heart set on a particular place, do call to verify their hours. Unless noted, none of the places listed below has a cover charge.

Best Bars & Cocktails

Note that there's an entire section earlier in this book on the best bars and cocktails in New Orleans. Yes, we realize that's a nearly impossible topic in which to stick an, um, olive pick, but you need to start somewhere. So refer to p. 7 and p. 8 in addition to those listed here, and let the imbibing—and debating—begin.

THE FRENCH QUARTER & THE FAUBOURG MARIGNY

In addition to the places below, you might consider the clubby bar at **Dickie Brennan's Steakhouse,** 716 Iberville St. (✆ **504/522-2467;** p. 123), a place where manly men go to drink strong drinks inside, smoke smelly cigars outside on the street (they have a vast selection for sale, but don't allow smoking in the establishment), and chat up girlie girls.

PAT O'BRIEN'S & the mighty hurricane

Pat O'Brien's, 718 St. Peter St. (✆ **504/525-4823;** www.patobriens.com), is world-famous for the hefty, rum-based drink with the big-wind name. The formula (according to legend) was stumbled upon by bar owners Charlie Cantrell and George Oechsner during World War II. The drink is served in signature 28-ounce hurricane lamp–style glasses.

On weeknights, the bar also offers a 3-gallon magnum Hurricane that stands taller than many small children—it's served with a handful of straws and takes a group to finish (we profoundly hope), all of whom must drink standing up. Naturally, this attracts the tourists and college yahoos in droves. The line can stretch down the street, despite the plethora of drinking options mere feet away.

Pat's is nonetheless worth a stop—it's a reliable, rowdy, friendly introduction to New Orleans and no trip to the city is complete without sampling the famous red scare (they do have other drinks, too). Some prefer doing so in the large lounge with the dual piano players (starting at 7pm), but the highlight, on nonrainy days at least, is the attractive, sprawling tropical patio. Don't look there for a quiet respite, though. It's where the party atmosphere thrives, and on pretty days, tables can be hard to come by. There's no minimum and no cover, but if you buy a drink and it comes in a glass, you'll be paying for the glass until you turn it in at the register for a $3 refund.

The Abbey Despite the name, this place is more basement rumpus room (walls covered with stickers and old album covers) than Gothic church (well, there are some motley stained-glass windows). But it's been a bar since the 1930s, the jukebox plays the Cramps and Iggy Pop and the Stooges' "I Wanna Be Your Dog," and the clientele is very David Lynchian (maybe still left over from the place's heyday 20-plus years ago!). Still, you might find this a scary dump rather than a cool dump. Open 24 hours. 1123 Decatur St. ✆ **504/523-7177.**

Apple Barrel You can find refuge from the hectic Frenchmen scene (catch your breath and have a beer) at this small, dusty, wooden-floored watering hole or kick it off (they're open by 2pm-ish). Or join said scene, as they have live music (tending toward local blues acts like Coco Robicheaux) nightly. 609 Frenchmen St. ✆ **504/949-9399.**

The Bombay Club This noted martini bar (serving over 115 different versions) features grown-up jazz nightly. The wood-paneled bar bills itself as casually elegant—a polite way of saying don't wear jeans or shorts—but it's not at all snooty. It's also a restaurant (the food is not great) but the romantic, curtained booths in the back are awfully inviting. 830 Conti St. ✆ **800/699-7711** or 504/586-0972. www. thebombayclub.com.

Cat's Meow Actually, cocktails aren't the attraction here. It's a karaoke mecca—one of the first and still foremost locales in the nation to popularize this *Idol*-age form of self-aggrandizing art (or artlessness, as the case may be). The drinks and drink specials flow aplenty—the better to loosen the larynx. Whether or not you plan to take the mic, the scene can be as entertaining as it is crowded. The action starts at 4pm Monday through Thursday, 2pm Friday through Sunday. 701 Bourbon St. ✆ **504/523-2788.** www.catskaraoke.com.

Chart Room ★ This is one of the only bars on Chartres Street in the French Quarter. Dark and mysterious, this sometimes-seedy place is the perfect spot to be left alone and escape the hustle and bustle of Bourbon Street. This place is popular with the local Quarter crowd. 300 Chartres St. ✆ **504/522-1708.**

Crescent City Brewhouse When this place opened in 1991, it was the first new brewery in New Orleans in more than 70 years. It still holds up as a decent microbrewery, and comes with live jazz. 527 Decatur St. ✆ **504/522-0571.** www.crescentcitybrewhouse.com.

Dickie Brennan's Bourbon House Seafood and Oyster Bar ★★ Step up to this clean and convivial horse-shoe-shaped bar for raw seafood, house specialty drinks (some with fresh fruit, others called "new-fashioneds"!), or, naturally, bourbon (even if the street is named for the French royal family, not the liquor). They serve many kinds in many ways, including the award-winning frozen bourbon milk punch. 144 Bourbon St. ✆ **504/522-0111.** www.bourbonhouse.com.

Don't miss the raw bar at Dickie Brennan's Bourbon House Seafood and Oyster Bar.

Fahy's Irish Pub One night we went looking for a bar with pool tables, and you know what? New Orleans (or at least the Quarter) doesn't have a lot of 'em. So it was with relief we found Fahy's, a corner neighborhood pub (which attracts a pool-playin' crowd) that keeps its two tables in good condition. 540 Burgundy St. *©* **504/586-9806.**

Feelings Café ★ Here's a funky, low-key neighborhood restaurant and hangout set around a classic New Orleans courtyard, which is where most folks drink—unless it's Friday and they're hanging out upstairs with the piano player. (See p. 133 for the restaurant listing.) It's a bit out of the way in the Faubourg Marigny, but authentic in the right ways and also more cheerful than some of the darker, hole-in-the-wall spots that deserve that adjective. *Note:* Open only Thursday through Sunday, only from 5pm; the balcony piano bar is open Fridays only. 2600 Chartres St. *©* **504/945-2222.** www.feelingscafe.com.

Hermes Bar at Antoine's Everything old *is* new again: New Orleans's oldest restaurant recently opened this smallish, more casual adjunct room (no cover, no jacket required). It's well stocked, so yes, you can have soufflé potatoes and other food. Even with the attractive old-school tile and woodwork it feels like it's still finding its footing (give it another 150 years or so), with weekend live music somewhat haphazardly stuck at one end of the room. But classic cocktails, good local bands, and a chance to ogle some of Antoine's storied collection of Mardi Gras memorabilia make it worth a visit. 713 St. Louis St. *©* **504/581-4422.** www.antoines.com.

Kerry Irish Pub ★ This traditional Irish pub has a variety of beers and spirits but is most proud of its properly poured pints of Guinness and hard cider. "The Kerry" is a good bet for live Irish and alternative folk music, and to throw darts and shoot pool. For that last nightcap on your way back through the Quarter, Kerry specializes in very-late-night drinking. 331 Decatur St. *©* **504/527-5954.** www.kerryirishpub.com.

Lafitte's Blacksmith Shop ★★ It's some steps away from the main action on Bourbon, but you'll know Lafitte's when you see it. Dating from the 1770s, it's the oldest building in the Quarter—possibly in the Mississippi Valley (though that's not documented)—and it looks it. Legend has it that the privateer brothers Pierre and Jean Lafitte used the smithy as a "blind" for their lucrative trade in contraband (and, some say, slaves they'd captured on the high seas). Like all legends, that's probably not true.

The owner managed to maintain the exposed-brick interior when he rescued the building from deterioration in the 1940s (and later lost it). At night when you step inside and it's entirely lit by candles, you can understand why *Offbeat* magazine claims Lafitte's patented the word *dank.* In other towns, this would be a tourist trap, a jukebox does overblare, and an exterior renovation badly falsified the previous genuine plaster-and-exposed-brick look. Yet it still feels authentic (Tennessee Williams did drink here, after all), and it's almost always easy to get into, even on Mardi Gras day. Definitely worth swinging by for atmosphere, but drink only beer; their mixed drinks appall cocktail aficionados. 941 Bourbon St. *©* **504/593-9761.**

Mimi's in the Marigny It started out feeling a bit like an L.A. club impresario's idea of a Marigny bar: clean, perfectly lit, not out of place in a New York hipster hotel that wanted a New Orleans–themed club. But it's gained some grit, the initial trendiness has mellowed, and now it's perhaps the veritable beating heart of the Marigny area. Still a step up from our beloved but shabbier New Orleans

A lively scene at Molly's on the Market.

clubs, with tapas, tunes, and late, late hours, but with a welcoming, largely local crowd and a serious dance scene upstairs. When legendary DJ Soul Sister spins rare soul on Saturday and Sunday nights, *everyone* gets their groove on. 2601 Royal St. ℰ **504/872-9868.**

Molly's on the Market ★★★ This is *the* hangout for boho and literary locals who chew over the state of their world and their city, and who will get mad at us for broadcasting the location of their clubhouse. They consider it the best bar in the French Quarter. It's noted especially for being one of the only bars to remain open during Hurricane Katrina. Part eccentric English bar, and yet accessible enough to make it popular with firefighters and policemen, this place has a cool, East Village feel. Molly's also serves as the starting point for the French Quarter Halloween parade, a must-see should you happen to land in New Orleans during what many locals hail as the Second Biggest Party of the year. 1107 Decatur St. ℰ **504/525-5169.**

Orleans Grapevine Wine Bar & Bistro ★★ Locals know about this wonderfully intimate venue—dark, cool, and surprisingly quiet so close to the bustle of Bourbon Street. There's a staggeringly extensive wine list and a small but delightful seasonal dining menu. 720 Orleans Ave. ℰ **504/523-1930.** www.orleansgrapevine.com.

Pirate's Alley Café and Absinthe Bar Its tucked-away locale around the corner from St. Louis Cathedral and plenty of outdoor tables lend this cafe-bar a European feel. Purists will balk at their absinthe service, but others will have fun with it—flaming sugar cube and all. The food's nothing much, but it's there. 622 Pirates Alley. ℰ **504/524-9332.** www.piratesalleycafe.com.

Pravda ★ A bit high-concept, with its Soviet-era lounge kitsch, it is nonetheless the best place in town for vodka drinkers and the absinthe-curious. While other bars in town stock this once-banned liquor, Pravda has the best selection and the

Those looking for a pool table should head to R Bar and Royal Street Inn.

correct service paraphernalia. And they know better than to set it on fire (well, unless you ask), a silly party trick that gained favor in 1990s Eastern Europe. A limited but interesting menu features seasonal, local-focused small plates Tuesdays through Sundays. 1113 Decatur St. ✆ **504/581-1112.** www.pravdaofnola.com.

R Bar and Royal Street Inn ★★   The R (short for Royal St.) Bar is a little taste of New York's East Village in the Faubourg Marigny. It is a quintessential, cool neighborhood bar in a neighborhood full of artists, wannabe artists, punk-rock intellectuals, urban gentrifiers, and well-rounded hipsters (and it's their designated headquarters on Mardi Gras). It's a talkers' bar, with crowds gathered in layers along the bar, and a haven for strutting, overconfident pool players. There's a large imported beer selection and a fine alternative and art-rock jukebox, and dudes can get a haircut and a shot for $10 on Mondays. The R Bar fronts the Royal Street Inn, otherwise known as the R Bar Inn, a bed-and-beverage (p. 94). 1431 Royal St. ✆ **504/948-7499.** www.royalstreetinn.com.

ELSEWHERE AROUND THE CITY

In addition to those listed below and chapter 1 under "The Best Bars Beyond Bourbon," (p. 8), hang with the local beautiful people at **Loa** or **Le Phare** (neither of which is particularly New Orleans–like, but that might come as a relief for Los Angeles refugees): Loa, the bar at the International House hotel, 221 Camp St., in the Central Business District (hotel review p. 102), is a hip and happening hangout with a very non–New Orleans, deeply attractive atmosphere and superb craft cocktails; it's a good place to meet a date (just bring a full wallet). Hot on its hip heels and with a slightly higher energy level, Le Phare's good-looking crowd beautifully shows off the old timbers of this former warehouse (in the Loft 523 hotel, p. 99). Several small restaurant bars, all of which feature house-made ingredients, are definitely noteworthy as well: **Delmonico** (1300 St. Charles Ave.); **A Mano** (870 Tchoupitoulas St.); **Iris** (321 N. Peters St., in the Bienville Hotel), and **Rio Mar** (800 S. Peters St.).

Bar Uncommon ★★ Mixologist Chris McMillan may be the best bartender in a town of greats, so take advantage of his (and his colleagues') talent. That is, do *not* order a Stoli Red Bull; *do* order a classic mint julep, his specialty, or another craft cocktail off their menu of updated classics (we dig the Winkle). Then appreciate what a difference fine ingredients, balance, tools, and technique can make in a cocktail, and savor the end product. Aaah. The room is minty fresh, too: almost anachronistically sleek, black and white and red all over. Not too big, sometimes too loud, excellent (not inexpensive) bar snacks are available. 817 Common St. (in the Pere Marquette Hotel). ℓ **504/525-1111.** www.baruncommon.com.

The Bulldog ★ This local haunt has an incredible beer selection, and some of the best bar food in the city. Wednesday is buy a pint, keep the glass night (a great souvenir). Both locations have nice outdoor patios for sippin' in the hot, muggy New Orleans evenings, and both get very full. 2 locations: Uptown, 3236 Magazine St.; ℓ **504/891-1516.** Old Metairie, 5135 Canal Blvd.; ℓ **504/488-4191.** http://bulldog.draftfreak.com.

Circle Bar ★★ This tiny dive is among the most bohemian-hip in town, courtesy of the slightly twisted folks behind Snake & Jake's. Ambience is the key, so we're anxious to see how the ever-popular "elegant decay" look (peeling wallpaper, glowing neon K&B drugstore sign) fares after a mid-2011 renovation. The jukebox keeps the quirky romantic vibe going, thanks to mood-enhancing selections from the Velvet Underground, Dusty Springfield, and Curtis Mayfield. The clientele is laid-back and Marlboro loving. No stage (for now), just an alcove where good live local music goes on at 10pm nightly, or so they say. Bet you'll see us there. Bet we will be complaining about how late the acts come on, again. 1032 St. Charles Ave., in the CBD at Lee Circle. ℓ **504/588-2616.** www.myspace.com/thecirclebar.

Delachaise ★ A rare free-standing bar on its own little island on St. Charles, it became known for its terrific bar-food menu by chef Chris DeBarr, who left to open Green Goddess restaurant (p. 127). The menu is still quite good but it's still first and foremost a bar—a long, lean, tin-ceilinged one, with a fine selection of spirits and an excellent wine and beer list. A good thing, since there's not a lot of seating for its size, the servers can have attitude, and the A/C is usually set to frigid. 3442 St. Charles Ave. ℓ **504/895-0858.** www.thedelachaise.com.

Dos Jefes Uptown Cigar Bar Dos Jefes has a post-college, young clientele (mostly men, it seems), from yuppie to scruffy. The patio outside has banana trees and iron chairs, and it's nicer than inside—carpet and cigars are a bad combination. The full bar has a good selection of beer on tap and piano music until midnight-ish Monday through Saturday. 5535 Tchoupitoulas St., Uptown. ℓ **504/891-8500.**

Hi-Ho Lounge ★ A thorough overhaul to this age-old neighborhood dive has made it a comfortable hang once again. While not a must-go destination, for something completely different we dig the no-cover Monday-night bluegrass jam. It's BYOB (banjo), but they provide the red beans and rice, gratis. They have random live music on other nights, too. The area is a bit dicey—proceed with caution. 2239 St. Claude Ave. ℓ **504/945-HIHO** (945-4446). www.hiholounge.net.

Kingpin ★★ This place is for that *Barfly* experience, without the smelly drunks, but in the company of other like-minded, 20-something folks. Nominally Elvis-themed (expect bashes on key dates in the King's timeline), this absurdly small space is increasingly popular among hipster/rocker/Dave Navarro types—when they can find it, that is. (***Hint:*** It's across from the Upperline restaurant and behind the market.) 1307 Lyons St., Uptown. *C* **504/891-2373.**

Monkey Hill Bar ★ Sleaze is fun, but there are limits. When this bar hit theirs, it was converted from a seedy old tavern into something quite nice on the inside, and while we can do without the yuppie meat-market weekend scene, the rest of the time it has a very good happy hour (though the drinks are only so-so in quality), best enjoyed from comfy sofas and chairs. 6100 Magazine St. *C* **504/899-4800.**

Pal's Lounge ★★ This used to be Yvonne's, a nondescript corner neighborhood bar that was only open for a couple of hours in the afternoon. It's still a neighborhood bar, whose well-heeled backers (including Rio Hackford, son of director Taylor) turned it into a retro hipster bar for a bit. Lately it's slunk back into a welcome comfort zone as a mixed-bag watering hole for the gentrifying Bayou St. John neighborhood. The buzzer on the right side of the door gets you in, 2 bucks gets you a can of Pabst Blue Ribbon, 5 or 6 gets you something fruity and froufrou. Vintage barflies mingle with neighborhood bohos who come with their dogs or on bikes. It's too smoky for some, and it can be hard to find a seat, but there's a good jukebox, air hockey, tacos on Tuesdays, and friendly regulars. The place still flies below the tourist radar—which is part of the reason Jude Law, Sean Penn, Philip Seymour Hoffman, and Steve Zahn drink there while filming in town. 949 N. Rendon St., Bayou St. John. *C* **504/488-PALS** (488-7257).

The Polo Lounge ★★ The **Windsor Court** is one of the city's finest hotels (p. 100), and the Polo Lounge is ideal if you're feeling particularly stylish (jeans

The Polo Lounge.

were just recently allowed) or just feel like feeling important. Sazeracs and cigars are popular here, and if you like to seal your deals with a drink, this is likely to be your first choice. In the Windsor Court hotel, 300 Gravier St., in the CBD. ✆ **504/523-6000.**

Ralph's on the Park ★★ Ralph's was once the site of a tavern frequented by the ladies of Storyville, though in being spiffed up it's lost most of that particular ooh-la-la flavor. Still, who cares? Look how gorgeous that bar is! A grown-up but not stuffy place to drink, with a gorgeous view of the oak trees in City Park, plus very good food (it's a Brennan family restaurant, after all). If you're lucky, Joe Krown will be tickling the ivories at happy hour. 900 City Park Ave. ✆ **504/488-1000.**

St. Joe's Bar ★★ An agreeably dark (but not pretentious), nonseedy corner bar, this is a very typical New Orleans friendly place. It has the right vibe without trying for the vibe at all, and its Upper Magazine location means it's more neighborhood- than business- or tourist-oriented. Folk-art crosses hang from the (apparently) hammered tin ceiling, and chandeliers are strung over the patio. At Halloween, the cobwebs look as if they should be permanent. It has a sweet, well-stocked jukebox (Ray Charles, Grateful Dead) and a pool table. 5535 Magazine St., Uptown. ✆ **504/899-3744.**

Saturn Bar ★ The Saturn Bar is among the hipster set's most beloved dives, but it's hard to decide if the love is genuine or comes from a postmodern, ironic appreciation of the grubby. It's been cleaned up a bit from the art-project (we hope) interior that its late owner, an irascible hoarder, cultivated, but it's still worth a visit, and they've added live bands a couple of times a week. The neighborhood demands that caution be exercised—get someone to walk you to and from your car, especially if you are a woman alone. 3067 St. Claude Ave., in the Bywater. ✆ **504/949-7532.**

Snake & Jake's Christmas Club Lounge ★★ Though admittedly off the beaten path, this tiny, friendly, serious dive is the perfect place for those looking for an authentic neighborhood bar. Owned by local musician Dave Clements, decorated (sort of) with Christmas lights, this is the kind of place where everybody knows your name and your dog's too, 'cause you can bring 'em (on a leash, before midnight). There is almost no light at all, so make friends and be prepared to be surprised. Naturally, Snake & Jake's can get really hot, crowded, and sweaty—if you're lucky. 7612 Oak St., Uptown. ✆ **504/861-2802.** www.snakeandjakes.com.

GAY NIGHTLIFE

The LGBTQ community is quite strong and visible in New Orleans, and the gay bars are some of the most bustling places in town—full of action nearly 24 hours a day (and more during Southern Decadence, p. 33, or it just seems that way). We only have room to list some of New Orleans's most popular LGBTQ nightspots, not those for every ilk, but they're out there and they're all most welcoming.

For more information, check ***Ambush***, 828-A Bourbon St. (✆ **504/522-8049;** www.ambushmag.com), a great source for the gay community in New Orleans and for visitors. Once you're in New Orleans, you can call the office or pick up a copy at Faubourg Marigny Art and Books (600 Frenchmen St.; ✆ **504/947-3700;** www.fabonfrenchmen.com) or at any of these bars.

Bars

In addition to those listed below, you might also try the **Golden Lantern,** 1239 Royal St. (☎ **504/529-2860**), a nice neighborhood spot where the bartender knows the patrons by name. It's the second-oldest gay bar in town, and one long-time patron said that "it used to look like one-half of Noah's Ark—with one of everything, one drag queen, one leather boy, one guy in a suit." If Levi's and leather is your scene, then **Rawhide 2010,** 740 Burgundy St. (☎ **504/525-8106;** www.rawhide2010.com), is your best bet.

The Bourbon Pub—Parade Disco This is more or less the most centrally located of the gay bars, with many of the other popular gay bars nearby. The downstairs pub offers a video bar and is the calmer of the two; it's open 24 hours daily and usually gets most crowded in the hour just before the Parade Disco opens. (**Note:** Sun nights the cover charge gets you all the draft beer you can drink 5–9pm.) The Parade Disco is upstairs and features a high-tech dance floor complete with lasers and smoke. It usually opens around 9pm, except on Sunday, when it gets going in the afternoon. 801 Bourbon St. ☎ **504/529-2107.** www.bourbon pub.com.

Café Lafitte in Exile This place is one of the oldest gay bars (if not *the* oldest) in the United States, having been around since 1953 and claiming Tennessee Williams as a former patron (believe what you will). There's a bar downstairs, and upstairs you'll find a pool table and a balcony that overlooks Bourbon Street. The whole shebang is open 24 hours. This is a cruise bar, but it doesn't attract a teeny-bopper or twink crowd. Mondays are campy movie nights; Wednesdays there's karaoke. 901 Bourbon St. ☎ **504/522-8397.** www.lafittes.com.

The Corner Pocket While the boast that they have the hottest male strippers in town may be perhaps too generous, you can decide for yourself by checking out this bar nightly after 9pm. The bar itself is none too special (and despite the name, the only draw for the pool table is that players might not be especially clothed), and draws a well-seasoned clientele. 940 St. Louis St. ☎ **504/568-9829.** www.cornerpocket.net.

Country Club ★ It's a bar, it's a pool, it's a restaurant, it's a club. It's a place you can sip a cocktail while soaking in a Jacuzzi, without having to stay in a fancy hotel (though there is an entry fee, ranging $7–$15; more for special events). Everyone's welcome at this Bywater neighborhood swimming hole, set in a converted Creole cottage with a pretty veranda and dining room. Best of all (or worst, depending), you don't have to worry about those pesky tan lines since clothes are a mere suggestion around the pool (fear not, they're required in the bar and dining room). 634 Louisa St. ☎ **504/945-0742.** www.thecountryclubneworleans.com.

1135 Decatur At this best-known lesbian club in the Quarter (formerly Whirling Dervish and Rubyfruit Jungle, and still a bit confused about its bar identity), all are welcome but you'll see more ink than lipstick. It's Goth-y and dark but for the dance floor lights. Various alternative nights rotate in and out, from burlesque to metal, but there's always dancing, strong drinks, and friendly regulars. 1135 Decatur St. ☎ **504/571-1863.**

Good Friends Bar & Queens Head Pub This bar and pub is very friendly to visitors and often wins the Gay Achievement Award for Best Neighborhood Gay Bar. The local clientele is happy to offer suggestions about where you might find the type of entertainment you're looking for. Downstairs is a mahogany bar and a

Oz is the city's best gay dance club.

pool table. Upstairs is the quiet, Victorian-style Queens Head Pub, open Friday through Sunday only (well, Sun's 6pm singalong is not so quiet). Open 24 hours on weekends and during Mardi Gras weekend; closes at 2am during the week. 740 Dauphine St. ✆ **504/566-7191.** www.goodfriendsbar.com.

LeRoundup LeRoundup attracts the most diverse crowd around, welcoming drag queens, the transgendered, and all persuasions—even well-groomed men in khakis. Expect encounters with working boys. It's open 24 hours. 819 St. Louis St. ✆ **504/561-8340.**

Dance Clubs

Oz Oz is the place to see and be seen, with a primarily young crowd. It was ranked the city's best dance club by *Gambit* magazine, and *Details* magazine named it one of the top 50 clubs in the country. The music is great, there's an incredible laser-light show, and from time to time there are go-go boys atop the bar. 800 Bourbon St. ✆ **504/593-9491.** www.ozneworleans.com. Cover varies.

THE PERFORMING ARTS

In addition to the resources below, culture vultures may want to see what the local universities have on tap: Check Loyola's website at www.loyno.edu/calendar and Tulane's at http://tulane.edu/calendar. We're awfully hopeful that the extensive renovations of the once-glorious **Saenger Theatre** (143 N. Rampart St. at Canal; ✆ **504/525-1052;** www.thesaengertheatre.com) will be completed by mid- to late 2012.

A performance put on by the New Orleans Opera Association.

Performing Arts Companies

OPERA

It wasn't until 1943 that the **New Orleans Opera Association** (✆ 504/529-2278; www.neworleansopera.org) was formed. They present several operas a season. Stars from New York's Metropolitan Opera Company frequently appear in leading roles, supported by talented local voices. The Met's touring company occasionally performs here, too. For most performances, seats start at $20. Performances are at the Mahalia Jackson Theater, 801 Rampart St. (enter from Basin St.).

DANCE

The **New Orleans Ballet Association** (✆ 504/522-0996; www.nobadance.com) presents excellent dance programs and runs a much-lauded educational program. Visiting dance companies, including some top names, perform regularly. Check the newspapers for current performances. The ballet's season generally runs from September through April. Performances are at the Mahalia Jackson Theater, 801 Rampart St. (enter from Basin St.) or NOCCA, 2800 Chartres St.

CLASSICAL MUSIC

The **Louisiana Philharmonic Orchestra** (✆ 504/523-6530; www.lpomusic.com) plays a subscription series of concerts during the fall-to-spring season and offers pops concerts on weekends in June and July; tickets start at $10. Performances take place at various locales including City Park, a suburban church, halls at Loyola and Tulane, and the Mahalia Jackson Theater.

Theaters

Contemporary Arts Center Located in the Warehouse District, the Contemporary Arts Center is best known for its changing exhibitions of contemporary art. Also on the premises are two theaters that frequently feature dance performances and concerts as well as experimental works by local playwrights. Call for the current schedule. 900 Camp St. © **504/528-3805.** www.cacno.org.

Le Chat Noir ★★ This cool-cat, swanky, cabaret-style theater in the Warehouse District (with tables, cocktails, and candles) features rotating performances of a variety of entertainment: jazz, cabaret shows (think Broadway tunes), musical revues, and plays, plus local actors doing play readings. They usually, but not exclusively, feature local talent. Prices run from free to $35, depending on the act featured, and reservations are suggested. Come early or stay late for cocktails and mingling. 715 St. Charles Ave. © **504/581-5812.** www.cabaretlechatnoir.com.

Mahalia Jackson Theater for the Performing Arts This cultural hub (located in Armstrong Park bordering the French Quarter) is home to the Louisiana Philharmonic Orchestra, the New Orleans Opera Association, and the New Orleans Ballet Association. Following a post-flood rehab with close attention paid to acoustics and lighting, the 2,100-seat theater's 2009 reopening gala featured performances by Itzhak Perlman, the New York City Ballet, and Placido Domingo. The handsome, bi-level theater also hosts Broadway touring companies, dance troupes, rock concerts, and other live acts. If you're considering mixing some highbrow into your visit, check the website to find out what's playing. 801 N. Rampart St. © **504/525-1052.** www.mahaliajacksontheater.com.

Southern Repertory Theatre ★ Focusing on the works of Southern playwrights and actors, the Southern Rep Theater is comfortable, intimate, and easily accessible from all downtown and French Quarter hotels. Expect to find productions by or (occasionally) about famous Southern playwrights (though not

Le Chat Noir hosts a variety of jazz, cabaret, and musical revue acts as well as readings and plays.

exclusively), projects by local playwrights, and even world premieres. It's located in Canal Place Shopping Centre, with ample parking available. *Tip:* Anything written by, starring, or otherwise mentioning the hyper-talented Ricky Graham is probably worth catching. Canal Place Shopping Centre, Level 3. (℗ **504/522-6545** or 504/891-8332. www.southernrep.com. Ticket prices vary by production, but usually $23–$35.

AN EVENING CRUISE

The *Creole Queen* (℗ **800/445-4109** or 504/524-0814; www.neworleans paddlewheels.com) and the slightly smaller *Steamboat Natchez* riverboat cruisers both host lovely (if a bit touristy) jazz cruises nightly, with extensive if mediocre Creole buffets, but much better live jazz and dancing against a backdrop of the city's sparkling skyline. The *Creole Queen* departures are at 8pm (boarding at 7pm) from the Canal Street Wharf; it's $64 per person including dinner or $40 without. The *Natchez* leaves at 7pm (boarding at 6pm) from the Toulouse Street Wharf behind Jax Brewery in the French Quarter; cost is $68 with dinner, $41 without ($34 and $21 for kids 6–12). Schedules are subject to change and reservations are required, so call ahead.

11

SIDE TRIPS FROM NEW ORLEANS

f you have time (an overall trip lasting more than 3 days, say), you should strongly consider a sojourn into the countryside outlying New Orleans. It makes for an interesting cultural and visual contrast to the big city. This chapter starts off by following the River Road and the plantation homes that line the banks of the Mississippi, heading upriver from New Orleans; the second part will take you a little more than 100 miles west of New Orleans to the heart of Acadiana, or Cajun Country.

On the River Road trip, you can see many of the highlights in a day trip, but it's quite possible to keep rambling north to visit the plantation homes in the St. Francisville area. That exploration calls for an overnight stay (more if you can), as does the Cajun Country trip (more if you can).

PLANTATIONS ALONG THE GREAT RIVER ROAD

If your image of plantations comes strictly from repeated viewings of *Gone With the Wind,* you may well be disappointed when you go plantation hopping. That particular Tara was a Hollywood creation. That said, you can get reasonably close visiting this picturesque area; imagine life as it was when these were working plantations—for better and worse.

Plantation houses, at least the existing ones that you can tour, are mostly humble in scale (they got grander after 1850, which most of these predate). The Creole style tends to be a low-slung, simple affair; the showier American style is closer to classic antebellum grandeur. Nevertheless, they're smaller than you might think, even cramped compared with the lavish mansions of turn-of-the-20th-century oil barons and today's nouveau riche. If your fantasies would be dashed without pillars and porticos, stick to Destrehan, San Francisco, Oak Alley, and Madewood. (The listings follow.)

The early planters of Louisiana were rugged frontier people. As they spread out along the Mississippi from New Orleans, they energetically cleared vast swamplands, to create unhindered waterways for transporting indigo and other cash crops. Rough flatboats moving produce to market could be capsized by rapids, snags, sandbars, and floating debris, or captured by river pirates. If they made it to New Orleans, these farming men (and a few extraordinary women) collected their pay and then went on wild drinking, gambling, and brawling sprees—earning them a reputation as barbarians among the French Quarter Creoles.

By the 1800s, Louisiana planters (and their slaves) had introduced large-scale farming, and brought more and more acres under cultivation. King cotton, rice, and sugar cane arrived on the scene around this time, bringing huge monetary returns. But natural dangers, a hurricane or swift change in the capricious Mississippi's course, could wipe out entire plantations and fortunes with little warning.

PREVIOUS PAGE: **Madewood plantation.**

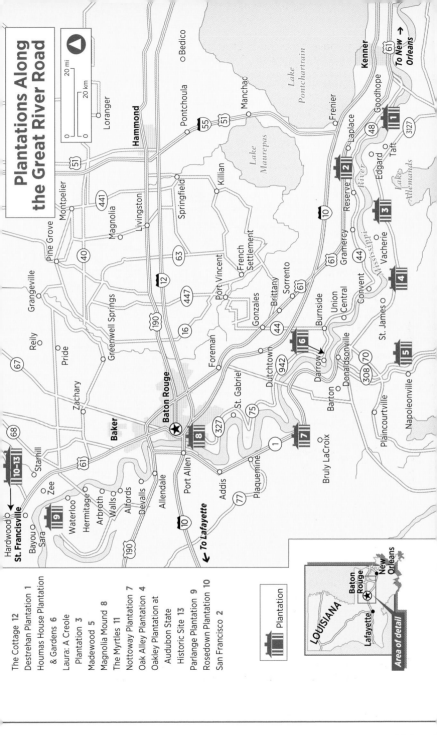

Plantations Along the Great River Road

The Cottage 12
Destrehan Plantation 1
Houmas House Plantation 6
Laura: A Creole
  Plantation 3
Madewood 5
Magnolia Mound 8
The Myrtles 11
Nottoway Plantation 7
Oak Alley Plantation 4
Oakley Plantation at
  Audubon State
  Historic Site 13
Parlange Plantation 9
Rosedown Plantation 10
San Francisco 2

Plantation

THE RIVERBOATS After 1812, the planters turned to speedier and safer new steamboats to transport their crops to the market. When the first steamboat (the *New Orleans,* built in Pittsburgh) chugged downriver belching sooty smoke, it was so dirty, dangerous, and potentially explosive that it was dubbed a "floating volcano."

Over a 30-year period, however, vast improvements were made, and the steamboats came to be viewed as veritable floating pleasure palaces. Moving goods to market may have (literally) floated the boat, but the lavish staterooms and ornate "grand salons" put a whole new face on river travel. Family and slaves could now take the trip in comfort, set up dual residences, and spend the social season and winters in elegant New Orleans town houses. Also, it became possible to ship fine furnishings upriver to plantation homes, creating a more elegant lifestyle amid the fields.

The riverboats had a darker side, however. The boats were the realm of some cunning and colorful characters: the riverboat gambler and "confidence" (or "con") man. Huge fortunes were won from, and lost to, these silver-tongued professional gamers and crooks, and no doubt a few deeds to plantations changed hands at the table on a river steamboat.

BUILDING THE PLANTATION HOUSES During this period of prosperity, from the 1820s until the beginning of the Civil War, most of the impressive plantation homes were built, as were many grand town houses in cities like New Orleans and Natchez.

The plantation home was the focal point of a self-sustaining community and generally was located near the riverfront; most were modest, but some had wide, oak-lined avenues leading from their entrances to a wharf. On either side of the avenue would frequently be *garçonnières* (small houses, sometimes used to give adolescent sons and their friends privacy or as guesthouses). The kitchen was often behind the main house, separated from the house because of fire danger; close by was the overseer's office. Some plantations had pigeon houses or dovecotes—and all had the inevitable slave quarters, in twin lines along the lane to the crops or across the fields and out of sight. The first houses were simple "raised cottages," with long, sloping roofs; cement-covered brick walls on the ground floor; and wood-and-brick (brick between posts) construction in the living quarters on the second floor. Influenced by West Indian styles, these colonial structures suited the sultry Louisiana climate and swampy building sites and made use of native materials.

In the 1820s, homes that combined traces of the West Indian style with some Greek Revival and Georgian influences—a style that has been dubbed Louisiana Classic—began to appear. Large, rounded columns and wide galleries usually surrounded the main body of the house, and the roof was dormered. Inside, two rooms flanked a wide central hall. They had few imported interior details like fireplace mantels, and they were constructed of native materials, such as local cypress and bricks of river clay, sealed with cement.

GRAND & GRANDER By the 1850s, many planters were quite prosperous, and their homes became more grandiose and much larger—some with 30 to 40 rooms. Many embraced extravagant Victorian architecture and gave it a unique Louisiana flavor; others borrowed features from northern Italian villas, and some followed Gothic lines (notably the fantastic San Francisco plantation, sometimes called "steamboat Gothic;" p. 309). Planters and their families traveled to Europe during this period, and brought back ornate furnishings and skilled artisans (until Louisiana artisans such as Mallard and Seignouret developed skills that rivaled the Europeans). Glittering crystal chandeliers and *faux marbre* (false marble) mantels appeared.

Families and social life grew—and so did houses and egos. The Madewood house on Bayou Lafourche was built for no other reason than to outshine Woodlawn, the beautiful home of the builder's brother (unfortunately, not open to the public).

The planters' enormous wealth stemmed from an economy based on human servitude. The injustice and frequent cruelty of slavery, however, were the seeds of its own demise. After the Civil War, emancipation had an inestimable effect on Southern plantations. Farming became impossible without that large, cheap labor base. During Reconstruction, lands were often confiscated and turned over intact to people who later proved unable to run the large-scale operations; many were broken up into smaller, more manageable farms. Increasing international competition began to erode the cotton and sugar markets. The culture represented by the few houses that remain today emerged and died away in a span of less than 100 years.

THE PLANTATION HOUSES TODAY Where dozens of grand homes once dotted the landscape along and around the river, relatively few remain. Several that survived the Civil War fell victim to fires, floods, or industrial development. Others, too costly to be maintained, have been left to the ravages of dampness and decay. A few, however, have been saved, preserved, and upgraded with plumbing and electricity. Most of the old houses are private residences, but some are open to visitors, the admission fees supplementing upkeep.

Tours of plantations are a hit-or-miss affair—much depends on your guide. If you visit several, you'll begin to hear many of the same facts about plantation life after a while, sometimes as infill for missing or boring history. We describe the best experiences below.

Planning Your Trip

All the plantation homes shown on the map on p. 305 are within easy driving distance of New Orleans. How many you can tour in a day will depend on your endurance (in the car and on your feet), how early you set out, how many of the same details you can stand to hear repeated, and how late you want to return (the small highways get a little intimidating after dark). You'll be driving through sugar cane fields and land ravaged by oil and chemical development. Don't expect to enjoy broad river views along the Great River Road (the roadway's name on *both* sides of the Mississippi); it's obscured by tall levees. But you'll pass through little towns that date from plantation days, and have the luxury of detouring to inspect them—and take a chance on finding your favorite new road food.

If you have minimal time, we suggest viewing just Laura and Oak Alley (see below); they are a mile apart, and each offers a different perspective on plantation life (Laura being classic understated Creole, while Tara-esque Oak Alley represents the showy Americans) and the tourism industry (Oak Alley is slick and glitzy, while Laura is more low-key but a superb presentation). Both are approximately an hour's drive from New Orleans.

If you're in New Orleans on **Christmas Eve,** consider driving along the River Road to see the huge bonfires residents build on the levees to light the way for the Christ child and Papa Noël (who rides in a sleigh drawn by—what else?—eight alligators!).

Some grand plantations were alongside bayous, which also provided water transportation. These are farther away from New Orleans, and listed separately, with some lodging recommendations. There are also listings for lodgings in St. Francisville, which can serve as a convenient plantation-tour base.

Organized Tours

A plantation-house bus tour is a stress-free way to visit the River Road region from New Orleans (someone else deals with planning and transportation), though most of the tours visit only one or two of the houses described below. In general, tour guides are well informed, and the buses are an easy, comfortable way to get around in unfamiliar territory. Almost every New Orleans tour company operates a River Road plantation tour.

The 4½-hour tours offered by **Gray Line** (© 800/535-7786 or 504/569-1401; www.graylineneworleans.com) are a reliable choice, visiting either Oak Alley or Laura Plantation, and prices include admission and transportation from Toulouse Street at the Mississippi River in the French Quarter. Tours depart around noon for Oak Alley on Monday, Wednesday, Friday, and Saturday, and for Laura on Tuesday, Thursday, and Sunday. Exact times vary during the year, so call ahead. The price is $52 for adults and $26 for children 6 to 12.

If you prefer a smaller group, **Tours by Isabelle** (© 888/223-2093 or 504/398-0365; www.toursbyisabelle.com) takes up to 13 people in a comfortable van on an 8-hour expedition to Oak Alley and Laura Plantations, plus a bayou tour. The $146 cost includes lunch at Oak Alley's restaurant; for $180 the swamp tour is done via speedy airboat. The tour runs only when six or more people request it, so you might have to wait a day or two for a large enough group. Isabelle offers many other tour permutations, including an All Day Plantation tour, from 8am to 5pm, and visits Destrehan, San Francisco, and Houmas House, where one can purchase lunch. The cost is $125.

Plantations Between New Orleans & Baton Rouge

The plantations below are listed in the order in which they appear on the map, running along the Mississippi north, out of New Orleans. Many people choose one or two homes—Oak Alley, Nottoway, Laura, and Madewood are popular ones—and find the quickest route (get a good map). If you choose to follow the route along the riverbanks, know that you will have to cross the Mississippi bridge a few times to see every plantation. The windy river makes distances deceiving; give yourself more time than you think you'll need. All the plantations discussed in this section are roughly 1 hour from New Orleans and approximately 15 minutes from each other.

Destrehan Plantation ★★ Its proximity to New Orleans (about 30 min. away), in-character docents, and appearance in *Interview with the Vampire* have made Destrehan Manor a popular plantation jaunt. It's the oldest intact plantation home in the lower Mississippi Valley open to the public. It was built in 1787 by a free person of color for a wealthy Frenchman and was modified between

Destrehan Plantation is the oldest intact plantation home in the lower Mississippi Valley open to the public.

1830 and 1840 from its already dated French colonial style to Greek Revival. Its warmly colored, graceful lines are aesthetically pleasing.

The tour, led by costumed guides (it's better than it sounds) is worth taking. The house stayed in the original family's possession until 1910 (some female descendants are still on the board that oversees the place), so a fair amount is documented, and some of the furnishings (including a table used by Lafayette) are original. One of the rooms has been left deliberately unrenovated, and its messy deconstructed state shows you the humble rawness under the usual public grandeur. ***Important note:*** This is perhaps the only plantation that is truly accessible for those with disabilities; there are entrance ramps and an elevator to the second floor.

13034 River Rd., La. 48, Destrehan. © **877/453-2095** or 985/764-8758. www.destrehan plantation.org. Admission $15 adults, $5 children 6–16, free for children 5 and under. Daily 9am–4pm. Closed New Year's Day, Mardi Gras, Easter, Thanksgiving, and Dec 24–25.

San Francisco ★ This fanciful mansion, a brightly colored creation known as steamboat Gothic, is farther from Destrehan than it seems on the map. But it's worth the trip if you want to see something other than a cookie-cutter plantation home. Located 2 miles north of Reserve, the house was built between 1853 and 1856 by Edmond B. Marmillion. Unfortunately, Marmillion died shortly after its completion and never occupied the home, which was willed to his sons, Valsin and Charles. In 1855, while on a grand tour of Europe, Valsin met and married Louise Seybold. They redecorated, after which Valsin jokingly declared that he was *sans fruscin,* or "without a cent." Thus its first name, St. Frusquin. When Achille Bougère bought the estate, the name was changed to San Francisco.

The three-story Gothic house has wide galleries resembling a ship's double decks, and twin stairs lead to a broad main portal. Inside, the owner created beautiful carved woodwork, and paintings alive with flowers, birds, nymphs, and cherubs, on walls and ceilings of cypress tongue-and-groove boards.

San Francisco plantation home.

2646 Hwy. 44, Garyville. ☏ **888/509-1756** or 985/535-2341. www.sanfranciscoplantation.org. Admission $15 adults, $14 military with ID and AAA members, $7 children 7–17, free for children 6 and under. Daily Apr–Oct 9:30am–5pm, tours start at 9:40am and last tour at 4:40pm; Nov–Mar 9am–5pm, tours start at 10am and last tour at 4pm. Closed New Year's Day, Mardi Gras, Easter, Thanksgiving Day, and Dec 24–25.

Laura: A Creole Plantation ★★★ If you see only one plantation, make it Laura: the very model of a modern plantation (well, for today's "tourism" crop). Instead of the hoop-skirted tours found elsewhere, Laura delivers a comprehensive view of daily life on an 18th- and 19th-century plantation, a cultural history of Louisiana's Creole population, and a dramatic, in-depth look at one Creole family.

Fortunately, much is known about this house and the family that lived here, thanks to extensive records (more than 5,000 documents researched in France), particularly the detailed memoirs of Laura Locoul (for whom the plantation is named). Hundreds of original artifacts, from cookware to jewelry, are on display in this classic Creole house: simple on the outside but with real magic within. Still, all of the outbuildings are slowly being renovated.

A huge fire hit the plantation in 2004. Fortunately, employees saved many artifacts and much of the original house. During the restoration, they returned the house to the 1805 period, with new accurate details and Louisiana-made furniture. Basic tours of the main building and the property start at 10am, run approximately every 40 minutes, and are organized around true (albeit spiced-up) stories from the history of the home and its residents. (*Of special note:* The stories that eventually became the beloved B'rer Rabbit were first collected here by a folklorist in the 1870s.) Special 1½ hour tours on subjects including Creole architecture, Creole women, children, slaves, and the "Americanization of Louisiana" can be scheduled in advance; tours in French are offered Tuesday and Saturday. Handouts in several additional languages are available. *Note:* To

Hundreds of original artifacts are on display at Laura: A Creole Planation.

learn about Laura's family's life in New Orleans, go on the **Le Monde Creole** tours (p. 205).

2247 La. 18, Vacherie. ✆ **888/799-7690** or 225/265-7690. www.lauraplantation.com. Admission $18 adults, $16 for military and AAA members, $5 children 6–17, free for children 5 and under. Daily 10am–4pm. Last tour begins at 4pm. Closed Jan 1, Mardi Gras, Easter, Thanksgiving, and Dec 25.

Oak Alley Plantation ★★★ This is precisely what comes to mind when most people think "plantation." A splendid white house, its porch lined with giant columns, approached by a magnificent drive lined with stately oak trees—yep, it's all here. Consequently, this is the most famous plantation house in Louisiana—and the location of several Hollywood movies. It's also the slickest operation, with an expensive lunch buffet (we say BYO picnic), hoop-skirted guides, and golf carts traversing the blacktopped property. It's an interesting contrast with Laura (above), and they are just a mile apart, so we highly recommend that you visit both.

The house was built in 1839 by Jacques Telesphore Roman III and was named Bon Séjour—but if you walk out to the levee and look back at the ¼-mile avenue of 300-year-old live oaks, you'll see why steamboat passengers quickly dubbed it "Oak Alley." To match the 28 trees, Roman planned his house with 28 fluted Doric columns. Oak Alley lay disintegrating until 1914, when the Hardins of New Orleans bought it. It passed to Mr. and Mrs. Andrew Stewart in 1925, whose loving restoration is responsible for its National Historic Landmark designation.

Little is known about the families who lived here, so tours focus on general plantation facts. Recent renovations have helped return the house to its 1830s roots, with accurately reproduced furnishings. The plantation hosts a bonfire party in December.

Overnight accommodations are available in five really nice century-old Creole cottages complete with sitting rooms, porches, and air-conditioning.

Oak Alley is recognizable to many because of its long drive lined with stately oaks.

Rates are $130 to $175 and include breakfast but not a tour. A few acres away is the Rene House, with four pretty bedrooms (each with private bathrooms) and a kitchen. The whole place goes for $410 a night, or rooms can be let individually. The overpriced restaurant is open for breakfast and lunch daily from 8:30am to 3pm.

3645 La. 18 (60 miles from New Orleans), Vacherie. © **800/44-ALLEY** (442-5539) or 225/265-2151. www.oakalleyplantation.com. Admission $18 adults, $7.50 students 13–18, $4.50 children 6–12, free for children 5 and under. Discounts for 65 and over, AAA members, and active military. Grounds open daily at 9am; tours begin every half-hour at 10am; Mon–Fri last tour at 4pm; Sat-Sun tours until 5pm. Closed Jan 1, Thanksgiving, and Dec 25.

Madewood ★★ This imposing house, a two-story Greek Revival on Bayou Lafourche, just below Napoleonville, is one of the best-preserved plantation mansions. Tours are only offered for groups of 10 or more, but an overnight stay lets you fulfill your own plantation dreams—literally. Accommodations, unlike those offered by other plantation homes, are in the main house, so after hours you and the other guests get to pretend the 20 rooms are yours, all yours (or you can stay in Charlet House, a detached cottage on the grounds). When you hear the recent history, however, you might be rather glad it's not.

A youngest brother originally built Madewood for the sole purpose of out-doing his older brother's elegant mansion, Woodlawn. It took 8 years to con-struct, but the owner never got to gloat—he died of yellow fever just before it was finished in 1848. Later, Madewood fell into disrepair and stood empty. It was bought in 1964 by the parents of the present owner, Keith Marshall, whose laborious renovation tales demonstrate how much work it is to maintain these glorious houses.

Guests enjoy grand canopied or half-tester (curtains at the head end) beds, wine and cheese in the library, a multicourse Southern dinner (sometimes served by a charming woman whose family has worked at Madewood for seven generations; be sure to chat with her), brandy in the parlor, and coffee in bed the next morning followed by a full plantation breakfast. Now that's gracious Southern living. Rates are $265 for two Sunday through Thursday, $298 Friday and Saturday; the honeymoon suite is $329. Unnamed celebrities make this a getaway spot, and Brad Pitt slept here while filming *Interview with the Vampire.*

4250 La. 308, Napoleonville. © **985/369-7151.** www.madewood.com. Tours available for groups of 10 or more; call for appointment and rates. Closed Thanksgiving Eve and Day, Christmas Eve and Day, New Year's Eve and Day.

Houmas House Plantation & Gardens ★★ Houmas is actually two houses joined together. The original house was a four-room structure built in 1775. In 1828 a larger, Greek Revival–style house was built next to it, and subsequently a roof was put over both. A former sugar plantation, little is known about most of its owners, until the late Dr. George Crozat of New Orleans purchased and restored it as a home. Recent owner Kevin Kelly now lives there, and the place feels like an active home.

Live oaks, magnolias, and beautifully landscaped formal gardens frame Houmas House. The inside has been lovingly brought back to early-1800s detail, including period-accurate paint, 19th-century paintings, and antique rugs. Costumed guides deliver stories from the house's busy past. Because scenes from *All My Children* were shot here, be sure to ask for those Susan Lucci stories (they've got 'em). A casual cafe and an excellent upscale restaurant are also on the grounds.

40136 La. 942, Burnside (58 miles from New Orleans). © **888/323-8314** or 225/473-9830. www. houmashouse.com. Admission (including guided tour) $20 adults, $15 children ages 13–18, $10 children ages 6–12, free for children 5 and under; gardens and grounds only $10. Mon–Tues 9am–5pm; Wed–Sun 9am–8pm. Closed Dec 25 and Jan 1. Take I-10 from New Orleans or Baton Rouge. Exit on La. 44 to Burnside and turn right on La. 942.

Nottoway Plantation ★★ Nottoway is everything you want in a dazzling Old South mansion. Dating from 1858, it's the largest existing plantation house in the South, a mammoth structure with 64 rooms (covering 53,000 sq. ft.) and pillars to rival the White House's. Saved from Civil War destruction by a Northern gunboat officer who had once been a guest here, the still-handsome interiors feature marvelous curlicue plasterwork, hand-carved Corinthian columns of cypress wood in the ballroom, beautiful archways, and original crystal chandeliers.

You can (and should) stay here, in rooms with period furnishings and luxurious bathrooms ($190–$360 per night, including breakfast; room service is available). Some rooms are on the tour and may require late check-ins and early checkouts.

Mississippi River Rd., White Castle. © **866/LASOUTH** (527-6884) or 225/545-2730. www. nottoway.com. Admission $20 adults, $6 children ages 6–12, free for children 5 and under. Daily 9am–4pm, tours begin on the hour. Closed Dec 25. From New Orleans, follow I-10 west to La. 22 exit, then turn left on La. 70 across Sunshine Bridge. Exit onto La. 1 and drive 14 miles north through Donaldsonville. From Baton Rouge, take I-10 west to Plaquemine exit and then La. 1 south for 18 miles.

WHERE TO EAT

Note that many of the plantations operate their own so-so restaurants.

In Vacherie

B&C Seafood Market & Cajun Restaurant ★ CAJUN/SEAFOOD We believe in "when in Rome," so join the locals at this decidedly low-atmosphere family operation for some fresh seafood (the house specialty—boiled or fried), gumbo, jambalaya, po' boys, and our favorite, fried *boudin* (sausage) balls (they make a great car snack).

2155 Hwy. 18. ✆ **225/265-8356.** All items $5–$24. AE, DISC, MC, V. Mon–Fri 10am–6pm; Sat 10am–5pm.

St. Francisville & Surrounding Plantations

St. Francisville, 30 miles northwest of Baton Rouge, doesn't look like much on approach, but by the time you get to the center of town, you are utterly charmed. Many of the plantations described below are nearby. It's roughly a 2-hour drive from New Orleans and pretty much requires an overnight stay. There is lodging in town if you don't stay at one of the plantations described below, or you could decamp to Baton Rouge, but only if you have to. Contact the **St. Francisville tourism information office** for more information (✆ **800/789-4221** or 225/635-4224; www.stfrancisville.us; Mon–Sat 9am–5pm, Sun 9:30am–5pm), or the **Baton Rouge Area Convention and Visitors Bureau** (✆ **800/LA-ROUGE** [527-6843]; www.visitbatonrouge.com). Request their useful *Baton Rouge Visitors Guide*. It's worth pointing out that this is *not* Cajun Country; the area has American plantations only and no French history at all.

Magnolia Mound ★ This plantation home was built in the late 1700s as a small settler's house, taking its name from its setting amid a grove of trees on a bluff overlooking the Mississippi. As prosperity came to the lower Mississippi Valley, it was enlarged and renovated, eventually becoming the center of a 900-acre plantation. Its single story is nearly 5 feet off the ground and has a front porch 80 feet across. The hand-carved woodwork and the ceiling in the parlor are authentically restored. One of the oldest wooden structures in the state, it is typical French Creole in architecture. Costumed guides take you through the slave cabins and house, authentically furnished in Louisiana and early Federal styles (though the roof is ca. 2011).

2161 Nicholson Dr., Baton Rouge. ✆ **225/343-4955.** www.magnoliamound.org. Admission $10 adults 49 and under, $8 50 and over and students 18–22, $4 children 5–17, free for children 4 and under. Mon–Sat 10am–4pm; Sun 1–4pm. Tours begin on the hour; last tour begins at 3pm.

Inside the kitchen at Magnolia Mound.

Parlange Plantation ★ This plantation is one of the few that still functions as a working farm (and as such, is only open by appointment). Built in 1750 by Marquis Vincent de Ternant, the house is one of the oldest in the state, and its two stories rise above a raised brick basement. Galleries encircle the house, which is flanked by two brick *pigeonniers* (pigeon houses). Indigo was planted here at first; in the 1800s, sugar cane became the main crop. It's still grown, along with corn, soybeans, and cattle. During the Civil War, this house hosted generals from both sides (General Nathaniel Banks of the Union and General Dick Taylor of the Confederacy)—not, of course, at the same time. Parlange is a National Historic Landmark and is owned by relatives of the original builders.

8211 False River Rd., New Roads. ✆ **225/638-8410.** www.nps.gov/history/nr/travel/louisiana/ par.htm. Admission $10 adults; call for appointment and children's rates (may not be appropriate for young children). From Baton Rouge, take U.S. 190 19 miles west and then La. 1 another 8 miles north.

Oakley Plantation at Audubon State Historic Site ★ Oakley Plantation, 3 miles east of U.S. 61, is where John James Audubon came to study and paint the wildlife of this part of Louisiana. Built in 1799, it is a three-story frame house with the raised basement typical of that era. A curved stairway joins the two galleries, and the whole house has a simplicity that bespeaks its age. When Audubon was here, he tutored a daughter of the family and painted some 32 of his *Birds of America* series. Some original prints from his portfolio and many fine antiques are displayed, and a walk through the gardens and nature trails will explain the location's appeal to Audubon. Oakley is part of the 100-acre Audubon State Commemorative Area, a wildlife sanctuary that would have gladdened the naturalist's heart.

La. 965, St. Francisville. ✆ **225/635-3739.** Admission $4 adults, free for seniors (63 and over) and children 12 and under. Daily 9am–5pm. Guided tours of the house hourly 10am–4pm. Closed Jan 1, Thanksgiving, and Dec 25.

Rosedown Plantation ★★ By far the most impressive and historic of the more far-flung plantations, Rosedown is notable for its dramatic gardens and a tour stuffed with intriguing trivia, courtesy of more than 8,000 documents in their archives. Just east of St. Francisville, Rosedown was completed in 1834 for Daniel Turnbull (whose son, William, married Martha Washington's great-great-granddaughter) on land granted by the Spanish in 1789. The two-story house, flanked by one-story wings, combines classic and indigenous Louisiana styles. A wide avenue of ancient oaks, their branches meeting overhead, leads up to the house. The 28 acres of historic gardens, dotted with marble statuary, date to 1835 and came to be one of the great horticultural collections of the 19th and 20th centuries. Unfortunately, Rosedown's

Rosedown Plantation is notable for its dramatic gardens.

ownership is now in the hands of the state of Louisiana, and many of its wonderful family treasures have been lost (well, sold, but don't get anyone started on *that* scandal). Still, you can easily spend 2 hours wandering here.

12501 Hwy. 10 (at La. 10 and U.S. 61), St. Francisville. © **888/376-1867** or 225/635-3332. www. lastateparks.com. Admission (house tour and historic gardens) $10 adults, $8 seniors, $4 students 6–17, free for children 5 and under. Daily 9am–5pm; tours begin at 10am. Closed Jan 1, Thanksgiving Day, and Christmas Day.

WHERE TO STAY IN ST. FRANCISVILLE

Lodging options in St. Francisville include two other worthy (if slightly less interesting) plantations with rooms to let: The **Cottage,** at 10528 Cottage Lane, St. Francisville, LA 70775 (© **225/635-3674;** www.cottageplantation.com), is a rambling country home 5 miles north of St. Francisville, built between 1795 and 1859. It's nothing grand, but the two-story cypress house has a long gallery out front, a nice relaxing place to imagine life when General Andrew Jackson stayed here (after his victory in the Battle of New Orleans). The Cottage's interior looks very much as it did back in the 1800s, and is still a working family farm of some 360 acres. The six guest rooms are a mix of elegant (huge four-poster canopy beds) and funky (icky motel room carpeting) and there's a small pool open during summer. Breakfast is served in the elegant main house dining room. Room prices range from $115 to $130; no kids under 12 are allowed.

There's also the **Myrtles,** at 7747 U.S. 61 (PO Box 1100), St. Francisville, LA 70775 (© **225/635-6277;** www.myrtlesplantation.com). The 1795 home is beautiful and well-preserved, if slightly dull, and rooms and baths (some shared) vary in size. But it has the great selling point of being haunted, and Friday and Saturday night there are kitschy fun "mystery" tours with guides telling spooky sighting tales. Rooms range from $115 to $230.

Rooms should be booked well in advance. The St. Francisville **tourism information office** (p. 314) can also provide a list of (and suggestions regarding) local B&Bs.

Barrow House Inn ★★ The Barrow House Inn is actually two guesthouses: the Barrow House and the Printer's House. Both are listed on the National Register of Historic Places and located in the heart of St. Francisville's charming historic district. The Printer's House, dating from the 1780s, is the oldest in town and was built and occupied by the monks for whom St. Francisville is named. Across the street is the New England saltbox–style Barrow House (ca. 1809). Owned and operated by Shirley Dittloff and her son Christopher, the houses have been restored and furnished with mid-1800s antiques. Each room has fine furniture, and many have claw-foot tubs. The Empire Suite is the most popular, but we'd go for the Peach Suite just to try the

 Grandmother's Buttons

Once in St. Francisville, stop by **Grandmother's Buttons** ★, at 9814 Royal St. (© 800/580-6941 or 225/635-4107; www.grandmothersbuttons.com). The owner makes jewelry from antique and vintage buttons (from Victorian brass picture buttons to 1940s Bakelite)—one-of-a-kind, amazing creations. We've bought more earrings, brooches, and other gewgaws from here than we could ever possibly wear. Don't overlook their fascinating (really) Button Museum. They're open Monday to Saturday from 10am to 5:30pm, Sunday 11am to 5pm.

authentic Spanish-moss mattress—the only one in the country! The upstairs Hideaway Suite has modern furnishing but displays the results of a Civil War cannonball hit on the exposed joists. The kitchen is well stocked with drinks and munchy snacks, while the Dittloffs offer breakfast in the historic dining room. In addition to numerous pampering touches, guests also have access to a mini space exploration museum dedicated to Shirley's father, Jim Chamberlin, a pioneer in American space history.

9779 Royal St. (PO Box 2550), St. Francisville, LA 70775. www.topteninn.com. © **225/635-4791.** Fax 225/635-1863. 7 units, all with private bathroom. $115–$135 double; $160 suite. Extra person $30. Rates include complimentary wine. AE, DISC, MC, V. **Amenities:** Dining room (breakfast only). *In room:* A/C, TV/DVD player, movie library (w/more than 400 movies!), Wi-Fi (free).

Butler Greenwood Plantation B&B ★★ This is a dynamite place to stay (as a plantation tour, it's nothing you won't see elsewhere—though it is one of few that is still owned and occupied by the original family, and still a full-time family home), starting with the setting: There are extensive grounds full of tangled oak trees, plus a pond with resident ducks. The front main house (tours can be arranged for $5) is full of original family furnishings. The guest quarters are private cottages, each stocked with breakfast supplies and with its own personality, from the **Old Kitchen** (with the original 150-ft. well, covered by glass so guests can peer down it), to the **Gazebo,** with old church windows, to the storybook-cunning three-story **Dovecot.** Some rooms have Jacuzzis, fireplaces, and decks overlooking a minigorge; it's a splendid romantic retreat. Be sure to ask the owner, a prolific author, about her true-crime book that details a true crime she herself survived.

8345 U.S. 61, St. Francisville, LA 70775. www.butlergreenwood.com.© **225/635-6312.** Fax 225/635-6370. 8 units, all with private bathroom. $135 double. Rates include continental breakfast. AE, MC, V. **Amenities:** Pool. *In room:* A/C, cable TV, kitchen.

St. Francisville Inn ★ This budget alternative to local B&Bs has a pool; plain, motel-comfortable rooms (the top-end choice is the king with the Jacuzzi tub); and a few antiques tossed into the mix. But the owners inject plenty of family-friendly hospitality, and offer a small but top-heavy breakfast buffet (also open to locals), with choices like bacon, grits, filled crepes, and pastries. There's also a "wine parlor," a good vibe, and enough space for a small group. The owners can also prepare tasty group dinners.

5720 Commerce St., St. Francisville, LA 70775. www.stfrancisvilleinn.com. © **800/488-6502** or 225/635-6502. Fax 225/635-6421. 10 units. $90 single; $100 double; $115 Jacuzzi room. Rates include full buffet breakfast. AE, DC, DISC, MC, V. **Amenities:** Pool. *In room:* A/C, TV, Wi-Fi (free).

3 V Tourist Court ★★★ 🛏 Not much space, but good value and of oddball interest, this genuine 1930s tourist court consists of wee cottages with their original interior fixtures and wood ceilings untouched. Each has a spiffy color scheme, with sweet bed linens topping excellent queen-size mattresses (which nearly take up the whole adorable room), teeny kitchenettes, and nice basic bathrooms. Additionally, there's a two-bedroom cabin with full kitchen, and a coffee shop, restaurant, eco-friendly hair salon, and massage therapist on the grounds. Don't expect five-star service, but it's a great deal for a weekend jaunt, and you're right in the middle of the fun local scene.

5689 Commerce St., St. Francisville, LA 70775. © **225/721-7003.** 9 units. $75 double; $125 cabin. AE, MC, V. *In room:* A/C, TV, fridge, Wi-Fi (free).

WHERE TO EAT IN ST. FRANCISVILLE

For a light snack or drink, consider **Bird Man Coffee & Books** (5687 E. Commerce St.; ℭ **225/635-3665**), on the same grounds as the 3 V Tourist Court and Magnolia Cafe. "It's got the best espresso around," a visiting Polish man told us, and who are we to disagree with such a coffee authority? This small bookstore/coffeehouse, open from 7am to 5pm on weekdays, 8am to 6pm on Saturdays, 8am to 4pm on Sundays, offers excellent drinks and decent baked goods.

Magnolia Cafe ★★★ 🎁 CAFE This sweet cafe has become the center of a local scene thanks to a newish bar and airy patio that features live music on Friday nights. Those who have to eat étouffée and jambalaya may be disappointed by the less-than-local-centric menu, but everyone else should be thoroughly pleased. Don't be deceived by the seemingly ordinary menu, which is heavy on salads and sandwiches—even a humble turkey on pita is fresh and striking. Look also for a spicy garlic shrimp po' boy with pepper jack cheese, muffulettas, and even enchiladas. Dinner brings steak and fish entrees, and fancy-ish appetizers.

5687 E. Commerce St. ℭ **225/635-6528.** Everything under $25. MC, V. Sun–Wed 10am–4pm; Thurs–Sat 10am–10pm. Bar opens and closes with restaurant usually.

CAJUN COUNTRY

The official name of this area is Acadiana, and it consists of a rough triangle of Louisiana made up of 22 parishes (counties), from St. Landry Parish at the top of the triangle to the Gulf of Mexico at its base. Lafayette is Acadiana's "capital," and it's dotted with such towns as St. Martinville, New Iberia, Abbeville, and Eunice. You won't find its boundaries on any map, nor the name "Acadiana" stamped across it. But those 22 parishes are Cajun Country, and its history and culture are unique in America.

Meet the Cajuns

The Cajun history is a sad one, but it produced a people and a culture well worth getting to know.

THE ACADIAN ODYSSEY In the early 1600s, colonists from France began settling the southeastern coast of Canada in a region of Nova Scotia they named Acadia. They developed a peaceful agricultural society based on the values of a strong Catholic faith, deep love of family, and respect for their relatively small landholdings. This pastoral existence was isolated from the

 tuning in TO CAJUN COUNTRY

Our standard soundtrack for the drive from New Orleans to Cajun Country begins with the excellent **WWOZ 90.7** FM (to which we're assiduously tuned while in the city). After an hour on the road, static takes over, signaling the unwrapping of whatever new music we've wisely recently purchased from Louisiana Music Factory (p. 263). In about half a CD's time, we can usually pull in **KBON 101.1** FM for some rollickin' Cajun and zydeco tunes. At that point we know we've arrived, as much in geography as mood. (Even the ads are good!)

THE REAL evangeline

You may know Henry Wadsworth Longfellow's epic poem *Evangeline*—the story of Evangeline and Gabriel, Acadian lovers who spent their lives searching for each other after being wrenched from their homeland. In real life, Evangeline was Emmeline Labiche, and her sweetheart was Louis Pierre Arceneaux. Their story has a different ending from the poet's—Emmeline found Louis Pierre, after years of searching, in Cajun Country, in St. Martinville. The tragedy was that, by then, Louis had given up hope of finding her and was pledged to another. She died of a broken heart in Louisiana, not Philadelphia. (***Note:*** Sorry, probably none of the above is true at all. Emmeline and Louise Pierre were yet another fictional couple, invented to build a "real life back story" for the popular poem. But who cares? It's a good yarn!)

mainstream of European culture for nearly 150 years, until 1713 when Acadia became the property of the British under the Treaty of Utrecht. For more than 40 years, the Acadians were harassed by the king's representatives, who tried to force them to pledge allegiance to the British Crown, renounce Catholicism, and embrace the king's Protestant religion. When the Acadians steadfastly refused, the British governor of the region sent in troops. Villages were burned; husbands, wives, and children were separated as ships were loaded to deport them; and a 10-year odyssey began.

Some Acadians returned to France, some went to England (some to return to America decades later), many were put ashore along America's East Coast, and some wound up in the West Indies. Hundreds of lives were lost to the terrible conditions onboard.

Louisiana, with its strong French background, was a natural destination for Acadians hoping to reestablish a permanent home. In 1765, Bernard Andry brought a band of 231 men, women, and children to the region now known as Acadiana.

The swampy land differed greatly from what they had left in Nova Scotia. Bogs interlaced with bayous and lakes; thick forests teemed with wildlife. They built small levees (or dikes) along the banks and drained fields for small farms and pastures.

A NEW PRIDE After many decades during which Cajuns shied away from their roots (children were beaten in school for speaking French, which was considered a sign of ignorance; Cajun music was considered primitive or hokey), the Cajun culture has experienced a resurgence of popularity and respect, and gained a new sense of community pride.

Cajun Language

This essay was provided by two-time Grammy nominee Ann Allen Savoy, who is, along with her husband, Marc, a musician in the Savoy-Doucet Cajun Band and in her own groups, the Magnolia Sisters and Ann Savoy and the Sleepless Knights. Ann and Marc have also spawned a musical dynasty, including their son Joel (founding member of the Red Stick Ramblers and head of Valcour Records), their son Wilson (of Pine Leaf Boys fame), and their daughter Sarah (of the Paris-based Sarah Savoy and the Francadians)—all stellar musicians leading the charge of a new generation.

The French influence in Louisiana is one of the things that sets the state apart from the rest of the United States. As soon as you get west of Baton Rouge, you can cruise down the Louisiana highways listening to French radio. The accent is sharp and bright with occasional English words thrown in (*"On va revenir right back"*—"We'll be right back"), so it is fun to see how much even Anglophones can follow the French story lines.

Though French is spoken by most of the older Cajuns (ages 60 and up), most middle-aged and young Louisianans don't speak the language. This is partially because the knowledge of the French language, from the 1930s on, became associated with a lack of business success or education, and therefore was stigmatized. Today, however, there is a resurgence of pride in being bilingual. French immersion programs are cropping up and people of all ages are learning to speak French.

CAJUN FRENCH & THE CREOLE LANGUAGE Cajun French is peppered with beautiful old words dating from Louis XIV, unused in France and historically intriguing. Cajun French is not a dialect of the French language, nor are there actual dialects of Cajun French from town to town in southwest

GROWING UP cajun

Growing up immersed in Cajun culture was rewarding but alienating. My heroes weren't football jocks or rock-'n'-roll stars but rather my old neighbors, farmers who spoke French, and played the accordion or fiddle. When fiddler Dennis McGee farmed for my grandpa, I didn't play with his children, even though they were my age—I hung around Dennis. I followed him in the fields while he plowed with his mule team. I wanted to hear his stories.

None of my classmates shared my love for what these old-timers had to offer. On my best days, my peers' attitude toward me was indifference. Even though it was difficult being Cajun in the '40s and '50s, I never felt any anger about the negativity of the non-Cajuns or by those Cajuns who had given up their heritage, but rather frustration and disappointment. They were turning away from this wonderful heritage in pursuit of the mainstream. They were turning their backs on a delicious bowl of gumbo in favor of an American hot dog. I think my ulterior motive in opening up a music store that specialized in Cajun music in 1966 was that I had an ax to grind. I wanted to destroy the stigma of being Cajun, to prove to the locals that heritage and success could coexist,

that being Cajun and speaking French was okay. I wanted to tell outsiders how good our food was and about all these wonderful, warm, friendly, and sincere people who were called Cajuns.

That year was a turning point—Cajun music was first presented to the outside world at the Newport Folk Festival. A three-piece group of old Cajuns was up against names such as Bob Dylan and Joan Baez. The Cajuns played their first simple tune, "Grand Mamou," and before they were halfway through, an audience of 10,000 gave them a standing ovation.

This experience reinforced the passion that had kept the fire burning in the musicians' hearts, while the audience and press reaction surprised even the local non-Cajuns. This brought

Louisiana. However, many words refer to particular items, and certain areas prefer particular words over others: a mosquito can be called a *marougouin* in one area, a *moustique* in another, or a *cousin* elsewhere. Since Cajun French is not a written language (it's only spoken), certain words that were originally mispronounced have become part of the language. Similarly, some English words are part of the language today because when the Acadians first came to Louisiana, there were no such things as pickup trucks, typewriters, and other modern inventions, so the English words are used.

Additionally, the fascinating Creole language is still spoken by many black Louisianans. A compilation of French and African dialects, it is quite different from standard French, though Cajuns and black Creoles can speak and understand both languages.

Cajun Music

It's hard to decide which is more important to a Cajun: food or music. In the early days when instruments were scarce, Cajuns held dances to a cappella voices. With roots probably found in medieval France, the strains usually came in the

outside interest—and visitors—to Cajun Louisiana. In turn, this "relegitimized" Cajun culture among locals. What was once considered a stigma—to be Cajun—was now considered an asset. Sadly, some took it to a commercialized extreme, hawking a Hollywood-ized caricature to tourists. Cajun music comes from the flat, rice-farming prairie regions. The Germans brought the button accordion from their homeland, and some say they brought rice as well. My theory is this: Prosperity equals permanence, and permanence equals roots. Having been raised on a rice farm, with 6 feet of topsoil in some places, the first settlers here could easily sustain themselves without having to move after the first spot was depleted. We also don't have big rivers, which bring in big industry and masses of people diluting the existing culture. So we stayed and dug in—literally and figuratively.

I don't think modern Cajuns are much different from the early Cajuns in the past. For any other ethnic group, it's not about one aspect of a culture—whether or not you play music, eat spicy food, or speak a certain language. It's about having a foundation that was cultivated in good times and bad. And because of devotion and love, those roots sink deep, deep, deep and produce a strong, strong, strong tree, which gives protection and comfort to all those who come into its embrace. It's a matter of vision, being from a certain ethnic minority. It's about how you see yourself in your environment and how you relate and function in that environment, and having a deep sense of the past in order to know your direction. It's about having respect and love for the things that make you who you are and prevent you from being someone else. It's not about being a crowd-pleaser. It's about being natural.

—Marc Savoy
Marc Savoy supports his Cajun heritage through the craftsmanship of accordions, as a musician with the highly acclaimed Savoy-Doucet Cajun Band and the Savoy Family Band, and by keeping Cajun community traditions alive.

form of a brisk two-step or a waltz. Traditional groups still play mostly acoustic instruments—a fiddle, an accordion, a triangle, and maybe a guitar.

The best place to hear real Cajun music is on someone's back porch, the time-honored spot for eating some gumbo and listening to several generations of musicians jamming. If you don't have access to a back-porch gathering, there are dance halls with something going on just about every weekend, full of willing dance coaches for newbies. Locals come to dance and socialize (and so should you). And don't be shy, everyone will be watching the really good dancers (and so should you). Talk to the people around you, too. Cajuns love to tell stories and jokes, and do it well.

Mulate's, Randol's, and **D.I.'s** restaurants (see listings later in this chapter) offer regular live music and dancing. The regular Saturday morning jam session at the **Savoy Music Center** (p. 327) in Eunice is a sheer delight that's not to be missed—it's the closest you will get to that back-porch experience.

Zydeco also thrives in this region. Zydeco bands share the bill at the weekly live show at Eunice's **Liberty Theater, Slim's Y Ki-Ki** in Opelousas, the **Zydeco Hall of Fame** in Lawtell, and **El Sido's** in Lafayette. (More information on these venues can be found later in this chapter.)

Planning Your Trip

A circular drive will allow you to take in one or two of the plantation homes en route to Baton Rouge (if you take the River Rd. instead of I-10) before turning west on I-10 to reach Lafayette and the land of the Cajuns. Go north of Lafayette on I-49 to reach Opelousas; Eunice is about 20 minutes west of there on Hwy. 190. A return to New Orleans on U.S. 90 is a trip through the history, legend, and romance of this region. There is more than a day's worth of interest in this area, so you'll probably want to plan at least an overnight stay. On I-10 the distance from New Orleans to Lafayette is 134 miles; Lafayette to New Orleans on U.S. 90 is 167 miles. Listed below (in alphabetical order) are lodging and restaurant options, and some of the places you should not miss, but some adventurous wandering will reward you with scores of other Cajun Country attractions on your own.

For tons of good detailed information, contact the excellent **Lafayette Convention and Visitors Commission** (𝄐 **800/346-1958** in the U.S., 800/543-5340 in Canada, or 337/232-3737; fax 337/232-0161; www.lafayette travel.com), open weekdays 8:30am to 5pm, weekends from 9am to 5pm. (See the "Lafayette" section, later in this chapter, for driving directions.)

Hands down, the best time to visit Acadiana is during Cajun Mardi Gras (p. 51), as the Cajuns celebrate with gusto. Festival International de Louisiane (p. 32) and Festivals Acadiens et Creoles (p. 55) are also outstanding, but every weekend seems to bring a smaller festival somewhere else in the area—and plenty of music through the year.

Tours

If you just can't stay over in Cajun Country, a 1-day guided tour can introduce you to the area. **Tours by Isabelle** (𝄐 **888/223-2093** or 504/391-3544; www. toursbyisabelle.com) offers small tours in comfortable, air-conditioned passenger vans. You'll cross the Mississippi to visit Cajun Country and then take a 1½-hour narrated swamp tour. The Cajun Bayou Tour ($76) leaves New Orleans at 1pm

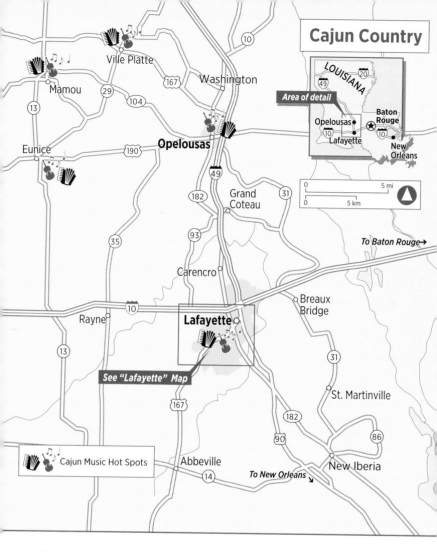

<figure>
Cajun Country

LOUISIANA

Area of detail

Opelousas • • Baton Rouge
Lafayette
New Orleans

0   5 mi
0   5 km

To Baton Rouge →

10   Ville Platte
Washington
Mamou   167
29   104
13   190   Opelousas
Eunice   49
182   Grand Coteau   31
35   93
Carencro   Breaux Bridge
10   Rayne   Lafayette
13   **See "Lafayette" Map**   31
St. Martinville
167   182   86
Cajun Music Hot Spots   90   New Iberia
Abbeville   14
To New Orleans ↘
</figure>

and returns around 5:30pm. Isabelle's Grand Tour ($146) adds plantation tours and lunch. Each year in the days between Jazz Fest weekends, **Festival Tours International** provides a stellar 3-day, music-focused tour of Cajun Country (p. 55). Also see "Organized Tours" in chapter 7, "Sights to See & Places to Be," beginning on p. 203.

A Cajun Weekend

For roots music lovers, a trip to the source of Cajun and zydeco music is essential. Though it's especially tempting to go during an organized event such as Lafayette's Festival International, Breaux Bridge's Crawfish Festival, or any of dozens of small-town niche festivals, there is always plenty of music happening.

Here are our suggestions for a good Cajun Country weekend itinerary (all specifics can be found in more detail later in this chapter):

FRIDAY Drive out from New Orleans (avoid rush hour, when it can take a very long time to get through Baton Rouge). Stay in Lafayette, Eunice, or Washington, pretty towns with nice B&Bs (and some basic chain hotels). That night, check out the music at the **Blue Moon Saloon** in Lafayette or Opelousas's **Slim's Y Ki-Ki.**

SATURDAY Get up early and head to the **Savoy Music Center** in Eunice for the weekly jam session. Leave before noon and drive to Mamou, where **Fred's Lounge** should be jam-packed till around 1pm. Then head to Ville Platte and **Floyd's Record Shop** to buy some of what you've heard. Have a bite at the **Pig Stand.** That night, go to Eunice's **Liberty Theater** for the live (French) radio broadcast and plenty of Cajun folk tales and jokes. Consider dinner at **D.I.'s,** which also has live music.

SUNDAY Spend the morning checking out picturesque Washington, strolling the wonderful gardens at **Magnolia Ridge,** or combing the many antiques shops before heading back to New Orleans.

Breaux Bridge ★

Just off I-10 on La. 31, this pretty, little town, founded in 1859, prides itself on being the Crawfish Capital of the World. Its Crawfish Festival and Fair, held the first week in May, has drawn as many as 100,000 to the town of 4,500 for music, crawfish races, and crawfish-eating contests. Little antiques shops of varying price and charm line the main drag (we notice they tend to close early on Tues afternoons). The standout is **Lucullus** (107 N. Main St.; © **337/332-2625**), a branch of the terrific New Orleans culinary- and dining-oriented shop.

WHERE TO STAY

Note: If the B&B listed below is full, you may be directed to the also charming Bayou Teche B&B, next door.

Maison Des Amis ★★ The winner of a national preservation award, this one-story Creole-Caribbean cabin (ca. 1860) is one of the best B&Bs we've ever stayed in, for sheer comfort and style. We can't decide which we like best: the front room, with the towering half-canopy bed; the middle room with the nearly 300-year-old four-poster; or the small room with the mosquito-net-draped plantation bed. A fine bonus: Housekeeping will do your laundry on-site. Best of all, guests get breakfast at the well-known **Café Des Amis** (see below) or, on the mornings the former is closed for breakfast, at Chez Jacqueline. There is also a nicely painted gazebo down by the bayou.

111 Washington St., Breaux Bridge, LA 70517. www.maisondesamis.com.© **337/507-3399.** Fax 337/332-2227. 4 units, all with private bathroom. Mon–Thurs $100; Fri–Sun $125. Rates include full-service breakfast and complimentary beverages. AE, DISC, MC, V. **Amenities:** Restaurant. *In room:* A/C, cable TV, Wi-Fi (free).

Maison Madeleine ★ This lovely Creole cottage is filled as much with antiques as with proprietor Madeleine Cenac's hospitality. She and her family moved the 1840s house from its original location, brick by literal brick, and opened it as a B&B after housing Katrina relief workers. Comfortable rather than elegant, there aren't many fancy amenities—but the unmanicured gardens and woodsy setting near Lake Martin are a birder's delight (and breakfast includes locally made sausage). The two guest rooms share a bath—rent them both to ensure privacy.

1015 John D. Hebert Dr., Breaux Bridge, LA 70515. www.maisonmadeleine.com.℃ **337/332-4555.** 2 units. $125 single (shared bath); $160 double (private bath). Rates include breakfast and complimentary cookies. **Amenities:** Wi-Fi throughout (free). *In room:* Fridge.

WHERE TO EAT

For less formal dining, head to **Poche's Market Restaurant & Smokehouse** (3015 Main Hwy. No. A—call ℃ **800/3-POCHES** [376-2437] or 337/332-2108 for directions!) for excellent spicy *boudin,* cracklins (fresher earlier in the day), weekend barbecue plates, and other regional meaty delicacies. They also ship, in case you want to cook like a Cajun at home. Open Monday through Saturday 5am to 8pm, Sunday 5am to 6pm.

There's also an outpost of **Baby's Coffee,** the Key West cult coffee roaster, in Breaux Bridge, offering a small selection of pastries and cookies. Look for the Quonset hut at 282 Rees St. (℃ **337/442-6359**). Open Monday through Friday 8am to 5pm.

Café Des Amis ★★★ CAJUN Not even a devastating fire could keep down the pride and joy of Breaux Bridge, a charming cafe that features local art and often live music in addition to meals good enough for one recent customer to drive up from New Orleans for eggs Begnaud—eggs on a grilled biscuit topped with crawfish étouffée. They also offer *orielle de couchon*—fried dough in the shape of pigs' ears! You can get them stuffed with *boudin,* or the omelets stuffed with tasso, with a side of andouille-cheese grits. The dinner menu changes frequently but most anything with the fresh local crawfish or shrimp will be good to great.

Breaux Bridge is the self-proclaimed Crawfish Capital of the World.

Save room for the superb creamy white-chocolate bread pudding. This restaurant is hugely popular, so expect a wait on the weekends. Weekends they start seating at 7:30am; the band starts at 8:30am Saturday.

140 E. Bridge St. © **337/332-5273.** www.cafedesamis.com. Main courses $9–$28. AE, DISC, MC, V. Tues 11am–2pm; Wed–Thurs 11am–9pm; Fri–Sat 7:30am–9:30pm; Sun 8am–2:30pm.

Chez Jacqueline ★★ CAJUN/FRENCH This cafe next door to higher-profile Café des Amis is a small, unfussy restaurant, where the busy chef is also the bartender; eat here only when you can linger. The food is sufficient though not exceptional, but Jacqueline is a hoot. Her menu is divided into two parts, Cajun and French. Try *les huitres au gratin* (oysters baked with garlic, butter, and Parmesan cheese), or a nicely crisped veal *cordon bleu*. Banana cake is moist and not overly sweet. They also serve a zydeco breakfast on weekends and can create special menus with advance request.

114 E. Bridge St. © **337/277-4938** (Jacqueline's cellphone, not always answered!). Reservations suggested. Main courses $11–$30. DC, DISC, MC, V. Wed–Mon 8am–2pm (including Sat zydeco jazz breakfast); Thurs–Sat 4pm–"whenever" (it depends on how busy they are; call ahead). Closed Tues.

Crawfish Town USA Restaurant and Fresh Market ★★ SEAFOOD/CAJUN Guess what the house specialty is? Yup: crawfish! The food is as pleasant as the heavily decorated dining room and is prepared to your taste: from mild to extra hot. The staff says they serve the biggest crawfish in the world—and the steaming platters are loaded with what look like small lobsters. The crawfish étouffée, gumbo, and bread pudding are delicious. Indecisive? Go for the Seafood Festival Platter, for a bit of everything. There's a free *fais-do-do* on the second Saturday of each month and a market next door.

2815 Grand Point Hwy. © **337/667-6148.** www.crawfishtown.com. Reservations recommended. Main courses $13–$28. AE, DISC, MC, V. Sun–Thurs 11am–9pm; Fri–Sat 11am–10pm. From Lafayette, take I-10 to Henderson (exit 115). Go north ½ mile and follow the signs; you can't miss it.

Mulate's the Original Cajun Restaurant ★★ ☺ CAJUN Skip the unaffiliated Mulate's in New Orleans, and come here instead. It's gotten a bit touristy, but the food, music, and prices are reasonable—it's a great introduction to Cajun music and food. Stuffed crab and the catfish are the specialties here. They have live music nightly and at noon on Sundays.

325 Mills Ave. © **800/422-2586** or 337/332-4648. Reservations recommended for parties of 6 or more. Main courses $16–$20. AE, DC, DISC, MC, V. Sun–Thurs 11am–9pm; Fri–Sat 11am–10pm.

Eunice ★★★

Founded in 1894 by C. C. Duson, who named the town for his wife, Eunice is a prairie town and the cultural center of Cajun country. Here, the Saturday-morning jam sessions at the Savoy Music Center, the Liberty Theater's live radio broadcasts, and the exhibits and crafts demonstrations at the Prairie Acadian Cultural Center will greatly enrich your understanding of Cajun life. That is, if you aren't having too much fun to notice that you're also getting an education.

Liberty Theater ★★★ 📷 This classic, restored 1927 theater showcases Cajun music most nights, but Saturday attracts the big crowds for the *Rendezvous des Cajuns* radio show. Running from 6 to 7:30pm and simulcast live on local radio, it features Cajun and zydeco bands, from up-and-comers to big names, as

Memorabilia from the Liberty Theater in Eunice.

well as folktales and jokes. Oh, and it's all in French (neighbors will be happy to translate). Locals and tourists alike pack the seats and aisles, with dancing on the sloped floor by the stage.

Second St. and Park Ave. © **337/457-7389.** www.eunice-la.com. Admission $5 adults, $3 children 7–12, free for children 6 and under. Tickets on sale at 4pm Sat; doors open at 4pm; show runs 6–7:30pm.

Prairie Acadian Cultural Center ★★★ 🏛 A terrific small museum devoted to Cajun life and culture. Exhibits explain everything from the history of the Cajuns to how they worked, played, and married. Most objects on display were acquired from local families who owned them for generations. There might be quilting or other crafts demonstrations going on (including cooking if you're lucky), and the center has a collection of videos about Cajun life available for viewing in the small theater (just ask). Anything by Les Blanc is a good choice, but then there's *Anything I Can Catch,* about the nearly lost art of hand-fishing. (You *need* to see someone catch a giant catfish with his bare hands!)

250 W. Park. © **337/457-8490.** www.lsue.edu/acadgate/lafitte.htm. Free admission; donations accepted. Tues–Fri 8am–5pm; Sat 8am–6pm. Closed Dec 25.

Savoy Music Center ★★★ 📷 On weekdays, this is a working music store with instruments, accessories, and a small but essential selection of Cajun and zydeco CDs. In the back is the workshop where musician Marc Savoy lovingly crafts his Acadian accordions—fine musical instruments and works of art coveted by musicians worldwide—amid cabinets bearing his observations and aphorisms.

On most Saturday mornings, though, this nondescript faded-green building on the outskirts of Eunice becomes the spiritual center of Cajun music. Keeping alive a tradition that dates from way before electricity, Marc and any of his talented, Grammy-nominated family host a jam session where you can hear some of the region's finest music and watch as tunes are literally passed from generation to

On the grounds at Prairie Acadian Cultural Center.

generation. Here, the older musicians are given their due respect, with octogenarians often leading the sessions while preteen players glean all they can—if they can keep up. Meanwhile, guests munch on hunks of *boudin* sausage and sip beer while listening or socializing. All comers are welcome, but bringing a pound of *boudin* or a six-pack of something will earn *you* respect. Players who bring instruments can join in—well, actually, they request just one triangle player at a time. Don't try to show off, just follow along and revel in the joyfulness of real music, played real well, by real people.

Hwy. 190 E. (3 miles east of Eunice). © **337/457-9563.** www.savoymusiccenter.com. Tues–Fri 9am–5pm (closed for lunch noon–1:30pm); jams Sat 9am–noon.

WHERE TO STAY

The once-fabulous Seale Guest House, recently reopened as **Le Village Guesthouse,** is the best choice with any character. Set amid sprawling greenery, the main house plus a separate bridal suite feature antique country furnishings; room prices range from $85 to $125 (125 Seale Lane; © **337/457-3573;** www.levillagehouse.com). There's also a **Days Inn and Suites,** with microwaves and fridges in the consistently clean rooms (1251 E. Laurel Ave. [Hwy. 190 E.]; © **337/457-3040**); the **Holiday Inn Express,** in our experience, a very reliable chain (1698 Hwy. 190; © **337/546-2466**); or the newish, basic **Best Western** (1531 W. Laurel Ave.; © **337/457-2800**). All three have complimentary continental breakfasts.

WHERE TO EAT

D.I.'s Cajun Restaurant ★★ CAJUN Even when you follow the directions to D.I.'s Cajun Restaurant, you will think you are about to drive off the face of the earth, particularly if you're driving there in the dark. You'll know you're there—and that you are not alone—when you see all the cars in the gravel parking lot. Located on a back highway, D.I.'s is more or less what Mulate's was before the tourists found it: a

An accordion at the Savoy Music Center.

homey family restaurant full of locals dancing to live music (Thurs–Sat) and stuffing themselves with crawfish, catfish, and fresh crabs in season. Some items are not fried, but most are—or they're stuffed or topped with a sauce—and it's all good.
6561 Evangeline Thruway, Basile. ℂ **337/432-5141.** www.discajunrestaurant.biz. Main courses $7.95-$22. AE, DISC, MC, V. Mon–Fri 10:30am-1:30pm; Tues-Sat 5-10pm. Take Hwy. 190 to Hwy. 97, then drive 8 miles south.

SHOPPING

Lejeune's Sausage Kitchen Look for the signs or just ask, but do find your way here for a delicious, if perishable, souvenir (serious buyers show up with a cooler and ice packs). In addition to tasso (Cajun ham) and pounce (stuffed pig stomach), family-run Lejeune's sells a variety of sausages, including a memorable garlic pork. It all freezes well, but alas, they don't ship. Old Crowley Rd., 108 Tasso Circle. ℂ **337/457-8491.** Mon–Fri 7am-5:30pm.

Grand Coteau ★

Grand Coteau seems like just a wide spot in the road, but it won't take long to explore it. First see the beautiful, more than 180-year-old **Academy of the Sacred Heart,** 1821 Academy Rd. (ℂ **337/662-5275;** www.ashcoteau.org; tours by appointment only, offered 9am–2pm on school days but other times may be arranged), and its gardens. Then stop off for a quick bite and a few gifts.

WHERE TO EAT

Creola Cafe CAFE This cute country-ish newcomer serves simple but satisfying homemade soups, salads, and sandwiches (the roast beef po' boy is gaining quite a reputation), and tasty homemade desserts vary each day. They serve lunch only.
284 E. Martin Luther King Dr. ℂ **337/662-3914.** Entrees $6-$10; desserts $3-$4. Wed-Sat 11am-4pm.

Kitchen Shop ★ CAFE The name is misleading because this is actually a well-stocked, cute gift store that features kitchen, cooking, and nice food items as well as having a much larger room stuffed with local books, upscale knickknacks, jewelry (including Grandmother's Buttons [p. 316], a line made from antique buttons), and vintage-looking clothes. There is also a tiny cafe with a sweet little

boudin JOINTS

Boudin is Cajun sausage made of pork, usually mixed with rice, onions, and spices, and stuffed inside a chewy casing. If it's done right, it's spicy and sublime. You can get *boudin* (warm) at just about any grocery store or gas station, and we've spent many a day taste-testing. Disputes rage about who makes the best. Visit **www.boudinlink.com** for hard-core ratings and listings of dozens of *boudin* shops in the area. Try several to compare for yourself—it's a cheap (just over $2 per lb.), filling snack, best eaten while leaning against a car, chased with a Barq's root beer. For the less intrepid, we recommend the following, relatively easy places to locate:

Best Stop ★★★, 615 Hwy 93 N., Scott 9 (℃ 337/233-5805), truly is, in our much-researched opinion, the best *boudin* around, with just the right balance of pork-to-kick (spice). They're always busy, which means the links are always fresh, and their cracklins are equally superb. Look for the bright red building with a parking lot full of pickup trucks. Open Monday through Saturday 6am to 8pm, Sunday 6am to 6pm.

Don's Specialty Meats ★★, 730 I-10 S. Frontage Rd., Scott (℃ 337/234-2528), or 104 Hwy. 726, Carencro (℃ 337/896-6370), is a bit less country funk and a bit more sanitized grocery store—but the semispicy *boudin* rocks. There's also a yummy pork chop sandwich for the *boudin*-averse (but really, you should just leave them behind). There's a good selection of sausages and meats for shipping, too. Both stores are open Monday through Saturday 6am to 7pm, Sunday 7am to 6pm.

At **Eunice Poultry,** 125 E. Laurel, Eunice (℃ 337/457-5614), don't let the "poultry" thing throw you—they also have tasty, mildly rice-y *boudin* that's worth seeking out. And yes, they have

all variety of winged deliciousness, including authentic turducken (a chicken in a duck in a turkey, each dressed), and a really good spice blend. Open Monday through Friday 6am to 5pm, Saturday 6am to noon, and closed Sunday.

Others swear by **Bubba Frey's,** 29017 Crowley Eunice Hwy., Mowata; **Eunice Superette Slaughterhouse** ★, 1044 Hwy. 91, Eunice (℃ **337/546-6041**), open Monday through Friday, 6am to 5:30pm, and Saturday from 6am to noon; **Poche's** (p. 325); and the convenient drive-through window at **Ray's Grocery,** 904 Shortvine off Hwy. 190, across from Town Center, Opelousas (℃ 337/942-9150), open Monday through Friday 7:30am to 6pm, Saturday 8am to 5pm, and Sunday 8am to 2pm.

patio. The owner is a New York–trained pastry chef who serves quiches, delicious pastries (the specialty is Gateau Nana), and terrific café au lait. It's all packed into an 1840 building that used to be a stagecoach stop.

296 Martin Luther King Dr. ✆ **337/662-3500.** Entrees $6.50–$9.50; desserts $5–$7; coffee and tea $2–$3. DISC, MC, V. Tues–Sat 10am–5pm; Sun 1–5pm.

Lafayette

Stop by the **Lafayette Convention and Visitors Center,** 1400 NW Evangeline Thruway (✆ **800/346-1958** in the U.S., 800/543-5340 in Canada, or 337/232-3808; www.lafayettetravel.com). The helpful staff will assist with everything you could possibly want to know about the region. Turn off I-10 at exit 103A, go south for about a mile, and you'll find the office in Cajun-style homes in the center of the median. It's open weekdays from 8:30am to 5pm and weekends from 9am to 5pm.

We also highly recommend the **Festival International de Louisiane** ★ (✆ **337/232-8086;** www.festivalinternational.com), a 5-day music-and-art street festival in late April that many find to be a good alternative to New Orleans's increasingly crowded Jazz Fest. Not quite as big or broad in scope, there's always an interesting lineup, emphasizing music from French-speaking lands. It's low-key, manageable—and free!

The **Blue Moon Saloon** ★★★, 215 E. Convent St. (✆ **337/234-2422;** www.bluemoonpresents.com), is filled pretty much every night with cool people who know a good hangout when they see one. Some of the best local bands, Cajun and otherwise, play here Wednesdays through Saturdays and sometimes on Sundays (catch Feaufollet or the edgier Lost Bayou Ramblers if you can). They also operate cheap (but likeable) hostel-style and private lodging. The zydeco hot spot is **El Sido's,** 1523 N. Martin Luther King St. (✆ **337/235-0647**), where combos such as Nathan & the Zydeco Cha Chas hold sway. Hours are irregular so call ahead (or just ask a local), but when it jumps, it jumps high.

SEEING THE SIGHTS

You shouldn't leave this area without exploring its bayous and swamps. Gliding through misty bayous dotted with gnarled cypress trees that drip Spanish moss, seeing native water creatures and birds in their natural habitat, and learning how Cajuns harvest their beloved crawfish is an experience not to be missed.

To arrange a voyage, contact **McGee's Landing Atchafalaya Basin Swamp Tours,** 1337 Henderson Levee Rd., Henderson (✆ **337/228-2384;** www.mcgees landing.com; $20 adults, $18 seniors, $16 children ages 4–12, free for children 3 and under). The 90-minute tours, at 10am, 1pm, and 3pm, go to Henderson Lake in the Atchafalaya Basin, with "extreme" private airboat tours also available ($50 for adults, $35 children; these last 2 hr.); and nighttime tours by prearrangement. There's a cafe, shop, campground, and some floating guest cabins at McGee's, too.

There's a lovely natural swamp environment in the very heart of town on the grounds of the University of Louisiana at Lafayette. Although it's small, it gives the effect of being in the wild, with several varieties of water birds and turtles almost always on hand. Spring brings Louisiana irises and gators. It's used as a teaching tool; contact the **Communications and Marketing Department,** University of Louisiana at Lafayette, Lafayette, LA 70504 (✆ **337/482-6397**). If you just want to get closer to the sort of swampland seen most often from highways, you'll like **Cypress Lake,** next to the Student Union on the ULL campus, between St. Mary Boulevard and University Avenue and Hebrard Boulevard and McKinley Street.

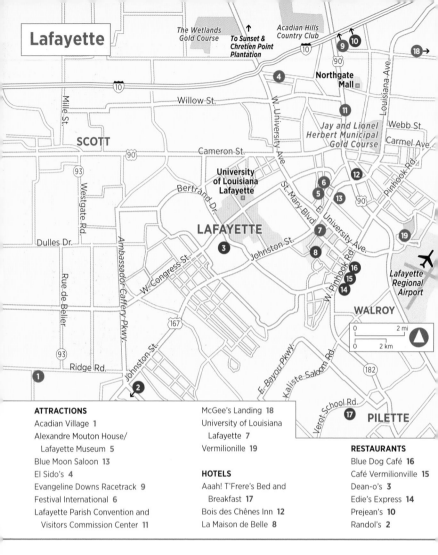

Lafayette

The Wetlands Gold Course
Acadian Hills Country Club
To Sunset & Chretien Point Plantation
Northgate Mall
Jay and Lionel Herbert Municipal Gold Course
Willow St.
SCOTT
Cameron St.
University of Louisiana Lafayette
Bertrand Dr.
LAFAYETTE
Dulles Dr.
W. Congress St.
Johnston St.
Ridge Rd.
WALROY
Lafayette Regional Airport
PILETTE

Mille St.
Westgate Rd.
Rue de Belier
Ambassador Caffery Pkwy.
St. Mary Blvd.
W. University Ave.
E. University Ave.
Louisiana Ave.
Webb St.
Carmel Ave.
Pinhook Rd.
W. Pinhook Rd.
Kaliste Saloom Rd.
E. Bayou Pkwy.
Verot School Rd.

0   2 mi
0   2 km

Acadian Village ★ Just south of La. 342 is a reconstructed (actually, reassembled) Cajun bayou community that looks a little prefab at first, but it grows more alluring as you wander the footpath through period-furnished houses beside a sleepy bayou. There is a dear small church and a proper Cajun dance hall, all in a setting that isn't radically different from 200 years ago. The Blackpot music and cooking festival, where traditional meets steampunk cool, is held here in October (see www.blackpotfestival.com for info), and Santa—plus a gajillion lights—lands here each holiday season.

200 Greenleaf Dr. ℂ **800/962-9133** or 337/981-2364. www.acadianvillage.org. Admission $8 adults, $7 seniors, $5 children 7–14, free for children 6 and under. Mon–Sat 10am–4pm. Closed

A look inside life at the Acadian Village.

major holidays; tours closed in Nov. Take I-10 to exit 97. Go south on La. 93 to Ridge Rd., turn right, and then turn left on W. Broussard.

Alexandre Mouton House/Lafayette Museum ★ Louisiana's first Democratic governor, Alexandre Mouton, once lived in this antebellum town house with square columns and two galleries. Today it is home to the Lafayette Museum. Inside, in addition to the antiques, paintings, and historical documents, there's a colorful collection of Mardi Gras costumes worn by Lafayette's krewe kings and queens.

1122 Lafayette St. ✆ **337/234-2208.** Admission $3 adults, $2 seniors, $1 students. Tues–Sat 10am–4pm. Closed major holidays.

Vermilionville ★★ This reconstruction of a Cajun-Creole settlement from the 1765-to-1890 era sits on the banks of the brooding Bayou Vermilion. While it may sound like a "Cajunland" theme park, it's actually quite a valid operation. Hundreds of skilled artisans labored to restore and reconstruct original Cajun homes and to reconstruct others, representing varying levels in society from humble to well-to-do. (It *must* be authentic: One Cajun we know refuses to go, not because he dislikes the place or finds it offensive but because "I already *live* in Vermilionville!") The costumed staff and traditional, performers and craftspeople give vivid demonstrations of daily life back then. Vermilionville is both bigger and better than Acadian Village (see above).

Vermilionville is a reconstruction of a Cajun-Creole settlement from more than 200 years ago.

300 Fisher Rd., off Surrey St. © **866/99-BAYOU** (992-2968) or 337/233-4077. www.vermilion ville.org. Admission $8 adults, $6.50 seniors, $5 students, free for children 5 and under. Tues–Sun 10am–4pm; admission desk closes at 3pm. Closed New Year's Eve, New Year's Day, Martin Luther King Day, Mardi Gras, Thanksgiving, and Dec 24–25. Take I-10 to exit 103A. Take Evangeline Thruway south to Surrey St. and then follow signs.

WHERE TO STAY IN & AROUND LAFAYETTE

As always, we tend to direct you to stay at local B&Bs—mainly because they are more interesting than the chain hotel alternatives. However, prices and personal preferences can make said chain hotels even more attractive than an antique bed. As a small city with a good-size college, Lafayette has several such options, including the **Holiday Inn Lafayette—Central,** 2032 NE Evangeline Thruway (© **800/942-4868** or 337/233-6815), and the **Lafayette Hilton & Towers,** 1521 W. Pinhook Rd. (© **800/TILSONS** [846-7667] or 337/235-6111).

Aaah! T'Frere's Bed & Breakfast ★★★ Everything about this place cracks us up, from the name (it's so they're first in any alphabetical listing) to the evening "T'Juleps" to the owners' handsome son/breakfast cook/part-time model, to the cheerful owners themselves, Pat and Maugie Pastor. The latter would be adorable even if she didn't preside over breakfast in red silk pajamas every day (a former restaurateur, she wanted a radical change from chef's whites). Oh, wait, did we mention the goofily named (but superb) breakfasts, like the "Ooh-La-La, Mardi Gras"—eggs in white sauce on ham-topped biscuits, with cheese, and garlic grits, tomato grille, sweet potatoes, and chocolate muffins? After-dinner drinks in the parlor? The rooms (and grounds) are gorgeous (the public areas may be a bit Grandma-cluttered for our tastes); the ones in the Garconniere in the back are a bit more country plain than Victorian fancy. We particularly like Mary's Room, with its priceless antique wood canopy bed and working fireplace.

1905 Verot School Rd., Lafayette, LA 70508. www.tfreres.com. © **800/984-9347** or 337/984-9347. Fax 337/984-9347. 8 units, all with private bathroom. $135 double. Extra adult $35, extra children $20. Children 3 and under stay free in parent's room. Rates include full breakfast, complimentary beer, wine, after-dinner drinks, soft drinks, and Cajun canapés (hors d'oeuvres). AE, DC, DISC, MC, V. *In room:* A/C, TV, Wi-Fi (free).

Bois des Chênes Inn ★ Three rooms here are in the carriage house, and two rooms, one with an open fireplace, are in the 1820s Acadian-style plantation home known as the Charles Mouton House. Now listed on the National Register of Historical Houses, Bois des Chênes was once the center of a 3,000-acre cattle and sugar plantation. Rooms are plain if you are used to the more lavish, travel magazine offerings, but some have fireplaces. The third-floor room with its long skinny bathroom and claw-foot tub is the most appealing. The grounds are quite pretty. Owner Marjorie, a noted cook, prepares a Louisiana-style breakfast, and all guests get a bottle of wine and house tour. Marjorie's husband, a geologist, can conduct weekend nature and birding trips into the Atchafalaya Swamp by prearrangement. *Note:* At press time, the facility was for sale and may have different owners by now.

338 N. Sterling (at Mudd Ave.), Lafayette, LA 70501. www.boisdechenes.com. © **337/233-7816.** Fax 337/233-7816. 5 units. $110–$150 double. Rates include breakfast. Extra person $30. AE, MC, V. *In room:* A/C, TV, fridge, Wi-Fi (free; in 2 guest rooms and public areas).

La Maison de Belle ★★ This restored 1898 house was moved to this large, pretty property near the university. The downstairs suite is a knockout, with its own parlor, private porch, and enormous bathroom—just right for a honeymoon. The two upstairs rooms have garret ceilings, a queen-size or king-size bed, and one has the original dinky cast-iron tub. The coolest thing (if available—it's booked through May 2012) is the cottage in back: a two-bedroom, dark cypress wood–paneled dwelling where author John Kennedy Toole wrote part of *A Confederacy of Dunces*. It has a full kitchen so it's a good choice for families, though it's not particularly spacious or light (the effect is cozy at night). The entertaining chef-owner's tasty new breakfast may include eggs Benedict with crawfish étouffée or fresh beignets.

610 Girard Park Dr., Lafayette, LA 70503. © **337/235-2520.** 5 units. $100–$125. Rates include breakfast. No credit cards. Limited Wi-Fi access from public areas only (free). *In room:* A/C, TV, hair dryer.

WHERE TO EAT IN & AROUND LAFAYETTE

Blue Dog Cafe CAJUN Yes, it's that Blue Dog, told ya he was everywhere (p. 254; painter George Rodrigue is from these parts). Expect dogs on walls, white cloths on tables, pretty wood beams, music on weekends, crowds at brunch. The extensive menu is based in local ingredients, done traditionally (gumbo, fried seafoods) or slightly gussied up (smoked duck quesadillas, Asian grilled pork chops). Either way is pretty darn good, though the spicy, creamy zingy Crabmeat Florentine reeled us in, and the Sunday brunch buffet is nearly awesome.

1211 W. Pinhook Rd. © **337/237-0004.** www.bluedogcafe.com. Reservations accepted and recommended for 10:30am and 11am brunch seatings. Entrees lunch $8–$15, dinner $13–$30; brunch

$23, kids $8. AE, DC, DISC, MC, V. Mon–Thurs 11am–2pm; Mon–Thurs 5–9pm; Fri–Sat 5–10pm; brunch Sun 10:30am–2pm.

Café Vermilionville INTERNATIONAL/CAJUN Though it's highly touted locally, and set in a beautifully restored 1799 Acadian cypress house, we find this place a bit disappointing. The fussy food layers on the ingredients, many of which are cream-sauce intensive. Having said that, the crawfish beignets are a perfect appetizer. Service can be inexplicably slow.

1304 W. Pinhook Rd. ℂ **337/237-0100.** www.cafev.com. Reservations and appropriate attire recommended. Main courses $12–$18 lunch, $22–$33 dinner. AE, DC, DISC, MC, V. Mon–Fri 11am–2pm; Mon–Sat 5:30–9:30pm. Closed major holidays.

Dean-o's ★ ☺ PIZZA Yeah, yeah, you're supposed to be eating jambalaya and red beans, but let's say you have already, or that you've got an unwilling kid. Dean-o's offers up the best pizza in Lafayette, with homemade sauces and olive oil crust. The sampler—up to four of their elaborate specialty combos on one pizza, is perfect for split opinions: one person gets the T. Rex (for "ultimate meat eaters") half of the pie, the other gets the Marie Laveau, with bluepoint crab. Next meal, have some étouffée, okay?

305 Bertrand (at Johnston St.). ℂ **337/233-5446.** Takeout but no delivery. Main courses $6–$24 (for a giant specialty pizza). AE, DC, DISC, MC, V. Mon–Thurs 11am–10:30pm; Fri–Sat 10:30am–midnight; Sun 10:30am–9pm.

Edie's Express ★★ CAJUN This is Lafayette's favorite breakfast place, and for good reason. Things will be smothered, but they will also be melt-in-your-mouth. And the biscuits? They're all you can ask for in baked dough.

1400 W. Pinhook Rd. ℂ **337/234-2485.** All main courses under $7. AE, MC, V. Mon–Fri 5:30am–11am.

Prejean's ★★ CAJUN This likable, unpretentious, and once-glorious family restaurant serves hearty meals that still make it worth a drop-in, and there's live Cajun music nightly. Their smoked duck and andouille gumbo and crawfish enchiladas are justly Jazz Fest favorites. Recognizable Cajun dishes come with elaborate flourishes, sometimes erring on the gloppy side. Look for fried crawfish *boudin* balls and the seafood-stuffed mushrooms (think a sort of mini crab cake stuffed into a 'shroom) for appetizers, and shrimp stuffed with tasso and jack cheese and then wrapped in bacon, or more staid blackened fish entrees. Matters are cheaper and lighter at lunch. If the menu still lists the "fresh" Louisiana strawberry shortcake, verify that: The one we had featured hideous gelatinous syrup instead of actual fruit (it was out of season, but still).

3480 I-49 N. ℂ **337/896-3247.** www.prejeans.com. Reservations for groups of 8 or more only. Children's menu $5–$8.95 lunch and dinner, $3.50 breakfast; main courses $17–$30; breakfast $7 and up. AE, DC, DISC, MC, V. Daily 7am–9:30pm. Take I-10 to exit 103B and then I-49 north to exit 2/Gloria Switch.

Randol's Restaurant and Cajun Dance Hall ★ CAJUN In addition to better-than-average Cajun food, Randol's offers a good-size, popular dance floor. The star of the menu is fresh seafood from bayou or Gulf waters, served fried, steamed, blackened, or grilled, and their gold-medal winning crawfish étouffée. (With fried as the only option at most Cajun restaurants, the other alternatives alone make Randol's an attractive stop.)

Plenty of Cajun flavor is on hand at Prejean's.

2320 Kaliste Saloom Rd. © **800/YO-CAJUN** (962-2586) or 337/981-7080. www.randols.com. Reservations accepted only for parties of 8 or more. Main courses $14–$27. MC, V. Sun–Thurs 5–9:30pm; Fri–Sat 5–10:30pm. Closed major holidays. From New Orleans, take I-10 west to exit 103A. Follow Evangeline Thruway to Pinhook Rd., turn right, and follow Pinhook to Kaliste Saloom Rd. (on the right). Randol's will be on your right.

Mamou ★

There is one darn good reason to come to Mamou and that's Saturday mornings at **Fred's Lounge ★**, 420 Sixth St. (© **337/468-5411;** open Sat 9am–2pm only). At the other end of the Cajun music scale from the Savoy Music Center (p. 327), this small-town bar nonetheless offers just as essential an Acadiana Saturday-morning experience. For half a century, Fred's has hosted Saturday daytime dances, with the band in a roped-off area in the middle of the floor and couples waltzing and two-stepping around them. This is pure dance-hall stuff (leaning toward the country-western side of Cajun, but much of it in French), where hardworking locals blow off steam and let loose. It won't be the same (or maybe it will) now that legendary bartendress Tante Sue, schnapps flask firmly holstered to her hip, has retired, but it still airs from 9 to 11am on radio station KVPI (1050 AM).

Opelousas ★

Opelousas, the third-oldest city in Louisiana, is the seat (and heart) of St. Landry Parish, but for the average tourist, there isn't that much to see. It's such a pretty town, though—particularly the main drag, Landry Street—that passers-through often find themselves pulling over to have a look around.

The **Tourist Center,** 828 E. Landry St. (✆ **800/424-5442** or 337/948-6263), is open Monday through Friday from 8am to 4:30pm, Saturday and Sunday 10am to 4pm. Famed frontiersman Jim Bowie lived in the building for a (really) short time as a child, and there is a small collection of ephemera devoted to him. Don't go out of your way for that, but do drop in for other tourist and lodging advice. You can also call the **St. Landry Parish Tourist Commission** (✆ **877/948-8004;** www.cajuntravel.com). Spring and fall bring frequent live music events so check the website. Notably, the last weekend in October, Opelousas features its delightful **Yambilee Festival,** a salute to everyone's favorite Thanksgiving side dish.

If you need a proper tourist experience, drop by the **Opelousas Museum and Interpretive Center,** 329 N. Main St. (✆ **337/948-2589;** www.cityofopelousas.com; Mon–Fri 8am–4:30pm, Sat 10am–3pm). In passing, admire the 300-year-old oak across the street from City Hall; its branches have gotten so heavy that in spots they not only touch the ground but are buried beneath the sod. The ultimate spot for zydeco, **Slim's Y Ki-Ki** (✆ **337/942-6242**) at 8393 Hwy. 182, fills up to hot and sweaty capacity most weekends. Just down the highway in Lawtell, the **Zydeco Hall of Fame** (formerly Richard's) is doing its best to keep the dance-hall traditions of its legendary predecessor going, while mixing in DJs spinning hip-hop (11154 Hwy. 190, Lawtell; ✆ **337/349-8827;** open only sporadically; search "zydeco hall of fame" in www.facebook.com for upcoming shows there and elsewhere in the region).

WHERE TO STAY

Opelousas has a **Super 8,** 5791 I-49 Service Rd. S. (✆ **337/942-6250**); a **Days Inn,** 5761 I-49 Service Rd. S. (✆ **337/407-0004**); and a **Holiday Inn,** 5696 I-49 Service Rd. N. (✆ **337/948-3300**).

Country Ridge Bed and Breakfast This contemporary house is a throwback to the classic B&B, in which nice people rent you a room in their house and make yummy banana muffins. The Southern Belle room (more feminine) and the Southwest Room (more masculine) have private bathrooms and also share a Jacuzzi for an extra fee. The Acadiana Suite is significantly larger, with a king-size bed, access to a patio, washer and dryer, sound system, and Jacuzzi tub. All rooms have queen-size beds, and the pool area backs up to a thoroughbred horse farm. There is no smoking allowed.

169 Country Ridge Rd., Opelousas, LA 70570. www.cajunbnb.com. ✆ **337/948-1678.** 4 units. $85–$165 double. Rates include continental breakfast. AE, DISC, MC, V. Free parking. No children. Small crated pets allowed. **Amenities:** Jacuzzi; pool; Wi-Fi (free). *In room:* A/C, TV, hair dryer.

WHERE TO EAT

Back in Time ★★ LIGHT FARE This cafe and gift store is run by Wanda Juneau, only the second owner of the building since 1921. The first, shoe repairman Mr. Grecco, may still be haunting the place; ask Wanda to tell you her ghost stories. The cafe has homemade diner-type selections: sandwiches (including muffulettas with their own olive dressing), salads, and gooey desserts including award-winning brownies.

123 W. Landry St. ✆ **337/942-2413.** All items under $14. AE, MC, V. Mon–Sat 11:30am–4pm (lunch stops at 2:30pm).

Palace Cafe ★★ CAJUN/GREEK Owned by the same family since 1927, this no-frills spot on the main drag will sate your crawfish cravings—it serves a heck of an étouffée, not to mention textbook versions of other local favorites and daily lunch specials.

135 W. Landry St. ℰ **337/942-2142.** Main courses $6–$18. AE, DISC, MC, V. Mon–Fri 6am–9pm; Sat 7am–8pm.

St. Martinville ★

This lovely, historic town dates from 1765 when it was a military station known as the Poste des Attakapas. There was a time when it was known as la Petite Paris—many French aristocrats fled their homeland during the Revolution and settled here, bringing with them such high-living traditions as fancy balls and lavish banquets.

SEEING THE SIGHTS

Three of St. Martinville's main attractions revolve around Longfellow's epic poem *Evangeline.* Understandably, over time it was adopted with great pride by local Cajuns as part of their heritage. Yet the poem's content and characters are entirely fictitious, with only a vague connection to any historical personage.

The **Evangeline Monument,** on Main Street, is a statue next to St. Martin's Church. It was donated to the town in 1929 by a movie company that came here to film the epic; the star, Dolores del Rio, supposedly posed for the statue. This also reportedly marks the spot of the grave of the "real-life" Evangeline, Emmeline Labiche, herself a work of fiction by a local author in the early 20th century. (Don't say that out loud, though!)

The Evangeline Monument.

The Evangeline Oak.

At Port Street and Bayou Teche is the ancient **Evangeline Oak,** where self-proclaimed descendants say Emmeline's boat landed at the end of her long trip from Nova Scotia and she learned of her lover's betrothal to another. It's a pretty sight, with a very nice mural and memorial to the original Cajun settlers nearby.

Also on the banks of Bayou Teche, just north of St. Martinville on La. 31 at 1200 N. Main St., is the **Longfellow-Evangeline State Historic Site** (℗ **888/677-2900** or 337/394-3754). The 157 acres that make up the park purportedly once belonged to Louis Pierre Arceneaux, allegedly Emmeline's real-life Gabriel, but we know better. The 1765 **Olivier Plantation House** here is typical of larger Acadian homes, with bricks made by hand and baked in the sun, a cypress frame, and pegs (instead of nails). You can also see the *cuisine* (outdoor kitchen) and *magazin* (storehouse) out back. Admission is $4 for adults, free for seniors and children 12 and under. Open daily 9am to 5pm. Tours start on the hour until 4pm.

The Petit Paris Museum Next to the church, this establishment often has unexpectedly interesting displays—a recent visit found a terrific St. Martinville Mardi Gras exhibit with splendiferous costumes and the extraordinary local story that inspired the theme that year.

103 S. Main St. ℗ **337/394-2233.** Call for rates and information on guided tours, by reservation only.

St. Martin de Tours Church ★ This is the mother church of the Acadians; the building was constructed in 1836 on the site of a previous church building. It is the fourth-oldest Roman Catholic church in Louisiana. You'll also see the original box pews, an ornate baptismal font (which some say was a gift from King Louis XVI of France), and the lovely old altar. Outside is a cemetery that purportedly holds the grave of Evangeline herself.

A piece of work on display at the African-American Museum.

The original pew boxes at St. Martin de Tours church.

201 Evangeline Blvd. ℰ **337/394-6021.** Daily 8am to 5pm for viewing; guided tours by reservation.

St. Martinville Cultural Heritage Center, African-American Museum, and Museum of the Acadian Memorial ★ Just doors down from the Acadian Memorial (where an eternal flame commemorates the expulsion of French immigrants from Canada, the same ones who eventually made their way to Louisiana and became Cajuns) is a small but well-designed exhibit discussing the various roles of African Americans within the local Cajun communities, both as slaves and free people. The other side of the building does the same for the Cajun people. Both are simple but exceedingly well done.

125 S. New Market St. ℰ **337/394-2258** or 337/394-2233. www.acadianmemorial.org/english/area.html#african. $3 for adults, free for children 11 and under. Daily 10am–4:30pm. Closed major holidays.

WHERE TO STAY

Old Castillo Bed & Breakfast ★★ This place reminds us of a rooming house—it used to be a Catholic girls' school—though the generously sized rooms (especially no. 3), with four-poster beds and pretty quilts, are quite a bit nicer than boarding school accommodations. They're appealing but not lavish; nor are the rates. Its porch sits practically underneath the Evangeline Oak and it's right next to the town square. Bathrooms (though private) are dinky, and one has no tub. The hot breakfast in the morning is most satisfying, though the food smells can linger in the rooms.

220 Evangeline Blvd., St. Martinville, LA 70582. www.oldcastillo.com. ℰ **800/621-3017** or 337/394-4010. Fax 337/394-7983. 7 units. $80–$150 double. Rates include breakfast. AE, DISC, MC, V. Free parking. *In room:* A/C, Wi-Fi (free).

Ville Platte ★

Floyd's Record Shop ★★ Long before Cajun and zydeco were known outside the region, Floyd Soileau was recording and releasing Cajun, zydeco, and swamp pop (see below) records on his three labels. Eventually, he built a whole operation of recording, pressing, and selling records. For fans of the music, this is a must-stop locale with a fine selection of releases by such great artists as D. L. Menard (the Cajun Hank Williams) and Clifton Chenier (the King of Zydeco), as well as other hard-to-find local musicians and new releases in all genres.

434 E. Main St. ✆ **800/738-8668** or 337/363-2138. www.floydsrecordshop.com. Tues–Sat 8:30am–5pm.

Swamp Pop Museum ★ If you're not a swamp pop devotee, it's probably because you just haven't heard it (remember "Lonely Days and Lonely Nights?"). Popular in the late 1950s to mid-1960s, it's experiencing some latent, well-deserved respect and popularity. The genre's name is pretty accurate: It's an infectious, oozy stew of early rock swagger, country Cajun sway, and R&B swoon. Fans have pilgrimaged to Ville Platte for years: Now it's the official "Swamp Pop Capital of the World" and the small museum (an old railroad depot) commemorates the music with well-presented, informative photos and memorabilia.

205 SW Railroad St. ✆ **337/363-0900.** www.vpla.com/site13.php. Admission $3, $2 seniors, $1 kids 12 and under. Fri–Sat 10am–3pm.

WHERE TO EAT

The Pig Stand ★★ BARBECUE/SOUTHERN As you might guess, the Pig Stand serves pig—oh, and such pig! It's no longer a deep dive (and we mean that nicely), a new owner spruced it up some just last year, and while he brought in some New Orleans po' boys and other big-city dishes, he didn't mess with the divine pork, tangy barbecued chicken, and other Southern specialties. Prices are great and locals hang out here now as they have for nearly 4 decades.

318 E. Main St. ✆ **337/363-2883.** Main courses $14 and under. AE, DISC, MC, V. Tues–Thurs 6:30am–9pm; Fri–Sat 6:30am–10pm; Sun 6:30am–2pm.

12

PLANNING YOUR TRIP TO NEW ORLEANS

N o matter what your idea of the perfect New Orleans trip is, this chapter will give you the information to make informed plans about getting there, getting around, and the essentials for an easy Big Easy vacation. We'll also point you toward additional resources, so you can let the bons temps begin even before you arrive.

GETTING THERE
By Plane

Most major domestic and some international airlines serve the city's **Louis Armstrong New Orleans International Airport (MSY).**

The airport is 15 miles west of the city, in Kenner. You'll find information booths scattered around the airport and in the baggage claim area, as well as a branch of the **Travelers Aid Society.**

Some large airlines offer transatlantic or transpacific passengers special discount tickets under the name **Visit USA,** which allows mostly one-way travel from one U.S. destination to another at very low prices. Unavailable in the U.S., these discount tickets must be purchased abroad in conjunction with your international fare. This system is the easiest, fastest, cheapest way to see the country.

GETTING INTO TOWN FROM THE AIRPORT

For $20 per person (one-way), the **Airport Shuttle** (✆ 504/522-3500) van will take you directly from the airport to your hotel in the French Quarter, Garden District, Central Business District, or Faubourg Marigny. There are Airport Shuttle information desks (staffed 24 hr.) in the airport.

Note: If you plan to take the Airport Shuttle *to* the airport when you depart, you must call a day in advance to arrange a pick-up time. You can also book and pay for a round-trip ($38) in advance, via phone or online at www.airportshuttle neworleans.com.

A **taxi** from the airport to most hotels will cost $33 for one to two people; for three or more passengers, the fare is $14 per person. Taxi stands are outside the baggage claim area.

To ride in style from the airport to your hotel, try **New Orleans Limousine Service** (✆ 504/288-1111; www.limoserviceneworleans.com). Express transfer service for a six-passenger stretch limo starts at $75 plus 20% gratuity.

From the airport, you can reach the **Central Business District** by Jefferson Transit public bus No. E-2 for $2. The bus goes to Tulane Avenue and Carrollton Avenue daily, or Tulane and Loyola Monday through Friday, where riders can transfer to the Regional Transit Authority lines for an additional $1.25. Buses run from 5:20am, departing from the upper level of the airport about every 25 minutes. The Tulane/Carrollton line runs until 9pm daily; the line to Loyola runs

PREVIOUS PAGE: **The St. Charles Avenue streetcar.**

until 6:30pm Monday through Friday only. For more information, call **Jefferson Transit** (☎ **504/818-1077;** www.jeffersontransit.org) or the **Regional Transit Authority** (☎ **504/248-3900;** www.norta.com).

By Car

You can drive to New Orleans via **I-10, I-55, U.S. 90, U.S. 61,** or across the Lake Pontchartrain Causeway on **La. 25.** From any direction, you'll see the city's distinctive and swampy outlying regions; if possible, drive in during daylight and allow time to enjoy the scenery. U.S. 61 or La. 25 offers the best views, but the larger roads are considerably faster.

It's a good idea to call your hotel in advance for directions and parking fees and instructions. Most hotels have parking facilities or can refer you to a garage nearby. Daily fees can be hefty.

AAA (☎ **504/367-4095** or 504/837-1080; www.aaa.com) will assist members with trip planning and emergency services.

Approximate drive time to New Orleans from Atlanta is 8 hours; from Houston it's 6 hours; Chicago, 15 hours; Baton Rouge is an hour and a half away.

Driving in New Orleans can be a hassle, and parking is a nightmare. It's a great city for walking, and cabs are plentiful and not too expensive, so you really don't need a car unless you're planning several day trips. Nevertheless, most major national car-rental companies are represented at the airport.

International visitors should note that insurance and taxes are almost never included in quoted rental-car rates in the U.S. Be sure to ask your rental agency about additional fees for these, as they can be significant. See "By Car" under "Getting Around" below for more on rental-car age and payment requirements.

By Train

As with the interstates and highways into New Orleans, the passenger rail lines cut through some beautiful scenery. **Amtrak** (☎ **800/USA-RAIL** [872-7245] or 504/528-1612; www.amtrak.com) trains serve the city's **Union Passenger Terminal,** 1001 Loyola Ave.

The New Orleans train station is in the Central Business District. Plenty of taxis wait outside the main entrance to the passenger terminal. Hotels in the French Quarter and the Central Business District are just a short ride away.

International visitors can buy a **USA Rail Pass,** good for 15, 30, or 45 days of unlimited travel on **Amtrak,** as well as various regional passes. They're available online or through many overseas travel agents. See Amtrak's website for the cost of travel within the western, eastern, or northwestern United States. Reservations are generally required and should be made as early as possible.

By Boat

While not a traditional means of getting to or from New Orleans, several major cruise lines do embark from the Port of New Orleans. A visit to the Crescent City followed by a Caribbean cruise sounds like a right fine vacation. Contact **Royal Caribbean** (☎ 866/562-7625; www.royalcaribbean.com), **Carnival Cruises** (☎ 888/227-6482; www.carnival.com), or **Norwegian Cruise Line** (☎ 866/234-7350; www.ncl.com) for information. **Blount Small Ship Adventures** plies

12

PLANNING YOUR TRIP TO NEW ORLEANS

Getting There

the Mississippi River to New Orleans (© 800/556-7450; www.blountsmallship adventures.com).

GETTING AROUND

By Car

Unless you're planning extensive or far-flung explorations outside the major tourist zones, you really don't need to rent a car during your stay in New Orleans. Not only is the town made for walking (it's flat and ultrapicturesque), but most places you want to go are also easily accessible on foot or by some form of the largely excellent public transportation system. Indeed, a streetcar ride is as much entertainment as a practical means of getting around. At night, when you need them most, cabs are easy to come by (less so during Mardi Gras and Jazz Fest). Meanwhile, driving and parking in the French Quarter bring grief. Many streets around town are narrow, potholed, and crowded, and some go only one way. (This is easily the most confusing city we have ever driven around in, and we've driven in Rome.) Street parking is minimal and parking lots are fiendishly expensive. That said, this book still recommends a few outlying destinations for those who can access them.

If you're visiting from abroad and plan to rent a car in the United States, foreign driver's licenses are usually recognized, but you should get an international one if your home license is not in English.

Car-rental agencies with a presence in New Orleans include Advantage, Avis, Budget, Dollar, Enterprise, Hertz, National, and Thrifty. Rental rates vary according to the time of your visit and from company to company, so do some advance comparison shopping. Try different dates and pickup points, and ask about corporate or organizational discounts (such as AAA or frequent-flier-program memberships). Rates decrease for weekly (or longer) rentals. Also, check the major online travel sites, like Expedia, Orbitz, Hotwire, Travelocity, or Priceline.

To rent a car in the United States, you need a valid driver's license and a major credit card (and a passport for foreign visitors). Some will accept a debit card with a cash deposit. The minimum age is usually 25, but Enterprise and Budget will rent to younger people and add a surcharge; they may also require proof of ability to pay (such as paycheck stubs and utility bills). It's a good idea to buy maximum insurance coverage unless you're certain your own auto or credit card insurance is sufficient. Stick to the major companies because what you might save with smaller companies might not be worth the headache if you have mechanical troubles on the road.

At press time in New Orleans, the cost of gasoline (also known as gas, but never petrol), is about $3.90 a gallon, but prices are in wild flux and could change significantly by the time you read this. Generally, the cost of gas in New Orleans tends to be at or slightly below the U.S. average. Taxes are already included in the printed price. One U.S. gallon equals 3.8 liters or .85 imperial gallons. Fill-up locations are known as gas or service stations; they are readily available on major streets (none are located within the French Quarter). Most accept credit or debit cards right at the pump or via prepayment to the clerk (clerks will also accept cash, of course). Change is given inside if your tank fills up before you reach your prepaid amount.

When driving in New Orleans, right turns on a red light are legal except where "No right turn on red" signs are posted, so keep your eyes open for those.

Similarly, many major intersections restrict left turns. Drive past the intersection, make a u-turn at the next allowable place, then double-back and turn right (a maneuver sometimes referred to as the "Louisiana Left").

Streetcars run down the center of St. Charles Avenue, Canal Street, and Carrollton Avenue, requiring motorists to cross their paths frequently. Look *both* ways for streetcars, yield the right of way to them, and allow ample time to complete track crossings. They'll brake between stops if you're in their way, of course, but it's best not to get stuck on the tracks and impede their progress.

It is illegal to have an open container of alcohol, including "go cups," in a moving car, and, of course, driving while under the influence of alcohol is a serious offense.

Keep doors locked and never leave belongings, packages, or gadgets (GPS, iPods, and the like) visible in parked cars.

By Taxi

Taxis are plentiful in New Orleans, and except during the busiest times (we're looking at you, Mardi Gras and Jazz Fest) they can be hailed easily on the street in the French Quarter and in some parts of the Central Business District. They are also usually lined up at taxi stands at larger hotels. Otherwise, call and expect a cab to appear in about 15 minutes. The rate is $3.50 when you enter the taxi and $2 per mile thereafter. During special events, the rate is $5 per person (or the meter rate if it's greater) no matter where you go in the city. The fee for transfers between hotels is $10 no matter how short the ride.

Most taxis can be hired for a special rate for up to five passengers (many are minivans). It's a hassle-free and economical way to tour far-flung areas of the city (the lakefront, for example). Within the city you pay an hourly rate; out-of-town trips cost double the amount on the meter.

The city's most reliable company is **United Cabs** (✆ **504/524-9606;** www.unitedcabs.com). They accept credit cards if you tell the operator when you call to request a cab. Some drivers will accept credit cards if you hail them on the street, but ask when you first get in, as cash is the norm for taxi service.

On Foot

We can't stress this enough: Walking is by far the best way to see New Orleans (besides, you need to walk off all those calories!). You'll miss the many unique and sometimes glorious sights if you whiz past them. Slow down. Get a drink or snack to go. And stroll. Take one of our walking tours (see chapter 8, "City Strolls"). If it's just too hot, humid, or rainy to make walking attractive, there's always a cab or bus nearby.

By Bike

One of the best ways to see the city is by bike. The terrain is flat, the breeze feels good, and you can cover ground pretty swiftly on two wheels. But the streets can be bumpy and potholed, and as yet there are only a few designated bike corridors, so some experience and comfort with city riding is helpful. **Bicycle Michael's,** 622 Frenchmen St. (✆ **504/945-9505;** www.bicyclemichaels.com), near the French Quarter, rents good quality, multigear hybrids and mountain bikes for $25 for a half-day (4 hr.), $35 a day, and $120 for 5 days. A lock is included; helmets (recommended, but not required) are additional. At the other end of the French

Quarter, **American Bicycle Rentals,** 317 Burgundy St. (℗ 866/293-4037; www.amebrc.com), has supersturdy, cushy American-made, Worksman single-speed bikes for $30 for a half-day, $40 full day, including a lock, helmet, and rack or basket; discounts are available for longer-term rentals. **Joy Ride Bicycles** (℗ 504/982-1617; www.joyridebikerentals.com) rents lightweight, single-speed Carmel cruiser bikes and delivers to hotels. Rates of $30 a day and $130 for 5 days include a lock and helmet. All companies require credit card deposits and waivers. Also see the section on bicycle tours in chapter 7 (p. 211).

By Ferry

The Canal Street ferry is one of the city's secrets—and it's free for pedestrians and cars. The ride takes you across the Mississippi River from the foot of Canal to Algiers Point (25-min. round-trip), and affords great views of downtown. Once in Algiers, you can walk around the old Algiers Point neighborhood. At night, with the city's glowing skyline reflecting on the river, a ride on the ferry can be quite romantic.

By Bus

DISCOUNT PASSES If you won't have a car in New Orleans, we strongly encourage you to invest in a **JazzyPass,** which entitles you to an unlimited number of rides on all streetcar and bus lines. It costs $5 for 1 day, $12 for 3 days, or $20 for 5 days. Many visitors think this was the best tip they got about their New Orleans stay and the finest bargain in town. One-day passes can be purchased when boarding; get multiday passes at Walgreens drug stores and other locations. To find the nearest one, ask at your hotel or guesthouse or contact the **Regional Transit Authority** (**RTA;** ℗ 504/248-3900; www. norta.com).

BUSES New Orleans has a good public bus system, so chances are there's a bus that runs exactly where you want to go. The local fare at press time is $1.25 (you must have exact change in bills or coins), transfers are an extra 25¢, and express buses are $1.25 (or you can use a JazzyPass; see above). For route information contact the RTA (℗ 504/248-3900; www.norta.com) or pick up one of the excellent city maps available at the Visitor Information Center, 529 St. Ann St., in the French Quarter.

By Streetcar

Besides being a National Historic Landmark, the **St. Charles Avenue street-car** is also a convenient and fun way to get from downtown to Uptown and back. The iconic green cars click and clack for 6½ miles, ending at South Carrollton and South Claiborne avenues. It runs 24 hours a day at frequent intervals, and the fare is $1.25 each way. All streetcars take exact change in bills or coins only, or JazzyPasses (see above). Streetcars can get crowded at rush hour and when school is out for the day. Board at Canal and Carondelet streets (directly across Canal from Bourbon St. in the French Quarter) or anywhere along St. Charles Avenue, sit back, and look for landmarks or just enjoy the scenery.

The streetcar line extends beyond the point where St. Charles Avenue bends into Carrollton Avenue. The end of the line is at Palmer Park and Playground at Claiborne Avenue (there's decent shopping in the Riverbend shopping area,

p. 249). It will cost you another $1.25 for the ride back to Canal Street. It costs 10¢ to transfer from the streetcar to a bus.

The **riverfront streetcar** runs for 2 miles, from the Old Mint across Canal Street to Riverview, with stops along the way. It runs from 7:30am to 10:30pm, and is a great foot saver as you explore the riverfront. The fare is $1.50, and there's wheelchair ramp access (but not on the St. Charles line).

The **Canal Street** line has spiffy newish (air-conditioned!) bright-red cars. Check the destination sign, because one branch, Cemeteries, goes to several of the older cemeteries and runs from 5am to 3am, while the other, labeled either City Park or Beauregard Circle, is the one you want if you are taking it to Mid-City, City Park/the New Orleans Museum of Art, or Jazz Fest. Be prepared for jammed cars during Jazz Fest, because the line runs to within a few blocks of the Fair Grounds. If your destination is strictly Canal Street/Carrollton, any of the cars will take you there. One-way fares are $1.25, and the line runs between 7am and 1:15am.

A short, new line opening in mid-2012 will run along Loyola Street, connecting the Union Passenger Terminal (and Amtrak and Greyhound passengers) with the Canal Street line, and more streetcar line expansions are in the offing.

[Fast FACTS] NEW ORLEANS

African-American Travelers New Orleans's African-American history is rich with important milestones, from the joyous nascence of jazz to the horrors of the slave trade (to say nothing of the essential contributions to the city's cuisine, politics, and literature). The **historic Treme neighborhood** is a touchstone itself, with a number of worthy sights within its bounds (see box, p. 207). The statewide **African American Heritage Trail** is an excellent network of cultural and historic points; information and downloadable maps are available at www.astorylikenoother.com. A tour of the **9th Ward** may be of interest (see "Organized Tours," p. 203), and the **House of Dance and Feathers** (1317 Tupelo St.; ✆ **504/957-2678**) is essential for anyone interested in the Mardi Gras Indian tradition (p. 43), though open by appointment only. The *Essence Festival* is a huge draw (p. 55), and the restaurant and music options relevant to black heritage could fill a weeklong vacation without repetition.

Area Codes The area code for New Orleans is 504.

Business Hours Most stores are open 10am to 6pm; bars can stay open until the wee hours, and restaurants' hours vary depending on the types of meals they serve. Expect breakfast to start around 8am, lunch around 11am, and dinner at 6pm.

Car Rental See "By Car" under "Getting There," earlier in this chapter.

Cellphones See "Mobile Phones," below.

Crime See "Safety," later in this section.

Customs For U.S. Customs details, consult your nearest U.S. embassy or consulate, or **U.S. Customs** (www.cbp.gov).

For information on what you're allowed to bring home, contact one of the following agencies:

U.S. Citizens: U.S. Customs & Border Protection (CBP), 1300 Pennsylvania Ave. NW, Washington, DC 20229 (✆ **877/287-8667;** www.cbp.gov).

Canadian Citizens: Canada Border Services Agency, Ottawa, Ontario, K1A 0L8 (✆ **800/461-9999** in Canada, or 204/983-3500; www.cbsa-asfc.gc.ca).

U.K. Citizens: HM Customs & Excise, Crownhill Court, Tailyour Road, Plymouth, PL6 5BZ (✆ **0845/010-9000;** from outside the U.K., 020/8929-0152; www.hmce.gov.uk).

Australian Citizens: Australian Customs Service, Customs House, 5 Constitution Ave., Canberra City, ACT 2601 (✆ **1300/363-263;** from outside Australia, 612/6275-6666; www.customs.gov.au).

New Zealand Citizens: New Zealand Customs, The Customhouse, 17–21 Whitmore St., Box 2218, Wellington, 6140 (✆ **04/473-6099** or 0800/428-786; www.customs.govt. nz).

Disabled Travelers Most disabilities shouldn't stop anyone from traveling in New Orleans. Thanks to provisions in the Americans with Disabilities Act, most public places are required to comply with disability-friendly regulations. Almost all public establishments (except a few National Historic Landmarks) and at least some modes of public transportation provide accessible entrances and facilities.

Be aware, however, that despite extensive efforts toward improvement, in New Orleans you are still dealing with many older structures created before thoughts of ease for those with disabilities. Before you book a hotel, **ask questions** based on your needs. If you have mobility issues, you'll probably do best to stay in one of the city's newer, more accommodating hotels.

Like the sometimes potholed or cobblestoned streets, maneuvering wheelchairs and walkers on the often bumpy and uneven sidewalks can be challenging (though most have curb cuts), and getting on the St. Charles streetcar might be too great a challenge. Other streetcar lines have lifts. Some French Quarter streets are closed to cars during certain parts of the day and allow pedestrian traffic only.

For information about specialized transportation systems, call **LIFT** (✆ **504/827-7433**).

Drinking Laws The legal age for purchase and consumption of alcoholic beverages is 21; proof of age is required and often requested at bars, nightclubs, and restaurants, so bring ID when you go out (but don't be surprised if people much younger take a seat next to you at the bar). Alcoholic beverages are available round-the-clock, 7 days a week. Bars can stay open all night in New Orleans, and liquor is sold in grocery and liquor stores. You're allowed to drink on the street but not from a glass or bottle. Bars will provide a plastic "go cup" that you can transfer your drink to as you leave (and some have walk-up windows for quick and easy refills).

A warning: Although the police may look the other way if they see a pedestrian who's had a few too many (as long as he or she is not bothering anyone), there is zero tolerance for intoxication behind the wheel. Don't even think about driving (car, motorcycle, *or* bicycle) while intoxicated. Further, do not carry open containers of alcohol in your car or any public area that isn't zoned for alcohol consumption. The police can fine you on the spot.

Driving Rules See "Getting Around," p. 346.

Electricity Like Canada, the United States uses 110–120 volts AC (60 cycles), compared to 220–240 volts AC (50 cycles) in most of Europe, Australia, and New Zealand.

Downward converters that change 220–240 volts to 110–120 volts are difficult to find in the United States, so bring one with you.

Embassies & Consulates All embassies are in the nation's capital, Washington, D.C. Some consulates are in major U.S. cities (including a few in New Orleans), and most nations have a mission to the United Nations in New York City. If your country isn't listed below, call for directory information in Washington, D.C. (✆ **202/555-1212**), or check **www.embassy.org/embassies**.

Australia: 1601 Massachusetts Ave. NW, Washington, DC 20036 (✆ **202/797-3000**; www.australia.visahq.com). Consulates are in New York, Honolulu, Houston, Los Angeles, and San Francisco.

Canada: 501 Pennsylvania Ave. NW, Washington, DC 20001 (✆ **202/682-1740;** www.canadianembassy.org). Other Canadian consulates are in Buffalo (New York), Detroit, Los Angeles, New York, and Seattle.

Ireland: 2234 Massachusetts Ave. NW, Washington, DC 20008 (✆ **202/462-3939;** www.embassyofireland.org). Irish consulates are in Boston, Chicago, New York, San Francisco, and other cities. See website for complete listing.

New Zealand: 37 Observatory Circle NW, Washington, DC 20008 (✆ **202/328-4800;** www.nzembassy.com). New Zealand consulates are in Los Angeles, Salt Lake City, San Francisco, and Seattle.

United Kingdom: 3100 Massachusetts Ave. NW, Washington, DC 20008 (✆ **202/588-6500;** http://ukinusa.fco.gov.uk). Other British consulates are in Atlanta, Boston, Chicago, Cleveland, Houston, Los Angeles, New York, San Francisco, and Seattle.

Emergencies For fire, ambulance, and police, dial ✆ **911** from any phone. This is a free call from pay phones. Calls from land lines will route to the local emergency dispatch center. From mobile phones, immediately tell the operator your location and the nature of the emergency.

Family Travel New Orleans doesn't spring to mind as the first place to take a child, but there are plenty of activities and sights appropriate for children, who often get a kick out of the city (and love Mardi Gras!). They, too, probably dislike the heat, so summer months may not be best. Look for the "Kids" icon throughout this guide for accommodations, restaurants, and attractions that are particularly kid-friendly.

Gasoline Please see "By Car" under "Getting Around," earlier in this chapter.

Health No widespread mold and floodwater-related illnesses that were feared after Katrina ever materialized, nor have any ill effects on air or water supply from the Deepwater oil spill. (New Orleans is, after all, 150 miles from the spill; booze and butter overindulgence pose greater dangers.)

Healthcare is sufficiently but not extensively available (there are fewer available facilities than before Katrina, though construction recently began on a major new medical complex). If you have a medical condition that may require care, make appropriate arrangements before traveling to New Orleans. See "Hospitals" below for **hospitals, urgent-care centers,** and an **emergency number.** If you need a doctor for less urgent health concerns, try **Ochsner Physician Referral Service** (✆ **504/842-3155** or 842-4106; www.ochsner.org), or visit **New Orleans Urgent Care,** 900 Magazine St. (✆ **504/552-2433;** www.neworleansurgentcare.com), Monday to Saturday from 11am to 7pm, Sunday from 9am to 1pm.

Pollen, sun, uneven sidewalks, overindulgence, and mosquitoes (especially near the swamps and bayous) are the most common medical annoyances. Packing the following items may help prevent minor health problems: insect repellent, especially during the hot or rainy periods; sunscreen; digestive aids; and antihistamines.

Hospitals In an emergency, dial ✆ **911** from any phone to summon paramedics. For nonemergency injuries or illnesses, call or go to the emergency room at **Ochsner Baptist Medical Center,** 2700 Napoleon Ave. (✆ **504/899-9311**), or the **Tulane University Medical Center,** 1415 Tulane Ave. (✆ **504/588-5800**).

Insurance Travel insurance is a good idea if you think for some reason you may be cancelling your trip. It's cheaper than the cost of a no-penalty ticket and it gives you the safety net if something comes up, enabling you to cancel or postpone your trip and still recover the costs.

For information on traveler's insurance, trip-cancellation insurance, and medical insurance while traveling, please visit www.frommers.com/planning.

Internet & Wi-Fi Nearly all major hotels have free Wi-Fi in their lobbies, as do many cafes and all Starbucks (there's one in the French Quarter in the Canal Place Mall, 365 Canal St.; ✆ **504/566-1223**). The vast majority of hotels also offer some form of in-room Internet access, usually high speed, often wireless. A few include the cost in the room charge, but most add a usage fee between $5 and $15 daily. Most larger hotels have business centers with computers for rent.

To find public Wi-Fi hot spots, try **www.jiwire.com**; its Hotspot Finder holds the world's largest directory of public wireless hot spots. It may be nearly as easy to boot up and see what signals you get; or walk down any commercial street and look for "Free Wi-Fi" signs. It's a pretty well-wired city.

The **Riverside Internet Café** in the Riverwalk mall (✆ **504/299-1945**) has rental computers, as does the **Krystal Burger** at 116 Bourbon St. (available 24 hr.; $5 for 20 min.).

FedEx Offices with fully loaded rental computer stations with Internet can be found at 555 Canal St. (✆ **504/654-1057**) and 762 St. Charles Ave. (✆ **504/581-2541**). **Louis Armstrong Airport** has Internet kiosks that provide basic Web access for a per-minute fee that's usually higher than cybercafe prices. To find other cybercafes, check **www.cybercaptive.com** and **www.cybercafe.com**.

Language English is spoken everywhere, while French, Cajun French, and Spanish are heard occasionally in New Orleans.

Legal Aid If you are pulled over by the police for a minor infraction (such as speeding), never attempt to pay the fine directly to an officer; this could be construed as attempted bribery, a much more serious crime. Pay fines by mail, or directly into the hands of the clerk of the court. If accused of a more serious offense, say and do nothing before consulting a lawyer. Here in the U.S., the burden is on the state to prove a person's guilt beyond a reasonable doubt, and everyone has the right to remain silent, whether he or she is suspected of a crime or actually arrested. Once arrested, a person can make one telephone call to a party of his or her choice. The international visitor should call his or her embassy or consulate.

LGBT Travelers New Orleans is a very welcoming town with a high-profile homosexual population that contributes much to the color and flavor of the city. You'll find an abundance of establishments serving every alternative interest, from bars to restaurants to community services to certain businesses. For resources, start with *Ambush Magazine,* 828-A Bourbon St. (www.ambushmag.com), which covers the scene; the website offers plenty of links to other interesting sites. The **Gathering Place Worship Center,** 3151 Dauphine St. (© **504/944-9836**), and the **Big Easy Metropolitan Community Church,** 1333 S. Carrollton Ave. (© **504/214-4340;** www.bigeasymcc.com), serve primarily gay and lesbian congregations. The website **www.gayneworleans. com** provides information on hotels, restaurants, arts, and nightlife. The local **Lesbian and Gay Community Center,** 2114 Decatur St. (© **504/945-1103;** www.lgbtccno.org), is staffed part-time by volunteers, but they can provide a wealth of info if you catch them when they're in.

Mail At press time, domestic postage rates were 28¢ for a postcard and 44¢ for a letter. For international mail, a first-class letter of up to 1 ounce costs 98¢ (75¢ to Canada and 79¢ to Mexico); a first-class postcard costs the same as a letter. For more information go to **www.usps.com**.

If you aren't sure what your address will be in the United States, mail can be sent to you, in your name, c/o General Delivery at the main post office of the city or region where you expect to be. (Call © **800/275-8777** for information on the nearest post office.) The addressee must pick up mail in person and produce proof of identity (driver's license, passport, and so on). Most post offices will hold mail for up to 1 month, and are open Monday to Friday from 8am to 6pm, and Saturday from 9am to 3pm.

Always include ZIP codes when mailing items in the U.S. If you don't know the ZIP code, visit www.usps.com/zip4.

Medical Requirements Unless you're arriving from an area known to be suffering from an epidemic (particularly cholera or yellow fever), inoculations or vaccinations are not required for entry into the United States.

Mobile Phones Mobile (cell) phone and texting service in New Orleans is generally good, with AT&T/T-Mobile and Verizon faring best, and Sprint lagging a bit behind. Some dead zones still exist around the city and inside old brick buildings. International mobile phone service can be hit-or-miss (despite what you may have been told before you began your trip). If you plan to use your phone a lot while in New Orleans, it may be worthwhile to invest in an inexpensive "pay as you go" phone from a local outlet. There's an **AT&T** store at 201 St. Charles Ave. (© **504/581-2900**) and a **Verizon** store at 109 St. Charles Ave. (© **504/524-8888**). Depending on the current offers, you may even get a generous credit for calls when you buy the phone—enough to last through your trip, perhaps. Various calling plans are available. Most no longer charge for roaming but additional costs for texting or data downloading can add up. Definitely discuss the options to determine which one best suits your needs before making a commitment, and read the agreement to make sure you're not purchasing more services or a longer-term agreement than you need.

If you have a computer and Internet service, consider using a broadband-based telephone service (**Voice over Internet protocol,** or **VoIP**) such as Skype (www.skype. com) or Vonage (www.vonage.com), which allow you to make free international calls from your laptop or in a cybercafe. Neither service requires the people you're calling to also have that service (though there are fees if they do not).

Money & Costs Frommer's lists prices in the local currency. The currency conversions quoted above were correct at press time. However, rates fluctuate, so before departing consult a currency exchange website such as **www.oanda.com/convert/ classic**.

THE VALUE OF THE U.S. DOLLAR VS. OTHER POPULAR CURRENCIES

US$	C$	£	€	A$	NZ$
1.00	0.97	0.62	0.70	0.96	1.31

Costs in New Orleans are generally right in the middle of, and sometimes lower than, other midsize U.S. "destination" cities—less than New York, more than Phoenix. For the quality of the accommodations, attractions, and particularly of the restaurants, it actually offers slightly better value. As with any destination, costs can vary greatly by season. There are often superb hotel deals in the heat of summer, while prices can soar during big events. December's prix-fixe Réveillon deals can get you into restaurants for dinners that might otherwise be prohibitive.

With a few cash-only exceptions, major credit cards are accepted everywhere (some don't accept American Express, Discover, or Diners Club). Cash is king anywhere, and ATMs are plentiful throughout the city (including inside many bars and souvenir shops). Expect a $2.50 to $4.00 charge to use an ATM outside your network. To avoid the fee, most grocery and convenience stores will allow you to get a small amount of cash back with your purchase (from $10–$100, depending on store policy).

WHAT THINGS COST IN NEW ORLEANS   US$

Taxi from airport to the Quarter	33.00 (for two people)
Shuttle from airport to the Quarter	20.00 (per person)
Cost of bus/streetcar one-way	1.25
Day pass for bus/streetcar	5.00
Standard room at Ritz-Carlton	199.00–329.00
Standard room at International House	119.00–379.00
Standard room at Drury Inn	119.00–139.00
Order of 3 beignets or cup of café au lait at Café du Monde	2.14
Dinner at Commander's Palace (3 courses)	70.00 (per person)
Dinner at Irene's Cuisine	40.00 (per person)
Muffuletta sandwich at Central Grocery	13.00
Ticket to a show at Tipitina's	10.00–25.00
Cost of a Hurricane at Pat O'Brien's with souvenir glass	11.00
Cost of a Pimm's Cup at Napoleon House	6.00

Beware of hidden credit card fees while traveling. Check with your credit or debit card issuer to see what fees, if any, will be charged for overseas transactions. Recent reform legislation in the U.S. has curbed some exploitative lending practices, but many banks have responded by increasing other fees. For example, fees for customers who use credit and debit cards while out of the country, even if those charges were made in U.S. dollars, can amount to 3% or more of the purchase price. Check with your bank before departing to avoid surprise charges on your statement.

For help with currency conversions, tip calculations, and more, download Frommer's convenient Travel Tools app for your mobile device. Go to www.frommers.com/go/mobile and click on the Travel Tools icon.

Newspapers & Magazines To find out what's going on around town, pick up a copy of the daily *Times-Picayune* (www.nola.com) and an *Offbeat* (www.offbeat.com) or *Where Y'at,* two monthly entertainment guides with live music, art gallery, and special event listings. Both can usually be found in hotels and clubs, and get scarce toward the end of the month. *Gambit Weekly* (www.bestofneworleans.com), which comes out every Sunday, is the city's free alternative paper and has a good mix of news and entertainment information.

Packing What to pack depends largely on what you plan to do while visiting New Orleans. But comfortable walking shoes are a must year-round. A compact umbrella will often be put to use, as will other raingear during the wetter months and a sun hat for much of the year. A light sweater or jacket is needed even in the hottest weather, when the indoor air can get frigid. Casual wear is the daytime norm, but cocktail wear is appropriate in nicer restaurants, and some of the old-liners require jackets for gentlemen. Also see the suggestions under "Health" and "Safety" in this section.

Passports Every air traveler entering the U.S. is required to show a valid passport (including U.S. citizens). *Note:* U.S. and Canadian citizens entering the U.S. at land and sea ports of entry from within the Western Hemisphere must now also present a passport or other documents compliant with the Western Hemisphere Travel Initiative (WHTI; see www.getyouhome.gov for details). Children 15 and under may continue entering with only a U.S. birth certificate or other proof of U.S. citizenship.

It is advised to always have at least one or two consecutive blank pages in your passport to allow space for visas and stamps that need to appear together. It is also important to note when your passport expires. Many countries require your passport to have at least 6 months left before its expiration in order to allow you into the destination.

Australia Australian Passport Information Service (☏ **131-232;** www.passports.gov.au).

Canada Passport Office, Department of Foreign Affairs and International Trade, Ottawa, ON K1A 0G3 (☏ **800/567-6868;** www.ppt.gc.ca).

Ireland Passport Office, Setanta Centre, Molesworth Street, Dublin 2 (☏ **01/671-1633;** www.foreignaffairs.gov.ie).

New Zealand Passports Office, Department of Internal Affairs, 47 Boulcott St., Wellington, 6011 (☏ **0800/225-050** in New Zealand, or 04/474-8100; www.passports.govt.nz).

United Kingdom Visit your nearest passport office, major post office, or travel agency, or contact the **Identity and Passport Service (IPS),** 89 Eccleston Sq., London, SW1V 1PN (☏ **0300/222-0000;** www.ips.gov.uk).

United States To find your regional passport office, check the U.S. State Department website (travel.state.gov/passport) or call the **National Passport Information Center** (☎ **877/487-2778**) for automated information.

Petrol Please see "By Car" under "Getting Around," earlier in this chapter.

Police Dial ☎ **911** for emergencies. This is a free call from pay phones. Calls from land lines will route to the local law emergency dispatch agency. From mobile phones, immediately tell the operator your location and the nature of the emergency.

Safety It's true that New Orleans has a high crime rate. But most of the serious crime is drug-related, and confined to areas where tourists do not go. Still, we urge you to be very cautious about where you go, particularly at night. In short, behave with the same savvy and street smarts you would demonstrate in any big city: Travel in groups or pairs, take cabs if you're not sure of an area, stay in well-lighted areas with plenty of street and pedestrian traffic, follow your instincts if something seems "off." Stay alert and walk with confidence; avoid looking distracted, confused, or (sorry) drunk. Speaking of which, one way to ensure you will look like a tourist—and thus, a target—is to wear Mardi Gras beads at any time other than Mardi Gras season.

Don't hang that expensive camera around your neck when it's not in use. Put it out of sight. Use camera cases and purses with a shoulder strap, carried diagonally over the shoulder so a simple tug won't dislodge them. Consider using a money belt or other hidden travel wallet. Women may want to ditch the trendy enormous bag and invest in a cute little shoulder-strappy thing for clubbing, one you can dance with rather than leave on your seat (better yet, go purse-free). And never leave valuables in the outside pocket of a backpack. Should you stop for a bite to eat, keep everything within easy reach—of you, not a purse snatcher. If you must store belongings in a car, place them in the trunk, do not leave items visible through the window. It's always a good idea to leave expensive-looking jewelry and other conspicuous valuables at home anyway. And by all means, don't look for or buy drugs or engage in any illegal activity.

The **French Quarter** is fairly safe, especially during the daytime, thanks to the number of people typically present, but some areas are better than others. (Rampart and the north part of Esplanade have bad reputations.) On Bourbon Street be careful when socializing with strangers, and be alert to distractions by potential pickpocket teams. Dauphine and Burgundy are in quiet, lovely parts of the Quarter, but as you near Esplanade, watch out for purse snatchers. At night take cabs down Esplanade and into the **Faubourg Marigny.**

Conventional wisdom holds that one should not go much above Bourbon toward Rampart alone after dark. Nowadays, with the adjacent Armstrong Park and Treme neighborhood experiencing a bit of renaissance, more crowds and safer streets are in the offing. Still, for the time being, it's best to stay in or near a group if you can, and consider taking a cab, even if it seems silly, for the (very) short ride.

In the **Garden District,** as you get past Magazine toward the river, the neighborhoods can be rough, so exercise caution (more cabs, probably).

Single Travelers Single travelers, both male and female, should feel comfortable in New Orleans. Many restaurants, including some of the city's finest, will serve meals at the bar—a personal favorite spot when dining solo (NOLA, Coquette, Cochon, and Acme come to mind). Still, single women travelers in particular should heed the warnings in the "Safety" section, above.

Smoking Technically, smoking is not allowed in most public places, with some exceptions, such as free-standing bars. Restaurants are nonsmoking (though many bars serve some food, and thus smoking is allowed), thus often the nearest courtyard or street becomes an impromptu smoking section. Hotel lobbies are nonsmoking, but guest rooms can be designated as smoking or nonsmoking (be sure to make your preference clear when reserving a room; some hotels are entirely smoke-free). Historically, nightclubs have been smokers' havens, but there's a growing trend toward nonsmoking clubs (see www.letsbetotallyclear.org for a list of them). While recent attempts to tighten smoking restrictions have failed, renewed efforts are likely, so this situation is in flux.

Taxes The United States has no value-added tax (VAT) or other indirect tax at the national level. Every state, county, and city may levy its own local tax on all purchases, including hotel and restaurant checks and airline tickets. These taxes will not appear on price tags. The sales tax in New Orleans is 9%. Add 4% tax to hotel bills, for a total of 13%. There is also a nightly tax of 50¢ to $2 based on the number of rooms a hotel has.

On the upside, international travelers who purchase goods in Louisiana to take to their home countries can often get the sales tax refunded in full. When you make your purchase, keep your receipt and also request a "tax back" voucher (you'll be asked to show your passport). Before you leave the state, bring your receipts and vouchers to the Refund Center at the Riverwalk Mall or New Orleans Airport (near American Airlines ticketing). You'll be rebated in cash up to US$500 (larger rebates are mailed; see www.louisianataxfree.com for instructions and more information). Not all stores participate, so ask first.

Also, many original works of art purchased in New Orleans are tax-exempt. Do inquire, as this applies in designated cultural districts only.

Telephones Hotel costs for long-distance and local calls made from guest rooms vary widely. Local calls can be complimentary, or astronomically expensive; long-distance calls typically fall into the latter category. If you intend to use the room phone, definitely inquire about phone charges. You may be better off using a mobile phone, **prepaid calling card** (available at convenience and grocery stores in denominations up to $500), or a public pay telephone, which cost 25¢ or 35¢ for local calls (and are increasingly scarce). Many public pay phones at airports accept credit cards. Most long-distance and international calls can be dialed directly from any phone. **To make calls within the United States and to Canada,** dial 1 followed by the area code and the seven-digit number. **For other international calls,** dial 011 followed by the country code, city code, and the number you are calling.

Calls to area codes **800, 888, 877,** and **866** are toll-free. However, calls to area codes **700** and **900** (chat lines, bulletin boards, "dating" services, and so on) can be absurdly expensive.

For **reversed-charge or collect calls,** and for person-to-person calls, dial the number 0 then the area code and number. An operator will come on the line. Specify whether you are calling collect, person-to-person, or both. If your operator-assisted call is international, ask for the overseas operator.

For **directory assistance** ("Information"), dial 411 for help finding numbers in the U.S. and Canada; for long-distance information, dial 1, the appropriate area code, plus 555-1212.

Time New Orleans is in the Central Standard Time (CST), which is 1 hour earlier than Eastern Standard Time and 5 hours earlier than Greenwich Mean Time. The continental United States is divided into **four time zones:** Eastern Standard Time (EST), Central

Standard Time (CST), Mountain Standard Time (MST), and Pacific Standard Time (PST). Alaska and Hawaii have their own zones. When it's 9am in Los Angeles (PST), it's 7am in Honolulu (HST), 10am in Denver (MST), 11am in New Orleans and Chicago (CST), noon in New York City (EST), 5pm in London (GMT), and 2am the next day in Sydney.

Daylight saving time (summer time) is in effect from 1am on the second Sunday in March to 1am on the first Sunday in November, except in Arizona, Hawaii, the U.S. Virgin Islands, and Puerto Rico. Daylight saving time moves the clock 1 hour ahead of standard time.

For help with time translations, and more, download our convenient Travel Tools app for your mobile device. Go to www.frommers.com/go/mobile and click on the Travel Tools icon.

Tipping Tips are a very important part of certain workers' income, and the standard way of showing appreciation for services provided (it's certainly not compulsory if the service is poor!). In hotels, tip **bellhops** at least $1 per bag ($2–$3 if you have a lot of luggage) and tip the **chamber staff** $1 to $2 per day (more if you've been extra messy). Tip the **doorman** or **concierge** if he or she has provided you with some specific service (for example, calling a cab for you or obtaining tickets or reservations). Tip the **valet-parking attendant** $1 every time you get your car.

In restaurants, bars, and nightclubs, tip **service staff** and **bartenders** 15% to 20% of the check, tip **checkroom attendants** $1 per garment, and tip **valet-parking attendants** $1–$2 per vehicle. Some restaurants will automatically add a tip to the bill for larger parties (typically 18% for six or more guests, but this can vary). Check your bill or ask your server if gratuity has been included in your bill.

As for other service personnel, tip **cabdrivers** 15% of the fare, tip **skycaps** at airports at least $1 per bag ($2–$3 if you have a lot of luggage), and tip **hairdressers** and **barbers** 15% to 20%.

For help with tip calculations, currency conversions, and more, download our convenient Travel Tools app for your mobile device. Go to www.frommers.com/go/mobile and click on the Travel Tools icon.

Toilets You won't find public toilets or "restrooms" on the streets in most U.S. cities but they can be found in hotel lobbies, bars, restaurants, museums, department stores, railway and bus stations, and service stations. Large hotels and fast-food restaurants are often the best bet for clean facilities. Restaurants and bars may reserve their restrooms for patrons.

Tours Various special-interest tours of New Orleans are addressed in chapter 7, "Sights to See & Places to Be." These include tours geared toward antiquing, literature, history, gay and lesbian culture, ghosts, and voodoo, along with tours of the fabled, stunning swamps, plantation homes, cemeteries, and various areas of New Orleans. Also see the bicycle, kayak, and self-guided walking tours in "City Strolls," chapter 7, and voluntourism opportunities on p. 36.

Festival Tours International offers group trips to the Jazz & Heritage Festival, with an optional side trip to Cajun Country (p. 318). The New Orleans Cooking Experience (p. 210) offers half-day and 3-day trips with on-site bed-and-breakfast lodging and hands-on classes by master chefs.

VAT See "Taxes," earlier in this section.

Visas The U.S. State Department has a **Visa Waiver Program (VWP)** allowing citizens of the following countries to enter the United States without a visa for stays of up to 90 days: Andorra, Australia, Austria, Belgium, Brunei, Czech Republic, Denmark, Estonia, Finland, France, Germany, Greece, Hungary, Iceland, Ireland, Italy, Japan, Latvia, Liechtenstein, Lithuania, Luxembourg, Malta, Monaco, the Netherlands, New Zealand, Norway, Portugal, San Marino, Singapore, Slovakia, Slovenia, South Korea, Spain, Sweden, Switzerland, and the United Kingdom. (**Note:** This list was accurate at press time; for the most up-to-date list of countries in the VWP, consult http://travel.state.gov/visa.) Even though a visa isn't necessary, in an effort to help U.S. officials check travelers against terror watch lists before they arrive at U.S. borders, visitors from VWP countries must register online through the Electronic System for Travel Authorization (ESTA) before boarding a plane or a boat to the U.S. Travelers must complete an electronic application providing basic personal and travel eligibility information. The Department of Homeland Security recommends filling out the form at least 3 days before traveling. Authorizations will be valid for up to 2 years or until the traveler's passport expires, whichever comes first. Currently, there is one US$14 fee for the online application. Existing ESTA registrations remain valid through their expiration dates. **Note:** Any passport issued on or after October 26, 2006, by a VWP country must be an **e-Passport** for VWP travelers to be eligible to enter the U.S. without a visa. Citizens of these nations also need to present a round-trip air or cruise ticket upon arrival. E-Passports contain computer chips capable of storing biometric information, such as the required digital photograph of the holder. If your passport doesn't have this feature, you can still travel without a visa if the valid passport was issued before October 26, 2005, and includes a machine-readable zone, or if the valid passport was issued between October 26, 2005, and October 25, 2006, and includes a digital photograph. For more information, go to **http://travel.state.gov/visa**. Canadian citizens may enter the United States without visas, but will need to show passports and proof of residence.

Citizens of all other countries must have (1) a valid passport that expires at least 6 months later than the scheduled end of their visit to the U.S., and (2) a tourist visa.

For information about U.S. Visas go to **http://travel.state.gov** and click on "Visas." Or go to one of the following websites:

Australian citizens can obtain up-to-date visa information from the **U.S. Embassy Canberra,** Moonah Place, Yarralumla, ACT 2600 (✆ **02/6214-5600**), or by checking the U.S. Diplomatic Mission's website at **http://canberra.usembassy.gov/visas.html**.

British subjects can obtain up-to-date visa information by calling the **U.S. Embassy Visa Information Line** (✆ **09042-450-100** from within the U.K. at £1.20 per minute, or ✆ **866-382-3589** from within the U.S. at a flat rate of $16 and is payable by credit card only) or by visiting the "Visas to the U.S." section of the American Embassy London's website at **http://london.usembassy.gov/visas.html**.

Irish citizens can obtain up-to-date visa information through the **U.S. Embassy Dublin,** 42 Elgin Rd., Ballsbridge, Dublin 4 (✆ **1580-47-VISA** [8472] from within the Republic of Ireland at €2.40 per minute; **http://dublin.usembassy.gov**).

Citizens of **New Zealand** can obtain up-to-date visa information by contacting the **U.S. Embassy New Zealand,** 29 Fitzherbert Terrace, Thorndon, Wellington (✆ **644/462-6000; http://newzealand.usembassy.gov**).

Visitor Information Even a seasoned traveler should consider writing or calling ahead to the **New Orleans Metropolitan Convention and Visitors Bureau,** 2020 St. Charles Ave., New Orleans, LA 70130 (✆ **800/672-6124** or 504/566-5011; www.new

orleanscvb.com). The friendly, helpful staff will help with advice and decision-making; if you have a special interest, they'll help you plan your visit around it—this is definitely one of the most helpful tourist centers in any major city.

Once you've arrived, you also might want to stop by the **Visitor Information Center,** 529 St. Ann St. (② **504/568-5661**), in the French Quarter. The center is open Tuesday to Saturday from 9am to 5pm and has walking- and driving-tour maps and booklets on restaurants, accommodations, sightseeing, special tours, and pretty much anything else you might want to know.

The following websites are also excellent information sources:

- **www.NOLA.com**: The *Times-Picayune* newspaper's site, has news plus nightlife, culture, and festival information, and good links.
- **www.neworleansonline.com**: Detailed info from the Tourism Marketing Corporation.
- **www.gonola.com**: Fun videos to get you in the mood for a visit.
- **www.wwoz.org/livewire**: To-the-minute nighttime music show listings.
- **www.artsneworleans.com**: Good source for arty events and plenty more.

Among the many blogs about New Orleans, **www.myneworleans.com** and **www.blogofneworleans.com** keep good track of the goings-on; **www.appetites.us** has excellent NOLA food coverage; perennial fave **www.gumbopages.com** still has plenty of information about New Orleans–related food and music, though of late it's taken a sharp turn toward cocktail mania. The following literate locals offer musings (and sometimes rantings) about food, music, politics, and the gamut of aspects of their beloved city:

- **www.BlackenedOut.com**: Food, food, and more food—from a chef who knows it well.
- **www.Fleurtygirl.com**: Fun flirty videos-about-town.
- **http://homeofthegroove.blogspot.com**: Terrific music blog.
- **www.HesaidShesaidNOLA.com**: A local couple agree (or don't) on subjects about the city.
- **http://redstreetcarline.wordpress.com**: Good New Orleans ideas and finds.
- **www.noladefender.com**: Commentary and info on the city.
- **http://b.rox.com**: A catchall of politics, culture, warts, beauty spots, and so on.
- **http://humidcity.com/**: More interesting commentary for the post-Katrina era.

As for **apps,** all the big festivals have them, complete with helpful schedules (French Quarter Fest, Jazz Fest, *Essence,* Voodoo, and so on). For ongoing general information, we also like the apps from Nola.com, Offbeat, GoNola, the GuidePal New Orleans map, and the cool Experience Mardi Gras parade-tracker. All are available for iPhones, some for Android, and we remain hopeful for the Blackberry users.

Water Tap water is safe to drink in New Orleans, although bottled water is still popular. There are no indications that the water supply has been tainted as a result of either Hurricane Katrina or the Deepwater oil spill.

Wi-Fi See "Internet & Wi-Fi," earlier in this section.

INDEX

Accommodations

Restaurants

PHOTO CREDITS